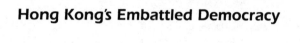

Hong Kong's Embattled Democracy

Hong Kong's

Embattled

Democracy

A SOCIETAL ANALYSIS

Alvin Y. So

The Johns Hopkins University Press

Baltimore and London

© 1999 The Johns Hopkins University Press
All rights reserved. Published 1999
Printed in the United States of America on acid-free paper
9 8 7 6 5 4 3 2 1

The Johns Hopkins University Press
2715 North Charles Street, Baltimore, Maryland 21218-4363
www.press.jhu.edu

Library of Congress Cataloging-in-Publication Data will be found
at the end of this book.
A catalog record for this book is available from the British Library.

ISBN 0-8018-6145-4

To my three loving children: **Alina, Nadia, and Andre**

Contents

Tables

Preface

It was in late 1983 that I decided to write a book about Hong Kong's political development. After spending seven years in the United States for my graduate training, I returned to Hong Kong in August 1983, just in time to observe the dramatic impact of the upcoming 1997 event. In 1983, the Hong Kong dollar fell from six in September 1982 to an unprecedented low of 9.55 against the U.S. dollar; the Hang Seng index of the Hong Kong stock market stood at an all-time low of 690. In early 1984, a riot erupted—looting, burning, an attack on a police station. Later that year, students at the University of Hong Kong held marathon debates on what they should do to influence the negotiations over the future of Hong Kong, and a new political group called the Meeting Point pushed for democracy before Hong Kong's reunification with China. I was fascinated by these political developments and wanted to understand more about Hong Kong's transition to Chinese rule in 1997.

The prevailing explanation of Hong Kong's political development was based on the power dependency theory: because Hong Kong was controlled by London and Beijing, there was not much the Hong Kong people could do to influence the 1997 transition. I found myself disagreeing with that theory, because it neglected the role of social forces and civil society in the shaping of Hong Kong's democratization.

Coming from a class perspective and having written about class analysis (So and Hikam 1990; So and Suwarsono 1989; So 1991, 1995c, 1996), I initially concentrated on new middle-class politics in Hong Kong, and I wrote several papers from that perspective (So and Kwitko 1990, 1992; So 1993b, 1995a). I discovered, however, that the term *new middle class* is highly controversial (see So 1993a; Lui 1993a; Wong 1993). The new middle class is composed of two contradictory segments: service professionals (e.g., teachers and social workers) and corporate professionals (e.g., managers and accountants). Service professionals favor democracy; most corporate professionals stand against it. To lump these contradictory segments into a single "new middle class" is confusing rather than illuminating. As a result, I dropped the "new middle class" framework in recent studies.

Instead, I now frame my project as a study on Hong Kong's democracy. The process of democratization in Hong Kong has been highly dynamic, going from empowerment to alienation at short notice. To explain the changing contour of Hong Kong's democracy, I examine not just Beijing and London but also service professionals, big businesspeople, and the grassroots population. One of the most interesting aspects of Hong Kong's democracy is the constant shifting of political alliances since the early 1980s. Antidemocracy alliances regularly dissolved, realigned, and reconstructed themselves, and so did prodemocracy alliances. The aim of this book is to explain how shifting political alliances led to the rise and transformation of the democratization project in Hong Kong.

I want to take this opportunity to express my sincere thanks for the support I have received from many institutions and persons throughout this project. Several joint appointments with the Social Science Research Institute at the University of Hawaii greatly reduced my teaching load. Three research grants from the Institute for Peace and the Office of Research Administration at the University of Hawaii enabled me to make several trips to Hong Kong to collect data and conduct interviews. My friends in Hong Kong—Karen Joe, Lee Kin-sum, Lee Yok-siu, Maria Tam, and Tsui Fung-kwok—sent me useful material on short notice whenever I called upon them. In addition, I have benefited enormously from reading the work of many first-rate researchers on Hong Kong politics, among them Ming K. Chan, Joseph Cheng, Lau Siu-kai, Lee Ming-kwan, Lo Shiu-hing, Lui Tai-lok, Ian Scott, and the many others I cite in the reference section. Their studies have provided numerous insights and pertinent information, and my book has benefited from them. Ming K. Chan, Chang Heng-hao, Choi Young-jin, Diane Davis, John Lie, Hagen Koo, and Chun Liu have read one or more draft chapters, and their critical comments were very useful in the revision of the book.

Finally, I express my gratitude to my wife, Judy Chan So, who has sustained me unfalteringly over the past two decades. It was during the writing of this book that my three children were born, so I would like to dedicate this book to my three loving children — Alina, Nadia, and Andre.

A note on style: I use the pinyin system to write the names of mainland Chinese persons and places, but I use the Cantonese system for Hong Kong names. Chinese personal names consist of a surname followed by two characters that make one given name. Hong Kong given names are hyphenated; mainland Chinese names are not. If a Hong Kong Chinese has an English name, I use that name whenever possible.

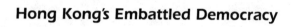

Hong Kong's Embattled Democracy

1 | Introduction

The so-called third wave of democratization (e.g., Huntington 1991a, 1991b; Shin 1994) finally reached East Asia in the 1980s. In Taiwan, democratization came from above. The Guomindang lifted martial law, allowed the opposition party to compete in the electoral arena, revised the constitution, and made key legislative and government posts elective. In South Korea, democratization came from below. Prolonged strikes and urban protests first forced the military Chun government to step down, then helped institute competitive elections in the South Korean polity.

Consequently, the literature takes note of democratic breakthroughs in Taiwan and South Korea by the 1990s (Chao and Myers 1998; Cheng and Kim 1994; Tien 1992). Not only did those countries enjoy a high level of civil liberties, political participation, and competition for key positions of government power, but their election rules were institutionalized. In Taiwan and South Korea, therefore, political actors focused on winning elections and working through the electoral rules rather than challenging the nascent democratic constitutions.

At first it seemed that Hong Kong would follow the path of Taiwan and South Korea toward democratization, because it had attained most of the prerequisites for democratization (Lipset 1994). Like other East Asian newly industrializing economies (NIEs), Hong Kong had considerable wealth and a rising middle class, without extreme or intolerable inequalities. It had also maintained a high level of socioeconomic development since the 1960s. Hong Kong's GNP had grown an average of more than 8 percent a year from the 1960s to the 1980s. Its per capita gross domestic product soared from U.S.$894 in 1971 to U.S.$5,609 in 1989. According to Lipset's (1959) and Huntington's (1984) wealth explanation, Hong Kong's robust economy should make possible high levels of urbanization, industrialization, education, literacy, and mass media exposure, all of which are conducive to democracy. In addition, Hong Kong's wealthy economy should have moderated political tensions and facilitated accommodation and compromise for democratization.

Unlike other East Asian NIEs, Hong Kong has not undergone any authoritarian rule, military regime, or political censorship. Although it was a British colony, its government was very liberal. Its citizens were free to form political organizations, free to criticize the state, free to engage in public political protest. A widely differentiated and articulated social structure developed, with autonomous business, professional, and labor organizations. According to Diamond's (1989) argument, such a civil society should lay a firm foundation for Hong Kong's democratic transition.

Hong Kong's century as a British colony has also been seen as an advantage. Weiner (1987) observed that the developing countries with the most successful democratization since independence are, by and large, former British colonies. Weiner attributed this phenomenon to the rule of law and some system of representation within British colonialism. If Taiwan and South Korea, whose colonial histories were more uniformly authoritarian, can achieve a democratic breakthrough, observers would certainly expect Hong Kong to follow the same path.

Hong Kong's political development in the mid-1980s also seemed to indicate bright prospects for democratization. In 1984 the London government signed a joint declaration with the Beijing government, allowing China to resume the sovereignty of Hong Kong by 1997. The declaration raised strong expectations of democratization in Hong Kong, because it stated that "the chief executive . . . shall be selected by election or through consultations held locally," that "the legislature . . . shall be constituted by elections," and that "the executive authorities shall . . . be accountable to the legislature."

Moreover, just before signing the Joint Declaration in late 1984, the Hong Kong government issued a Green Paper promoting democratic reforms. The aim of the reform was "to develop progressively a system of government the authority for which is firmly rooted in Hong Kong, which is able to represent authoritatively the views of the people of Hong Kong, and which is more directly accountable to the people of Hong Kong." The Green Paper also called for grassroots elections at the level of the local District Board, and it suggested that the Hong Kong government would institute direct elections to the legislature in 1987, so that the Hong Kong people would be running their own government by the time of the hand-over in 1997.

In these circumstances, new political actors who favored democratization quickly emerged. The democrats formed political groups, participated in local elections in 1985, won big victories, got elected to the District Boards and the Legislative Council (Legco), and began to act like an opposition party. They called for direct elections of the Legco, the popular election of the future chief executive of Hong Kong (one person, one vote), supervision of the chief executive by the Legco, and incorporation of all those political reforms into the Basic Law (Hong Kong's miniconstitution).

Developments since the mid-1980s, however, revealed that the transition to democracy was much less successful in Hong Kong than in the other NIEs (So and May 1993). Late in 1985 the Beijing government formally declared that it would not tolerate the formation of any independent political party in Hong Kong and that there should be no major political reform in Hong Kong before the promulgation of the Basic Law in 1990. The Hong Kong government responded by withdrawing its promise to establish direct elections to the Legislative Council in 1988, citing the need to postpone any reform until the content of the Basic Law was approved in China.

Since the Basic Law would define the political structure of Hong Kong after 1997, it became the bone of contention among Beijing, London, the Hong Kong democrats, and the conservatives (E. Lau 1988). The democrats were unable to influence the drafting of the Basic Law. Instead of adopting the populist democracy proposed by the democrats, the Beijing government endorsed the conservatives' choice of a restricted democracy. Rather than adopt one-person, one-vote direct elections, the Basic Law endorsed indirect elections. Since 1997, then, the governor of Hong Kong is indirectly selected by a 600-member electoral commission. In the sixty-seat legislature, only one-third of the seats are filled by popular election; half of the members are elected indirectly by "functional constituents" (occupational and industrial groups), and the remaining ten by an electoral commission. In addition, the Basic Law favors an executive-led government rather than the democrats' model of a legislature-led government (M. Chan 1991). Frustrated by losing so many battles, many middle-class democrats turned their thoughts from the political struggle to their families and careers and left Hong Kong in the late 1980s. The brain drain deprived the democracy movement of its most active leaders, and it demoralized those who had not yet emigrated.

There was even a lack of consensus on exactly what the electoral rules in Hong Kong were. The Basic Law, passed in 1990, right after the Tiananmen incident of 1989, was plagued by resignations and the purging of key members of the Basic Law Drafting Committee. In 1992, Chris Patten, the last

British governor of colonial Hong Kong, further delegitimized the electoral rules by introducing his own version of democratic reforms, which deviated from the constitutional framework set by the Basic Law. The Beijing government abolished Patten's reforms, asked most directly elected legislators to step down, and imposed its own Provisional Legislative Council when it resumed sovereignty on July 1, 1997 (Pepper 1997). In defiance of Beijing's authority, the democrats strongly protested that the Provisional Legislative Council was unconstitutional, because no provision for it had been written into the Basic Law, and they challenged its legality in court in mid-1997. In the mid-1990s, then, Hong Kong's democracy was marred by a feud over electoral rules.

Just before the hand-over on July 1, 1997, however, the democrats reluctantly accepted the restricted democracy model of the Basic Law after Beijing made it clear that new elections to replace the Provisional Legislative Council would be held in mid-1998 and that the democrats would be allowed to run for seats in the post-1997 Legislative Council. It seemed that Hong Kong's democracy was to have narrow electoral competition in the remaining years of the twentieth century.

The aim of this book, therefore, is to trace the origins and development of this embattled democracy in Hong Kong. In particular, it seeks to explain why, despite Hong Kong's favorable structural conditions and promising political development, its democracy has been so restricted and contested. What explains the rise of democratic expectations in the mid-1980s and the democrats' frustration in the mid-1990s? What obstacles stood in the way of Hong Kong's democratization over that decade? And what is the prospect for Hong Kong's democratization in the twenty-first century?

The Power Dependence Explanation

In the literature, there is a prevailing power dependency explanation of Hong Kong's democracy. This explanation emphasizes the dependence of Hong Kong' polity on London and Beijing, fragmented local political elites, the salience of political issues, and the political alienation of the masses.

Power Dependence

Kuan (1991) characterizes the Hong Kong government as a dependent polity controlled by London and Beijing. Before 1997 the incumbent London government was responsible for the current state of affairs; the Beijing government controlled Hong Kong's future. Both London and Beijing commanded overwhelming resources, especially coercive ones. The people of Hong Kong had no credible bargaining power against either of them, except perhaps by voting with their feet. In this situation of power dependence, London and Beijing set the rules of democratization in Hong Kong, while the people were denied the right to participate in shaping their own future.

Lau (1995) further explained that since Hong Kong was going to have decolonization without independence, the London government felt no urgent political need to install democracy there. On the contrary, London's paramount goal was to maintain governmental authority and effective rule in Hong Kong before the change-over. London had to ensure that the maximum amount of political power was still in its own hands, so that neither Beijing nor the people of Hong Kong could use the power transferred out of the colonial regime against it. The Beijing government, too, contemplated limited democratic changes in Hong Kong. Beijing was afraid that democratization would lead to an anti-China movement and the rise of political groups antagonistic to China's resumption of sovereignty. Besides, China was deeply suspicious of a British conspiracy to transfer power to pro-British political groups so that London could still control Hong Kong after 1997.

Since the interaction between London and Beijing determines the agenda of democratization in Hong Kong, what results is a pattern of centripetal and upward political dynamics. Lau (1995) observed that democratization, rather than transferring power to the Hong Kong people, served to shift the center of political gravity upward and outside of Hong Kong, as the most important decisions on democratic reforms are made by two superior governments, one in London and the other in Beijing.

Fragmented Local Elites

Had the Hong Kong people united, they might have exerted stronger influence on the course of democratization. But Kuan (1991) points out that the middle class, which usually provides leadership to the democracy movement, was fragmented in Hong Kong. Although some political activists came from the new middle class, the class as a whole was rather conservative; its members had vested interests in the existing system.

Kuan stressed that the Hong Kong people were split into at least three political camps: democrats, conservatives, and moderates. These elites disparaged one another as viable political contenders in the Hong Kong government. They were not prepared to compromise with any competitor whose political future was uncertain at best, dismal at worst. Lau (1995) noted that in the minds of the elites, relative gains for individual political actors overrode considerations of absolute gains available to all through cooperation. Worse, there was no political force in Hong Kong that could play the role of mediator to moderate conflict among the power contenders or to facilitate cooperation among them.

Lau (1995) explained the lack of unity among Hong Kong's elite by "the politics of the vortex": Hong Kong's political dynamics resembled a strong vortex that swept all local political elites upward toward London and Beijing, away from the masses. This politics of the vortex was devastating to unity because elites vied with each other for favors and patronage from London and Beijing. On the other hand, both London and Beijing viewed local elites as groups to be manipulated, selectively using them as pawns against each other, thus widening the gulf that separated them. The result was a fragmented and weak political leadership.

The Salience of Political Issues

Lau (1995) pointed out that a prominent feature of Hong Kong's democratization was the predominance of "pure" political issues to the neglect of the social and economic issues that affected people's lives. After 1984, public disputes were propelled largely by political issues: the pace of political reform, electoral arrangements for the Legislative Council, the mode of selection of the future chief executive, the relationship between the executive and the legislature, the need for and the role of political parties, legislation on human rights, the establishment of a court of final appeal.

The political issues centered on the formulation of the rules of the political game for the present and for the future. As the rules of the political game would determine the distribution of power in Hong Kong, all the political forces concerned were obsessed with establishing rules that would work to their own advantage. The conflicts over the rules of the game are intensified by the continuous erosion of the existing rules and the insecurity of new ones. Moreover, changes in the rules in turn triggered further attempts to change them.

Lau (1995) noted that the preoccupation with "pure" political matters and the neglect of social and economic issues set Hong Kong's democracy apart both from the democratization-cum-decolonization processes in other colonies and from most of the nations involved in third-wave democratization.

Political Alienation of the Masses

Lau and Kuan (1988) found that in respect to "civic culture" (Almond and Verba 1963), the political culture of Hong Kong was subject-parochial rather than participant-oriented. The people exhibited a limited sense of political efficacy, and they were neither prone to political action nor aggressive in challenging authority. In addition, surveys showed that the people's idea of democracy was neither coherent nor correct.

Lau (1995) argued that public acceptance of Hong Kong's nondemocratic system, widespread satisfaction with the social and economic status quo, and worries about the destabilizing effects of democratic changes weakened aspirations for democracy and hindered the rise of a strong democratic movement.

Since democratization in Hong Kong has basically been a top-down process, since the politics of the vortex pulled the elites away from the masses, and since democratization remained a "pure" political matter that did not address matters that affected people's livelihood, the struggle for power both before and after 1997 is still a preoccupation of the elites, with the masses largely playing the role of spectators.

Lau (1992a) further warned that the disparity between the priorities of the elites and those of the people has somewhat alienated the former from the latter, whose trust and confidence in their leaders have been low from the beginning. Incessant bickering among the political elites has led to their mutual delegitimation and to the further erosion of their already limited support base. As a result, democratization in Hong Kong may engender even more political alienation. The empirical studies of Lau and his colleagues (1991, 1992b) revealed that the people of Hong Kong have become less optimistic about the territory's democratic prospects and more cynical about authorities in general.

Restricted and Contested Democracy

In view of these analyses, Lau (1995) found it not surprising that all the bitter and prolonged political struggles among London, Beijing, and local political elites achieved only a modicum of success for democratization; that is, a level of restricted democracy below that of most nations undergoing third-wave democratization. Furthermore, since a binding agreement on democratization among contending parties was not reached, political actors dissatisfied with the existing arrangement were sure to contest the rules of democratization in the future if opportunities arose. Thus the level of consolidation of Hong Kong's restricted democracy was not high enough to warrant its survival.

Lau and Kuan have made a significant contribution to our understanding of Hong Kong's democracy. Their investigations point to the crucial role of external forces in the shaping of democracy in Hong Kong. Their emphasis on power dependence and elite divisions in Hong Kong's contested and restricted democracy is well taken. Furthermore, they have raised many pertinent issues, such as the salience of political issues and mass apathy, that ought to be investigated further. Nevertheless, more recent research on democratization has formulated a different approach, raised different questions, and highlighted different issues.

Critical Issues on Hong Kong's Democratization

A Single Democratic Transition or a Triple Transition?

For Lau and Kuan, democratization was a purely political phenomenon. They conceptualized democracy as an institution that involved a distribution of power among London, Beijing, and local elites. In more recent literature, however, democracy is not an isolated political phenomenon but an institution embedded in the economy and the nation-building process. In this framework, democratization involves not just a political transition but economic and national transformations as well. Thus, studies on Eastern Europe discuss the experience of a triple transition: a simultaneous transition from one-party authoritarian rule to democracy, from a statist economy to a market economy, and from the rule of the Soviet Union to the rise of new nation-states (Przeworski 1991). Since democratization is a part of the triple transition process, it is inevitably affected by economic transformation and nation-building.

In Hong Kong, democratization in the 1980s and 1990s took place side by side with such profound economic transformations as industrial upgrading (from low value-added, labor-intensive activities to high value-added, technology-intensive activities), industrial relocation (from Hong Kong to the Pearl River Delta across the border), and sector diversification (from manufacturing industries to service and financial industries). Observing such economic changes over`little more than a decade, researchers (e.g., Lam and Huque 1995) can't help asking: What was the impact of such profound economic transformations on the transition to democracy in Hong

Kong? In what ways have industrial upgrading, industrial relocation, and sectoral diversification affected the political transactions among Beijing, London, local political elites, and the masses?

Democratization coincided with the process of national reunification with China. After 1997, Hong Kong was no longer a British colony; it became a Special Administrative Region (SAR) of China. Like other national reunification processes, the leap to the status of China's SAR invoked a "Hong Kong" ethnic identity in Hong Kong and a "Chinese" identity in China. Gordon Mathews (1997) is interested in determining how such new ethnic identities and identity politics have interacted with democratization in Hong Kong.

External Constraints or Societal Agencies?

Lau presented a picture of powerless local elites and apathetic masses. Manipulated by external forces, both groups could play only the role of spectator, watching London and Beijing setting the agendas for and making decisive resolutions about democratization. More recent democracy studies see social forces as agencies and actors. Although societal structures and external constraints may determine the range of options available to political participants, it is still the participants that define the political space within which transitions to democracy can occur. Karl and Schmitter (1991) point out that the transition to democracy is a period of great political uncertainty. It is subject to unpredictable events, unforeseen processes, and unintended outcomes. The expected constraints of social structures and external powers seem temporarily suspended. Social sectors often forced into hurried and confused choices. But those choices, no matter how minor and seemingly irrelevant, may produce major effects and channel a democratic system in quite new directions that are not easily reversed. Similarly, Przeworski (1991) formulates a micro approach to democratic transitions in which actors have choices that matter.

Although Beijing and London are more powerful than local Hong Kong social groups, the latter are certainly not powerless. Local political forces have exercised their power and influence in various ways: they lobbied London to pick up the pace of democratization; they provided vital information and resources that Beijing needed; they delegitimized London and Beijing in the mass media; and they mobilized the grassroots population during the Tiananmen incident and the elections. The bargaining power of Hong Kong's social forces was at its height during the long transition period of national reunification, from 1984 to 1997, through which the British have agreed to return the sovereignty of Hong Kong to China, but the Chinese have yet to claim Hong Kong as an SAR.

Now the questions that need to be raised are: To what extent and in what ways have local forces played a role in shaping the form, speed, and extent of democratization in Hong Kong? Why were some social forces more influential than others in shaping the policies of London on some issues during some periods?

Political Elites or Social Classes?

In Lau's conceptual scheme (1995:85), elites were political actors interested in purely political matters. They sought power, with the result that "relative gains for individual political actors [overrode] consideration of absolute gains available to all through cooperation." Lau, then, stressed the need for strong leadership in the democratization of Hong Kong.

Nevertheless, like other elite theorists, Lau took a one-sided view of democracy; he saw democracy as rule not by the people but by elites. Here the inequality of power obviates democracy. Therefore, Lau's elite theory turns a blind eye to the class inequalities that have been very much in evidence in all democratic regimes. Lau also underestimated the role of class in either promoting or blocking democracy. As Eva Etzioni-Halevy points out, elites' "positions depend to a considerable extent on the interests they represent, and on the support they can therefore gain among different social classes. Hence elite analyses that neglect these interests afford but an imperfect understanding of the social forces that contend with each other in the struggle for democratization and the stabilization of democracy" (1997:xxxii).

Huber and her colleagues (1993) and Rueschemeyer and his co-workers (1992), in contrast, emphasized the crucial importance of classes in democratization. For Huber and her colleagues, capitalist development is related to democracy because it shifts the balance of class power, weakening the power of the landlord class and strengthening subordinate classes. Democracy, they pointed out, is not a creation of the bourgeoisie. Although the bourgeoisie made important contributions to the move toward democracy in their struggle with the feudal aristocracy, they were hostile to further democratization when their own class interests seemed to be threatened by the nascent working class. It is important to note that the bourgeoisie often come around to supporting democracy once it turns out that their class interests can be protected within the system.

A class perspective shifts our focus from external constraints to the critical role of social classes in Hong Kong's democratization. Hong Kong was well known as a capitalist paradise, for example, and its big business monopolized access to the colonial government for over a century; how, then, did business leaders react to democratization? Did they view it as an opportunity to strengthen or challenge their class interests? What did they do to retain their hegemonic control of the state during the transition period?

A Conservative Middle Class or Democratic Service Professionals?

Kuan pointed out that Hong Kong's middle class was rather conservative and its members had vested interests in the status quo. In the mainstream literature of third-wave democracy, however, the middle class is a crucial actor in the promotion of democratization. As Huntington (1991b) asks, what changes in plausible independent variables in the 1960s and 1970s produced the dependent variable of democratizing regime changes in the 1970s and 1980s? Huntington's answer is that economic development promotes the expansion of the middle class: a larger and larger proportion of society consists of businesspeople, professionals, shopkeepers, teachers, civil servants, managers, technicians, and clerical and sales workers. As the process of modernization continued, the leverage of rural radical movements on the political process weakened, and the urban middle class grew while the industrial working class declined. The potential threat that democracy posed to middle-class groups thus abated, and these groups became increasingly confident of their ability to advance their interests through electoral politics.

However, Huntington never clarifies the concept of the middle class. In the nineteenth century, businesspeople could be classified as middle class, because there was an aristocracy above them. But in the late twentieth century, businesspeople are surely the upper class: they have no class above them. In addition, there are profound differences between the so-called old middle class of small owners and shopkeepers and the new middle class of professionals and technicians. In fact, the new middle class can further be differentiated into a corporate segment of accountants and managers (who work in the business sector) and a service segment of college professors and social workers (who work in the state and nonprofit sectors). Huntington's middle class, therefore, includes such highly heterogeneous groups as upper-class businesspeople, the old middle class, and new middle-class corporate and service professionals.

In Huntington's middle class, only service professionals can be counted on to be key promoters of democratization. Businesspeople, the old middle class, and corporate professionals, because they work in the capitalist economy, are rational actors who weigh their options with respect to democratization, calculate the costs and benefits associated with each option, and then bargain and compromise accordingly. Service professionals, for their part, consider democracy a sacred value to keep on fighting for regardless of the outcome. Thus service professionals belong to a group of value-committed actors who are loyal to "principled democracy." They strongly support democracy on value grounds.

Instead of viewing the middle class as generally active in promoting democratization, a class perspective highlights the conflicting interests and values between service professionals on the one hand and businesspeople, the old middle class, and corporate professionals on the other in their orientations and commitment to democracy.

Elite Fragmentation, Elite Settlements, or Class Alliance?

Lau argued that serious fragmentation and disunity existed among local political elites in Hong Kong. They ended up weak and powerless because they competed with one another for patronage from Beijing and London; they did not compromise; and they cast doubts on the others.

The mainstream democracy studies, in contrast, stress that democracies are made through negotiations, compromises, and agreements. Huntington (1991b) argued that compromises, elections, and nonviolence made up the third-wave democratization syndrome. Field and his colleagues (1990) formulated an "elite settlement" concept in which the warring factions of a fragmented national elite suddenly and deliberately reorganized by negotiating compromises on their most basic disagreements, thereby achieving consensual unity and laying the basis for a stable representative regime. Similarly, Karl and Schmitter (1991) pointed to the critical role of "foundational pacts" — explicit (though not always public) agreements between contending elites, which define the rules of governance on the basis of mutual guarantees for the vital interests of those involved.

Although elite theorists have contributed insight by highlighting the importance of an "elite settlement" in democratization, they are vague about the specific basic disagreements or vital interests on which elites must compromise. A class perspective spells out those interests. Przeworski (1986), for instance, discusses the conditions of class compromise necessary to establish and maintain capitalist democracy. Capitalist democracy constitutes a form of class compromise in the sense that in this system, neither the aggregate interests of individual capitalists nor the interests of organized wage earners can be violated beyond specific limits. Profits cannot fall so low as to threaten the reproduction of capital, and wages cannot fall so low as to make profits appear to be the only interest of capital.

Przeworski (1986) suggested further that the elements of a Keynesian economic project—the endorsement of private capital, redistribution of income, and a strong state—constitute a perfect combination for guiding a tolerable compromise between capitalists and workers. Moreover, Huber and her colleagues (1993) noted that rapid economic growth, or an expanding economic pie, facilitates compromise between capital and labor and that, conversely, slow growth makes it almost impossible to satisfy both parties.

A lack of unity does not leave all groups forever static. In fact, one of the most interesting aspects of Hong Kong's democracy has been the constant shifting of political alliances over the 1980s and 1990s. Antidemocracy alliances regularly dissolved, realigned, and re-formed, and so did the prodemocracy alliances. Big business entered an unholy alliance with the Communist government in Beijing in order to safeguard its hegemonic domination of the Hong Kong state. Big business and service professionals, despite their major differences over democracy, worked together temporarily right after the Tiananmen incident in 1989 to quicken the pace of democratization. Furthermore, rapid economic growth before 1997 provided a good foundation for some form of class compromise between big business and service professionals.

In this respect, the crucial questions are: What are the indicators of class alliances? What are their characteristics, how long do they last, and what is the basis of their strength? What explains their rise, transformation, and dissolution? And how exactly have shifting elite alliances shaped democratization in Hong Kong?

Predetermined Outcome or Changing Phases of Democratization?

Lau was more interested in examining structural outcomes than in tracing the processes of democratization. He seemed to endorse a view of structural determination—that is, he viewed power dependence on two superior governments as having hampered democratic development in Hong Kong. In the end, Lau was quite pessimistic about the prospect of democratization in Hong Kong, because it divided the people, increased political alienation, and delegitimized political elites.

More recent investigations, however, have focused on the dynamics between pro- and antidemocratic forces. The future of democratization is uncertain and contingent on historical events and the strategic interaction of those forces. These investigators express an optimistic sense that democracy can be crafted and promoted in a structurally unfavorable environment (Kitschelt 1993; Di Palma 1990).

Przeworski (1986) lamented that establishing democracy is a process of institutionalizing uncertainty. Capitalists do not always win conflicts processed in a democratic manner; indeed, they have to struggle continually in pursuit of their interests. In a democracy, no one can win once and for all; if one group is successful once, the victors immediately face the prospect of further struggle in the future. Outcomes of democratic conflicts are not simply indeterminate: they are uncertain, and unlikely outcomes do occur.

The contour of democratization in Hong Kong has taken many surprising turns over the past two decades. The negotiations between London and Beijing from 1982 to 1984 led to the genesis of the democracy project; the Hong Kong government's democratic reforms and elections in 1985 gave a strong boost to the democracy movement; and the drafting of the Basic Law in the late 1980s signaled the democratic transition. Then, in 1989, the Tiananmen incident suddenly exploded, creating a crisis of confidence and the rebirth of democratization in Hong Kong. In the early 1990s, Governor Patten's democratic reforms further empowered the democrats and intensified the conflict between London and Beijing. The process of democratization in Hong Kong has been highly dynamic, constantly shifting from empowerment to alienation at short notice.

In view of this dynamic process, we must ask: What are the critical phases of democratization in Hong Kong? How can we explain the transition from one phase of democratization to another? And what explains the trend toward a restricted and contested democracy in Hong Kong?

Toward a Societal Explanation

The dependency explanation of Hong Kong's democracy highlights the crucial role of Beijing and London; thus, the Hong Kong government is characterized as a dependent polity controlled once by London, now by Beijing. In this view, it is London and Beijing that set the rules of democratization in Hong Kong, while the Hong Kong people were denied the right to participate in the shaping of their own future. This explanation tends to overlook Hong Kong's social forces, because local elites are seen as power-seeking and preoccupied with "pure" political issues; they have been divided and manipulated by Beijing and London, while the masses have remained alienated from the political process. Consequently, focusing on the structural outcome of democratization, proponents of the power dependence theory have taken a pessimistic view of democracy's prospects in Hong Kong.

However, more recent studies point to the crucial role of social forces and their shifting alliances in the democratization process. Instead of seeing democratization as a purely political phenomenon, these investigators situate it as one part of a triple transition, embedded in and interacting with the processes of economic restructuring and nation-building. The triple transition has released new social groups that can make strategic decisions affecting the outcome of democratization. Rather than characterizing the elites as power-seeking, these writers emphasize that elites are situated in a class hierarchy, have class interests, and raise class issues in their quest for democratization. Finally, instead of focusing on predetermined structural outcomes, they examine how social forces and their shifting alliances have complicated the genesis and transformation of democratization.

This aim of this book is to bring social forces, political alliances, and their impact on the changing phases of democratization back in when we study Hong Kong's democracy.

Social Forces

This book has identified six key players in Hong Kong's democratization: (1) London and the Hong Kong government, (2) Beijing and the pro-Beijing forces, (3) big businesspeople, (4) corporate professionals, (5) service professionals, and (6) the grassroots population.

For brevity, let us speak of the London government simply as London. Although the Hong Kong government had considerable autonomy before the 1980s, its independence sharply eroded as the 1997 issue loomed. Consequently, let us assume the coherence of London's and the Hong Kong government's policies unless otherwise stated. London and the pro-British forces were powerful because they controlled the colonial government and enlisted the support of other Western states. London's interests were to maintain effective administration of Hong Kong up to 1997 and then to retreat gracefully.

Similarly, I shall speak of the Beijing government simply as Beijing. Pro-Beijing forces in Hong Kong include the Xinhua News Agency (Beijing's unofficial consulate), the leftist Hong Kong Federation of Trade Unions (HKFTU), the leftist newspapers (*Wen Wei Po* and *Ta Kung Po*), the leftist schools, and so on. I call these forces "pro-Beijing" rather than "pro-China" (*qinzhong*) because many democrats in Hong Kong are also highly patriotic, and although they have protested against the policies of the present Beijing government, they are pro-China too. Beijing and the pro-Beijing forces are powerful because they are now Hong Kong's rulers. Beijing's interests are to use Hong Kong to promote the Four Modernizations and to prevent it from becoming a counterrevolutionary base.

The power dependency theory contributes to our insight by identifying London and Beijing as the key actors in Hong Kong's democratization, but if we are truly to understand the changing path of Hong Kong's democratization, we have to bring social forces and state-society relationships back in. Big businesspeople have played crucial roles in blocking democratization in Hong Kong. I use the terms *big businesspeople* and *big capitalists* interchangeably to refer to a small group of tycoons who own or direct the transnational corporations of Hong Kong, such as the Bank of East Asia, the Worldwide Shipping Group and Kowloon Wharf, and Jardine & Matheson. Before the 1980s, the British hongs (large, traditional trading companies) were key players in Hong Kong politics. After the 1997 issue arose, the power center gradually shifted to the Hong Kong Chinese tycoons who were patronized by Beijing. Big businesspeople are powerful because they own Hong Kong's economic resources and were the ruling class before democratization. Business's interests are to promote economic prosperity and political stability as well as to retain control of the Hong Kong government.

Instead of calling them *new middle class,* I prefer to use the term *service professionals* when I speak of social workers, teachers, journalists, lawyers, and the like, because the new middle class is deeply divided between two contradictory segments: service professionals and corporate professionals (managers, accountants, engineers, architects, etc.). Corporate professionals tend to ally themselves with big business to slow democratization and restrict its scope. Only service professionals have been key promoters of democratization. They are influential because they have symbolic power to shape public opinion through the mass media, their track record in winning direct elections is a distinct asset, and a few have the popular power of charisma. Service professionals' interests are to ensure autonomy, freedom, the rule of law, and respect for human rights, and to promote social welfare and lessen class inequalities.

Finally, I use the term *grassroots population* to describe the urban masses.

I avoid the term *working class* because Hong Kong's urban masses are not class-conscious and have yet to form a political class. For historical reasons, Hong Kong's workers are divided into pro-Beijing and pro-Taipei camps, and they are more interested in national reunification than in workplace issues. While there has been no shortage of community protests, large-scale strikes and workers' violence are almost unheard of. Hong Kong's urban masses are more interested in raising issues that impinge on their daily lives than in fighting for class issues in the workplace. The grassroots population's strength lies in their sheer numbers at the ballot box. Their interests are to safeguard their livelihood, expand their entitlements, and minimize the harmful impacts of industrial relocation and upgrading.

Shifting Alliances

Naturally, these social forces seldom acted on their own. They formed alliances with one another and with the state actors, and they shifted alliances as the democracy project unfolded. In the 1970s, colonial officials formed an alliance with pro-British big businesspeople. In the early 1980s, a temporary patriotic alliance between Beijing and service professionals emerged during the negotiations over the future of Hong Kong. In the late 1980s, an unholy alliance was forged between Beijing and big businesspeople. Finally, in the early 1990s, a populist alliance between service professionals and the grassroots population was formed for the 1991 and 1995 elections.

We must distinguish, however, between two kinds of alliance. An *institutional alliance,* based on common class interests and values, is formalized through institutional channels and therefore is highly stable and has lasting impact. A *strategic alliance,* in contrast, is based on political convenience. As it has no institutional basis, it easily falls apart when the political situation changes. Different types of alliances have led to changing phases of democratization in Hong Kong.

Changing Phases of Democratization

I adopt the narrow concept of democracy formulated by Schumpeter (1950:269), for whom "the democratic method is that institutional arrangement for arriving at political decisions in which individuals acquire the power to decide by means of a competitive struggle for the people's vote." In this formulation, democracy is simply a political method, a mechanism for choosing political leadership. The citizens are given a choice among rival political leaders who compete for their votes. The ability to choose between leaders at election time is democracy (Sorensen 1993:10). The merit of this narrow definition is that, by not overloading the term *democracy* with social and economic rights, it enables us to investigate why some democratic governments are more prone than others to promote welfare policies and safeguard human rights.

Hong Kong has quickly gone through several phases of democratization since the 1970s. As a British colony, Hong Kong before the mid-1980s was a *nondemocracy*. The governor was appointed by the queen on the advice of Parliament, and the governor in turn appointed members of the Legislative Council. There was simply no meaningful election, and Hong Kong citizens had no voice in their political leadership.

By the mid-1980s, however, the Hong Kong government began to be transformed into a quasi-democracy or a *restricted democracy* when elections were introduced to select some political leaders. And Hong Kong's democracy continued to be restricted because the London government, and later the Beijing government, set severe limits on meaningful and extensive competition for all positions of government power. Under this restricted democracy, only one-third of the legislature's seats would be directly elected, and the governor could not be directly elected at all.

In the 1990s, as the democrats gained power, they pushed for a *populist democracy,* in which all positions of real power (such as the governorship and seats in the legislature) would be opened to meaningful competition through direct elections by Hong Kong's citizens. As Governor Patten tried to accommodate the democrats' wishes by reinterpreting the Basic Law, and as Beijing condemned Patten for violating the Basic Law and decided to replace the 1995 popularly elected legislature with a provisional legislature on July 1, 1997, a *contested democracy* was evolving in Hong Kong, because these key political actors had failed to arrive at a consensus to institutionalize the rules of electoral competition. In the late 1990s, however, after Beijing not only agreed to hold new elections in 1998 to replace the provisional legislature but also assured the democrats that they would be allowed to run for office, the democrats tactically accepted the restricted democracy imposed by Beijing.

The task of this book is to explain the origins and the transformation of the democracy project in Hong Kong. In other words, what explains the metamorphosis of the Hong Kong state from a nondemocracy before the 1980s to a restricted democracy in the late 1980s, then to a contested democracy in the early 1990s, then back to a restricted democracy in the late 1990s? What prevented the evolution and consolidation of populist democracy in Hong Kong? What roles have Hong Kong's social forces and their alliances played in the genesis and transformation of Hong Kong's democracy project?

Chapter Outline

After this chapter reviews the dependence explanation, critical issues, and a societal approach to examine Hong Kong's democratization, the next chapter will examine the historical setting in which Hong Kong's democratization took place.

Chapter 2 argues that the Hong Kong government was a nondemocracy, its political stability based upon an expatriate alliance between British officials and pro-British big businesspeople. However, as Hong Kong became a newly industrializing economy in the 1970s, the numbers of college students also increased. In response to the overseas Diaoyutai movement and the "China heat" in the early 1970s, these students started a nationalist movement to visit China and for promoting Chinese as the official language of Hong Kong. When student activists graduated in the mid 1970s, they entered social work, teaching, and journalism and became service professionals. Trying to forge a populist alliance with the grassroots population, the service professionals promoted a community movement to challenge the political hegemony of the expatriate alliance. Nevertheless, service professionals still had to wait until the advent of the 1997 event in the early 1980s before they could actively push for democratization.

Chapter 3 examines how the negotiations over the future of Hong Kong between Beijing and London led to the genesis of the democracy project in Hong Kong. During negotiation politics from 1982 to 1984, Beijing proposed a package of "Hong Kong People Ruling Hong Kong" to craft a strategic alliance with the service professionals. In response, the service professionals were politicized, forming new political groups, and developing a pro-welfare, democratic platform to prepare for the 1997 transition. After London decided to accept Beijing's demands, it pushed for inserting some democratic clauses in the Joint Declaration to sell the package to the Hong Kong service professionals and the British Parliament.

Once London let the democratic genie out, it proposed modest democratic reforms in 1984. Chapter 4 studies how societal forces in Hong Kong react to the transformation of a nondemocracy into a quasi, restricted, corporatist democracy. The service professionals seized the democratic openings and actively participated in local District Board and Legislative Council elections. They were empowered by defeating the business conservatives in the local elections. Once they were elected into the Legislature, they began to impose their pro-welfare, pro-environmental agenda in the Legislative Council in the late 1980s. This growing power of the service professionals alarmed the big businesspeople. Threatened by the prospect for losing power during democratic elections, big businesspeople were determined to regain their political hegemony in the Hong Kong government through slowing down and restricting the scope of democratization.

Chapter 5 traces the formation of an "unholy alliance" between Hong Kong's big businesspeople and the communist Beijing government. This alliance was institutionalized by the economic integration of Hong Kong and China as well as by the appointment of big businesspeople into the drafting committee for the Basic Law. The constitution-drafting process was then used by the big businesspeople to impose a probusiness, pro-Beijing political agenda. The service professionals did fight for their model of populist democracy; they wanted the Hong Kong government to fulfill its promise to institute direct elections in 1988, and protested against the business model both in the drafting committee and in the streets. Nevertheless, after London joined Beijing and the big businesspeople to form a strategic conservative alliance, the service professionals' package was defeated, and a restricted, corporatist democracy was stipulated in the Basic Law.

Chapter 6 examines how this conservative alliance was suddenly torn apart by the Tiananmen incident in 1989. The Tiananmen incident discredited Beijing and the pro-Beijing forces, frightened some big businesspeople, pressured London and the Hong Kong government to speed up the pace of democratization in Hong Kong, and empowered the service professionals who emerged as popular leaders against Beijing's Tiananmen policies. Seizing this opportunity, the service professionals deepened community bonding with the grassroots population. Through this populist alliance, the service professionals had a landslide victory at the first direct election to the Hong Kong Legislature in 1991. Alarmed again by the growing influence of the service professionals in the Legislature, the big businesspeople returned to the unholy alliance with Beijing.

Chapter 7 shows that London abruptly changed its decolonization policy in the early 1990s. It dropped its cooperative policy and adopted an antagonistic policy toward Beijing. In 1992, Governor Patten crafted a strategic alliance with the service professionals by appointing them to the Executive

Council and promoting a pro-welfare policy. Then Patten reinterpreted the grey area of the Basic Law to fit the populist democracy model of the service professionals. With Patten's support, the service professionals again had an overwhelming victory in the 1995 elections. But Beijing, with the blessing of the big businesspeople, decided to dismantle the popularly elected Legislature and set up a provisional Legislature after the resuming of sovereignty, laying the conditions for a contested democracy during the 1997 transition.

However, contested democracy did not materialize during the July 1, 1997 transition. The aim of Chapter 8 is to explain why the service professionals suddenly dropped their radical stand and decided to tactically work with Beijing during the July 1 transition. On the one hand, Beijing announced that new elections to the Legislature Council would take place as early as mid-1998. Beijing also ensured the Democratic Party that its members would be allowed to run in elections in the post-1997 SAR government. Furthermore, the Chief Executive Elect, Tung Chee-hwa, successfully maintained a communication channel with the Democratic Party and personally appealed to the democrats for a smooth transition on July 1. On the other hand, the Democratic Party was weakened by the departure of radical members to form a new Frontier organization and by the pro-welfare stand of Tung's SAR government. Subsequently, the Democratic Party accepted a class compromise with Beijing and Tung's SAR government over democratization.

Before we examine the origins and transformation of Hong Kong's democracy, it may be helpful to provide a brief overview of Hong Kong's history in order to provide background information for discussion.

Hong Kong in British, Chinese, and Hong Kong History

Situated in the coastal area of Guangdong Province, Hong Kong was a frontier region of southern China up to the mid–nineteenth century. After losing several wars to Britain, however, China was forced to cede the island to Great Britain "permanently" in 1842 and a part of the Kowloon peninsula in 1860. In 1898, a large part of Hong Kong's hinterlands, called The New Territories (covering 92 percent of the Hong Kong territory), was leased to Great Britain for ninety-nine years.

During the long years when Hong Kong was a British colony, its history was written largely from a British perspective: Hong Kong was viewed from outside and from above. British observers (e.g., Eitel 1895) tended to portray the British as the principal actors, the initiators of action. The development and execution of British policy were the main concerns of the colonial historians; they had little to say about the Chinese people in Hong Kong. In the picture they presented, most Hong Kong Chinese saw themselves as willing subjects of a foreign government rather than as involuntary slaves of a conquering colonial regime. The aim of those historians was to show how the colonial government and the British elites created an economic miracle that transformed Hong Kong from a traditional fishing village in the nineteenth century to a modern global city in the twentieth.

In sharp contrast to the colonial approach, Tsai (1993) explored the social crises, conflicts, and political activism of Chinese laborers, merchants, and intelligentsia in Hong Kong. To the masses of Hong Kong's workers, the "foreign devils'" rule often seemed arbitrary and unjust. They sarcastically called St. John's Cathedral Hung-mo-miu (the Red Hair Temple, or the temple of red-haired foreign devils) and Governor Sir Reginald E. Stubbs *si-tap-si* ("shit Stubbs"). The Chinese merchants in Hong Kong, too, were nationalists to a degree and were worried about China's possible partition and absorption by foreign powers. They thus developed an ambivalent relationship of collaboration and resentment with the colonial government and foreign business during the popular insurrection in 1884, the anti-American boycott in 1905, and the boycott of the Hong Kong Tramway in 1912. Up to the 1940s, the proximity of Hong Kong to the Chinese mainland and the close socioeconomic connections across the border gave China considerable influence over Hong Kong's society.

Nevertheless, in 1949 Hong Kong and mainland China went their separate ways. After the Communist revolution, mainland China sealed off its border with Hong Kong by installing barbed wire and strict border controls to prevent its socialist domain from being infected by the capitalist disease of Hong Kong. Mainland China then actively promoted Mao Zedong's revolutionary policies—collectivization, nationalization, self-reliance, politics in command, and the Cultural Revolution.

Hong Kong, for its part, rapidly pursued export-led industrialization in the 1950s and 1960s (So 1986a). The Communist revolution on the mainland brought windfall profits to Hong Kong as Chinese capitalists transferred capital, international connections, and machinery from Shanghai to the British colony and laborers fled to Hong Kong to avoid the turmoil of the revolution. Mainland China was quite willing to supply food, raw materials, and even drinking water to Hong Kong in exchange for much-needed foreign currency. This unequal exchange of cheap Chinese products for

Hong Kong currency subsidized Hong Kong's economy, lowered its cost of living, strengthened its competitive position in the world market, and quickly established Hong Kong as a newly industrializing economy.

Because Hong Kong's political economy diverged so sharply from mainland China's, its people began to develop a distinctive lifestyle, set of cultural values, and identity that set them apart from the mainland Chinese. Skeldon (1997) notes that high fertility in the postwar decades led to increasing numbers of Hong Kong Chinese who had been born in Hong Kong and had little contact with mainland China. Faure (1997) also notes that up to the 1960s most Hong Kong Chinese had migrated from mainland China, but from then on were viewed as Hong Kong people of Chinese descent. Wu (1996:161–62) recalls that "people like myself no longer associated with China in the same way that our parents had. I've never thought of myself as someone who was a Chinese national. I thought of myself as a Hong Kong person, and there were many who thought like me. . . . We were the second generation. We had grown up in Hong Kong. We were more affluent, better educated, more inquisitive, and it was quite natural to want to have a role in the running of Hong Kong, whether through community affairs, social affairs, or politics. It was one of the major issues that I, and others, became concerned with while I was at university in the early 1970s."

In the 1970s, then, members of the second generation became politically active; they began to promote Hong Kong's interests and a Hong Kong identity; and they wanted to make, write, and interpret history from a Hong Kong point of view. In Chapter 2 we will see how this 1970s generation became the pioneers of the democracy movements in the 1980s and 1990s.

Part I | **The Genesis of the**

Democracy Project

2 | The Prelude to Democratization

> We must clearly understand the call of nationalism and the responsibility of Chinese youth, strongly resist bullying from foreigners, unite all nationalist forces, and continue to struggle for wealth, power, and the great unification of China!
>   Bun-fong Kwan [1971] (1982), student activist

> SoCO [the Society for Community Organization] hopes to enhance social justice, raise citizen power, and help people to know that they are not mere passive beneficiaries but active participants in formulating social policies.
>   Ho-lup Fung (1982), director of SoCO

The Social Origins of Hong Kong's Democracy Movement

What are the social origins of Hong Kong's democracy movement? Who were its leaders and who took active part in it? When did they take up the political cause of challenging the authority of the colonial government?

Studies on Hong Kong's democracy tend to focus on the 1980s. The first half of the 1980s is usually said to be the starting point of the democracy project. Lo (1990), for instance, divides Hong Kong's democracy movement into a "background phase" from 1982 to 1984, a "preparatory phase" from 1984 to 1988, and a "decision phase" from 1989 to 1990. Scott (1989), too, focuses on how the negotiations over the future of Hong Kong in the early 1980s and the democratic reforms of mid-decade affected the contour of democratization in Hong Kong.

In contrast to the literature's focus on the 1980s, I argue that the origin of Hong Kong's democracy project can be traced to the nascent social movements of the 1970s. That was the decade in which the postwar baby-boomers entered college, became politically active, and began to intervene in Hong Kong's historical development. The 1970s political generation was historically significant because it was the first that grew up in Hong Kong and identified itself as HongKonger rather than sojourner Chinese. This local-born generation was different from the postwar sojourner generation, which viewed Hong Kong as a lifeboat in a sea of political turmoil. As Lui and Chiu (1997:100) pointed out, the sojourner generation tended to view "Hong Kong politics as an extension of the Communist-Nationalist struggle, and was based on a fear that China would intervene in Hong Kong. The 1966 disturbances and the 1967 riots marked the end of an era and the beginning of a new one — a (temporary) farewell to politics phrased within the framework of 'Chinese politics.' "

In the early 1970s, however, the Hong Kong–born generation suddenly rediscovered its cultural links to the Chinese motherland. The 1970s generation initiated a national movement for identification with China. In the mid-1970s, when the China Heat died down, this local-born political generation turned its attention to the inequalities in Hong Kong society. It then engaged in a robust community movement on behalf of the urban grassroots.

This chapter presents a "continuity thesis," arguing that this generation's participation in the nationalist and community movements had a profound impact on the techniques, values, and leadership of the democrats in the 1980s (see also Leung 1986b; B. Leung forthcoming). The nationalist and community movements provided training in the techniques and strategies of the democracy movement. The 1970s were the formative years in which the democrats acquired the values of nationalism and community orientation: they not only pushed for democratic reforms but also accepted reunification with China and advocated welfare policies for the grassroots population. Furthermore, there was continuity in movement participants, as the 1970s political generation became the leaders, activists, and key supporters of the democracy movement in the 1980s and the 1990s (W. T. Lee 1996).

Let us examine the rise of the nationalist and community movements in the 1970s and see how they served as a prelude to the democratization of Hong Kong in the 1980s (Lo 1997:43).

The Early 1970s

The Interstate Setting

Hong Kong's nationalist movement was a response to the changing political situations in the United States and China as well as to the political, economic, and educational setting of Hong Kong in the early 1970s (So and Kwitko 1992).

In the United States the antiwar movement was at its height, and students were not alone in condemning the Vietnam War as an act of imperialism and demanding that the U.S. government pull its troops out of Vietnam. The antiwar movement quickly connected with the civil rights and women's liberation movements, because many radical students thought that imperialism, racism, and sexism were inevitably linked to U.S. capitalism.

China, too, underwent political turmoil in the late 1960s as the Cultural Revolution abolished university entrance examinations, sent city people to the countryside, set up May 7 cadre schools, and turned workers into managers. The Maoists stressed "redness" at the expense of technical expertise and glorified the virtues of selflessness and self-sacrifice in service to the people. Their self-proclaimed mission was the eradication of all vestiges of foreign imperialism, of which Hong Kong was the most blatant. Beijing always insisted that it reserved the right to reassert control of Hong Kong whenever it chose. Still, Beijing preferred not to interfere with the colonial status quo for economic and geopolitical reasons. The official Beijing position was that Hong Kong was a question left over from history to be settled in an appropriate way when the time was ripe; reunification would be accomplished peacefully and through negotiations. During the Cultural Revolution, Beijing even warned the radical Red Guards not to incite disturbances in Hong Kong (Roy 1990).

By the early 1970s, the Beijing government began to scale down its revolutionary fervor and engaged in pragmatic diplomacy. It succeeded in luring President Nixon to pay China a visit and in replacing the Taiwan government as the sole government representing China in the United Nations. Beijing also opened its doors to visitors sympathetic to Mao Zedong's programs. In 1972 Beijing made clear to the United Nations Committee on Decolonization that Hong Kong was "entirely within China's sovereign right," and therefore should not be included in the list of colonial territories to be granted independence (Roberti 1994:10). As a result of the Chinese protest, the United Nations agreed to delete Hong Kong from its list of colonies. With U.S. backing and a seat on the U.N. Security Council, the prestige of the Beijing government had risen to unprecedented heights in the early 1970s.

The Political Setting

Despite these tremendous political changes in China and the interstate system, there had been little departure from traditional nineteenth-century methods of colonial administration in Hong Kong. The colonial government can be called a *corporatist bureaucratic state* for these reasons:

First, the colonial government was a bureaucratic rather than a democratic state. As King (1981:133) noted, "strictly speaking, there [were] no politicians in Hong Kong." Like other British colonies, Hong Kong failed to institute a competitive electoral system for the selection of its governor and legislators. The governor was appointed by the Queen on the advice of the Secretary for Foreign and Commonwealth Affairs in London for a renewable term of five years. The governor, in turn, appointed senior government officials such as the chief secretary, the financial secretary, and the commissioner of police. The governor also appointed "unofficial members" to the Executive Council (Exco) and the Legislative Council (Legco). In reality, the Exco had no administrative functions; it simply advised the governor on all administrative decisions. The Legco, on the other hand, did legislate, and it passed government budgets. In this respect, the essence of the Hong Kong bureaucratic state was "the wide executive and legislative powers of the governor under the supervening authority of the Colonial Office" (Ghai 1991:798).

Second, the bureaucratic state adopted a corporatist strategy to promote political stability. At the top level, senior government officials and the British hongs formed a close *expatriate business alliance.* The administrative ranks of the Hong Kong government were occupied almost exclusively by officers on expatriate terms of service (Davies 1977). These expatriate officials ruled Hong Kong with the help of a small group of merchants and bankers affiliated with such big British hongs as Jardine & Matheson, John Swire, and the Hong Kong and Shanghai Bank. Scott (1989) points out that as early as the 1850s, large hongs and the Chamber of Commerce, which represented the interests of British merchants, had an informal process of nominating unofficial members to the Legislative Council. By the 1890s, after many Chinese businesspeople were appointed to lower-level municipal councils and advisory boards, a few prominent Chinese with extensive economic ties to British hongs were also appointed to the Legco. The system of appointments to the government bodies, therefore, served as a vital institutional link between the expatriate officials and British (or pro-British) businesspeople, guaranteeing that British business interests would be the only ones represented in the colonial government (Ghai 1991). In Miners's (1996:248) account, of the 102 unofficials who sat on the Legislative Council between 1850 and 1941, at least 74 were businesspeople, and most of the remainder were lawyers closely connected with business interests. There was a similar preponderance of businesspeople in appointments made to the Executive Council. After World War II, the majority of the unofficials on the Legislative and Executive Councils continued to be businesspeople until 1985. This institutionalization of the expatriates' business alliance gave rise to the saying that "Hong Kong is run by the Jockey Club, Jardine and Matheson, the Hong Kong and Shanghai Bank, and the Governor—in that order" (Miners 1996:247).

Chan (1997:575) remarks that the appointment system not only enabled British businesspeople to enjoy special access to power, information, and policy inputs, and in crisis situations the support of the colonial state against the local Chinese grassroots movements, but also distorted the basic orientation of the state in its larger responsibility to the society. The colonial state was at fault for its subservience to business interests. Until the mid-1980s, there was no legislation to enforce competition, to check trade monopolies, or to break up cartels (Miners 1996:253).

Under this expatriates' alliance, there was naturally a consensus mode of operation in the Legco. The unofficials were chosen not for their ability to represent the society's interests but for their conservatism and likely support for the governor. Consequently, although the unofficials could affect government policy by raising questions and creating select committees to scrutinize legislation, these initiatives, when they were actually employed, rarely gave rise to noticeable changes in government policy or to impassioned public controversy (Wesley-Smith 1987). Miners (1994a) comments that the meetings of the Legco were short, polite, and very boring. Most important policies were made behind closed doors, with no accountability to the Hong Kong public. Castells and his colleagues (1990:120) similarly note that the role of the Legco was "purely symbolic, rubber-stamping the laws and decrees submitted to it by the Exco without debate."

Third, the bureaucratic state failed to incorporate labor, community groups, and the grassroots population into its governing bodies (Joe Leung 1990, 1994). The expatriate officials and the big businesspeople preferred policies of laissez-faire and fiscal conservatism. They did not feel it necessary to provide social services to the grassroots population, and they saw little need for government officials to come into contact with them so long as the society remained politically stable. As a result, the relationship between the colonial state and the local civil society had been characterized throughout Hong Kong history by externality, distrust, and distance (Castells et al. 1990).

When the winds of the Cultural Revolution blew over Hong Kong in

1967, a political conflict arose between Hong Kong Maoists and the colonial government (B. Leung 1990). After the colonial government put down the 1967 riot with much violence, a climate of "white terror" was created. In the late 1960s, anyone who raised the issue of social problems or tried to organize a social movement was seen as a leftist — a radical who would disturb the peace and order of Hong Kong society. In such a repressive environment, the urban masses were politically apathetic. Lau (1982) formulated the concept of "utilitarian familism" to explain why the depoliticized Hong Kong people were more interested in satisfying the material needs of their families than in articulating their interests through official channels (see also Wong and Lui 1992:8).

The Economic Setting

That the repressive environment lingered after the 1967 riot was highly unfortunate, because Hong Kong was undergoing very rapid economic growth in this period. Howe (1983:512) reported that "the growth of Net Domestic Product accelerated from 6.8 per cent per annum in the 1950s to 9.6 per cent through the 1960s. . . . If we compare Hong Kong with other countries, World Bank data [show that] . . . no economy consistently outperformed Hong Kong on this indicator throughout both decades." Similarly, Chen (1980:14) pointed out that the GDP (at constant 1966 market prices) grew from H.K.$6.621 billion in 1961 to H.K.$15.704 billion in 1971; the labor force increased from 1.2 million to 1.6 million in the same period, while labor productivity jumped from H.K.$5,558 per person to H.K.$9,629. As Howe (1983) notes, the greatest growth of the Hong Kong economy occurred during the 1960s, when real per capita GDP increased by about 7 percent per year.

The rapid growth of the economy was mostly the result of an influx of refugee capital from Shanghai and refugee labor from South China, the provision of relatively cheap raw materials and consumer goods by the Beijing government, and the post–World War II economic boom of the capitalist West (So 1986a; Wong 1988). However, as the Hong Kong government was still dominated by British hongs, whose interests were mostly in the financial and commercial sectors, it maintained the colonial laissez-faire policy of neither engaging directly in strategic economic planning nor promoting exports for the industrial manufacturing sector to assist Chinese industrial capitalists (Chiu 1995). What the government wanted to do was simply to improve the colony's infrastructure (public housing, transportation, land reclamation, education) to provide a better investment climate for all capitalists.

The sudden influx of Chinese capitalists and workers in the postwar period, moreover, did not arouse much tension between the Chinese population and the British ruling class. As immigrants fleeing from Communist rule, the Chinese capitalists tolerated the British monopoly of the state machinery so as not to rock the boat. And whereas Western Marxist critics (e.g., Halliday 1974) observed terrible working conditions, to immigrant workers in Hong Kong their situations had improved remarkably in comparison with what they had known in mainland China. Most rank-and-file industrial workers were women, and their attachment to the job was often secondary to their family obligations. Rapid economic development and labor shortages led to continuous increases in real wages, and labor mobility was an acceptable alternative to collective bargaining and resolution of grievances (Chiu and Levin forthcoming). Of course, there were unions and strikes. But unions tended to be small and ideologically divided between procommunist and pronationalist factions. Lo (1997:55) remarks that the Hong Kong working class was weak not only because of the political dominance of capitalists but also because of the division of trade unions into rightist, independent, and leftist categories. Consequently, strikes were few and serious ones were almost unknown in the 1970s (Turner et al. 1980).

The Educational Setting

Even after the advent of industrialization in the 1950s, Hong Kong had only one institution of higher education—the University of Hong Kong. Like schools in other British colonies, the university was stamped with the trademarks of British elite education—British professors, British curricula, British textbooks, British-style comprehensive examinations with honors degrees, and the English language as the medium of instruction. The student body was small, and most students were the children of the rich; they could not have afforded the very steep tuition and boarding fees otherwise. In such an environment, the students were generally highly elitist and pro-British. They expected to work for the colonial government and British hongs after graduation, and they were more interested in the Miss University beauty contest and in hazing new students than in studying Chinese history and culture (*Guang Jue Jing* 1985:90; Yuandong Shimu 1982:195; HKU 66 Editorial Committee 1977:32–42). A student leader in the 1970s described the mood among students in the 1960s: "A stagnant, totally uncritical and despondent atmosphere pervaded the whole university campus. Material satisfaction and degenerate personal honour and status were what the students looked for" (quoted in Leung forthcoming).

The mid-1960s, however, brought a drastic change of official policy toward higher education. As Hong Kong's economy began to take off, the corporations sought desperately for professionals, technicians, and managers to hire. The government responded by expanding student enrollments at the University of Hong Kong, establishing a second university, the Chinese University of Hong Kong, and adopting a "sponsored education" policy: tuition fell to a level that working-class families could afford, and generous grants and interest-free loans became available to working-class students bright enough to pass the highly competitive entrance examinations. The number of university students increased from 1,312 in 1962 to 5,659 in 1972 (Xie 1982:45), and they were quite a different lot from the students of the 1960s (HKU Student Union 1987:158).

The laissez-faire policy of the Hong Kong government, moreover, provided enough space for Chinese culture not only to survive but even to flourish. While the University of Hong Kong continued on its traditional British course, instruction at the new Chinese University of Hong Kong was in Chinese, and its aim was "to raise the standard of Chinese education . . . [and] to revere and promote traditional Chinese culture" (Ngan 1966:3).

The college students who grew up in the early 1970s, therefore, were strongly influenced by their historical heritage and the changes their society's institutions were undergoing. They had grown up in a British colonial setting that allowed Chinese culture to flourish; they had observed rapid industrialization but lived in poor working-class neighborhoods. Supported by the government's generous grants and interest-free loans and knowing that a nice professional career would be waiting for them after graduation, the 1970s student generation engaged in serious academic studies, as they did not need to worry about bread-and-butter problems. Impressed by the increasing prestige of the Beijing government in the world, they felt pride in their Chinese ethnicity and developed an urge to be reunited with their motherland. Aroused by the students' movements in the West, they revived the traditional Chinese intellectuals' ethos: they would sacrifice themselves to build up a strong and powerful Chinese nation. Thus they were determined to become political activists to transform their society, their nation, and the world (Yuandong Shimu 1982). These students' ethos and experiences help explain their promotion of the nationalist movement in the early 1970s.

The Nationalist Movement

The Events

The nationalist movement was marked by a series of significant events:[1]

• *The campaign to promote Chinese as an official language.* In July 1970, student unions organized a public forum and gathered over ten thousand signatures on petitions for the adoption of Chinese as Hong Kong's official language. This first large-scale student movement caught public attention, and two years later the government officially acquiesced.

• *The Diaoyutai campaign.* In February 1971, the student unions organized a demonstration in front of the Japanese consulate to protest Japan's takeover of the Diaoyutai Islands. The protesters clashed with police in Victoria Park in July 1971, and twenty-one people were arrested. Many large-scale peaceful demonstrations followed.

• *China tours.* The student union of the University of Hong Kong organized its first official China tour in December 1971; the student union of the Chinese University of Hong Kong followed suit in July 1972. The unions' reports on their tours were very well received by the student bodies. Many student tours of mainland China soon followed.

• *China Week exhibitions.* Student unions organized the first China Week exhibition in 1973 to introduce mainland China to the Hong Kong public. More than ten thousand persons attended the exhibition. More China Week exhibitions followed.

The Discourse

The students' slogan, "Identification with China, pay attention to [Hong Kong] society," reveals several characteristics of the discourse of the Hong Kong student movement. Notice that the slogan put China first and Hong Kong second. Thus the student movement was more a nationalist and anti-

---

1. Like all student movements, the one in Hong Kong had many factions. In addition to the nationalist faction that identified with the Maoists in China, a "social action" faction emphasized the importance of helping the deprived and underprivileged members of the community, a "democratic freedom" faction stressed individualism and hedonism, and a "national rightist" faction identified with the Guomindang in Taiwan. These factions differed in lifestyle as well as in political attitudes and worldview. Nevertheless, most observers have agreed that at the height of Hong Kong's student movement in the early 1970s, the nationalist faction was in control of almost all student unions, and the program of the movement therefore largely reflected the nationalists' concerns and aspirations (see So and Kwitko 1992; B. Leung forthcoming).

colonial movement than a local reform movement. Even its first large-scale campaign, to promote Chinese as the official language, implied condemnation of the colonial government for neglecting the Chinese heritage of the Hong Kong population. Notice too that the slogan called only for "identification with China," not for any rational evaluation of the Beijing government. In this respect, the radical students not only took the existing Communist regime for granted but wholeheartedly endorsed the Maoist version of socialism. Moreover, the slogan asked Hong Kongers only to "pay attention to society," not to take any concrete actions to reform their society. The student radicals thought that only a total restructuring of Hong Kong society through revolution could eliminate colonial domination and social injustice. Since this total restructuring had to be deferred until China took over Hong Kong, and since the Beijing government made it clear that it tolerated the colonial regime in Hong Kong because of special historical circumstances, the student radicals felt that the only thing they could do for Hong Kong per se was to pay more attention to it.

The students rationalized their indifference to the colonial government by claiming than the plight of 700 million Chinese on the mainland was much, much more important that the affairs of 4 million Chinese in Hong Kong. Moreover, following the political line of the Chinese Communist Party, the students argued that the primary contradiction of the early 1970s was not British colonial domination but the imperialism of the United States and the Soviet Union. Thus the radical students' discourse placed global anti-imperialism higher on their agenda than local anticolonialism (Ma 1982). In short, the discourse of the Hong Kong student movement was marked by nationalism, Maoism, anti-imperialism, and radicalism in words but not in deeds. In this respect, the Hong Kong student movement was not unlike the student movements in the United States and China.

Participants, Organization, and Strategy

The participants in the movement were college students—young, enthusiastic, and highly committed. Though their numbers were small, they were willing to devote many hours and enormous energy to the nationalist movement; and though they lacked work experience, they believed they were intelligent enough to accomplish their mission.

The Hong Kong nationalist movement was promoted by such student unions as the University of Hong Kong Student Union, the Chinese University of Hong Kong Student Union, the Polytechnic Student Union, and the Hong Kong Federation of Students of Higher Education. The groups were loosely organized and even more loosely coordinated. They came together temporarily only when they saw a need for collective action. New officers of the student unions were elected every year, and there was no guarantee that the new officers would pursue the policies of the old.

As mentioned previously, the Hong Kong nationalist movement relied upon forums, exhibitions, collection of signatures, campus newspapers, China tours, and public demonstrations to propagandize its causes. With a few exceptions, the colonial government tolerated the students' activities, but the students failed to develop any institutional links with the grassroots population. Public support of the nationalist movement was sporadic and low-key; most people who supported it did little more than show up briefly at exhibitions and sign their names in support of the students' campaigns.

The Government's Response

Although most businesspeople were indifferent to the students' nationalist movement, the colonial government was highly suspicious of it, and showed that it would not hesitate to use force to suppress it if necessary. At the beginning of the Diaoyutai campaign in 1971, for example, the government arrested twenty-one demonstrators in April, arrested another twelve in May, and wounded a few dozen and arrested twenty-two protesters in the famous July confrontation (Yuandong Shimu 1982:4–5).

After the colonial government learned that the nationalist movement targeted the imperialism of the two superpowers more than British colonialism, however, and that the students were more interested in identification with mainland China than in transforming Hong Kong society, it became more tolerant. Although the government still kept close watch on the nationalist movement, it did not interfere with public protests and avoided open confrontation with demonstrators. Chan (1989:16) recalled that when the organizers of a public demonstration applied for a permit only a day before the scheduled event, the government bypassed its own regulations to issue approval in time.

Nevertheless, in order to curb the growing nationalist sentiment in Hong Kong society, the colonial government cultivated its own kind of "Hong Kong" ethnic identity movement in the mid-1970s (Yuandong Shimu 1982: 264, 283). Thus, the government earnestly promoted such events as "The Hong Kong Festival" and "The Keep Hong Kong Clean Campaign" in order to stress identity and loyalty to Hong Kong (in contrast to the nationalist calling by the students to unite with the Chinese motherland), to highlight the importance of economic prosperity and political stability for a healthy

Hong Kong society (in contrast to calling for political activism and commitment in the nationalist movement), and to encourage consumerism and hedonism as characteristics of the "Hong Kong man" (in contrast to the frugal and backward lifestyle of the "socialist man" presented by the Maoists). The government's efforts were not without success: what Hugh Baker (1983) calls the "Hong Kong people" identity began to take hold in the late 1970s.

Contributions and Limitations

The nationalist movement was the first large-scale social movement among Hong Kong college students. It aroused their interest in political participation and gave student leaders an opportunity to acquire skill in mobilization. In fact, the nationalist movement nurtured many activists who later became prominent leaders in the community movement in the late 1970s and the democracy movement in the 1980s.

The nationalists also helped break the climate of white terror. Their movement was a far cry from the violence of 1967 — peaceful, orderly, dedicated to a "good cause." After observing the students' peaceful demonstrations, the public no longer perceived social movements as threats to law and order.

Furthermore, the movement was successful in promoting nationalism. James Chui, president of the Hong Kong Federation of Student Unions, remarked in 1971 that the Chinese official language movement and the Diaoyutai movement "will provoke people to think seriously about their position as Chinese. They are turning points for Hong Kong" (FEER, May 5, 1971). Thus the nationalist movement of the early 1970s served as groundwork for a national alliance with Beijing in the early 1980s.

Nevertheless, the nationalist movement was not without weaknesses. As we have seen, the student unions were loosely organized and torn by factional rivalries. The rapid turnover of officers made any continuity of policy impossible. And the student unions were highly elitist. They had developed no institutional links to the grassroots population. Finally, the fortunes of the nationalist movement were tied to those of the Maoists in China. The Hong Kong nationalist movement was at its height when the Maoists were in power in the early 1970s; with the fall of the Maoists in the mid-1970s, the nationalist movement fell into decline. By the late 1970s, a vigorous community movement had emerged to take its place.

The Late 1970s

The Interstate System

Times had changed by the late 1970s. Economic difficulties in the United States, China, and Hong Kong gave rise to a new community movement.

The United States was suffering under "stagflation"—stagnation of productivity combined with high inflation. Good jobs were scarce. College students lost their enthusiasm for idealistic goals and turned their energies toward building careers. The radical student movement had largely disappeared by the late 1970s. Many radicals turned into yuppies (young, upwardly mobile urban professionals), typically embracing the values of hedonism and consumerism.

The death of Mao was followed by the arrest of the Gang of Four, and Deng Xiaoping's pragmatism took the place of Mao's socialism. Instead of condemning imperialism and colonialism, Beijing desperately searched for foreign investment, management expertise, and advanced technology. Thus in the late 1970s Beijing's image was transformed from that of a proud socialist state to that of a poor Third World nation. Beijing's top priority was to develop productive forces as rapidly as possible. Under the slogan of the "Four Modernizations" it set out to modernize agriculture, industry, science and technology, and the military in an effort to catch up with the advanced capitalist states. To achieve this developmental objective, Beijing promoted an open-door trade policy and brought market forces back in (So and Chiu 1995).

In 1978, a Hong Kong and Macao Affairs Office headed by Liao Chengzhi was set up to examine Beijing's policies toward Hong Kong. Then Beijing opened four "special economic zones" adjacent to Hong Kong and Macao where a semicapitalist system would prevail: they would retain their earnings from exports to promote rapid growth and would act as a bridge between Hong Kong and the mainland (So 1988; Chu 1996:86).

By and large, Beijing and the pro-China forces (the Xinhua News Agency, the leftist unions, newspapers, schools, banks, department stores, etc.) had tolerated the expatriate-business hegemony in Hong Kong because they advanced Beijing's Four Modernizations program. Beijing badly needed Hong Kong's capital investment, technology, management expertise, and foreign currency to jump-start its economic program. In order to improve its relationship with the London government, the Xinhua News

Agency, serving as Beijing's unofficial consulate, even invited Murray Mac-Lehose, the governor of Hong Kong, to visit the capital in 1979.

The Economic Setting

Despite the downward turn in the world economy and the stagflation in the United States, Hong Kong's economy reached another milestone as the third largest container port and the third largest financial center in the world. In the late 1970s the share of the industrial sector in the GDP began to fall, while that of real estate and financial and commercial services rose. In just a decade, the share of real estate, financial and commercial services in the GDP had almost doubled from 14.9 percent in 1970 to 25.9 percent in 1980 (Chen 1980).

A prosperous economy enabled the government to take a more active role in promoting infrastructure projects, public housing, and social services without raising taxes. Faced with the constraint of limited space in the territory on the one hand and the increasing momentum of economic development on the other, the government devised various means to extract land for development. Large-scale reclamation of land from the sea and excavation from hillsides were not enough to solve the problem. The government therefore turned its sights on the urban fringe where squatters, temporary housing, and resettlement projects had proliferated (Chui 1989:217). In 1972 Governor MacLehose announced an ambitious plan to build public housing for 1.8 million people over ten years and to eliminate the squatter huts clinging to the hillsides. Chiu and Levin (forthcoming) note that this policy had an adverse effect on Hong Kong's labor movement by disrupting the working-class squatter communities that had formed in the postwar period. As workers in these areas were dispersed among various housing projects, the spatial basis for reinforcement of group cohesion and collective consciousness was undermined.

Further, MacLehose extended free education from six to nine years and got the Legco to approve funds to build swimming pools, sports stadiums, concert halls, and cultural centers. He appropriated more money for social services, medical and health services, crime prevention, family planning, and pollution control. During the first eight years of his administration, spending on social welfare increased nearly twentyfold (Roberti 1994:13). The proportion of the Hong Kong government expenses grew dramatically to reach 23 percent of the GDP during the MacLehose years, while still ensuring a high rate of economic growth and a balanced budget. According to Castells and his colleagues, "Hong Kong became a welfare state within the limits and constraints of a colonial situation and the straitjacket of a noninterventionist ideology, increasingly refuted in the practice of government" (1990:138).

The increase in social services, however, led to an escalation of urban grievances and protests. The expatriates' state and the urban society were structurally at odds (Lui 1984). On the one hand, the government was compelled to provide public housing and other social services to lower the cost of labor and promote the peaceful labor-management relations that facilitated economic development (Chai 1993:138). On the other hand, the massive dislocation of people when the squatter huts and slums were demolished sparked resentment among the grassroots population. In addition, since low taxation, the government's laissez-faire ideology, and its philosophy of "positive noninterventionism" limited the help it could supply, the public housing it erected for the poor was of low quality and unable to satisfy their needs. Ernest Chui (1989:218) points out that such issues as the management and allocation of public housing were catalysts for urban social conflict throughout the 1970s. The lack of democratic representation as a means to channel grievances to the government aggravated the problem, igniting numerous, sporadic, violent public protests in the mid-1970s. Therefore, although the grassroots population did not protest as a working class in the factory, they participated in social movements against housing and urban issues.

Changing State-Class Relationships

In spite of the above increase of social services provided to the grassroots population, the colonial nature of the Hong Kong government remained intact. The goal of the MacLehose government was to build up political legitimacy on the basis of social programs without constitutional change in the government. Welfare reforms from above thus had not been followed by political reforms from above toward a more democratic, representative government. Hong Kong was still a corporatist bureaucratic state. What had changed in the mid-1970s, however, was the broadening of the corporatist strategy to appoint not just big businesspeople, but corporate professionals such as accountants and lawyers into the Executive Council (Exco) and the Legislative Council (Legco), and a small number of conservative service professionals into the Legco (Davies 1989).

The shift in the economy from labor-intensive to information-intensive, the rise of Hong Kong as the third largest financial center in the world, and the expansion of the state's responsibility for the people's welfare widened the gap between the corporate segment and the service segment of the nascent middle class (So 1993a). Upgrading the economy called for more corporate professionals (managers, accountants, architects, engineers) in the banking, real estate, and manufacturing industries. Employed by corporations and working in the business world, these people wanted to perpetuate the existing capitalist system, and shared big businesspeople's concerns for capital accumulation, profit maximization, commodification, and technical efficiency. As a result, corporate professionals had a closer relationship with big business than with either the working class or state administrators. Like the big businesspeople, the corporate professionals preferred a state that imposed fewer taxes and regulations on corporations and allowed business to influence state policies. The professional associations that administered the systems of accreditation, qualification for registration, and licensing and established guidelines for the professional conduct of their members were strong enough to ensure very high salaries and lucrative benefits. Corporate professionals embraced consumerism wholeheartedly because they had the money to do so. They strove for status symbols, became calculating and utilitarian in human relationships, and enjoyed the status quo.

On the other hand, state welfare policies recruited more service professionals (social workers, teachers, nurses, and journalists) in the state service sector and nonprofit sectors. Since service professionals do not work in the profit sector, they showed little interest in the perpetuation of the capitalist system. Instead, they were more concerned with the expansion of needs and services (e.g., welfare, education, health care, housing) to the grassroots population. From their daily contact with their clients, service professionals are socially closer to the grassroots population than they are to the big businesspeople. Service professionals also had more linkages with state officials, because they depended on the state for jobs, funding, and other facilities. For service professionals, then, the ideal state was a welfare state that redistributed resources from the rich to the poor through a progressive taxation system. They advocated stricter regulations on business to combat environmental abuses, consumer fraud, and tax evasion. They were critical of the consumerism and hedonism encouraged by capitalism. They valued egalitarianism, social justice, reform, and political participation. Chui (1989:227) noted that Hong Kong's social workers were highly politicized because "their constant interaction with government policies, principally through their involvement in welfare work for their clientele, . . .

gave them the justification of policy-relevance for their political participation" (1989:227). Unlike corporate professionals, service professionals failed to develop strong associations to monitor accreditation and licensing, so they were paid much less and had lower occupational prestige. Many service professional organizations, such as the 40,000-member Hong Kong Professional Teachers' Union (HKPTU), acted more like progressive trade unions than like the established professional groups.

Anthony Cheung (1987) further notes that many Hong Kong service professionals were first generation — born in Hong Kong after World War II — and tended to come from working-class and peasant family background, experiencing poverty and hardships during childhood. Growing up with such backgrounds and still maintaining close relationships with their relatives and childhood friends, service professionals wanted to improve the living standard of the grassroots population in Hong Kong. Subsequently, this first generation of service professionals began to participate in community movements in the late 1970s.

The Community Movement

From Student Activists to Community Organizers

The first generation of student activists graduated from college in the mid-1970s. Although no longer Maoist and revolutionary, many student activists still believed in social justice and equality. The mentality of this 1970s generation was thus quite different from that of the generations that grew up in the 1980s and 1990s, heavily influenced by the values of hedonism and careerism.[2]

Even so, a large number of the student activists of the 1970s entered such professions as social work and teaching because they saw them as represent-

2. The student movement so far declined after the 1970s that student unions had difficulty finding students to run for offices. Since the 1980s, Benjamin Leung (forthcoming) notes, students have played only a "marginal and inconspicuous role" in Hong Kong's political development. Leung points out that the small number of student participants, the short duration of each episode, and intermittent involvement without a clear and long-term commitment demonstrated the decline of the student movement in the 1980s. As the 1970s drew to a close, students' role in collective action was increasingly superseded and overshadowed by those of pressure groups and political groups. The dwindling number of student activists then became junior partners of those groups in confronting the established authorities. See also K. K. Leung 1993:161; Yuandong Shimu 1982; So and Kwitko 1992.

ing "the conscience of society" and "the force behind social reform" (Mak 1988:173; Law 1988:166). They had been heavily influenced by the Fabian socialism that was taught in the social work departments of the two universities, with its ideals of equality, freedom, fellowship, and justice. Once they had entered the social service professions, these young graduates' ties to the grassroots population strengthened. The grievances of the urban poor—the demolition of squatter neighborhoods, the debilitating environmental conditions of public housing, dislocation from urban centers to new towns in the New Territories, rapid increases in rent and bus fares—became their own. Highly dissatisfied by the government's responses, service professionals started a robust community movement in the late 1970s.

The Events

The activists in the community movement engaged in a variety of significant activities:

• *Protest against high rent.* The residents of old public housing were relocated to newer buildings with better facilities (they now had private toilets and kitchens) but rents were sharply increased. In 1976, the relocated tenants of six public housing projects organized a protest against the high rents.

• *Demand for participation in meetings on public housing policy.* The Public Housing Authority, the government agency responsible for policies affecting the lives of public housing residents, ignored the residents' complaints. In 1977 the residents of ten public housing projects protested in front of the authority's offices, demanding the right to participate in discussions on public housing policy.

• *The Golden Jubilee Secondary School incident.* After some teachers discovered irregularities in the financial accounts of the Golden Jubilee Secondary School, the principal was found guilty of forgery and a new principal, Miss Kwan, was appointed. Miss Kwan threatened to dismiss the dissenting teachers and tried to isolate new students from them. The dissenting teachers and students marched to Government House to demand Miss Kwan's dismissal. The Education Department's announcement that it would close the school set off a series of protest actions. University students and community activists held a series of sit-ins and demonstrations and engaged in a two-day hunger strike to demand the reopening of the school and a thorough investigation of the issue. In the end, a new school was opened to accommodate the Golden Jubilee Secondary School students.

• *The bus fare protest.* In February 1980, the two bus companies raised their fares by 70 percent. In October they asked for another increase, ranging from 30 to 100 percent. A committee representing two hundred pressure groups was formed to protest against the repeated increases in bus fare. The committee organized forums, surveys, and public demonstrations in Victoria Park, and it formulated a policy of "mass supervision of public enterprises."

Discourse, Organization, and Strategy

The discourse of the community movement in the late 1970s was differed from that of the nationalist movement in the early 1970s. The community movement was more interested in Hong Kongism than in Chinese nationalism. This movement focused on affairs that affected the lives of the Hong Kong community—housing, transportation, education, working conditions. Motherland identity politics was replaced by a discourse centered on allocating more resources to the grassroots population (Lui and Chiu 1997).

Rather than advocating a radical revolution, the community movement stressed reform. The Society for Community Organization (SoCO), as Fung (1982:7) explained, had high aims: "SoCO aims at raising the ability of people to solve problems and at building up citizen power through the process of community work so as to improve the livelihood of people, and, as a result, to change the social system. . . . SoCO hopes to enhance social justice, raise citizen power, and help people to know that they are not only passive beneficiaries, but also an active participant in formulating social policies."

Rather than emphasize theories and ideals, the community movement stressed political actions and practices that would enable powerless citizens to articulate their grievances, influence government policies, and achieve their rights (Joe Leung 1982).

When service professionals joined the movement, its organizational form changed. Whereas the nationalist movement had been organized by the student unions, the community movement was organized by pressure groups. The most important of them (Sing 1996:500–501; S. H. Lo 1988:619, 1997:43):

• People's Council on Public Housing Policy (PCPHP), which mobilized and organized public housing residents to protest rent increases.

- Society for Community Organization (SoCO), which organized community social actions and encouraged assertiveness in the grassroots population.

- Christian Industrial Committee (CIC), which focused on labor welfare policy and industrial safety and monitored public services.

- Hong Kong Professional Teachers' Union (HKPTU), which sought to protect the welfare of teachers and school administrators.

- Hong Kong Social Workers General Union (HKSWGU), which pressed for social services and other benefits for social workers.

Although there were no formal institutional links among these pressure groups, their members formed strong informal networks, because most of them were either former comrades in the nationalist movement or alumni of the two universities. Thus it was not difficult for them to form a temporary coalition to represent the interests of the urban poor before the colonial government when a community protest broke out.

In the late 1970s, the community movement developed three strategies: grassroots community organization, issue intervention, and policy intervention. First, the Society for Community Organization (SoCO) tried to organize squatters and tenants in public housing into permanent citizen organizations, in the hope that they would become independent and improve conditions in the community by themselves. Second, SoCO went directly to the community and helped people to organize political actions when problems such as the eviction of squatters arose. Third, SoCO helped establish the People's Council on Public Housing Policy to fight for fairer policies concerning such matters as roof insulation for top-floor residents, temporary housing, and rents (Fung 1982).

In general, the community movement heavily relied on protest strategies that could enlist public sympathy: mass gatherings, sleep-ins, sit-ins, petitions, peaceful demonstrations, letters to the editor, public posters, press conferences. The hope was that adverse publicity would embarrass the colonial government into changing its political stance. The government characterized the community movement as an attempt to use "group mobilization and propaganda to highlight government deficiencies in order to press for change in government policies" (Home Affairs Branch 1980:1). On the whole, the activists shied away from ugly confrontations; their main strategy was to arouse the sympathy of top government officials and the general public through the mass media (Joe Leung 1994).

Without freedom of the press, this strategy would not have been effective. If Hong Kong had been a democratic state, public protests need not have been carried so far, for the grievances of the urban grassroots population could have been directed through institutional channels. In this respect, these strategies of protest and adverse publicity were products of an undemocratic colonial state that tolerated a high degree of press freedom in an effort to soften its authoritarian image.

The Participants

Emerging in the early 1970s, the community movement gained in sophistication and frequency of activities, and reached its peak by the late 1970s. For example, in terms of numbers, there were only 6 demonstrations, 24 petitions, and 14 press conferences in the community movement between 1971 and 1975; but the numbers rapidly increased to 19 demonstrations, 68 petitions, and 48 press conferences between 1976 and 1980 (Lui and Kung 1985:80). In terms of goals, the early 1970s community movement tended to focus on specific complaints, such as poor facilities and relocation problems in public housing estates. However, in the late 1970s, it began to raise general policy issues and demand input into the decision-making process.

How can we explain the ripening of the community movement in the late 1970s? It may be due to the recruitment of new elements into the movement. As might be expected, the majority of participants were the grassroots population living in public housing. It was the urban poor who suffered most from relocation, from poor housing, and from the high cost of transportation. With no resources and no formal means to articulate their concerns, they usually resorted to violence to make their grievances known to the government in the early 1970s.

By the mid-1970s, however, service professionals had begun to take part in the community movement in large numbers. A Hong Kong government report (Home Affairs Branch 1980:3:5) pointed to two types of service professionals who actively supported pressure group activism: (1) Pressure groups "are served or led by young social workers, who have been trained to believe that they have an important role to play in identifying social problems and in helping the man in the street to organize himself to press his justifiable demands on the Government." Before the 1970s, the social work profession stressed consensus, cooperation, and community integration. With the arrival of student activists, however, emphasis shifted to protests and demonstrations in an effort to organize marginalized people into instruments of power. (2) Young reporters were "strongly motivated by modern theories on the role of the news media in society. . . . There is a tendency therefore for them to be suspicious and critical of Government policies and to slant their reports in favour of the pressure groups." As Margaret Ng, one of the activists, said, "My generation . . . grew up with a longing to understand politics and to play a much more positive role in society" (quoted in Chai 1993:140).

What service professionals contributed to the community movement was organizational skills, extensive social networks with other pressure groups, and the ability to mobilize the grassroots population (Lui 1984). In addition, service professionals brought symbolic power to the community movement. They helped articulate the grievances of the grassroots population to the public; they were able to get media people to cover their protest activities; they laid the foundation for more critical attitudes toward the business establishment; and they broke the "interpretive monopoly" of the government (Chai 1993:140).

When service professionals became part of pressure groups, the community movement had more resources than it had ever had before. It no longer needed to resort to violence to make its case to the public. Yet the combined resources of service professionals and the urban poor were still not enough to enable the activists to engage in direct confrontation with the government.

Government Responses

The community movement's public protests were concerned mainly with the specific allocation of government resources; they were not directed primarily against either the capitalist system, the Beijing government, or the Hong Kong government. As long as the movement was not directed against them, Beijing and big businesspeople in Hong Kong paid little attention to it. It is interesting to note that although Beijing developed a rudimentary network of local organizations in the 1970s, pro-Beijing forces maintained a very low profile in the community and took no part in government-sponsored institutions. These pro-Beijing forces essentially kept to themselves, sent their children to their own schools, read their own newspapers, and worked in China-oriented enterprises (England and Rear 1981:14; Pepper 1997:686–87).

By the late 1970s, however, the colonial government struck back with a policy of "community building" — providing more government-sponsored infrastructural support to residents' organizations, strengthening community programs such as sports and recreation, mobilizing the public in government campaigns, and taking public opinion into account in policy formulation. Joe Leung (1977) identified six programs by which the government strove to demonstrate its commitment to local community affairs: the Community Involvement Plan; the Fight Violent Crime campaign; a three-tiered system of city district committees; the Community and Youth Officers program of the Department of Social Work; the Recreation and Sports Officers program of the Education Department; and the Police Community Relations Offices program of the Police Department. The community-building policy was an attempt to extend government-sponsored participatory institutions to the grassroots population to make it harder for pressure groups to mobilize them.

John Walden, director of home affairs between 1975 and 1980, has revealed that the government and the Special Branch of the Hong Kong Police carefully monitored the activities of pressure groups that advocated political reforms or grassroots democracy, and obstructed their activities when they could do so discreetly (Dimbleby 1997:105). Pepper (1997:686) has pointed out that "public demonstrations were strictly controlled. Telephones were tapped and lists continually updated the better to monitor groups suspected of advocating political reform." In 1978 the Hong Kong government finally set up a Standing Committee on Pressure Groups (scopg) to monitor the groups' activities and place their leaders under surveillance. The committee was "a new and secret body . . . which has the job of coordinating government surveillance of any protest or campaigning group and of mounting counterattack." Specifically, scopg aimed to undermine, co-opt, or coerce any of eleven target groups and any others that came to its attention (Campbell 1980:8). Interestingly, among the groups that scopg considered obnoxious was the Christian Industrial Committee: "The Christian Industrial Committee's intervention in trade disputes not only usurps the role of the Labour Department but complicates issues, feeds erroneous ideas into workers' minds, and renders them less amenable to conciliation" (quoted in Lo 1988:622). The committee was highly critical of any group that could affect the government's credibility and instill "a spirit of defiance" or "a fashionable attitude of knocking the Government" (Home Affairs Branch 1980:10).

The government also attempted to incorporate the pressure groups into the administrative machinery. By the late 1970s, its attitudes toward the community movement "had moved from hostility and suspicion to tolerance and limited acceptance, with an emphasis on promoting informal dialogue and making co-optation attempts" (Joe Leung 1990:48). The Hong Kong government would recognize autonomous community organizations and even subsidize them, legitimize their work in the eyes of the public, and allow their influence to expand in various government advisory committees as representatives of the grassroots population. Through this corporatist strategy, a few service professionals were recruited into government committees, into providing information and advice to officials, and into exerting their influence inside the state rather than waging public protests outside it.

Contributions and Limitations

Through pressure groups and the community movement, then, service professionals had become a new political force that the colonial government could no longer ignore. In general, the community movement made the government more responsive to the needs of the urban poor. The pressure groups had become a form of "opposition" which could act as a check-and-balance mechanism on the colonial administration (Chui 1989:222), and they provided an arena where service professionals could acquire the skills of grassroots mobilization. Many of those professionals became well known to the Hong Kong public after they had won battles with the government on behalf of the urban poor. Participation in the community movement in the late 1970s, therefore, encouraged service professionals to engage in politics at a higher level in the 1980s.

Finally, the community movement changed the political culture of Hong Kong. As Lui (1994:4) has noted, before the mid-1970s, Hong Kong's grassroots population usually just swallowed their pride and kept their mouths shut, even though they were highly dissatisfied with the social services provided by the colonial government. After the rise of the community movement, however, more and more of them expressed their views in public through petitions, protests, and meetings in efforts to induce the colonial government to modify its positions.

Yet the community movement, too, had its weaknesses. First, it was more effective in rallying opposition to an impending threat (like a rent increase) than in organizing protests around long-standing conditions that required fundamental change. People's enthusiasm tended to subside after their immediate demands were met; few of them were interested in a long-term struggle. Moreover, when the community movement was not provoking some dramatic event, its news value subsided; and without mass media coverage, the movement failed to engage the public's interest in championing the urban poor.

Second, despite their formidable image, the pressure groups were still loosely organized. A coalition of more than two hundred pressure groups certainly looked good on paper, but most of those groups were "paper organizations with very small followings and leaders who [were] spokesmen rather than organizers" (Joe Leung 1986a:365). Thus pressure groups remained a collection of articulate spokesmen rather than organizations with the capacity for mass mobilization. The coordination of so many small groups was also a problem. As Joe Leung (1982:46) remarked, "the greater the number of organizations taking part, the less radical the action becomes."

Third, as a result, the community movement failed to develop an opposition ideology comparable to the *minjung* ideology in South Korea (see Koo 1993b), one that could unite the grassroots population and appeal to the general public at a higher level. Thus instances of social action tended to be reactive protests, and activists relied on short-term tactics rather than comprehensive plans or long-term strategies.

Fourth, although the community movement did manage to influence the government, it developed no strong and stable grassroots organization to articulate the interests of the urban poor. The coalitions were issue-specific; none of them went beyond the concerns of a small segment of the community. After they had won some benefits for the chosen segment, the participants' enthusiasm evaporated and the coalitions dissolved. As Joe Leung (1990:49) has pointed out, a "strong grassroots organization employing protest actions to advocate changes had not emerged even by the end of the 1970s."

Finally, the colonial government was not threatened by the community movement and pressure group politics. As Miners (1981:263) laments, "the absence of elections in Hong Kong means that, unlike the situation in Britain, the top decision-makers are permanent civil servants, not party politicians, and so they do not need to trim their policies to gain votes." Service professionals, of course, understood this fact very well. That was why they started the democracy movement in the 1980s to make the colonial government more responsive to their interests and programs.

The Prelude to Democratization

Up to the early 1980s, the Hong Kong government was still a nondemocracy. The governor was appointed by the Queen, and the governor in turn appointed expatriate officials and pro-British big businesspeople to the bureaucracy and the Legislature. British business interests had a monopolistic representation in the colonial government, while other classes had little control over government policies.

However, the political hegemony of this expatriates' alliance was challenged by new social forces emerging in the society in the 1970s. Influenced by student radicalism in the United States and China, Hong Kong college youngsters took the pioneering role of instigating a nationalist student movement in the early 1970s, calling for identification with the Chinese motherland, campaigning for Chinese as an official language in Hong Kong, and sponsoring China tours. The students relied upon public forums, campus newspapers, and student unions to propagandize their causes.

By the mid-1970s, however, the students' nationalist movement died down after the Maoists fell out of power in China. After many student activists entered service professions upon graduation, this new generation of service professionals started a community movement to criticize the policies of the colonial government of Hong Kong. They formed "pressure groups" to address the grievances of the urban poor (such as poor facilities in public housing estates and high bus fares). Their strategy of protest was community mobilization, which aimed to arouse mass media coverage to embarrass the colonial government.

What are the implications of these two social movements in the 1970s for the democracy movement in the 1980s and the 1990s? First of all, there is a continuity of values and beliefs among the three movements. For example, while nationalism subsided in the late 1970s, it did not fade away. The service professionals were still highly nationalistic and identified themselves as Chinese in the 1980s (Anthony Cheung 1994:2). That was why, despite the fact that public opinion was generally favorable for the continual administration of the colonial government, service professionals instead advocated the return of Hong Kong's sovereignty to China during heated negotiations in the early 1980s.

Another value that greatly influenced the democracy movement was community orientation. Although service professionals were absorbed in the constitutional reforms and Legislature debates in the 1980s and the

1990s, they were still very much concerned with the livelihood of the grassroots population. In fact, many activists perceived democratization as a populist project to develop a welfare state to regulate big business and redistribute societal wealth to the grassroots population. Thus, Joe Leung (1986b:6, 9) observes that social workers who were active in the 1980s elections advocated "wider democratization, accountable government and redistributive policies. . . . ." These democrats were often described by the business sector as " 'free lunch parties' which advocate redistributive policies and universal social services."

Moreover, there is a continuity of leadership and strategy among the three movements. Lo (1997:146) remarks that "many pressure group leaders and members in the 1980s were not only experienced political activists during the 1970s, but also imbued with an ideal of shaping Hong Kong's future through participation." It was through the experience of participating in nationalist and community movements that many activists acquired the skills of community organization, mass mobilization, street protests, and getting support from the mass media. Many 1970s movement activists became popular leaders after they won some battles against the colonial government. A decade later, making use of their local connections, skills in publicity and ability to mobilize resources, social movement activists were very active in orchestrating election campaigns in local District Board elections. After winning elections, many social movement leaders — such as Yeung Sum, Lee Wing-tat, Cheung Man-kwong, and Lau Chin-shek — became leaders of the democracy movement in the 1990s. "Such a historical linkage," Lui (1993a:264) remarks, "largely explains the populist and oppositional orientations of most of these political leaders and political groups." These popular leaders applied the techniques of the earlier movements to get signatures to support direct elections to the Legislative Council in 1988 and to protest the Tiananmen incident in 1989.

Furthermore, there was continuity of organizational forms among the three movements. The nationalist movement, the community movement, and the early phase of the democracy movement all were weakly organized. Whether in the form of student unions or pressure groups or political groups, these organizations tended to be highly fragmented. At best they formed temporary alliances on certain critical issues at the height of the movement, but the alliances quickly fell apart as enthusiasm died. Weak organization may help explain why the democracy movement ran into difficulties in the late 1980s after facing strong opposition from Beijing and the big businesspeople (So and Kwitko 1990).

In short, there was continuity of values and beliefs, leadership and strategy, and organizational forms between the nationalist and community movements of the 1970s and the democracy movement of the 1980s and 1990s. Anthony Cheung (1994:2), vice chair of the Democratic Party in the mid-1990s, declared that

the leaders of today's democratic parties are the group of people who have long participated in social reforms. This group of people, whether they were at school or at work, have taken active part in movements to reform society, such as the student and community movements in the 1970s. The target that this group struggled against was the colonial institutional system, and the means and ends of social reform that they proposed were a democratic political institution. That being the case, the democracy movement in Hong Kong was initiated not at the time London signed the Joint Declaration with Beijing in 1984 but in an earlier period (the 1970s).

Thus, although the term *democracy* was never articulated in the 1970s and the "colonial nature of the Hong Kong government was left unscathed" (Lui and Chiu 1997), the nationalist and community movements served as a prelude to the democracy movement of a decade after (So 1995a).

3 | Negotiation Politics and the Birth of the Democracy Project

> When I read [the Joint Declaration], I was thrilled, because it promised that the people of Hong Kong could elect their Chief Executive and legislature and, through them, hold the government accountable to the people. To me that meant democracy.
>
> Martin Lee (1996:236), leader of the Democratic Party

> The Joint Declaration is about establishing democracy in Hong Kong, the sort of democracy they have in Taiwan, Korea, Japan and — it has to be said — the same sort of democracy that we have in the United Kingdom. That's what China signed up to — the development of representative government.
>
> Governor Chris Patten (Dimbleby 1997:349)

Hong Kong's path of democratic development is quite different from other paths of third-wave democratization. In South Korea and Taiwan, for example, democratization resulted from a retreat from authoritarian rule; Hong Kong's democracy, however, was a historical product of its reunification with mainland China. The discourse on democracy emerged only in the early 1980s, during the last phase of the negotiations between the Beijing and London governments over the future of Hong Kong.

This chapter presents a "muddling through" thesis to explain the historical origins of the democracy project in Hong Kong. It argues that during the negotiation process over Hong Kong's future, uncertainty prompted a class formation of the service professionals in forming a strategic alliance with the Communist Beijing government to push for democratization. After losing the support of these service professionals, the London government was willing to sign a Joint Declaration to return the sovereignty of Hong Kong to the Beijing government. In order to sell its Joint Declaration to the British Parliament and Hong Kong society, London tactically pushed for democratization during the last phase of the negotiation process. Nevertheless, after Beijing and Hong Kong's big business interests voiced their opposition to the democracy project, the London government adopted a strategy of muddling through—inserting some vague terms like "election" and "accountability" into the Joint Declaration, but no longer pushing to define these terms in order not to antagonize Beijing and Hong Kong big business.

To understand the complex genesis of the democracy project, let us begin with the emergence of the 1997 issue in the early 1980s.

1997 and the Class Formation of Service Professionals

The Emergence of the 1997 Issue

Hong Kong had been a British colony for over a century. Although the island of Hong Kong was ceded "permanently" to Great Britain in 1842 and part of the Kowloon peninsula in 1860, a large part of its hinterland (around 92% of Hong Kong's territory), called the New Territories, was only leased to Great Britain for ninety-nine years. The lease expired in 1997.

In the late 1970s, influential businesspeople began to exert pressure on the Hong Kong government to renew the lease on the New Territories. The normal term of a mortgage on land in Hong Kong was fifteen years, so by the early 1980s, real estate developers hesitated to venture into the New Territories or into any long-term investment when there was no assurance that the lease would be renewed beyond 1997. Jimmy McGregor, director of the Hong Kong Chamber of Commerce, said that large-scale investors needed some indication by the Chinese government about Hong Kong's status before making a commitment to the colony (Tang and Ching 1994:155).

Governor MacLehose visited Beijing in March 1979 and returned with a message from Deng Xiaoping to investors in Hong Kong: they should "put their hearts at ease." With this rosy response in mind, Prime Minister Margaret Thatcher visited China in September 1982 to negotiate the extension of the lease on the New Territories (Tang and Ching 1994:155).

Although both China and Great Britain repeatedly stressed the continued political stability and economic prosperity of Hong Kong regardless of the outcome, the very commencement of the negotiation process induced a crisis of confidence in its political future. Suddenly the colony was hit by irrational fluctuations in the financial sector, massive emigration of investment and human capital, fiscal problems in the Hong Kong government, and political instability.

The booming property market turned sour; property prices dropped more than 50 percent between 1982 and 1983, and the entire property market came to a virtual standstill in 1983. Many construction projects were canceled for fear there would be no buyers. Giant real estate companies, such as Regal Land and Hong Kong Land, reported unprecedented net losses amounting to billions of Hong Kong dollars (*FEER Yearbook* 1984:166). When the Hong Kong dollar fell from 6 to the U.S. dollar in September 1982 to an unprecedented low of 9.55 in September 1983, the government moved to stem the tide by linking Hong Kong's currency to the United States' at a fixed rate of H.K.$7.8 to U.S.$1. Then a banking crisis developed in 1983. Tam (1983:23) reported that "some DTCs [deposit-taking companies] and banks which have heavy exposure to the property market have run into financial difficulties, in part because of the sudden need to write off bad debts and in part because they cannot obtain sufficient short term funds to finance their long term lending." The government revoked the licenses of twenty-one DTCs and took over the Hang Lung Bank. The Hang Seng index dropped from 1,800 in 1981 to 690 in 1983 (*FEER*, Jan. 13, 1983:61; Oct. 13, 1983:96; Apr. 26, 1984:87).

There were signs that capital was moving out of Hong Kong. *Asian Business* (Jan. 1983:57) reported that "1982 would mark the beginning of an outflow of an estimated U.S.$20 billion of investment capital . . . [believed] to be in the hands of Hong Kong investors." Public opinion polls revealed that over half of the respondents would emigrate if they could (Kwong 1984). The most likely to emigrate were married professionals (aged 25–39) with young children, and the most favored destinations were Canada and the United States. Many professionals were so eager to obtain permanent residence abroad that a brisk trade in counterfeit visas and fraudulent marriages developed.

The volatility of the economy affected living standards. Supermarket prices rose from 20 to 30 percent between 1982 and 1983. The government of Hong Kong energetically raised taxes to reduce its deficit. Of course every tax increase was followed by a rise in prices; every month in 1983 saw an increase in the cost of at least one major public or private service — electricity, telephone, water, postage, gas, licenses, public hospital services, parking, trains, metro-rail, buses. As a result, real wages declined significantly between 1982 and 1984 (*Pai Shing*, Jan. 1, 1984:15; *SCMP*, Jan. 13, 1984:11; Jan. 16, 1984:Bus. 1).

In such an unfavorable economic climate, more than seven thousand people gathered in Victoria Park in September 1983 to protest high inflation and the government's indifference to their plight. In January 1984 a riot broke out: a mob looted, set fires, attacked a police station. In early

1984 the taxi drivers and the metro-rail workers went on strike (*SCMP,* Jan. 14, 1984:1; *Pai Shing,* Sept. 16, 1983; May 1, 1984).

The Class Formation of Service Professionals

The downturn of the property market and the economy, the cutback in state expenditures, worries about worsening professional standards, and the prospect of censorship and central planning after Beijing took over in 1997 were nightmares to the service professionals. Their painful life experiences can be observed in the pages of *Candid Opinion,* a book published by The Outstanding Young Persons' Association (TOYPA 1984:38, 40, 48, 49, 66, 94).

First, facing economic recession, the government of Hong Kong needed to scale down its expenditures on social services. As a social worker lamented,

Unfortunately, in recent years, government seems to feel that too much money has been deployed in social welfare services. From 5.8% of the total annual expenditure for social welfare in 1976–77, the provision has decreased to 4.4% for 1983–84. . . . These financial restraints have brought some delays in developments in our field of service. The acute shortage of trained personnel has also delayed progress in our profession. The vicious cycle of overwork, poor career prospects, low job satisfaction has taken its toll. The attitude of government toward our profession does not help at all, especially with its recent decision in reducing the starting salary of beginning social workers and the employment of non–social work graduates to the professional grade.

Second, there were worries about the lowering of professional standards once China resumed sovereignty over Hong Kong in 1997. Doctors, for example, "fear a loss of freedom that will leave them no choice as to where they go and whom they treat. They also fear that the present standards which are fairly homogeneous may not be maintained. Some fear they may be asked to do qualifying examinations in herbal medicine. Medical practice in China does not seem to be tightly monitored and there may be inadequate postgraduate training. The doctors in Hong Kong would not like to see that happen here."

Third, many service professionals (urban planners, lawyers, and doctors among them) were certified and regulated by British institutions. If China did not recognize their British qualifications, many members of the service professionals might lose privileges and livelihoods after 1997. Even though China had promised that it would not discriminate against British-educated professionals, service professionals were very much concerned about the change in regime and its possible negative impact. Barristers and solicitors not fluent in written Chinese worried about the possible erosion of judicial independence under Chinese rule as well as about the need to cope with laws written in Chinese.

Finally, Chinese censorship and central planning were pervasive worries. A teacher reported, "Many of the teachers I've talked to . . . do not believe that China will keep things as they are. They believe Beijing will want to change the curriculum and the syllabus of the schools. They think there will not be freedom of speech. . . . The teaching of Confucianism will probably all go out of the window. New books will be put on the syllabus and the simplified words will be used for teaching purposes and all the teachers will have to go through a period of reorientation." Social workers feared that with the arrival of the socialist state in 1997, "there will be no room and perhaps no need for social work as everything is planned and controlled by the Socialist government." Many members of the service professions were highly critical of Beijing's human rights record during the Cultural Revolution and the suppression of the Democracy Wall movement in 1979.

In short, the 1997 issue aroused the class consciousness of service professionals in their fear that their interests—job security, good income, credentials, professional standards, freedom, creativity—were under threat. The fear of falling was so intense that anxiety, worry, uncertainty, and feelings of helplessness were pervasive among them. It was this fear that brought members of the group together as a class. They had begun to see that they shared the same fate, and they knew that they had to do something to protect their economic interests and their lifestyle before 1997.

Then exactly what did the service professionals do to protect their career, freedom, and class interests? And what role did they play in the inauguration of the democratic project in Hong Kong? This chapter examines the changing pattern of political participation of service professionals during the Sino-British negotiation process from 1982 to 1984. It argues that these professionals played an important role in determining the outcome of the negotiation process, and they have articulated a democracy project of "Hong Kong People Ruling Hong Kong" to protect their class interests.

Prenegotiation Politics in Early 1982

The Positions of London and Beijing

Before the negotiations began in September 1982, the London government was highly optimistic about gaining Beijing's agreement to renew the lease on the New Territories, because China, in the midst of the Four Modernizations, derived many benefits from Hong Kong's prosperity. The British repeatedly stressed that about 30 to 40 percent of China's foreign exchange earnings came from Hong Kong (Jao 1985:373; Scott 1989:179). They were sure that China would not want to block the renewal of the lease and earn the distrust of the business sector, for economic recession in Hong Kong would adversely affect China's economy. Besides, it seemed to London that many senior Chinese officials were ready to work with them to solve the 1997 problem. Percy Cradock (1994:165) explained: "We now had, in the person of Deng Xiaoping, a Chinese leader who was rational and pragmatic. The senior official in charge of Hong Kong and Macao matters, Liao Chengzhi, was similarly flexible." To the British team it seemed feasible "to exchange sovereignty over the island of Hong Kong in return for continued British administration of the entire Colony well into the future" (Thatcher 1993:259).

To China's leaders, however, national reunification was a historical mission that they were duty-bound to accomplish in their lifetime. As they grew older, the task became increasingly urgent: reunification was one of the great tasks of the 1980s (Nathan 1990). To the Beijing government, recovery of Hong Kong was the only means of wiping out the humiliation China suffered when the Qing government ceded the territory to Britain; "the status quo of Hong Kong therefore cannot be maintained permanently, and the New Territories lease cannot be simply forgotten or extended indefinitely" (J. Cheng 1984a:9).

To shore up support in Hong Kong, Beijing activated such leftist organizations as trade unions and newspapers, held interviews with Hong Kong Chinese tycoons such as Henry Fok and Lee Ka-shing, and had its senior officials meet with the vice chancellor of the University of Hong Kong.

All the same, the Beijing government continued to keep a low profile on the 1997 issue, and did not disclose its true position until a few months before Margaret Thatcher's visit to Beijing in September 1982 (J. Cheng 1984b). Since the Beijing government did not publicly reject the British position, they gave Hong Kongers the false impression that they intended to endorse the British position.

Reactions in Hong Kong

Misunderstanding the situation as they did, the people of Hong Kong were highly optimistic that the lease on the New Territories would be renewed and Britain would continue to administer Hong Kong after 1997 (J. Cheng 1984a:79). In their optimism they advanced all kinds of proposals on how to resolve the 1997 issue. Here is just a partial list (J. Cheng 1984a:8; *Seventies Monthly*, Sept. 1982:33–36):

- *Maintain the status quo* by renewing the lease for fifty more years.

- *Continue British administration under Chinese sovereignty.* China formally recovers the sovereignty of Hong Kong through a treaty negotiated between Beijing and London, both sides agreeing that Hong Kong will continue to be administered by the British until further notice.

- *Co-administration.* China formally recovers the sovereignty of Hong Kong and is responsible for diplomatic and military affairs, but asks Britain to administer the territory's internal political, economic, and social affairs.

- *Independence.* Hong Kong becomes an independent city-state, like Singapore.

- *British administration under the auspices of the United Nations.*

- *China's special economic zone.* The Chinese government takes back Hong Kong in 1997, and the territory becomes a special economic zone of China, like Shenzhen.

Service Professionals' Initial Responses

Service professionals shared in the general optimism. Two established service professional organizations—the Hong Kong Observers and the Hong Kong Prospect Institute—took the lead in publicly expressing their views of the 1997 issue.

The members of the Hong Kong Prospect Institute, mostly of the older generation of Chinese intellectuals who were highly suspicious of communism and wanted to maintain the status quo to avoid chaos and uncertainty, proposed a "Sino-British Treaty of Friendship and Cooperation" that stated that "China's claims to sovereignty are recognized and the

British are given responsibility for administration of the territory, paving the way for a very gradual transition over a period of thirty or more years" (J. Cheng 1984a:133).

Most of the Hong Kong Observers were British-educated professionals in their thirties and forties. Widely known as social critics of public policies on corruption, education, health care, and law reform and enjoying access to senior officials in the Hong Kong government, the Observers conducted a survey in May 1982 and reported that 95 percent of the respondents said the status quo was acceptable, while only 26 percent said a return to China was acceptable. When respondents were pressed for their preference, 69 percent pointed to the status quo as the most preferred solution and 55 percent named a return to China as the least preferred (J. Cheng 1984a:14). The pro-British faction interpreted these findings as showing the reluctance of Hong Kongers to return to Chinese rule.

Businesspeople in the Executive Council (Exco) feared that London would give up the colony without a fight, so they became involved from the start. A delegation of Exco councilors led by S. Y. Chung met with Prime Minister Thatcher at 10 Downing Street on September 8, 1982, to present their position papers. They made it clear that if China was intent on recovering sovereignty and administration of Hong Kong, the people of Hong Kong should expect the British government to make every effort to maintain administrative control. They would accept nothing less (Roberti 1994:46).

The Thatcher Visit and the Deadlock: September 1982

British-Chinese Negotiations

The first round of talks over Hong Kong's future took place in late September 1982.

Beijing's position was summarized in the slogan "Recover Sovereignty, Preserve Prosperity." Beijing reiterated its view that the documents signed by the Qing government in the nineteenth century, relinquishing the island of Hong Kong, the Kowloon peninsula, and the New Territories, were unequal treaties that China would not recognize: Beijing resolutely stated its intention to regain sovereignty over all three areas. It promised that after sovereignty was resumed, it would preserve the economic prosperity of Hong Kong. A policy of "one country, two systems" would allow capitalism to flourish under the red flag.

However, Margaret Thatcher, fresh from victory in the Falklands, insisted that the treaties signed between the Qing government and Britain were still legal and valid. The British government was prepared to negotiate only the renewal of the lease on the New Territories; the sovereignty of Hong Kong Island and the Kowloon peninsula were not negotiable. In addition, Thatcher (1993) stressed that Britain had a moral obligation to the people of Hong Kong, and that anything less than British administration would be followed by a flight of capital and economic collapse. Thatcher, looking distressed at the end of the negotiation sessions, slipped and fell on her hands and knees on her way out of the Great Hall (Cradock 1994).

As both sides refused to yield, the negotiations were deadlocked before they started (H. Chiu et al. 1987). As soon as Thatcher left Beijing, the Beijing government condemned Britain for wanting to continue its hold on Chinese territory, while the Thatcher government blamed China for its failure to respect the international treaties it had signed.

Since the content of the negotiations was confidential, the people of Hong Kong were kept in the dark about the progress of the talks. Nevertheless, judging by the shouting matches they witnessed in late September 1982, the people sensed serious differences between the two governments. What worried the people most was not China's resumption of sovereignty in 1997 (still fifteen years away) but the immediate prospect of a total breakdown in the talks. In that event, the People's Liberation Army might march across the border and take Hong Kong by force.

The Pro-British Faction on the Offensive

In this battle for public support, Joseph Cheng (1984a:50) observed, "the Chinese side was in an unfavorable position at first. The local media are generally conservative and pro–Hong Kong government. The three major left-wing newspapers, *Ta Kung Po, Wen Wei Po,* and the *New Evening Post,* do not have very large circulations. Leftist organizations such as the New China News Agency and the trade unions were not keen to make new contacts and tended to limit themselves to their established supporters."

The mass media tended to report the opinions of businessmen, notables, and councilors who were pro-London and anti-Beijing. Ronald Li, chairman of the Far East Stock Exchange in Hong Kong, stated on September 22, 1982 that

for commerce as much as industry, doubt and uncertainty always spell trouble. . . . What we need are a stable political system and a reliable legal system. Can China offer such systems? It isn't enough that China keeps telling us it wants to preserve our prosperity. We need more than mere words. The only solution I can see is for Britain to turn the whole colony back to China. That would resolve China's face-saving dilemma. The timing isn't important, as long as it's before 1997. Then China leases it back to Britain. (Cheng 1984a:183–84)

John Swaine said in the Legislative Council in October 1982 that "the continuation of British administration" was necessary for the preservation of stability and prosperity. "Change must come by evolutionary process, not through having it thrust upon us" (Cheng 1984a:192). Big business-people in the Exco advised Prime Minister Thatcher to stand tough and to fight for continued British administration after 1997. That was what Thatcher did from late 1982 through the first half of 1983; she promised that the Exco would be kept informed of developments at the negotiating table and asked for their advice.

In general, the pro-British faction presented two compelling arguments for the renewal of the lease and the continuation of the status quo under British administration. The first, called the "economic card," was that Hong Kong's prosperity and business confidence depended on a continuing British presence. The second, the "public opinion card," was that the Hong Kong people wanted the status quo or did not want to be ruled by the Communist regime in China. How did members of the service professions respond to these offensives?

The 1997 issue reactivated the enthusiasm of student leaders, although most college students still remained apolitical. In August 1982 the student leaders had protested against Japan's revision of World War II history in its textbooks. After the first round of talks ended in September 1982, they started another nationalist protest against Thatcher's visit to Hong Kong. The student activists confronted Thatcher with banners proclaiming "Down with the unequal treaties! Never forget the agony of our ancestors. The treaties forced upon China should never be recognized." Later the student unions issued a policy platform: "sovereignty over Hong Kong should ultimately be restored to China; . . . the future political, social, and economic system in Hong Kong should be incorporated in a more democratic and a more equitable autonomous region" (Cheng 1984a:170, 172).

The Hong Kong People's Model and the Showdown: October 1982–October 1983

Beijing Clarifies Its Position

To rebut Britain's position and calm the fears of the Hong Kong people, the Beijing government began to spell out its position in more detail in late 1982. To the principles of "recovering sovereignty and preserving economic prosperity" the Beijing government now added the principles of "establishing a special administrative zone, keeping the existing institutions unchanged, and letting the Hong Kong people rule Hong Kong" (*Guang Jue Jing*, Mar. 1983:10). The Beijing government insisted that in this "Hong Kong people ruling Hong Kong" model (*gangren zhigang;* hereafter "Hong Kong People's Model"), Hong Kong would have a high degree of autonomy and its post-1997 government would be staffed by Hong Kong people rather than Chinese officials from Beijing.

To show its sincerity, the National People's Congress (NPC) of China in November 1982 quickly promulgated a new constitution, whose article 31 provided for the establishment of special administrative regions. Article 31 laid the legal foundation for the Beijing government's "one country, two systems" policy. Because of its pledge of confidentiality, however, Beijing could not formally reveal the details of the special administrative region before the conclusion of the negotiation process.

In addition, the Beijing government intensified its united front strategy. Beijing appointed more Hong Kong residents to mainland political bodies, including the National People's Congress. As Mark Roberti (1994:63) has said, "like Britain's royal honors, the appointments gave face in exchange for loyalty."

On June 30, 1983, Xu Jiatun arrived to take up his post as the new director of the Xinhua News Agency in Hong Kong. He was now the highest official of the Beijing government in Hong Kong. Before Xu's arrival, the Xinhua News Agency had kept a low profile since its disgrace in the 1967 riot. Xu's contribution, therefore, was to institutionalize the united front strategy in Hong Kong. Xu met with Hong Kong leaders to establish a social network (Wong 1997:116). Xu was reported to dine "nearly every night with bankers and businessmen . . . relaying Peking's message that there is no need to worry, that there will be only minimal change after China recovers sovereignty and that China really wants Hong Kong's capitalist system to continue" (Scott 1989:205). Xu also used dinner diplomacy with publishers and editors of independent newspapers. The Xinhua News Agency sent them fresh lychees and sweet Hami melons from Xinjiang Province, often accompanying the gifts with handwritten notes from Xu Jiatun (Wilson 1990:207).

Through Xu's connections, many senior Beijing officials initiated a series of meetings with businessmen, community leaders, professional groups, notables from the New Territories, student activists, and journalists. The delegations from China included representatives of the Trade Development Council, the Factory Owners Association, the Chinese Manufacturers Association, and a host of others. The meetings served two purposes. On the one hand, they "were intended to be briefing sessions for the Chinese leaders, as well as demonstrating their concern to learn the views and desires of the local population." The visitors "often came back with a sense that their opinions had been considered and that there were forums in which Chinese leaders would consult them in future" (Cheng 1984a:49; Scott 1989:205). At the same time, the Beijing government made use of these meetings to leak, bit by bit, the blueprint of the post-1997 special administrative region as it was being worked on.

A Warm Reception by the Service Professionals

The Hong Kong People's Model received a warm reception among service professionals, for it promised to resolve their dilemma of nationalism versus democratic capitalism (So 1993b). On the one hand, these professionals were highly nationalistic. They were proud to be Chinese, and they wanted China to develop into a powerful nation free of foreign domination. In August 1982 they were further incited by the nationalist protests of university students against the Japanese textbook revisions on the invasion of China during World War II (Chen 1985:194–95). In September they were attracted to the student protests against Thatcher's visit. Like other Hong Kong citizens, service professionals generally believed that sovereignty over Hong Kong belonged to China, that the treaties between Britain and the Qing government in the nineteenth century had been unequal, and that Thatcher should not invoke the three unequal treaties during the first round of negotiations (Cheng 1984a:78–79). In this respect, the service professionals preferred China's resumption of sovereignty over Hong Kong in 1997.

On the other hand, the professionals were frightened by the prospect of Communist rule. They worried whether their interests, careers, status, and lifestyles — credentials, organizational expertise, career advancement, freedom and creativity—would be preserved after the Chinese Communists took over Hong Kong in 1997. They were also highly critical of the Beijing government's violations of human rights during the 1979 Democracy Wall movement. In this respect, they very much wanted to keep the present status quo.

In the face of this dilemma, the service professionals found the Hong Kong People's Model very attractive. It would not only satisfy their nationalist sentiments and safeguard their professional interests and lifestyles, but also provided a historical opportunity to be an ascending class. The service professionals could become the future political leaders of Hong Kong, democratizing the government and instituting welfare reforms. After all, who could more appropriately represent the Hong Kong people than service professionals?

The Formation of New Political Groups

In the first half of the 1980s, many new political groups sprang up in response to the uncertainty of Hong Kong's future: in 1982 the Hong Kong Prospect Institute and the New Hong Kong Society; in 1983 the Meeting Point; in 1984 the Hong Kong Forum, the Hong Kong Affairs Society, the Hong Kong People's Association, the Association for Democracy and Justice, and the Hong Kong Policy Viewers (Leung 1986:chap. 5; Cheng 1984a:chap. 4; Lo 1997:140–41).

These new political groups shared the following common traits. First, their members were former student activists in the nationalist and community movements of the 1970s. Political group members were linked to one another through friendship networks formed in their schooldays, giving an impression of old-boy associations. For example, members of the Meeting Point were activists in the society faction of the student movement in the early 1970s.

Second, members of political groups generally belonged to the service professional class. In other words, they were usually social workers, teachers, professors, journalists, doctors, etc. Unlike corporate professionals closely tied to the business sector, service professionals developed strong linkages with the grassroots population of Hong Kong through their professional practices.

Third, political groups had a loose organizational structure. Small in size, these groups depended on personal networks to carry out their activities. Formal rules and regulations were still undeveloped. Although the groups' outspoken leaders frequently showed up in the mass media, they had actually tiny organizational resources (some didn't even have a full-time staff) to carry out ambitious programs.

Fourth, although varied in different degrees of articulation, the platforms and the policy statements of these political groups revealed their common commitment to a set of values which can be labeled as "Nationalism, Democracy, and Welfare Capitalism." The Meeting Point (1984:1), for instance, advocated:

• *Nationalism:* not narrow, exclusive nationalism, but affirmation of the fact that we are Chinese, and Hong Kong is a part of China.

• *Democratization:* not wholesale democracy overnight, but affirmation of the direction toward democratization, and its installation as quickly as possible through gradual, step-by-step political reforms.

• *Rationalization of the economy:* not nationalization or overthrowing the capitalists, but after affirming the principle of private enterprise, we seek more rationalization of social resource distribution, so that Hong Kong citizens can enjoy the fruits of political stability and economic prosperity.

The political groups hoped that the Hong Kong People's Model would put these principles of nationalism, democracy, and welfare capitalism (rationalization of the economy) into practice after 1997.

Finally, the political groups relied on legal channels to achieve their goals. Common tactics were organizing a public seminar, holding a news conference, and presenting a position paper on important issues (Meeting Point 1984:46–49). In addition, these groups wanted to cultivate links to the Beijing government. They frequently sent delegations to high-ranking Beijing officials. While other groups (such as the New Territories Notables and the Chinese Chamber of Commerce) also made pilgrimages to Beijing, only the service professionals' political groups brought back crucial news concerning the blueprint of the future Hong Kong government. Maybe these political groups, whose members were mostly cultural professionals and well-connected to the mass media of Hong Kong, were more trusted by Beijing to act as a transmitter to leak out news than other groups.

Transmitters of the Hong Kong People's Model

In February 1983 the New Hong Kong Society visited Beijing and brought back news concerning the blueprint for a special administrative zone in Hong Kong (*Guang Jue Jing*, Mar. 1983). In April a delegation from the intellectual circles of the two universities also passed on Beijing's message (*Pai Shing*, May 1, 1983). In July a group of activists of the Hong Kong Federation of Student Unions brought back another message from Beijing (Cheng 1984a:52–53). All of the messages were strikingly similar, and they showed how the details of the Hong Kong People's Model developed as time went by. The latest blueprint, in July 1983, included the following key elements:

- A basic law or miniconstitution would be drafted with local participation and, after consultation with the local community, submitted to the National People's Congress for approval.

- The existing legal system and the rule of law would be maintained, and the court of final appeal would be located in Hong Kong.

- Hong Kong would enjoy a high degree of self-rule, but China would be responsible for the territory's defense (it would station troops there) and foreign relations. However, Hong Kong was to manage its own external economic and cultural affairs and maintain full control over immigration matters, issuing its own identity cards and passports.

- Hong Kong's capitalist economy and free enterprise system would not be disturbed, the free flow of capital was to be maintained, and the territory would have its own currency backed by its own reserves. The Chinese government would not impose taxes in Hong Kong or send its officials to administer the territory.

- In the initial stage of self-administration, local organizations were invited to nominate the chief executive, who would be appointed by the Chinese authority.

- Expatriates as individuals would be allowed to continue to work in public and private establishments, except for the highest public offices.

- These arrangements would remain unchanged for fifty years after 1997.

Another activity of the service professionals was a discursive struggle with pro-British elements during the second round of talks, which started in July 1983.

Engagement in Discursive Struggles

In May 1983 a delegation of young pro-British people led by the Exco councilor Alan Lee (Li Peng-fei) visited Beijing (Cheng 1984a:18, 197–203).

Most of its members were corporate professionals who had attended universities in Britain, Australia, and the United States. In the position paper they submitted to Beijing, they acknowledged that "some professionals and executives may have expressed a different view," but speaking from their "conscience," they declared that they had no confidence in the Beijing government because of its poor track record in the past few decades. They argued that there was "clear and visible panic in Hong Kong," as shown by the outflow of capital and the brain drain. If this trend continued, the position paper warned, it would threaten the prosperity and political stability of Hong Kong.

Further, the corporate delegation found the Hong Kong People's Model impractical, for the following reasons:

- The incompatibility between capitalist and socialist policies.

- The lack of successful precedents of special administrative regions.

- The difficulty of maintaining domestic stability under self-administration and the contradiction between self-administration and Hong Kong as a Special Administrative Region under Chinese sovereignty.

- The lack of confidence of international investors, which would deprive Hong Kong of its status as a major international financial center.

- The difficulty of guaranteeing the independence of existing legal and judiciary systems.

The delegation had widely publicized its views in Hong Kong's mass media in June 1983, in an effort to show the distrust of pro-British elements toward the Hong Kong People's Model. Since then, pro-British headlines commonly appeared in the mass media: "Renew the Lease for Another 30 Years"; "Chinese Sovereignty and British Administration"; "Hong Kong People Ruling Hong Kong Model Will Not Work"; "Without British Contributions, No More Prosperity for Hong Kong."

In response to this mass media campaign, the two university student unions offered their rebuttal that it was too early to conclude that the Hong Kong People's Model would not work. First, the student unions argued that the details of the Hong Kong People's Model had yet to be worked out. The professionals and other strata in Hong Kong could participate to enrich the model. Second, the student unions pointed out that instead of concentrating our attention on the past errors of the Beijing government (like the Cultural Revolution), Hong Kongers should look forward to the future prospects for the Four Modernization programs. Third, the student unions pointed out that in the real world, capitalism and socialism always coexisted like the welfare states in Western Europe. Finally, they pointed to many factors that entered into Hong Kong's economic recession in the early 1980s. Not just the loss of the confidence but also the inappropriate governmental policies needed to be examined. The student unions accused the colonial government of encouraging risky investments in real estate and the currency markets on the one hand, and of failing to promote the manufacturing sector on the other (Student Unions n.d.:62–64; *Guang Jue Jing*, July 16, 1984:81–82).

A group of college students published a report on a survey conducted in April 1983, which showed a significant shift in public opinion on Hong Kong's political future (*Seventies Monthly*, July 1983; Cheng 1984a:15). Whereas in 1982 more than 80 percent of respondents thought the status quo was the best proposal, in April 1983 this figure had plummeted to around 40 percent. In April 1983 more respondents (24%) favored self-administration under Chinese sovereignty than British administration under Chinese sovereignty (17%). When they were asked, "What do you think is the most likely outcome of the negotiation process?" again more respondents believed that Hong Kong would end up self-administrated (43%) than that it would be under British administration (19%). The findings of the students' survey and the rebuttal of the two student unions were reported in Hong Kong's mass media, and the Xinhua News Agency disseminated them widely in China (Student Unions n.d.:22–27). The Meeting Point, too, declared that "nationalism is a basic principle in considering the problem of Hong Kong's future" and that there was "no reason to believe the Hong Kong economy would suffer when British administration ends" (*FEER*, Feb. 3, 1983:2). The pro-China mass media generally interpreted the survey findings, the students' statements, and the Meeting Point's declaration as strong indications that Hong Kongers supported the Hong Kong People's Model.

In this respect, service professionals played a crucial role in influencing the mass media. Through clarifying the Hong Kong People's Model by transmitting Beijing's messages to Hong Kong, and through endorsing the Hong Kong People's model in the mass media, the service professionals contributed to a significant shift in public opinion. As Joseph Cheng (1984b:50–51) observed, attitudes in Hong Kong had shifted markedly since Thatcher's visit to China. The Hong Kong People's Model had gradually gained broader acceptance by late 1983, as Hong Kongers finally became convinced that British administration would have to be terminated by 1997.

The Formal Talks and the Showdown

The pro-British forces, of course, still wanted British administration to continue. After Thatcher sent a private letter in March 1983 to Zhao Ziyang, China's premier, and made a small concession in the language about sovereignty (from "consider" making a recommendation to Parliament on sovereignty to "would be prepared to" recommend to Parliament), Beijing was willing to hold formal negotiation sessions with London at a Foreign Ministry guesthouse in Beijing in July 1983. The British delegation, headed by Percy Cradock, and the Chinese delegation, headed by Yao Guang, met for two days at a time and only in the mornings. The proceedings were formal, with set speeches and presentations of papers followed by slightly less rigid rejoinders and rebuttals. The British delegation's goal was to convey to the Chinese how Hong Kong worked and to demonstrate that its remarkable prosperity and the confidence it enjoyed among investors were organically linked to British administration, British law, and British freedoms. The Chinese rejected these statements out of hand, and the sessions grew increasingly emotional. The Chinese could not accept the separation of sovereignty and administration. There could be no progress in the talks until the British acknowledged that both sovereignty and administration must return to China (Cradock 1994:186–89).

Finally in late September there was a showdown on the economic front when the Hong Kong dollar fell from 6 in September 1982 to an unprecedented low of 9.55 against the U.S. dollar. With this sharp drop, Hong Kongers rushed to switch their bank deposits into foreign currency. More bad news followed. The *Far Eastern Economic Review* reported: "The past two weeks have seen the arrest of two company directors subsequently charged under the Theft ordinance; the collapse of their empire which is believed to have ties with some 200 companies; the winding up of one of Hong Kong's largest garment manufacturers; the takeover by the government of an ailing local bank and the resignation of the chairman of Hong Kong's largest trading company" (Oct. 20, 1983:29). The Hang Seng index fell to an all-time low of 690 on October 4, 1983.

Cradock (1984:189), who participated in the talks, assessed the situation: "It was plain that we faced a crisis. The Chinese would not retreat and we assessed that they were wholly committed to this stand. We therefore had the choice of accepting either a breakdown, or negotiating for the maximum degree of autonomy for Hong Kong that we could get." What, then, would London decide?

The Politics of Settlement: November 1983–June 1984

The Move toward Settlement

The London government decided to concede to Beijing's demands. There was to be no British administrative presence after 1997, and China was to regain sovereignty under the Hong Kong People's Model. According to Scott's (1989:171–219) account, three factors may have persuaded London to abandon its position. First, the British negotiators believed that no further progress was possible unless it made concessions. "It was a highly unequal negotiation," Cradock (1994:211) explained. "The Chinese held virtually all the cards. They had only to wait until 1997, when, under a treaty we recognized, 92 per cent of the territory would pass to them, the remaining 8 per cent not being viable on its own. They possessed overwhelming military force, in addition to the capacity to cut off essential supply." Second, Mrs. Thatcher's direct influence on the negotiation process seemed to wane, and matters increasingly came under the control of the Foreign Office's China experts, who had a continuing interest in improving Britain's relationship with China. In late 1983 there were reports that the Foreign Office had begun to appreciate the benefits (investment in China, for instance) that Britain could gain from an amicable settlement. Third, during the showdown in September 1983, there was evidence that political confidence in Hong Kong would quickly erode if no agreement were reached. Faced with the further plunge of the Hong Kong dollar and panic buying in supermarkets, the pragmatists in the Foreign Office probably felt that they had little option but to concede both sovereignty and administration of Hong Kong.

On October 14, 1983, Thatcher (1993:490) sent a message to Zhao Ziyang expressing Britain's willingness to explore China's ideas about Hong Kong's future and holding out the possibility of a settlement along those lines. Once London made this critical decision, its tactics were to press for detailed provisions and a binding agreement that would put the Hong Kong People's Model into practice after 1997 (Overholt 1985; D. Wilson 1990:210). In addition, London wanted to include provisions for a Western-style democratic government, with an elected governor and legislature, in order to sell the agreement to the British Parliament and the people of Hong Kong.

Having shifted its position at the negotiating table, London had to shift its allies as well. Many pro-British big businesspeople in Hong Kong were still pushing for the status quo and the extension of the lease. Cradock (1994:189) recalled that the Unofficials of the Exco, "led by Sir S. Y. Chung, were also obdurate. A majority took the view that the Chinese were bluffing, that they depended on the Hong Kong economy and that, faced with the prospect of economic collapse, they would draw back." The Exco Unofficials demanded that Britain make no concessions to Beijing. Subsequently, these big businesspeople had to be abandoned by the London government in this settlement phase. The Beijing government, of course, was very pleased with Britain's concessions. Beijing's strategy now was to conclude the negotiations and sign the Joint Declaration as quickly as possible. All that was needed was to settle on the general principles; the details could be discussed later (Scott 1989:195). Like London, Beijing also wanted to lobby the service professionals in order to sell the Joint Declaration to Hong Kong's people.

The Making of the Service Professionals

At this historical conjuncture, the service professionals suddenly received special treatment from all sides: Beijing, London, and the Hong Kong government needed them to endorse the Hong Kong people's model to fend off attacks from pro-British business forces.

The Beijing government intensified its united front campaign and crafted a strategic alliance with the service professionals. In early 1984, Xu Jiatun, the newly appointed director of the Hong Kong branch of the New China News Agency, addressed a convocation of the University of Hong Kong, showed up at the anniversary celebration of the Meeting Point, chatted with the officers of the University of Hong Kong's student union for more than three hours, attended the annual banquet of the university's alumni association, and gave a talk to young managers at a luncheon of the Lions Club (Ye 1985:11–60; Chen 1982:III, 34). On all of these occasions, Xu repeatedly pointed to the very important role that Hong Kong intellectuals could play during the transition period:

After 1997, when the people of Hong Kong will have to administer Hong Kong themselves, they will not be able to do it without the intellectuals. Or I should say they will depend mainly on the intellectuals. In the past Hong Kong's intellectuals have made significant contributions to socioeconomic prosperity. And they will play a more important role and make a more significant contribution in the future. . . . The future development of Hong Kong will be determined chiefly by the Hong Kong people themselves, and the intellectuals are the central foundation of the people. The days ahead will provide ample scope for the intellectuals to display their expertise and vision. All the people in the motherland and their Hong Kong compatriots have relied on and have high expectations of the intellectuals of Hong Kong. I have never doubted them, and the intellectuals will surely not let us down. (Ye 1985:15)

Xu's speech was published on January 13, 1984, in the *People's Daily*, Beijing's official newspaper, under the heading "Xu Jiatun Praises the Patriotic Spirit of the Hong Kong Intellectuals."

Students at both of Hong Kong's universities were excited when Premier Zhao Ziyang officially replied to letters they sent him that spring. Zhao called upon them to "realize their social responsibility, so as to make continual contributions to the stability and prosperity of Hong Kong as well as to the grand project of national reunification" (Lu 1985:6–9, 20–23). Moreover, Zhao formally confirmed that China would support the democratization of Hong Kong after 1997: "Of course, the special administrative zone will in practice be a democratic political institution — what you students have called a democratic administration of Hong Kong — in the future" (*Guang Jue Jing*, June 1984).

To the students' amazement, even Margaret Thatcher replied to their letter, which was critical of her government. The students excoriated Britain for not introducing more Western democracy to Hong Kong, argued that the members of the Exco and Legco could in no way represent the Hong Kong people because they were not democratically elected, and urged Thatcher to stop taking such a hard line in the negotiations (Student Unions n.d.:134). Within two weeks, Thatcher's private secretary wrote back. While Thatcher reiterated that "the aim of the British Government is to seek an agreement on the territory's future that will be acceptable to the people of Hong Kong as well as to the British and Chinese Governments," she thanked the students for presenting "the views of Hong Kong people on the future of the territory, particularly those such as you who now and in the future have such an important role to play in it" (*Chinese University Students*, Nov. 21, 1983:7).

The above replies from the Beijing and London governments, naturally, appeared as headline news in the mass media of Hong Kong. As such, these "VIP" treatments by both the Beijing and London governments served to empower the service professionals, made them feel much more important than before, and tempted them to push forward their platform of democratization.

Toward Hong Kong People Democratically Ruling Hong Kong

Now that their views were taken seriously by Beijing and London, service professionals began to shift their focus. Though they had endorsed Beijing's resumption of sovereignty in the negotiation phase, now they wanted to push for the democracy project. The Meeting Point, for instance, stressed democratization in its support of the Hong Kong People's Model (*Guang Jue Jing*, Aug. 1983; Student Unions n.d.:136–37):

The Hong Kong People Ruling Hong Kong Model will be workable if it can meet the following three conditions: (1) the Hong Kong people, with their passion for Hong Kong, will work hard in democratically participating in building up Hong Kong; (2) China will provide guarantees on its political, economic, social, and legal proposals; (3) China and Britain will work together for a smooth transition to 1997. . . . The intellectuals and professionals should be those that bring the whole society forward. They should represent or reflect the opinion of the middle and lower strata and the passive citizens, and struggle for their interests.

The New Hong Kong Society, too, called for the democratization of Hong Kong before 1997: "During the transition period there should be gradual reforms of the existing political structure so as to enhance the political participation of Hong Kong citizens, so that step by step they may develop the capacity to administer Hong Kong and train to be the political leaders of Hong Kong" (Student Unions n.d.:80).

A Crack in the Expatriate-Businesspeople Alliance

The pro-British businesspeople in the Exco were naturally very unhappy about London's concessions to China's demands. On October 7, 1983, the Exco councilors flew to London to meet with Prime Minister Thatcher and Foreign Secretary Howe. It would be a mistake, they said, to concede British administration; no agreement was preferable to a bad agreement (Roberti 1994:77). Then in February 1984 came the so-called Lobo motion in the legislature, demanding that Hong Kong's future be debated in the Legco before any final agreement was reached between London and Beijing. The business sector aimed to exercise veto power over the final agreement through the Legco. To avoid a veto of the Joint Declaration in Hong Kong, London insisted that there would be no alternative to the final agreement and it could not be amended. In March 1984 Jardine & Matheson announced that it would relocate its headquarters to Bermuda. Since

Jardine & Matheson was one of the oldest and richest British corporations in Hong Kong, the media reported the announcement as a vote of no confidence by British capital. In May 1984 big businesspeople in the Exco sent another delegation to London to lobby for a continued British presence after 1997. The delegation asked what London intended to do if the agreement with Beijing was found to be unacceptable to the Hong Kong people. Could London maintain a residual presence in Hong Kong after 1997 to ensure that Beijing would abide by the agreement? The delegation received a hostile reception in London, and the British press and members of Parliament turned deaf ears to their appeal (Roberti 1994:89–90). In June 1984 the Exco businesspeople sent one more delegation to Beijing to spell out their preference for the colonial status quo. These delegates, too, failed to accomplish their mission: Beijing informed them that they did not represent the interests of the Hong Kong people (Scott 1989:210–12).

Yet London needed the Exco's support for the Joint Declaration. It had been privy to the secret negotiations. If the Exco rejected the accord, surely the Hong Kong people would not accept it. On July 26, 1984, Foreign Secretary Howe arrived to consult with S. Y. Chung and his Exco colleagues before going on to Beijing. Howe hoped to persuade the Exco to be realistic and endorse the Joint Declaration, even if it was not what they wanted. Howe returned to Hong Kong to brief the Exco on the outcome of his visit to Beijing: London and Beijing had agreed on a framework and on key clauses of an agreement that would preserve Hong Kong's unique way of life. The agreement and its annexes would be legally binding. The arrangements would be spelled out with enough clarity and precision to command the confidence of the people who lived, worked, traded, and invested in Hong Kong (Roberti 1994:105, 108).

What then could the pro-British businesspeople do after London and Beijing already settled on the content of the Joint Declaration? Since the businesspeople finally realized that they could no longer change the course of history, they reluctantly agreed to endorse the agreement to the people of Hong Kong. However, it is interesting to note that Lo Tak-shing, an Exco and Legco councilor who had close British ties, resigned in protest over Britain's failure to acknowledge its obligation to its subjects in Hong Kong. His departure marked the end of the expatriate–big businesspeople's alliance. Although big businesspeople still worked with the London and Hong Kong governments to preserve their class interests, many councilors joined Lo Tak-shing in shifting their allegiance to Beijing. After all, Beijing would be ruling Hong Kong after 1997 (Rafferty 1990:445). "When Britain and

China decided to return Hong Kong to China," Lo Tak-shing (1996:270) explains, "it was clear that if one wanted to do anything for Hong Kong, one would have to get along with the future sovereign. This was not difficult since naturally the future sovereign's interests coincided exactly with Hong Kong's, whereas the outgoing sovereign's did not. To switch allegiance from British to Chinese sovereignty was, in effect, what the Joint Declaration required of everyone in Hong Kong."

The Genesis of the Democracy Project: July–September 1984

In the summer of 1984, Beijing and London negotiators, headed by Ke Zaishuo and David Wilson, worked hard on the Joint Declaration to be announced that September. China's policies toward Hong Kong after 1997, the heart of the agreement, would be spelled out in an annex. After agreeing that the legal system, including British common law, would remain unchanged, Wilson and Ke discussed Hong Kong's constitutional arrangements.

In Mark Roberti's (1994:98) account, the Chinese team proposed during the early rounds that (1) the future legislature would be "constituted by elections or consultations to be held locally" and (2) the governor would be appointed by Beijing "on the basis of the results of elections or consultations to be held locally." The British team wanted to include provisions for a Western-style democratic government, with a directly elected governor and legislature. Given the service professionals' call for democracy and Beijing's poor human rights record, a Western-style democratic government would be crucial in the effort to secure the support of the Hong Kong people and of the British Parliament for an agreement with China. Wilson pushed hard but got nowhere. The issue was put aside for further consideration.

The question of accountability was also controversial. Wilson and the British negotiators knew that Beijing would oppose an executive who was accountable to an elected legislature. According to Roberti (1994:99), the British work group decided to slip the term *accountability* into the agreement by telling the Chinese that Hong Kong's governor was already accountable to the Legislative Council. The governor had to seek approval for all public expenditures and proposed laws, and he had to answer questions about policy in the council. The Chinese team had been instructed to maintain "existing systems," so it agreed to the term *accountability*, though the word's definition was not spelled out.

By the time the work teams finished negotiating the issues of civil aviation, land leases, and nationality, it was already September 6. Since London and Beijing were scheduled to announce the content of the Joint Declaration by late September, there was little time left to discuss the complicated issue of the structure of the Hong Kong government. Wilson tried again to persuade the Chinese team to drop "consultations" as a method of selecting the governor and legislators, but Ke would not budge. In mid-September, Foreign Secretary Howe pushed the issue again by writing to his Chinese counterpart, Wu Xueqian, to insist that the governor and legislature be democratically elected. Two days later, the Chinese team conceded that the legislature would be "constituted by elections" but refused to define *elections* in any way or to drop consultations as a method of selecting the governor. Realizing that this was Beijing's bottom line, the British finally accepted the Chinese offer (Roberti 1994:113).

The above account, in short, explains the genesis of the democracy project in Hong Kong. The Joint Declaration announced in September 1984 not only declared China's resumption of sovereignty over the entire territory of Hong Kong on July 1, 1997, but also included a clause on democratization: "the chief executive . . . should be selected by election or through consultations held locally and be appointed by the Central People's Government. . . . The legislature of the Hong Kong Special Administrative Region shall be constituted by elections. The executive authorities shall abide by law and shall be accountable to the legislature" (Draft Agreement 1984, Annex I:1). As Jonathan Dimbleby (1997:52) notes, however, that paragraph contained the only reference to the concept of democracy in the entire 8,000-word document.

Muddling Through the Democracy Project

The above account on the genesis of the Hong Kong democracy project, however, resembled more a "muddling through" than a grand inauguration. The term *accountability* was sneaked into the annex of the Joint Declaration with no clarification, and in the Chinese political lexicon, *election* could have meant almost anything (Cottrell 1993).

The phrase "the legislature shall be constituted by election" was one of the last concessions that the British wrung out of the Chinese. As Cradock (1996:52) explains, it "was only secured at the last minute after a personal message from the Foreign Secretary. There was no chance of going further and securing direct election at that time" (see also Cradock 1994:227). Tsim (1990:133) notes that "the sentence which deals with elections to the legislature was only inserted at the eleventh hour and only at the insistence of the British side. It was so late in the day when this point was accepted by the Chinese that an earlier draft of the Joint Declaration which a Hong Kong newspaper— *The Express*—had gotten possession of and published on the morning of 26 September 1984 did not carry this important provision." John Walden, a high-ranking Hong Kong officer, also believed that the election provision was inserted in the Joint Declaration at the last moment (Lo 1997:99).

Since the term *election* was not defined and there was no reference to direct elections, both Beijing and London could interpret the term *election* in whatever way they pleased. When controversies arose later, both the proponents and the opponents of the democracy project could go back to the Joint Declaration and dig out text that sustained their claims or refuted their opponents' (Scott 1995). For example, Governor Chris Patten claimed in the 1990s that "the Joint Declaration is about establishing . . . the same sort of democracy that we have in the United Kingdom. That's what China signed up to—the development of representative government" (Dimbleby 1997:349). The service professionals, too, greeted the Joint Declaration with delight, because they thought it spelled out what they wanted. "When I read [the Joint Declaration]," Martin Lee (1996:236) recalled, "I was thrilled, because it promised that the people of Hong Kong could elect their Chief Executive and legislature and, through them, hold the government accountable to the people. To me that meant democracy."

Why did London not push harder for the democracy project? How did they know that Beijing's bottom line had been reached? It must be conceded that the democracy project was never high on the British agenda. The British were not committed to promote democratization in Hong Kong. At the beginning of the negotiations, London bargained for the continuity of the colonial administration, not for democratization of the Hong Kong government. Only at the end of the negotiation process, when London thought seriously about how to sell the Joint Declaration to the service professionals, did the British Parliament came up with the democracy idea. "In the wake of the Sino-British agreement," Lo (1997:83) explains, "democratization was necessary in order to give some substance to the claim of achieving a 'high degree of autonomy' in post-1997 Hong Kong." Thus the democracy project was a tactic to enable London to claim victory at the negotiating table. So long as the terms *election* and *accountability* appeared in the Joint Declaration, London was satisfied that the declaration was sellable; it needed to push no further.

By covering up its disagreements with Beijing on the issue of democratization, London created the misleading impression that Beijing, too, endorsed a Western-style democracy in Hong Kong after 1997. In addition, London framed the Joint Declaration as a *democratic* instrument (Scott 1992:16). Governor Edward Youde said at a press conference on the day after the Joint Declaration was unveiled: "What China has undertaken to do is to respect certain principles, which are that there will be an elected legislature, that there will be an executive accountable to that legislature, and that the executive will be bound by law" (quoted in Roberti 1994:302). This democratic provision was also highlighted in the early publicity for the Joint Declaration. According to Brian Hook (1997:559), "Such publicity had the effect of dispelling some of the apprehension and misgiving felt in several constituencies including, for example, the House of Commons, the civil service, academe, the media and the established Church over the retrocession of 'free' Hong Kong to a Marxist-Leninist China."

By late 1984, therefore, there seemed to be a convergence of forces toward the democratization of Hong Kong. The service professionals pushed for democracy in order to promote their platform of welfare capitalism; London used democratization to sell the final agreement to Parliament and to Hong Kong's service professionals; Beijing tacitly allowed the British to insert *elections* and *accountability* into the Joint Declaration to speed the signing process and gain the service professionals' support. The big businesspeople were too weakened by the sudden shift in London's stand to voice open opposition to the democracy project.

Needless to say, once the democratic genie was let out of the bottle in late 1984, Hong Kong's political development would be totally different.

Negotiation Politics and the Genesis of the Democracy Project

This chapter examines the politics of negotiation in Hong Kong between 1982 and 1984. Although there is no lack of research on this topic (Bonavia 1985; Ching 1985; Chiu et al. 1987; Jao et al. 1985), the literature tends to focus mostly on the strategies and tactics of state actors, namely, London and Beijing. There is little examination of the politics of negotiation from the angle of societal forces, especially from the viewpoint of service professionals.

This chapter argues that the emergence of the 1997 issue in the early 1980s had threatened the class interests of these professionals. These professionals thus became class conscious and promoted a democracy project to protect their interests and lifestyles. Energized by the 1997 issue, these professionals played an important role in communicating, clarifying, endorsing, and democratizing the "Hong Kong People Ruling Hong Kong Model"—which was subsequently adopted by both London and Beijing in the Joint Declaration signed in 1984.

First, service professionals contributed by communicating the Hong Kong People's Model to the Hong Kong people. Due to confidentiality, the Beijing government could not formally reveal the content of the Hong Kong People's Model. Therefore, these professionals acted as a bridge for passing out the content of this model as it was worked out in Beijing.

Second, these professionals helped clarify the Hong Kong People's Model. When it was first formulated in Beijing, the Hong Kong People's Model was highly abstract, talking mostly general principles. Thus, service professionals pushed Beijing to provide for more specific details, more realistic policies, and more concrete procedures.

Third, these professionals endorsed the Hong Kong People's Model. They engaged in a discursive struggle with pro-British elements on the practicality of this model. And their endorsement helped shift Hong Kong public opinion from pro-Britain to pro-China, and from pro-status quo to pro-Hong Kong People's Model between 1982 and 1983.

Finally, most important from this book's viewpoint, service professionals democratized the Hong Kong People's Model. They were the first group that brought the democratic discourse into Hong Kong politics. Their insistence on democratic reforms in the 1997 transition compelled London to frame the Joint Declaration as a democratic declaration, Beijing to tacitly agree to insert "election" into the Joint Declaration, and big businesspeople to play the democratic game in the transition period.

Why were service professionals able to play such an important role in the negotiation phase? Why were they able to impose a democracy discourse over the business sector, Beijing, and London? First, this may be due to the institutional location of service professionals. Many members were cultural workers (e.g., teachers and journalists) and possessed "symbolic power" through their linkages with the mass media. In addition, being highly educated, they were skillful in articulating ideas and influencing discourse in the mass media. Thus, their class capacity enabled them to transmit, clarify, endorse, and democratize the Hong Kong People's Model, because these activities required little organizational strength or financial resources.

Second, this may be due to the historical conjuncture of the 1997 crises.

The pro-British big businesspeople were weakened by the economic recession in the early 1980s. The colonial government of Hong Kong faced a legitimacy crisis as soon as London and Beijing started to negotiate its future. The Beijing and London governments were in turn frustrated by the deadlock in the first and second rounds of the negotiation process. The big businesspeople later were frustrated by London's shift of bargaining position in late 1983. These power vacuums between 1982 and 1984, then, provided a golden opportunity for service professionals to emerge as a new political force in Hong Kong politics.

Finally, this may be due to the strategic alliance between service professionals and Beijing during the negotiation process. These service professionals were repeatedly told by Beijing that they were the future leaders of Hong Kong society and could play a very significant role in the transition period. Beijing's support, therefore, served to energize these professionals, tempted them to form political groups, aroused their political expectations, prodded them into a discursive struggle with the big businesspeople, and gave them a sense of empowerment.

Nevertheless, while this book stresses the making of service professionals as a new political force during the negotiation process, it must be pointed out that these professionals had not yet emerged as a dominating class. Most of these professionals' political groups had just been set up for less than a year; they were loosely organized and short of resources (Jane Lee 1994:274). Lo (1997:141) labels the New Hong Kong Society and Hong Kong Forum as "mosquito organizations," meaning that these political groups were small and lacked financial support. The Hong Kong Policy Viewers even lacked an office for their regular meetings, although they often contributed articles to newspapers and held press conferences. These service professionals relied upon personal networks to recruit members into their political groups, and the political groups still had not even institutionalized the procedures for membership, fund-raising, making policy statements, etc. In addition, there was very little coordination among political groups. While service professionals shared the basic premises of democratic welfare capitalism, these values alone were insufficient to unify various political groups into one big new middle class party.

Subsequently, although service professionals were able to place the democracy project as an agenda at the negotiation table, they were still too weak a political group to exert any direct influence on the content of the Joint Declaration. Hence, London and Beijing agreed to "muddle through" the democracy project in the Joint Declaration. Democratic terms such as *election* and *accountability* were inserted in the annex, but these terms were never clearly defined, leaving ample room for both Beijing and London to exercise their own interpretations of the democratic content of the Joint Declaration.

As explained in the next chapter, although service professionals were empowered during the negotiation process, they soon faced tough democratic battles ahead after the big businesspeople, Beijing, and London formed a conservative alliance against populist democracy in the mid-1980s.

Part II Formation of a

Restricted Democracy

4 | Electoral Reforms and Legislative Politics

Members of the professional middle class have prestigious social status and high income. If they enter into politics, their chance of winning the election will be high. I predict that the future political arena of Hong Kong will be dominated by the middle class.   Wong Yiu-chung (1984:14)

I believe that the legislature should play a more important role vis-à-vis the executive. . . . My constituents expect me to speak up — to criticize the government — and hence Unofficials such as myself are now increasingly becoming a de facto opposition government.

An elected member of the Legislative Council
(quoted in Cheek-Milby 1989:265)

The Golden Opportunity for Democratic Reforms

The Legislative Council elections in 1985 were historic: it was the first time that some members were elected rather than appointed, and among them were a few service professionals, many of whom won races in District Board elections. As a result, service professionals were highly optimistic about the prospects for democratization in Hong Kong.

For the London government, too, the mid-1980s provided a golden opportunity to push for democratic reforms in Hong Kong: its relationship with Beijing was cordial now that Hong Kongers had regained their confidence with the signing of the Joint Declaration and the economy was growing.

First, although Beijing and London had engaged in a war of words during the negotiations over the future of Hong Kong from 1982 to 1983 (King 1991), the two governments basked in unwonted good relations as soon as they had reached a settlement. Margaret Thatcher flew to Beijing in December 1984 to sign the Joint Declaration. Prime Minister Zhao Zi-yang paid an official visit to Britain in June 1985. There was talk of "new vistas" in Sino-British relations. Zhao discussed trade and economic issues, and Britain was eager to sell more goods to China, especially weapons. Hu Yaobang, the general secretary of the Chinese Communist Party, visited England in 1986, and Queen Elizabeth visited China.

Second, confidence returned to Hong Kong after the Joint Declaration was signed. Editorials, comments and reports in the press, and the survey findings of independent research institutes all indicated that the overwhelming majority of Hong Kongers were pleased by the declaration (King 1991:53). Even Derek Davies of the *Far Eastern Economic Review*, one of the harshest critics of the British Foreign Office, was full of praise: the Joint Declaration was a masterpiece of drafting; it provided a solid foundation on which the Hong Kong community and those who traded with it and invested in it could continue to build prosperity (Roberti 1994:116).

Third, Hong Kong's economic indicators in real growth rates, volume of trade, stocks, the Hang Seng index, and property values were all very encouraging in the mid-1980s. King (1991:56) remarked in 1986, "Although Hong Kong people have not returned to their previous level of optimism, the once rampant pessimism and defeatist attitudes are now something from yesterday. Hong Kong seems steadily returning to the normality of the pre-1997 issue era."

Capital had largely stopped flowing out of Hong Kong and begun to flow in again. Japanese banks that in earlier years had rented property now moved in to buy it. Motorola began construction of a major manufacturing plant. The Bank of China bought substantial amounts of real estate. Beijing made a major loan to finance the Hong Kong subway and funded a nuclear power plant that would service Hong Kong (Overholt 1985).

The mid-1980s, therefore, was a period of prosperity and political harmony. Since Beijing had yet to intervene actively in Hong Kong's political development, the mid-1980s should have provided a golden opportunity for the London government to fulfill its promise to transfer power from the expatriate officials to the Hong Kong people. Yet the colonial government proposed only a modest democratic reform package of indirect elections and a corporatist democracy.

The aim of this chapter is to examine the nature of the democratic reforms proposed by the colonial government. In particular, it seeks to explain the following questions: Why were the democratic reforms modest despite the favorable context? How were service professionals able to seize this modest democratic opening to win elections and articulate their populist democratic agenda in the Legislative Council? How did the big business sector fight back this populist democracy offensive in order to regain its hegemonic domination of Hong Kong politics?

Electoral Reforms: July–November 1984

Timing

The Green Paper titled *The Future Development of Representative Government in Hong Kong* (Hong Kong Government 1984a) was issued in July 1984, even before negotiations between Beijing and London were completed. The Hong Kong public was given only two months to debate it, and the White Paper bearing the same title was rushed into print November 21, 1984. What explains the timing of the Green Paper and the White Paper?

The Hong Kong government dashed off the Green Paper before negotiations were complete so that it could carry out its decolonization policy of democratic reforms without influence from Beijing. Since Beijing needed London's signature on the Joint Declaration as soon as possible, Beijing did not want to upset the harmonious cooperation between the British and Chinese governments by openly criticizing the democratic reforms proposed in the Green Paper.

Between July and October 1984, the Beijing government told visitors in private that it disliked the British proposals, which it believed had been worked out with the aim of leaving pro-British people to administer Hong Kong after 1997. Beijing, said Ji Pengfei, director of China's Hong Kong and Macao Affairs Office, was in favor of "stability and prosperity," not "prosperity plus reform." Ji later added that political reforms in Hong Kong must consider problems with links to the Basic Law (King 1991:64). Nevertheless, the Beijing government said nothing in public against the British democratic reforms until November 1985 (Miners 1989:21). For Beijing, the most crucial activity in late 1984 was the restoration of business and public confidence in Hong Kong after the signing of the Joint Declaration; other matters could be postponed for awhile. Through 1985 London still appeared to be relatively free to implement democratic reforms in Hong Kong before the hand-over.

The White Paper was rushed into print on November 21, 1984, to help sell the Joint Declaration to the British Parliament. On December 5 the House of Commons debated a motion to approve the government's intention to sign the Joint Declaration. In the course of the debate, Foreign

Minister Howe and members of Parliament made frequent references to the White Paper's constitutional reforms to justify the government's position, and the motion was passed with no votes recorded against it. The "Joint Declaration would not have had such an easy passage through Parliament," Miners (1989:23) pointed out, "if it had not been accompanied by an announcement of immediate constitutional reforms and the clear promise of further advances in the not too distant future."

The Green Paper

In the Green Paper the Hong Kong government proposed to replace the existing corporatist bureaucracy with a new system of corporatist democracy. First, the government seemed to be quite sincere in carrying out long-range reforms to democratize its political structure. The proposed reforms were aimed to "develop progressively a system of government the authority for which is firmly rooted in Hong Kong, which is able to represent authoritatively the views of the people of Hong Kong, and which is more directly accountable to the people of Hong Kong." Thus, in place of the existing practice of appointing pro-British big businesspeople to the Legislative Council (Legco) and the Executive Council (Exco), the government proposed to set up a new democratic institutional arrangement under which individuals and groups acquired decision-making power by contending for votes at the ballot box. The seats of the appointed Unofficial and Official members would be gradually decreased until their combined seats, numbering forty-seven in 1984, dropped to ten in 1991 (see Table 1).

Second, although the reforms moved in the direction of democratic elections, they still tried to preserve the existing corporatist system. The second aim of the Green Paper was to "build this system on our existing institutions, which have served Hong Kong well, and as far as possible, to preserve their best features, including the maintenance of the well-established practice of government by consensus." Consequently, the Green Paper favored indirect elections to the Legco and the Exco. The rationale was that "direct elections would run the risk of a swift introduction of adversarial politics, and would introduce an element of instability at a crucial time." For the Legco, the Green Paper proposed indirect elections through "functional constituents" (occupational groups). The governor would no longer appoint businesspeople and corporate professionals to the Legco; these groups would now "elect" their own representatives. From the business and corporate professional groups' point of view, this system was an improvement: now their monopolistic representation in the Hong Kong govern-

TABLE 1.   *Proposals in Green Paper (July 1984) and White Paper (November 1984)*

				1991	
	1984	1985	1988	Option 1	Option 2
Green Paper					
Legislative Council members					
Elected by Electoral College					
(geographical constituents)	0	6	12	14	20
Elected by functional constituents	0	6	12	14	20
Appointed by governor	29	23	16	12	0
Official Members	18	13	10	10	10
All members	47	48	50	50	50
Executive Council members					
Elected by Legislative Council	0	4			8
Appointed by governor	12	8			2
Ex officio members	4	4			4
All members	16	16			14
White Paper					
Legislative Council members					
Elected by Electoral College					
(geographical constituents)	0	12			
Elected by functional constituents	0	12			
Appointed by governor	29	22			
Official Members	18	10			
All members	47	56			
Executive Council members					
No change proposed					

Sources: Hong Kong Government 1984a:14–15, 1984b:8.

ment was institutionalized and mandated by law; they no longer had to rely on the goodwill of the governor. Furthermore, the functional constituents would serve to elevate the power and status of corporate professional bodies (e.g., the Hong Kong Society of Accountants, the Hong Kong Institute of Engineers, and the Hong Kong Institute of Surveyors) as close allies of the big businesspeople (Joan Leung 1990:146, 170).

Third, in contrast to the existing corporatist bureaucracy, which selected only big businesspeople and corporate professionals to the Legco and the Exco, the proposed reforms attempted to broaden the interests of representation by including a few service professions in the "functional constituency" category and by setting up a new electoral college comprising all members of the District Boards, the Urban Council, and the Regional Council. Service professionals, social activists, and union leaders were now included because their consent was seen as crucial for stability and prosperity (Joan Leung 1990:170). The rationale was to open up opportunities for political participation if necessary for the maintenance of social order, but not so far as to endanger the entrenched interests of big businesspeople and corporate professionals.

The strategy was to introduce indirect elections to the Legco in two stages: twelve indirectly elective seats would be added in 1985, and the number would rise to twenty-four in 1988. The Exco, whose main function was to advise the governor on all important matters of policy, would also see a reduction in the number of appointed members and the introduction of indirect elections in two stages. Four Unofficial Members of the Exco would be elected by the Legco in 1988, and another four would be elected in 1991 (see Table 1). The governor would no longer serve as president of the Legco; he should be replaced by a presiding officer to be elected by the Unofficials from among their own members. The Green Paper further suggested that in future the governor be selected "through an elective process, for example, through election by a college composed of all Unofficial Members of the Exco and Legco after a period of consultation among them" (Hong Kong Government 1984a:20).

Finally, the Green Paper insisted that its proposals "are not definitive," and encouraged the people of Hong Kong "to consider and discuss, so that they can comment on them." The Green Paper said it would "allow for further democratic development if that should be the wish of the community" (Hong Kong Government 1984a:22, 4). It further proposed that there be a review of the position in 1989 to decide what further developments might be pursued.

Responses from Hong Kong Civil Society

Since this was the first time the people of Hong Kong had been invited to comment on democratic reforms of such significance, and since the Green Paper was published at the tail end of the Sino-British negotiation process, it naturally attracted considerable attention. Service professionals were highly enthusiastic about the Green Paper. In July 1984 the Meeting Point cooperated with forty-two pressure groups, including the Christian Industrial Committee, the Policy Viewers, the New Hong Kong Society, the

Hong Kong Professional Teachers' Union, the Hong Kong Federation of Student Unions, the Hong Kong Social Workers General Union, and the Ad Hoc Delegation for the Promotion of Democracy and Welfare, to study the Green Paper (S. H. Lo 1997:44; Sing forthcoming). In the next two months these political groups organized a large number of public seminars, appeared on TV talk shows, issued policy statements at press conferences, and rallied a thousand people to demand the speeding up of democratization (Pepper 1997:691). They proposed, though still vaguely, a new system of *populist democracy* in contrast to the mode of corporatist democracy proposed in the Green Paper. First, these professionals challenged the basic premises of the proposed corporatist democracy. The Society for Community Organization, for example, criticized the Green Paper for overemphasizing the need for economic prosperity and political stability at the expense of sacrificing the public's call for populist democracy (*SCMP* July 17, 1984). Second, these professionals identified direct elections, not indirect elections, as the key component of populist democratization of Hong Kong. Indirect elections would perpetuate the dominance of business and corporate professional groups in the Legco. Only direct elections would ensure the full representation toward the interests of the grassroots population. The Meeting Point, for example, suggested that direct elections were the best reforms to gain the support of the grassroots population and meet the political challenge of 1997. Thus, it advocated that one-third of the Unofficial members of the Legco be directly elected (*SCMP*, July 14, 1984). Third, with respect to the speed of democratization, service professionals wanted to set up democratic institutions as soon as possible. The Hong Kong Professional Teachers' Union, the Education Action Group, and the Hong Kong Store House and Transport Staff Association petitioned the Legco for a review of the Green Paper to be conducted earlier—in 1987 instead of 1989, as had been proposed (*Hong Kong Standard,* July 31, 1984). Finally, these professionals stressed that the political education of the public should be strengthened. During the two months of consultation over the Green Paper there were many forums, workshops, summer camps, and courses in order to get the grassroots population more involved in the debate on the democratization of Hong Kong.

Big businesspeople's response to the Green Paper was also highly negative, though for totally different reasons. Stephen Cheong, an appointed Legco member, explained that the present corporatist bureaucracy functioned so well that any major change could only be harmful (*Hong Kong Standard,* July 31, 1984). If the 1997 transition required democratic reforms, they had to be implemented very gradually. Edmund Chow, an urban councilor, told a luncheon meeting of the Lions Club of Hong Kong Island that he preferred indirect elections to maintain Hong Kong's prosperity and stability (*SCMP*, July 14, 1984). Big businesspeople worried that if direct elections were introduced hastily and policies could not be insulated from direct popular pressure, free-lunch provisions might become common.

The big businesspeople's institutional links to the colonial government gave them an edge over the service professionals. In late October 1984, when the Exco convened to discuss the democratic reforms to be spelled out in a White Paper, big businesspeople urged the government to maintain a majority of appointed members in the Legco to ensure that it could get legislation approved. They also wanted no changes to the method of constituting the Exco; the governor should be allowed to pick his own advisers (Roberti 1994:119). Above all, big businesspeople were vehemently against proceeding with democratic reforms "too quickly." They wanted a step-by-step approach, with a review after each stage to see if the government was on the right track. Otherwise, the businesspeople asserted, it would be difficult to preserve Hong Kong's prosperity and stability. In sum, as Miners (1989:20) remarked, the Green Paper "raised exaggerated fears among businesspeople that Hong Kong was on the brink of developing into a parliamentary democracy where an elected assembly would quickly raise taxes and provide extravagant welfare benefits for the poor."

The White Paper

In November 1984, the Hong Kong Government (1984b) published the White Paper after two months of reviewing the public response to the Green Paper. According to the government, it had received 360 written submissions from various organizations, groups, and individuals; extensive consultation was carried on through the District Office; the mass media had carried out several surveys of public opinion; and comments were received from members of the District Boards, Area Committees, the Urban Councilor, and the Unofficial Members of the Legislative Council. Since the government published none of these submissions, surveys, or comments, we do not know who submitted them, what their opinions of democratization were, or how the government weighed them. Nevertheless, the White Paper seems to indicate that the government did try to find a middle ground between the service professionals' and big businesspeople's proposals.

On the one hand, service professionals could claim a victory. First, the

White Paper increased the number of Legco seats to be elected by both geographical and functional constituents in 1985 from the Green Paper's twelve to twenty-four, and reduced the number of Official Members and seats appointed by the Governor from thirty-six to thirty-two (see Table 1). Second, the White Paper hinted that the first direct elections would be held as early as 1988. The government would make "a gradual start by introducing a very small number of directly elected members in 1988 and building up to a significant number of directly elected members by 1997" (Hong Kong Government 1984b:8). Third, with respect to the speed of reform, the White Paper decided to bring forward the date of the review of political reforms from 1989 (as proposed in the Green Paper) to 1987, and suggested that it would reconsider the Governor's position as President of the Legco at that review. Finally, to promote democratic consciousness among the Hong Kong people, the White Paper agreed to develop civil education through the formal school curriculum and extracurricular activities, and to schedule visits of senior students to the District Boards, the Legco, and government departments. Clearly the Hong Kong government had accepted some of the service professionals' proposals.

On the other hand, conservative businesspeople could claim victories too. First, the White Paper echoed their concern that "the prosperity and stability of Hong Kong are not put at risk by introducing too many constitutional changes too rapidly" (Hong Kong Government 1984b:3). Second, the White Paper institutionalized the monopolistic representation of business and corporate professional groups in the Legislature. This is because most of the functional seats were reserved for such corporate organizations as the Hong Kong General Chamber of Commerce, the Hong Kong Association of Banks, the Chinese General Chamber of Commerce, the Federation of Hong Kong Industries, the Hong Kong Institute of Architects, etc. (Joan Leung 1990:147). Third, the White Paper rejected the service professionals' proposal of direct elections in 1985. Fourth, the White Paper no longer reflected the Green Paper's vision of long-term democratic reforms. The Green Paper had discussed reforms for 1991; the White Paper's vision stopped at 1985. The rationale was that the review in 1987 would take up the issue of future reforms. Finally, the White Paper narrowed the scope of reforms considerably. It focused only on the composition of the Legco; it omitted issues concerning the Exco, the governor, and the relationship among the governor, the Legco, and the Exco. Miners (1989:21) comments that the White Paper "could be more accurately described as moves toward developing a more representative legislature rather than a more representative government." These moves away from a long-term, thoroughgoing reform indicated that big businesspeople were still exerting strong influence on the Hong Kong government.

Still, big businesspeople in the Exco were not completely satisfied. On December 5, 1984, S. Y. Chung led a delegation from the Exco to meet with Prime Minister Thatcher at 10 Downing Street. Chung made a special plea for prudence in introducing political reforms in Hong Kong. Some members of Parliament might push to introduce a complete parliamentary system in haste, he warned, but to do so might jeopardize Hong Kong's stability and prosperity (Roberti 1994:124).

Nevertheless, once the government decided on reforms in 1985, it started a new wave of voting politics in Hong Kong. Martin Lee later recalled that "right after the Joint Declaration was signed, there was great enthusiasm in Hong Kong among young professional people in particular. Many of them joined together to form political groups and began to take part in elections and so on" (*Executive*, Mar. 1989:21). Hong Kong society in the mid-1980s was thus very preoccupied with the issues of elections and democratization.

The District Board Elections: March 1985

The Elections of 1982 and Subsequent Reforms

Eighteen District Boards were set up in 1982 to cover the whole of Hong Kong. The total membership consisted of one-third Official Members, one-third appointed Unofficials, and one-third directly elected Unofficials.

The District Boards provided a forum for public consultation and participation at the local level. They had a mainly advisory role, and were allocated a small amount of public funds for local recreational and cultural activities and for minor environmental works (Hong Kong 1984a:6). The District Board was the first institution in which direct elections based on universal adult franchise were practiced in Hong Kong. Before the era of the District Board, people eligible to vote for the Urban Council seldom went beyond 1 to 2 percent of the total population (Tang 1993:252).

Because of the District Boards' restricted advisory role and limited resources, however, the elections in 1982 did not attract much attention among either service professionals or the grassroots population. As Lau and Kuan (1985:8) observed, "many pressure groups even regarded the election as political trickery designed with the sinister motive of subjugating them." Consequently, despite the government's strenuous efforts to mobilize candidates and register voters, only 404 candidates came out to compete for 132 seats, and only 32 percent of 2.78 million qualified people registered to vote; and of these 0.9 million registered voters, only 0.34 million (38%) actually voted (Lau and Kuan 1984:305, 308).

The political status of the District Boards was suddenly upgraded by the reforms in the 1984 White Paper. The proportion of elected members rose from one-third to two-thirds, so the number of elected members almost doubled, from 132 to 237. Government officials would no longer serve as chairs of the District Boards; the members could elect chairs among themselves. The financial compensation and executive duties of the board members increased slightly. Most significant, the District Boards would elect ten of their members to the Legco in 1985. Candidates with political ambitions thus could use a District Board as a springboard to the Legco (Lau and Kuan 1985:6). As Cheng (1986:71) observed, "the ten legislative councilors elected by the District Boards in September 1985 are certainly political stars, as each represents a constituency of about half a million people." With these reforms, service professionals "made a complete turnabout and joined the game in earnest."

The 1985 Elections

A total of 501 candidates competed for 237 seats in 1985. Whereas the candidates in 1982 were dominated by traditional probusiness elites, the group of candidates in 1985 tended to be younger (11% were under thirty and 31% were between thirty-one and forty) and better educated, and the number of educators, professionals, and social workers among them had increased significantly (Cheng 1986:72; Lau and Kuan 1985:15). A new generation of service professionals had begun to emerge as a political force in local politics.

This emerging new political force can also be seen in political groups' sponsorship of candidates. There were twenty-eight candidates from the Professional Teachers' Association, eleven from the People's Council on Public Housing Policy, four from the Public Policy Study Center, and one from the New Hong Kong Society (S. H. Lo 1997:179). Although lacking in resources, these groups still managed to organize training sessions and orientation camps both for candidates and for campaign workers. As Cheng (1986:74) observed, political groups and candidates were linked in an informal social network, as "most of them were acquaintances through participation in student and social movements in earlier years." In addition, Lau and Kuan (1985:14) pointed out that the political groups "gave symbolic support, with substantial support (campaign workers, training facilities, letters of support, endorsement of celebrities, etc.) devoted to selected candidates in selected constituencies."

If there was a continuity in the social networks between community movements of the 1970s and voting politics in 1985, there was also a continuity of ideology. The candidates with service professional backgrounds tended to share a platform of welfare capitalism. They offered much the same campaign promises: they would be outspoken, act as critics of government policies, and try their best to improve community works by demanding such social services as a night clinic, a child-care center, and more recreational facilities; they would seek improvement in traffic control.

To gain support from the grassroots population, service professional candidates also relied on respected colleagues—school principals, social workers, religious leaders—to strengthen ties with the community. They enjoyed the support of the so-called district-based grassroots organizations, or "livelihood concerned groups." In 1985, there was a total of 26 district groups with labels such as the Concerned Group for the People's Livelihood of X District, District Service Centers, District Development Centers, District Research Centers, etc. These district groups were nascent organizations formed after 1984; social workers acted as core members; and these groups were essentially comprised of the representatives of local leaders who were still staying with their parents in public housing estates. These groups were very active in community politics; they had strong connections with outside organizations such as pressure groups and political groups (Joe Leung 1990:51; Chui 1989:224; Tang 1993:260).

Service professional candidates further developed such campaign strategies as home visits, handshaking, banners, handbills, mailed leaflets and pamphlets, posters, videos, public speeches, and limited mass media exposure. During their campaigns, they stressed their educational and professional backgrounds, their past record in promoting community service, and their differences from traditional, conservative leaders of the *kaifongs* (neighborhood associations) with respect to political ideology (Cheng 1986:73–78). With such campaign strategies, did service professional candidates do well in the 1985 District Board elections?

Election Results

More people registered to vote in 1985 than in 1982 (1.27 million vs. 0.9 million) and more people actually voted (0.48 million vs. 0.34 million). Furthermore, turnout was higher in the low-income housing projects than

TABLE 2.   *Occupational groups represented by candidates for District Boards, 1982 and 1985 (percent)*

Occupational group	1982	1985
Businesspeople	44%	28%
Service professionals		
Educators	17	18
White-collar employees	11	15
Professionals	4	13
Social workers	3	8
All service professionals	35	54
Workers and technicians	5	3
Retirees	2	3
Others	14	12
All occupational groups	100%	100%

Source: Adapted from Cheng 1986:80.

elsewhere (e.g., 51% in Shatin vs. 31% in the territory as a whole). The people in the public housing projects, Joseph Cheng (1986:78–79) explains, could be reached more easily through home visits, and they felt a greater need for effective representatives to articulate their interests and grievances (such as high rent and poor community service).

The people elected to the District Boards were generally younger, better educated, and more likely to have professional backgrounds than their counterparts in 1982. In 1985, 56 percent of elected members were forty years old or younger, compared to 34 percent in 1982; 54 percent were service professionals in 1985, compared to 35 percent in 1982 (see Table 2). The grassroots population in public housing, Cheng noted (1986:79–80), seemed to want "someone young, well-educated, with relevant professional expertise (social workers and teachers) to represent them and to help to solve their problems."

Furthermore, candidates sponsored by the political groups and pressure groups of service professionals won decisive victories in 1985. All of the Meeting Point's candidates and 80 percent of those backed by the Hong Kong Professional Teachers' Union were elected. The traditional probusiness groups, such as the Civic Association, did much less well (see Table 3). This is another indication that service professionals had managed to appeal to the grassroots population, who were impressed by their organizational skills, campaign strategies, and welfare platforms. Clearly the traditional,

TABLE 3.   *Candidates nominated by political groups and elected to District Boards, 1985*

	Number of candidates	Number elected	Success rate (percent)
Service professionals' political groups			
Hong Kong People's Association	8	8	100%
Meeting Point	4	4	100
Hong Kong Affairs Society	3	3	100
Service professionals' pressure groups			
Eastern District Coalition	11	11	100
Central Western District Coalition	12	10	83
Hong Kong People's Council on Public Housing Policy	11	9	82
Hong Kong Professional Teachers' Union	30	24	80
Traditional political groups			
Reform Club	33	17	52
Civic Association	54	21	39

Source: Based on Cheng 1986:81.

business-oriented groups could no longer maintain hegemony in local political arenas.

The Impact of the 1985 District Board Elections

Service professionals' political groups, naturally, were jubilant. The income derived from service on the District Boards enabled them to set up offices and employ full-time community organizers to carry out their campaign promises (Joe Leung 1994:260) and to establish a foothold in community politics. Their leaders now had higher prestige, better public recognition, and a much-improved public image. A survey (Lau and Wan 1987:6) on the public image of pressure groups had positive findings. A significant proportion of the respondents believed that these groups were motivated by a desire to serve society. Now that they had edged their way into the establishment, service professionals began to shift their focus from single-issue protests and mobilization tactics to more formal channels and sophisticated tactics based on rational arguments, research and surveys, lobbying, and elite alliances (Joe Leung 1990:56).

Their electoral victory confirmed that a cross-class alliance with the grassroots population could empower them to defeat the traditional elites.

These professionals, Cheng (1986:83) commented, "firmly believe that time is on their side and they have great confidence that they will turn the tide in the early 1990s, if not earlier. Because they are in their mid-30s, they can certainly afford to wait."

On the other hand, the District Board election in 1985 had revealed the limitation of this electoral victory. First, these political groups and alliances remained loosely organized. Lau and Kuan (1985:14) remark that even "the two most impressive alliances — those in Eastern and Central/Western — were loose *ad hoc* groups, based mainly upon expediency, convenience and mutual acquaintance, had no organization, no discipline and no common platform." Cheng (1986:73) also points out that many of the political groups were still in the early stages of development; they "were courting the more promising candidates and trying to recruit them, instead of candidates being anxious to seek the endorsement of various political groups. Moreover, some candidates were members of a number of groups which were too weak to exercise discipline and force the candidates to make a choice."

The small size of the constituencies in the District Board elections allowed the political groups to localize the issues. Thus Lau and Kuan (1985:21) observed that " 'national' issues were conspicuously missing from the platforms of the candidates. Issues such as the future of Hong Kong, political reform, Hong Kong's relationship with China and even the role of the D.B. [District Board] in the evolving political system were scarcely mentioned. Instead, the candidates focused mainly on local services and facilities, which they considered would appeal better to the constituents."

Finally, although service professionals had made significant inroads into the District Boards, they were still unable to bring a fundamental shift of power into the decision-making process. Alarmed by the impressive victory of service professionals in the election, the Hong Kong government tried to restore the balance by appointing a large number of traditional, probusiness, progovernment elites to the District Board after the election. Of the 132 appointees, 56 percent were from the business sector. Since most of the appointed members supported the same candidates for the District Board chairmanships, the appointed members won five of the ten chairmanships in urban areas, took all nine rural chairmanships, and six out of nine seats on the Regional Council (Cheng 1986:82). Thus the traditional political forces had yet to lose control of the District Boards.

Even so, the victory of service professionals in the 1985 District Board election had posed an enormous threat to probusiness forces. Thereafter, the District Boards had become politicized, turning into a battleground for service professional groups to compete for influence, resources, and public attention (Joe Leung 1994:260). Subsequently, probusiness forces grew determined to contain the tide of service professionals in the Legco elections the following September.

The Legco Elections: September 1985

The Geographical Constituents (Electoral College)

According to the White Paper (Hong Kong Government 1984b), the Legco was to have twelve councilors elected by an electoral college made up of members of the District Boards, the Urban Council, and the Regional Council. The District Boards were regrouped into ten election districts of about 500,000 people each. Since each Board would elect one councilor, the District Boards would return a total of ten members to the Legco. Of the remaining two Legco seats, one would be filled by the Urban Council and one by the Regional Council in the New Territories.

What were the rules that governed a District Board's election of one of its members to the Legco? To start with, a member needed to get only five signatures to be nominated. Since five signatures were easy to get, a large number of candidates would compete in each district. In the Eastern District of Hong Kong Island, for example, as many as six candidates competed for the seat in Legco.

If no candidate received a majority of the votes in the first round of voting, the candidate with the fewest votes would be removed from the ballot. There would then be a recess for forty-five minutes before the second round of voting. If again no candidate secured a majority, the remaining candidate with the fewest votes would be removed from the ballot. The voting would go on until a candidate managed to get a majority of the votes. This rule basically shifted the candidates' focus from getting the support of the grassroots population to getting the support of fellow members of the District Board. New middle-class traits such as academic degrees, professional backgrounds, and community experience that had played a decisive role in the March District Board elections were no longer assets in this type of election. Now what mattered most was rapport, friendships, patron-client relationships, and support from cliques (*Pai Shing,* July 1 and Oct. 1, 1985).

Influenced by these election rules, the indirect election to the Legco of geographical constituencies through the District Board yielded the following results. First, the competition was so intense that many District Boards required four rounds or more of balloting to determine a winner. Many candidates were angry when former supporters voted for another candidate in the third or fourth round, and angry at the other candidate for stealing their supporters (*Pai Shing*, Oct. 15, 1985). The indirect election had created distrust and personal conflicts among members of the District Boards.

The appointed and directly elected members won equal numbers of seats: five each. Despite the impressive victory of service professionals at the polls in March, the government's "balanced" tactic of appointing a large number of business elites to the District Boards after the election had been successful. Appointed members were able to gather enough votes to block many service professionals from winning Legco seats after the District Boards were regrouped (*Pai Shing*, Oct. 1, 1985).

Finally, whereas political groups were very active in endorsing candidates and mobilizing the grassroots population to vote in the District Board elections in March, these same groups decided that they would not endorse any candidate in the Legco indirect election in September. The groups may have felt helpless to promote their own candidates under the existing rules of balloting.

The Functional Constituents

In addition to the twelve councilors elected from geographical constituencies, the Legco was to have twelve councilors elected by functional (occupational) constituencies, and here business interests were overrepresented (Scott 1989:276–77). Five of the twelve functional constituencies were allotted to the commercial, industrial, and financial sectors, and all of them were associated with particular business organizations: the Hong Kong General Chamber of Commerce, the Chinese Chamber of Commerce, the Federation of Hong Kong Industries, the Chinese Manufacturers' Association, and the Hong Kong Association of Banks. The remaining seven functional constituencies went to labor (two seats, one for the leftist unions, another for the pro-Guomindang unions) and the legal, education, medical, engineering, and social service professions.

As in the geographical constituencies, election rules strongly influenced the patterns and outcomes of the elections for the functional seats. Five seats were assigned to business and the corporate professions, and twenty-two more businesspeople would be appointed to the Legco by the governor. The combination of functional constituencies and the appointment system guaranteed that the conservatives would remain a dominant force in the Legco.

In addition, the method of counting constituents for service professions would create tensions among members. For example, a representative from the social work profession would be elected through the one organization, one vote method instead of through one member, one vote. This election rule favored the election of the moderate leader of the Hong Kong Council of Social Services (an umbrella group of social work–oriented organizations) over the more radical leader of the Hong Kong Social Workers General Union.

Furthermore, by stressing functional constituencies, the government narrowed the representative's role to the protection and enhancement of his or her own occupational interests. Thus the functional representation category was a means to divide and conquer service professionals, forcing them to retreat into narrow occupational issues and discouraging them from raising issues that concerned the grassroots population.

The results of the Legco election in September were much less dramatic than those of the direct election of the District Boards in March. On the one hand, candidates in four functional constituencies were automatically elected, because they faced no competitors. Many candidates from the business sector were automatically elected or had few competitors. As Roberti (1994:153) observes, many of the business "constituencies were so small that the election was akin to running for the presidency of a social club." On the other hand, the candidates from the service professions faced stiff competition. In general, the Legco councilors elected through functional constituencies were older, were better established in their careers, and had more experience in working with the government than their colleagues elected through geographical constituencies (*Pai Shing*, July 1 and Oct. 1, 1985).

The geographical and functional modes of election, as King (1991:61) observes, "did not really add too much democratic respectability to the Legislative Council." The functional constituency system gave disproportionate weight to the interests of established elites, and the indirect election of the geographical electoral colleges ultimately provided little room for grassroots participation. Nevertheless, the Legco had a new face and a greatly transformed *modus operandi* after 1985.

The Transformation of Legislative Politics

The Legco before 1985

In 1984 the Legco was composed of the Governor of Hong Kong (as the president), three ex officio members (the Chief Secretary, the Financial Secretary, and the Attorney General), 15 Official Members, and 29 Unofficial Members. Its primary function was the enactment of legislation. It also monitored the administration on matters of public interest and debated questions of policy, and it exercised control over the expenditure of public funds through the Finance Committee (Hong Kong Government 1984a:5 and n.d.).

There were several characteristics of the Legco's model of operation before 1985. First, the Legco was an executive-dominated institution. The Governor not only presided over the Council but appointed all the Official and Unofficial Members. In addition, he had actual lawmaking power: he enacted legislation by and with the advice and consent of the Legco. A bill passed by the Legco did not become law until the Governor signed it. Cheek-Milby (1989:260) points out that "these compositional and functional limitations determined that the Legislative Council would remain a creature of the executive branch, utilized primarily as a legitimator of civil servant policymaking."

Second, the Legco was a business-dominated political institution. Of the fifteen Unofficial Members in 1975, nine were big businesspeople and four were corporate professionals. Even when MacLehose tried to diversify the representation in the late 1970s, the pattern of business dominance continued. Of the twenty-seven Unofficial Members of the Legco in 1982, eleven were businesspeople and seven corporate professionals, versus three labor union representatives and six service professionals (see Table 4).

Third, the Legco tended to operate by consensus. Historically, Wight (1946:30) observed, Unofficials were chosen "not for their representativeness, but for their conservatism and the likelihood of their supporting the governor." Thus "any sensible Councillor knows that if he does not give the best advice he can," as Lydia Dunn (1989:81) put it so well, "he will . . . be unlikely to be reappointed." Consequently, although Unofficials could affect government policy making by raising questions, participating in adjournment debates, and creating select committees to scrutinize legislation, these initiatives rarely, when actually employed, gave rise to visible changes in government policy or impassioned public controversy (Miners

TABLE 4.   *Occupational groups represented by Official and Unofficial Members of Exco and Legco, 1975–1986*

	Exco		Legco	
Occupational group	Number	Percent	Number	Percent
1975				
Officials: civil service	7	47%	15	50%
Unofficials				
Big businesspeople	6	40	9	30
Corporate professionals	2	13	4	14
Service professionals	0	0	2	7
Labor	0	0	0	0
All occupational groups	15	100%	30	101%
1982				
Officials: civil service	7	44	23	46
Unofficials				
Big businesspeople	6	38	11	22
Corporate professionals	3	19	7	14
Service professionals	0	0	6	12
Labor	0	0	3	6
All occupational groups	16	101%	50	100%
1986				
Officials: civil service	7	47	11	19
Unofficials				
Big businesspeople	7	47	23	41
Corporate professionals	1	7	10	18
Service professionals	0	0	11	19
Labor	0	0	2	4
All occupational groups	15	101%	57	101%

Source: Adapted from Davies 1989:50–55.

1981; Wesley-Smith 1987). Furthermore, since most of the discussions were carried on behind closed doors, it was difficult to judge if the Unofficials actually exercised any pervasive influence on policy. As a result, Unofficials were considered never to oppose government policy vigorously, and the Legco was considered a rubber stamp that always endorsed the government. A former acting governor noted that "the Governors before 1985 in

serving as the President of the legislature had quiet lives—they made ritu-
alistic appearances on Wednesday afternoon before a small chamber which
was more of a club. Things were always arranged in advance between civil
servants and Unofficials—so there was little dissent and even discussion"
(quoted in Cheek-Milby 1989:274).

Finally, although little political division existed in the Legco, a status
hierarchy crystallized among its members. Depending on their seniority,
Unofficial councilors were assigned positions that conferred differential
power and prestige on incumbents. M. K. Lee (1990:116) pointed out that
"status differences are indicated by seating arrangements, committee and
panel chairmanships, and honors conferred by the Queen. At the apex of
this stratified order is the Senior Unofficial Member, who enjoys deference
from his peers and expects them to listen to him and obey. . . . The status
hierarchy represents a ladder for upward mobility. It provides an important
source of incentives for conformity, application, and other modes of posi-
tively regarded conduct." Similarly, Cheek-Milby (1989:272) remarked that
the Unofficials were expected to conform to the old norms of "deference to
authority" and "respect for those with senior legislative experience."

In sum, the Legco in the pre-1985 era was dominated by the executive
branch and the business sector. It practiced consensus politics and its members were highly status-conscious. How did the democratic reforms of 1985
affect the Legco's composition, functioning, and mode of operation?

The Legco in 1985

The White Paper changed the composition of Legco. On the one hand,
it reduced the number of Official Members from eighteen in 1984 to ten
in 1985 and cut the number of appointed members from twenty-nine to
twenty-two. On the other hand, it created a new category of elected members, of whom twelve were elected by geographical constituents and twelve
by functional constituents (Table 1).

Although the Legco's functions remained the same (enactment of legislation, control of public expenditures, monitoring of the administration),
its mode of operation was so drastically transformed that the future of democratization of Hong Kong was to be profoundly affected. First, the dominance of the executive was substantially reduced. The governor no longer
had the authority to appoint all Unofficial Members. Twenty-four out of
a total of fifty-six seats (43%) in the Legco were filled by indirect election
through geographical and functional constituents; the Legco could now

have members highly critical of the government. In addition, the number of Official Members was reduced from eighteen to ten, so that they became a minority (18%).

Second, the class composition of the Legco changed. There were more members from the service professional class (six in 1982, eleven in 1985). With some support from corporate professionals and labor, service professionals could become a force to be reckoned with. At the same time, the number of Legco members with business backgrounds nearly doubled (from eleven in 1982 to twenty-three in 1985). In fact, the power vacuum opened by the reduction of Official Members was filled by business interests (see Table 4). Although service professionals were now ready to challenge the hegemony of business interests in the Legco, they were unable to undermine those interests because of the relatively small number of seats they won through indirect elections.

Third, the consensus mode of operation disappeared in 1985, as the elected members no longer needed to toe the government line (M. K. Lee 1987:1). The Unofficials' perception of their legislative role changed. Instead of serving as steadfast legitimators of government policy, some Unofficials, particularly those who were elected, began to look upon themselves as challengers of proposed policies. It began to seem that the Unofficial Members might eventually develop into an opposition. A member elected from a functional constituency said as much:

I believe that the legislature should play a more important role vis-à-vis the executive. Normally we are not consulted until a policy has been decided upon — then it is just put before us as a fait accompli. It is very difficult to change it once it is made, except in highly controversial matters. My constituents expect me to speak up — to criticize the government — and hence Unofficials such as myself are now increasingly becoming a de facto opposition government. (Cheek-Milby 1989:265)

The opposition came from service professionals, most notably Martin Lee (a lawyer), Szeto Wah (an educator), Hui Yin-fat (a social worker), and Richard Lai and Conrad Lam (doctors) (Scott 1989:278). This breakdown of consensus politics in the Legco can be seen in the sudden increase in the number of questions submitted (from 179 to 296), adjournment debates (from 3 to 6), ad hoc groups (from 5 to 38), ad hoc group meetings (from 30 to 89), and panel meetings (from 29 to 99) between the 1984–85 session and the 1985–86 session (Cheek-Milby 1989:263).

Fourth, the disappearance of consensus politics was accompanied by a breakdown of the status hierarchy. M. K. Lee commented that "the Senior Unofficial Member can no longer claim to be the indisputable leader among the Unofficials. He ceases to be the captain who exercises discipline, assigns tasks, and imposes consensus. The very basis of his own authority is now at stake as his elected colleagues come to question the principle, i.e., appointment by the Governor, which legitimizes his superior status" (1990:117). In fact, in the eyes of the newly elected members, the Officials and the appointed members were second-class citizens, because they were appointed by the governor and always toed the government line, whereas the elected members saw themselves as having a mandate to criticize the establishment, because they were "truly reflecting the people's views and pushing for policies that were truly reflective of those views" (Cheek-Milby 1989:264).

Fifth, there was more openness in the post-1985 Legco. It was impossible to keep the rule of confidentiality after the sudden recruitment of twenty-four new members with service professional backgrounds, so the Wednesday meetings were no longer conducted behind closed doors. Furthermore, press conferences were held after the Friday meetings to inform the public about the major decisions that had been reached. The Legco had never had so much media exposure before (*Pai Shing*, Aug. 1, 1986:9, 11).

Finally, issues raised in the Legco became politicized. As long as the appointed members were accountable to the governor, they felt no pressure to stage a performance for the general public and generally stayed within the narrow areas of expertise assigned to them by senior members. After 1985, as Lee and Lai (1988:11) pointed out, elected members, "in their enthusiasm to demonstrate their accountability to their constituents, would speak on any issue area if given the opportunity." Miners (1989:32) also noted that "groups of Unofficials who are unable to persuade their colleagues to accept their point of view are much more ready than in the past to make their disagreements public, to air their views vigorously in debates, and sometimes to impugn the motives of their opponents." After analyzing the content of the speeches in the 1984–85 and 1985–86 legislatures, Lee and Lai (1988:18) found that appointed members were most "legalist" (focusing on a legalistic definition of their responsibility), while members elected by functional constituencies were most "political" and "ideological" (focusing on mediating or resolving conflict and theorizing about political ideals), and those elected from geographical constituencies were most "advocative" (focusing on fighting for or representing the interests of a broad social group or protesting against specific injustices).

Nothing reveals the politicization of issues more clearly than the Daya Bay controversy, which split the Legco into factions for and against the establishment.

The Daya Bay Incident and Its Political Significance

Chronology

According to the succinct account of Chan and Lee (1991:106–7), the Daya Bay controversy had its origins in the late 1970s. The world oil crisis sent Hong Kong searching for cheaper energy sources. The solution seemed to be construction of a nuclear power plant at Daya Bay, on the Chinese side but only seventy miles from Hong Kong. The Hong Kong government promised not only to guarantee a loan but also to purchase 70 percent of the power to be generated. The China Light & Power Company, a British corporation in Hong Kong, reached a joint venture agreement with the Guangdong provincial government in March 1986. Sophisticated equipment was to be purchased from both British and French companies. The Daya Bay project received the endorsement of Hong Kong's Exco in early April 1986. The Chinese government saw the Daya Bay nuclear plant as a vital source of electricity and transferred technology. It would generate six times more power than the Chinese nuclear plant in Zhejiang Province, and the foreign corporations promised to hand over the needed technology and capital to China on favorable terms. The key players in the Daya Bay project, then, were the Hong Kong government, a major British utility company in Hong Kong, the Guangdong provincial government in China, and British and French transnational corporations. In addition, the project was intended to testify to Hong Kong's continued economic power and its close cooperation with China.

In late April 1986, however, the Chernobyl accident in the Soviet Union claimed many Soviet lives, contaminated water, air, and food beyond Soviet borders, and had a ripple effect in Hong Kong. Suddenly Hong Kong caught Chernobyl fever. Safety concerns that had been ignored earlier now became a rallying cry for antinuclear protesters.

By the end of May, members of 117 pressure and political groups had formed a Joint Conference for Shelving the Daya Bay Nuclear Plant. By July they had collected around a million signatures to a declaration opposing construction of the nuclear power plant (Chan and Lee 1991:107). They organized seminars, press conferences, public demonstrations, visits to the Legco, and a trip to Beijing to express their views on safety, maintenance, and the economics of the Daya Bay plant.

Service professionals later turned the antinuclear protest into a democracy movement in opposition to both the Chinese and Hong Kong governments. On the one hand, they regarded the Daya Bay dispute as a litmus test of the sincerity of China's "one country, two systems" policy: would Beijing take the will of a million Hong Kong people seriously and actually shelve the Daya Bay project? On the other hand, they used the Daya Bay dispute to question the legitimacy of the Legco, the Exco, and the Hong Kong government, charging them with sacrificing the safety of the Hong Kong people to protect the interests of British capital. Editorials in publications in the service professionals' camp "reprimanded some Executive and Legislative Councilors for trying to appease China at a rapid pace . . . [and] went too far when they defied their past record and the will of the public to please the new boss. . . . [They chided] the Hong Kong government as a lame duck that always says yes to China" (Chan and Lee 1991:112).

Before the political reforms of 1985, service professionals had no choice but to promote such antinuclear and democratic protests outside the state through pressure group politics. Nevertheless, after some service professionals were elected into Legco in 1985, they could exercise their influence inside the state. As such, it is interesting to see how service professionals had articulated their interests within the Legco and tried, even though they had suspected their mission would fail, to challenge the hegemony of business's interests.

Big Businesspeople Respond

Big businesspeople generally acknowledged the public's concern about the safety of the Daya Bay nuclear plant, but they defined the issue as a technical matter rather than a political problem. A decision on the construction of the Daya Bay plant, they argued, should depend on expertise, rational knowledge, and access to information, not on the unfounded fears of an uninformed public.

H. K. Cheng, a Legco councilor who represented the engineers' constituency, addressed the Legco on July 6, 1986: "As a professional engineer, Sir, I fully appreciate that a nuclear power plant is an extremely complex installation involving multi-disciplines of engineering and technology and designed to the highest possible international safety standard. The Pressurized Water Reactor supplied by Framatone in this instance is considered one of the best systems in the world with a proven record of performance and safety." Nevertheless, Cheng conceded that it might be necessary to incorporate provisions in the design and special procedures in the operation of the plant to maximize safety. Therefore, he called for the release of various reports that contained detailed information about safety assessments, the probability of accidents and their consequences, a contingency plan, and an assessment of environmental impact; and the commissioning of an independent nuclear installation inspectorate to monitor the operation and maintenance of the plant throughout its life span (*HK Engineer,* Aug. 1986:48).

From Pressure Group Politics to Legco Politics

The Legco sent two fact-finding committees to Europe and the United States to inspect nuclear power plants. Upon their return to Hong Kong, the committees issued a lengthy report listing the safety measures adopted by foreign plants. They were immediately invited to Beijing to discuss their report in their official capacity. Until late 1985, the Beijing government had insisted that most of the Legco members were appointed by the colonial government and so represented British interests. Beijing's invitation, then, could be interpreted as formal recognition of the Legco's legitimacy, and had the potential to serve as a foundation for a broad alliance between Beijing and the business sector.

Service professionals' political groups, led by Martin Lee, Szeto Wah, and Dr. Conrad Lam, moved to counter Beijing's offensive in the Legco. On September 3, the day after Beijing issued its invitation to the fact-finding committees, the Legco debated three issues: Should the Legco send the fact-finders to Beijing? Should the Legco adopt the fact-finders' report? Should the Legco call a special session to debate the Daya Bay issue? Forty-three lawyers had sent a letter asking the Legco members to endorse the call for an urgent debate: "In a free society, any issue which concerns the welfare of the whole society, and which its people feel strongly enough about to endorse one million signatures on a petition, should be properly aired in the open and debated without fear or reservation" (*FEER,* Sept. 18, 1986:28). The governor told reporters on the eve of the debate that the Hong Kong government remained committed to the project.

The Legco session on September 3 was explosive. During the five hours of heated debate, the members divided into two camps. The majority, consisting of the civil servant Official Members, the appointed Unofficial Members, and some of the indirectly elected Unofficial Members, defended the position of the establishment. They supported the fact-finders' visit to Beijing because they could influence the Chinese government on safety and supervisory issues. They thanked the fact-finders for producing a timely report on the design, construction, accidents, emergency planning, management, and safety of nuclear plants, and rejected a motion for a special

TABLE 5. *Votes by appointed and indirectly elected Legco members on issues in the Daya Bay controversy*

| | Appointed councilors | | Indirectly elected councilors | | | |
| | | | Functional constituencies | | Geographical constituencies | |
	Percent	Number	Percent	Number	Percent	Number
Send delegation to Beijing?						
Yes	94%	16	67%	6	67%	6
No	6	1	33	3	11	1
Abstain	0	0	0	0	22	2
All votes	100%	17	100%	9	100%	9
Did not vote (absent/late)		5		3		3
Accept delegation's fact-finding report?						
Yes	100%	16	67%	6	64%	7
No	0	0	33	3	36	4
Abstain	0	0	0	0	0	0
All votes	100%	16	100%	9	100%	11
Did not vote (absent/late)		6				1
Hold a special Legco session?						
Yes	7%	1	33%	3	60%	6
No	87	13	67	6	30	3
Abstain	7	1	0	0	10	1
All votes	101%	15	100%	9	100%	10
Did not vote (absent/late)		7		3		2

Source: Adapted from *Pai Shing*, Sept. 16, 1986:51.

session, because it would only lead to confrontation with China, a split between the Legco and the government, and divisions within the community (*FEER*, 18 Sept. 18, 1986:28).

The minority faction, consisting largely of directly elected Unofficial Members, questioned the need to send a delegation to Beijing, because the antinuclear coalition had sent one only a month earlier, with no result. They questioned the fact-finders' report because it said nothing about the suitability of the site. And they strongly endorsed the motion to hold a special session because the safety issue was of the utmost importance, because it would enhance the monitoring role of the Legco over the executive, and because it would enhance public awareness of the Legco's functioning (*Pai Shing*, Sept. 16, 1986:49–51).

When the votes were finally tallied, the majority faction won all three motions, as expected. Nevertheless, the vote on the motion for a special session was closer than expected (22 to 10; see Table 5). Such an opposition vote, unprecedented in Hong Kong's history, revealed clearly that the Legco was split into a business faction and a welfare faction.

After failing to influence the Legco, service professionals had once again to rely on pressure group tactics. Martin Lee and nine other Legco members lost no time in appealing to the governor for another chance to call a special session. When their appeal was rejected, the antinuclear coalition delivered a blank letter of protest to the governor's office.

Unmoved by these efforts, the Legco delegation went to Beijing with its fact-finding report. After receiving the Beijing government's promise to give full consideration to the report in augmenting safety measures at Daya Bay, the Hong Kong government formally refused to withdraw its commitment to the project. The Daya Bay contract was signed by the concerned parties in Beijing on September 23, as scheduled, and the antinuclear coalition held their last protest in Morse Park on October 5.

Why They Failed to Stop the Construction

What explains the failure of the service professionals to stop the construction of the Daya Bay nuclear plant despite more than a million signatures on a petition to shelve it? One factor was the establishment's strong, unified opposition to the antinuclear movement. The antinuclear movement threatened the deeply rooted economic interests of Hong Kong's big businesspeople, the Hong Kong government, the Beijing government, and the British and French transnational corporations. The establishment elites fought back on all fronts. They discounted the million signatures and declared that the people who signed their names were ignorant about nuclear energy and had been stirred up by a handful of people after the Chernobyl accident. They mobilized public support by holding press conferences and public exhibitions on nuclear energy, by inviting the public to Daya Bay to inspect the plant site, and by representing Beijing as having ample experience with nuclear energy. They hired French experts to supervise the management of the plant to calm fears about its safety. And they defeated the antinuclear forces in the Legco with their votes (Chan and Lee 1991:108; *Pai Shing,* Oct. 1, 1986:6–10).

On the other hand, the antinuclear movement, like other new middle-class movements, was weakly organized. It was impossible to persuade 117 organizations to agree on protest strategies. The leftist unions and many other organizations, though they supported the antinuclear stand, hesitated to criticize the Beijing government publicly or to send a delegation to Beijing. In addition, the coalition called too many press conferences in September; reporters grew weary of their insistence on the same issue again and again when they had no action to report. Moreover, the organizers of the coalition were not sufficiently confident of success. They held their final protest at the small Morse Park rather than at Victoria Park because they were afraid not enough people would show up, and they banned comments from the audience to prevent radicals from attacking Beijing in public (*Pai Shing,* Oct. 1, 1986:6–10).

The Daya Bay incident made the service professionals realize that there were very serious structural constraints on their activities in the Legco. If councilors continued to be appointed and elected indirectly, service professionals would always be a minority faction and would never be able to translate their democratic programs into government policies. They could shout, yell, and protest in public, but they could not challenge big business and Beijing under the present structure of restricted democracy. From 1986 on, they began to shift their attention from legislative politics to constitutional reforms.

Electoral Reforms and Legislative Politics in the Mid-1980s

Having let the genie of democracy out of the bottle, London proposed democratic reforms in Hong Kong. The mid-1980s was a golden opportunity for reforms, because prosperity and political harmony had been restored in Hong Kong. Moreover, Beijing had yet to reveal its opposition to democratic reforms, thus leading Hong Kongers to believe that they could settle the issue of democratization on their own terms.

Although the expatriates' alliance had started to show cracks during the negotiation process, big businesspeople quickly regrouped and settled their differences with London when they faced the challenge of the Democrats in the mid-1980s. Their institutional links to the Hong Kong government through the Exco and the Legco had enabled them to slow the democratization process and restrict it to a "corporatist democracy" model, thus guaranteeing that their business interests would have a monopolistic representation in the Legco.

In the mid-1980s the service professionals were still not strong enough to challenge the corporate sector. Their political groups were too small, too lacking in resources, and too fragmented to permit them to push for a "populist democracy" under which the governor and the Legco members would be directly elected. Yet their political struggles in the mid-1980s were not entirely in vain. They were able to make the Hong Kong government double the number of indirectly elected Legco members from 12 to 24 in 1985 and promise a direct election of the Legco would be held in 1988.

A small democratic opening (in the form of local District Board elections and indirect elections in the Legco) in 1985, nevertheless, had already empowered service professionals. They enthusiastically participated in the elections, mobilized their community networks to support their candidates, appealed to the grassroots population with their welfare platform, and won a landslide victory against traditional business candidates for the District Boards. Some service professionals even got selected for the Legco through the indirect elections in geographical and functional constituencies. The 1985 elections thus convinced service professionals that they had grassroots support and could win elections, and they were determined to push for a populist democracy of direct elections in the late 1980s.

Although the Legco still had a majority of Official and Unofficial Members from the business sector, the entry of a small number of service professionals transformed legislative politics. Consensus politics was replaced by opposition politics. The elected service professionals were not hesitant to criticize government policies, to challenge the leadership of the senior unofficial members, and to voice their dissent to the public through the mass media.

So long as the constitutional structure of the Legco remained unchanged, however, the service professionals would always remain a minority faction in the Legco. As the Daya Bay incident revealed, no matter how hard they tried to influence their colleagues, no matter how strong their support from the grassroots population (they had, after all, collected a million signatures!), they would never have a chance to challenge businesspeople's decisions in the Legco.

As discussed in the next chapter, the energy of service professionals, therefore, had shifted from legislative politics to constitution-building politics in the late 1980s. Since Beijing was in charge of the drafting of the Basic Law (the miniconstitution) for Hong Kong, Beijing began to emerge as a key political actor in obstructing these professionals' quest for Hong Kong's democracy.

5 | Constitution Building and
the Democrats' Frustration

The essence of the future "Hong Kong People Ruling Hong Kong" arrangement
is a cross-class united government under the leadership of the capitalists.
Xu Jiatun, director of the Hong Kong branch of the Xinhua
News Agency (quoted in Chiu and Lui forthcoming)

Now the hope is in the Basic Law. This last meeting was so bad, this present
draft is so bad, that effectively we are not going to have democracy at all. . . .
The high degree of autonomy will only be there on paper, it cannot be carried
out in practice.   Martin Lee, member of the Basic Law Drafting
Committee (*Executive*, Mar. 1989:25)

In the late 1980s the battleground of the democracy movement shifted from
the Legislative Council to the Basic Law Committee. Since the Basic Law
defined the political structure and the scope of democracy in the post-
1997 Special Administrative Region (SAR), the future of democratization
in Hong Kong would depend on who controlled its drafting.

It was at this critical juncture that new political actors and political
alliances emerged in the drama of Hong Kong's democracy. The Beijing
government, which had had little to say about the colonial government's
democratic reforms in 1984, took center stage in the drafting of the Basic
Law. Despite its claim to be a communist state, Beijing used the drafting process to form an unholy alliance with Chinese big businesspeople in
Hong Kong. This alliance worked hard to defeat the service professionals'
populist democracy project. By early 1989, the democracy lobby began
to acknowledge defeat as the Hong Kong government bowed to pressure,
withdrew its promise to call direct elections in 1988, and bowed to the business sector as it imposed its restricted democracy model on the draft of the
Basic Law.

The aim of this chapter is to trace the historical formation of the unholy
alliance between the communist Beijing government and Hong Kong's big

businesspeople, to examine the political struggles between the unholy alliance and service professionals over the drafting of the Basic Law, and to explain the defeat and democratic frustration of service professionals by the end of the 1980s.

The Emergence of the Unholy Alliance

The growing political influence of service professionals in the mid-1980s alarmed both big businesspeople and Beijing. The businesspeople feared that democratization would bring stronger unions, higher taxes, more state regulations, and less business freedom. The chairman of the Hong Kong General Chamber of Commerce declared, "Business is against the idea of direct elections. . . . Business is worried of [sic] ending up with a system in which we won't have any influence" (FEER, 16 Apr. 1987:44). Louis Cha, owner of the newspaper Ming Pao, expressed business's concern clearly: "If a system of one person, one vote is followed in [the] election, the government and councils thus elected will most probably be representatives of the interests of residents in housing estates, workers and low-salaried employees, as they form the majority among the population. An elected government is bound to introduce a large number of welfare schemes, and interfere with the operation of banks, big enterprises and factories" (quoted in S. H. Lo 1997:103).

On the other hand, Beijing wanted to slow the democratic process, because it feared that democratization would lead to a truly autonomous government that the Chinese government could not control. A common enemy in the democracy project of service professionals, then, triggered an "unholy alliance" between the communist Beijing government and big capitalists in Hong Kong.

This alliance was strengthened by the rapid economic integration of Hong Kong with mainland China. By the late 1980s, Hong Kong had become the center of the Pearl River Delta economy. Hong Kong's labor-intensive, low-value-added manufacturing industries (garments, footwear, plastics) shifted northward across the border to Guangdong Province. More than two million Guangdong workers were employed in Hong Kong–owned and –managed enterprises in the Delta, much more than the total manufacturing workforce in Hong Kong itself (estimated at about 0.74 million in 1991). This shift relieved the pressure on labor and land, both in short supply in Hong Kong, and allowed Hong Kong to concentrate its energy on economic diversification and structural transformation (So and Kwok 1995).

By the mid-1980s, mainland China emerged as the largest market for Hong Kong's re-export trade, despite the fact that it had always provided the most goods to be reexported in the opposite direction. In addition, mainland China surpassed Great Britain and West Germany as the second most important market for Hong Kong's domestic exports. As their trade relations grew closer, Hong Kong advanced to become the financier, investor, supplier, designer, promoter, exporter, middleman, and technical consultant to the Pearl River Delta and the mainland Chinese economy. Many American and Japanese corporations established branches in Hong Kong to facilitate their expansion into the Chinese market (Chu 1996:172).

Consequently, despite the stock market crash of October 1987, Hong Kong enjoyed one of the greatest boom years in its history. That year Hong Kong's GDP grew 13.6 percent to U.S.$29 billion, bringing the real growth rate in the two most recent years to 25 percent. Total exports, the vehicle of economic growth in Hong Kong, soared 33 percent. Re-exports (mostly to China) showed an immense gain of 46 percent. Economic growth in general was around 7 percent, and corporate profits rose 20 percent. The problem that Hong Kong's economy faced was not unemployment but a labor shortage (*FEER,* Apr. 7, 1988:63). Furthermore, Hong Kong's office and residential property market had rallied strongly since the October stock market crash. Low interest rates, a lack of damage to the real economy, and a continued inflow of foreign companies and foreign investment buoyed demand. Rentals in the central business district and residential areas in Mid-Levels and on the Peak were at historic highs in early 1988 (*FEER,* Mar. 17, 1988:75).

While Chinese businesspeople had gained economic strength by investing in mainland China, the power of the British hongs had been in steady decline since the 1970s. "The real financial muscle in Hong Kong," noted Rafferty (1990:272), "no longer belongs to the British tycoons but to local Chinese who are friends of China." Wong's (1991) study of interlocking directorships and business networks in Hong Kong demonstrated that the central position once occupied by the mighty hongs had been taken over by Hong Kong Chinese businesses. In 1976, all but two of the major business groups were owned and controlled by U.K. expatriate business families, but by 1986 the hongs had receded. The Jardine group shrank in size and economic importance. The Hutchinson and Wheelock Marden groups were taken over by the Li Ka-shing and Pao Yue-kong families, respectively

(Rafferty 1990:275). To some extent, the decline of the hongs reflected the decline of Britain's importance to Hong Kong's economy. Britain's sales accounted for 6.6 percent of Hong Kong's imports in 1972 but fell steadily to 3.4 percent in 1986, whereas China's sales to Hong Kong soared from an already high 17.7 percent in 1972 to almost 30 percent in 1986. Britain accounted for 14.4 percent of Hong Kong's exports in 1972 but only 3.4 percent in 1986, whereas China, not even among the top ten in 1972, soared to second place in 1986, taking 11.7 percent of Hong Kong's exports and 33.4 percent of its re-exports (Tang and Ching 1994:165).

Wong (1994) notes that the decline of British businesspeople in the economic sphere was accompanied by their decline in the political arena. The proportion of expatriates in the Exco and the Legco dropped substantially. By the mid-1980s, those expatriates held only 13 percent of the seats (Davies 1989). Furthermore, many former pro-British businesspeople (such as T. S. Lo) quietly shifted their loyalties from London to Beijing, because they knew that Beijing would be in control in 1997.

To demonstrate their loyalty to Beijing, many big businesspeople invoked their Chinese identity by making huge donations to their native towns. The tycoon Li Ka-shing donated U.S.$30 million to start a new university in Shantou, the shipping billionaire Pao Yue-kong poured money back into Ningbo for charitable purposes, and the "patriotic" entrepreneur Henry Y. T. Fok bankrolled a new Olympic-standard sports compound in a suburb of Canton (Chan 1995:51; Rafferty 1991:322, 327). Indeed, numerous clinics, schools, retirement homes, libraries, recreational facilities, training programs, and scholarship funds were established throughout Guangdong Province through the generosity of Hong Kong kin. By cultivating relationships and gaining the trust of mainland cadres, Hong Kong's big businesspeople resolved the inevitable problems in their mainland business operations speedily, without lengthy and legalistic negotiations (Smart and Smart 1991).

Thus the Hong Kong Chinese businesspeople who had failed to develop networks with British interests and so were treated as nobodies by the colonial government now became VIPs to Beijing. To court these people, Beijing appointed them to represent Hong Kong in the Chinese People's Political Consultative Conference and the National People's Congress (China's highest political organ) and treated them as honored guests at the National Day celebration in Beijing (J. Cheng 1989b:28; B. Leung 1994:211).

After gaining the support of the Hong Kong Chinese businesspeople, Xu Jiatun, director of the local branch of the Xinhua News Agency, articulated a new Chinese united front policy. Xu (1994:120–21) straightforwardly advocated an alliance of all classes in the SAR government — with the capitalist class as the main body. Xu also reinterpreted the Hong Kong People's Model (*gangren zhigang*) as "Hong Kong People Ruling Hong Kong" under the political leadership of the capitalist class (Chu 1996:141; Chiu and Lui forthcoming).

The Formation of Basic Law Committees

Beijing's main task during the transition was to draft the Basic Law, the miniconstitution under which the Hong Kong Special Administrative Region would function. The Basic Law would spell out how the provisions of the Joint Declaration would be implemented. The process of drafting the Basic Law provided an institutional basis for the consolidation of the Beijing-businesspeople alliance, and it became a tool to demonstrate to the people of Hong Kong that Beijing was sincere in granting them a high degree of autonomy (E. Lau 1988; S. H. Lo 1992).

The Basic Law Drafting Committee

With respect to timing, the first meeting of the Basic Law Drafting Committee (BLDC) was held in Beijing on July 1, 1985. This timing was important. As soon as Britain and China exchanged instruments of ratification and the Joint Declaration entered into force in May 1985, the Beijing government acted with unexpected speed to establish a committee to draft the Basic Law. This is because the Basic Law was used as a means to halt Hong Kong's democratic reforms. The Chinese authorities made known their disapproval of any further moves by the Hong Kong government to carry out democratic reforms before the future political structure, as determined by the Basic Law, was settled in 1990. Although this message had not yet been made in public, it was transmitted indirectly through "leftist" newspapers and magazines (Miners 1989:23).

With respect to the composition of the 59-member drafting committee, two-thirds (36) were from mainland China and one-third (23) from Hong Kong. This ratio was to ensure that mainlanders would have the final decision on the blueprint of the Basic Law, yet involve enough Hong Kong members to make their participation meaningful and to give the document credibility. Several of the mainland members had taken part in the drafting of the 1982 Chinese constitution, some had participated in the Sino-British negotiations, many were officials from the Xinhua News Agency's Hong Kong branch and the Hong Kong and Macao Affairs Office, and the rest were prominent personalities included to ensure broad political support.

The majority of the Hong Kong members were big businesspeople and corporate professionals; only a few were service professionals. Of the four Hong Kong deputy directors of the drafting committee, three (Pao Yue-kong, Ann Tse-kai, and David Li) were business tycoons and bankers known for their opposition to democratic measures. Pao, for example, publicly said that Hong Kong should be governed by those elites who contributed to the prosperity of the colony (S. H. Lo 1992). Of the few service professionals, most were known for their conservatism and pro-Beijing positions. Only two, Martin Lee (a lawyer) and Szeto Wah (an educator and veteran movement leader), could be counted on as liberals or democrats. The big businesspeople, then, had no trouble advancing their interests in the drafting committee (E. Lau 1988). The class composition of the drafting committee confirmed Beijing's wish to preserve the existing bureaucratic-businesspeople alliance and the corporatist democracy system in Hong Kong.

With respect to its goals, the Basic Law was to provide the constitutional basis for the establishment of Hong Kong as a Special Administrative Region (SAR) of China from July 1, 1997, through June 30, 2047. It would legally establish the principles, policies, and premises enshrined in the Sino-British Joint Declaration. Thus it shaped the future development of Hong Kong for more than half a century (M. Chan 1991:3).

With respect to assignments of tasks in the Basic Law Drafting Committee, five subcommittees were formed to examine the relationship between the central government and the SAR; the political system; the economy; the rights and duties of the SAR's inhabitants; and education, science, technology, culture, sports, and religion. After the subcommittees wrote up their sections, they presented these to the full committee for review and revision.

Finally, with respect to the schedule, the process would involve "two downs and two ups." April 1988 was set as the date for the first draft to be released in Hong Kong for public consultation; then it would go back to the drafting committee for revision and submitted to China's National People's Congress (NPC) as a draft law. In February 1989, the second draft of the Basic Law would be released in Hong Kong for consultation, and after discussion and revision in the drafting committee it would go up to the NPC again for approval. The NPC would promulgate the final draft in

April 1990. These procedures were intended to solicit enough input from Hong Kong society so that the Chinese government could claim legitimacy for the Basic Law. It was under such considerations that the Basic Law Consultative Committee was set up to collect and consult public opinion on the drafts and to advise the drafters of its findings in late 1985.

The Basic Law Consultative Committee

The Basic Law Drafting Committee (BLDC) members from Hong Kong were given the task of forming the Basic Law Consultative Committee (BLCC). There were three methods for selecting its members: through nomination by BLDC members, through nomination by Hong Kong's influential associations (which set up a subcommittee to look into the Basic Law), and through unexpected self-nomination by individuals and organizations. The BLCC was designed to be much larger than the BLDC, so it could recruit members from eight categories: industry and commerce, finance, law, the professions, the mass media, labor and the grassroots strata, religion, and foreign nationals. All told, 180 people were recruited into the BLCC (Zhang et al. 1991:47–48).

The recruitment process spurred a variety of associations to form subcommittees in an effort to gain seats in the BLCC. Organizations in the same general category but with no working relationship now wanted to work together to nominate candidates to the BLCC. Leaders of the six dominant religions (Protestant, Catholic, Muslim, Buddhist, Taoist, and Confucian), for example, called a joint conference and were assigned a seat each in the BLCC.

Emily Lau (1988:99) reports that a row erupted when the leftist union leader Tam Yiu-chung, a BLDC and Legco member, asked Lau Chin-shek, director of the independent Christian Industrial Committee and a well-known proponent of the democracy movement, to withdraw his nomination for one of the seven seats allotted to a joint labor conference. The leftist unionists reportedly disliked Lau's Christian Industrial Committee for its militancy in fighting for labor rights, and Lau was also said to be unpopular with business leaders. As a protest against the purge of Lau and discrimination against the independent unions, more than twenty labor and civil service unions withdrew their nominations. The incident shows the hostility of business and leftist forces toward independent unions and service professionals (Chan 1992:19; S. H. Lo 1992; Chiu and Levin forthcoming). Consequently, although more service professionals were admitted to the

BLCC than to the BLDC, the BLCC was still dominated by supporters of Beijing and business.

The BLCC's day-to-day affairs were handled by the secretariat, headed by a Chinese official in the local Xinhua News Agency branch, a member of the Chinese Communist Party. A nineteen-member executive committee would set the agenda, set policy guidelines, and oversee the operations of the secretariat.

Another controversy arose over the BLCC's executive committee. Although the charter of the BLCC stipulated that the nineteen members of its executive committee would elect seven officeholders from among themselves, the BLDC and the Xinhua News Agency officials simply hand-picked and installed seven officers without an election. When criticized for breaching the BLCC charter, Xu Jiatun, the director of the local Xinhua, declared that the seven officeholders were selected "by election through consultation." Consultation, it seemed, was equivalent to election. According to Emily Lau (1988:103), the service professional political groups shrank from an open confrontation on the issue because they still wanted to maintain a dialogue with the Chinese government.

The British Dilemma and the 1987 Constitutional Review

Beijing's Open Opposition to Democratization

After initiating the process to set up Basic Law committees, Beijing quickly made known its disapproval of any further moves by the Hong Kong government to carry out any more democratic reforms before the future political structure as determined by the Basic Law to be installed in 1990. On October 20, 1985, Ji Pengfei, director of the Hong Kong and Macao Affairs Office, stressed that there must be no drastic changes in Hong Kong during the transition period (*Ta Kung Po*, Oct. 20, 1985). On November 21 Xu Jiatun held his first public press conference to warn that current moves to institute political changes indicated a deviation from the spirit and principles of the Joint Declaration. Xu, too, insisted that there must be no drastic changes during the transition period, and any developments must "converge" with the Basic Law (Miners 1989:24). Xu's warning, of course, was amplified in leftist newspapers, which demanded that Britain cancel the promised 1987 review and freeze all further changes until the Basic Law was finalized. "The yet to be promulgated Basic Law," declared

Ming Chan (1991:6), "is the PRC's not so invisible hand that has already restricted domestic developments in Hong Kong more than a decade ahead of its effective date of jurisdiction, despite the Joint Declaration's promise that the British alone would be responsible for the administration of Hong Kong until June 30, 1997."

The Beijing government, Ian Scott (1989:285–86) comments, was clearly apprehensive about Britain's intentions in the remaining years of colonial rule, and may have thought that the Green and White Papers of 1984 were British strategies to establish a more autonomous government, not necessarily pro-Chinese, before 1997. Moreover, after observing the lively debates in the post-1985 Legco, the Chinese government seemed to believe that Hong Kong would develop into a much more turbulent place if there were further moves in the direction of representative government.

The British Dilemma

The political developments during 1984 and 1987 put Britain in a dilemma (Miners 1989:25). On the one hand, the London government, to ensure ratification of the Joint Declaration, assured Parliament that democratic reforms in Hong Kong would take place immediately. Richard Luce, the minister responsible for Hong Kong, said in the House of Commons on December 5, 1984, "We all fully accept that we should build up a firmly-based democratic administration in Hong Kong in the years between now and 1997" (*Executive*, Mar. 1989:24). Furthermore, when the Hong Kong government published the Green and White Papers in 1984, it promised that there would be a constitutional review in 1987 and further development of representative government "if that should be the wish of the community."

On the other hand, the British faced strong opposition from Beijing, which condemned British democratic reforms in Hong Kong as a breach of the Joint Declaration that Britain had just signed. Moreover, the British had to contend with Beijing's "convergence" weapon—any democratic reforms during the transition period must converge with the structure spelled out in the Basic Law.

The British, of course, could disagree with the Chinese on the interpretation of the Joint Declaration. But, as Miners (1989:31) explains, to do so "would have risked an open breach with China and possibly even the denunciation of the treaty, which had been hailed as a great achievement of British statesmanship. Even if this did not occur, it was clear that any democratic reforms carried through before 1997 without China's approval and agreement could and would be reversed by China when it recovered sovereignty in 1997, and so would not serve the purpose of protecting Hong Kong's autonomy thereafter." In an attempt to avoid public confrontation with China, the London government dispatched Edward Youde, the governor of Hong Kong, to Beijing to deal with the problem. But Youde suddenly died in Beijing on December 5, 1985, with the dilemma still unresolved.

In the face of such strong opposition, London began to realize that there could be no further development of representative government without at least the tacit approval of Beijing. Timothy Renton, now the British minister with responsibility for Hong Kong, spoke of "the need for convergence with the Basic Law" and declared that he felt "no moral commitment to the introduction of the Westminster system in Hong Kong" (*FEER*, Dec. 12, 1985; Scott 1989:287). Yet if the Hong Kong government bowed to Beijing's demand and put off the review in 1987, it would be perceived as a lame duck and would find it increasingly difficult to govern the colony during the transition to 1997.

Failing to achieve a diplomatic breakthrough, trying to avoid public confrontation with China, and unable to renege on its pledges to Parliament and to Hong Kong's service professionals, London had little choice but to issue contradictory assurances: the 1987 review would take place as scheduled *and* any development of the political system in the transition period would converge with the Basic Law.

The Green Paper

David Wilson arrived in Hong Kong in early April 1987 to take up his post as governor. In Wilson's (1996:180) account, "the Chinese were against a review because to them it pre-empted the Basic Law, the future constitution for Hong Kong. Equally, it was clear enough to me that we were committed to the review and that we should go ahead with it." At his swearing-in ceremony, however, Wilson said, "If there is to be change, it should be prudent and gradual. It must not disrupt the steady progress we have been making, nor the stability which we prize" (quoted in Roberti 1994:191).

In May 1987 a Green Paper titled *The 1987 Review of Developments in Representative Government* (Hong Kong Government 1987) was published. Its aim, scope, and tune were quite different from those of the 1984 document (Miners 1989:26–27; *FEER*, June 11, 1987:36–37).

First, it failed to endorse the aim announced in the 1984 Green Paper "to develop progressively a system of government the authority for which is firmly rooted in Hong Kong, which is able to represent authoritatively the views of the Hong Kong people and which is more directly accountable to the people of Hong Kong."

Second, it was much narrower in scope than the 1984 Green Paper. The 1987 document dealt only with issues concerning the legislature (whether and when there should be direct elections of Legco members; whether the governor should continue to be president of the Legco). It silently dropped such controversial issues as the role, function, and composition of the Exco; the powers of the governor, the Exco, and the Legco; and the relationship between Exco and Legco members.

Third, the 1987 Green Paper avoided recommending any particular proposal for constitutional reform. It simply listed a large number of alternative proposals for changes in the Legco. It revealed a conservative bias in the first option listed in each section: "to make no change." The controversial issue of direct elections was simply listed as subsection (e) of option iv in the section on the Legislative Council. As Scott (1989:293) criticized, the 1987 Green Paper sought to bury the direct election issue "in a welter of minor, non-controversial constitutional options and proposals. In a 47-page document, only one page was devoted to direct elections."

Finally, the 1987 Green Paper promised that the review would be genuine. All the options listed were open, and the public was invited to comment on them. The Hong Kong government said it would speed or slow democratization in accordance with the input it received from the public. To facilitate the widest public response, a survey office was specially set up to receive written communications from the public over a four-month period, and to submit a report based on the communications received. This move started the battle for public opinion in late 1987.

Beijing and the Pro-China Forces on the Offensive

The first major offensive against direct elections was a press release from Beijing that was echoed by the leftist forces in Hong Kong. Li Hou, the deputy director of the Hong Kong and Macao Affairs Office and secretary general of the BLCC, was quoted on June 18, 1987, as claiming that direct elections in 1988 would fail to "converge" with the yet-to-be promulgated Basic Law and was contrary to the spirit of the Sino-British Joint Declaration. Direct elections in 1988 would only sharpen the contradictions between the various classes and segments of Hong Kong society and lead to political, economic, and social instability, which would interfere with a smooth transfer in 1997 (M. Chan 1991:10, 1994:164).

Beijing organized a propaganda blitz. The pro-Beijing newspapers in

Hong Kong kept up a constant barrage of editorials against direct elections in 1988. A deputy secretary of the Basic Law Consultative Committee, writing under the pen name Sun Wai-sze, characterized political reform in 1988 as a "silent revolution" by which the British aimed to transform the colonial legislature into a representative one. Leaders of the leftist Hong Kong Federation of Trade Unions (HKFTU) claimed that the early introduction of direct elections would undermine confidence in Hong Kong and harm workers' economic well-being. A slogan was coined: "Hong Kong workers only want their meal tickets, not a ballot." Hecklers were sent to prodemocracy rallies (S. H. Lo 1989:210; Roberti 1994:197; M. Chan 1992:20, 1994:164–65).

Leftist organizations instructed their members and employees to sign and send in preprinted forms objecting to the introduction of direct elections to the Legco in 1988. The Survey Office received 69,557 identical letters (Miners 1989:28). It was suspected that many of the signatures were solicited by business organizations and China-owned institutions, such as the Bank of China, as evidence of good performance on the job (*FEER*, May 7, 1987).

Responses from the Corporate Sector

The business and professional groups in the BLCC campaigned strongly against direct elections in 1988. They enjoyed the support of such influential Exco members as S. Y. Chung, who asserted that the Hong Kong government should pay more heed to "quality rather than quantity" in the assessment of public opinion (*SCMP*, Apr. 1 and 26, 1987). Members of the group spoke at small meetings and to the media on the recurrent theme that direct elections might conflict with the Basic Law, were disruptive, and would lead to confrontational politics. They produced a video showing "scenes of disruption outside the Legco chamber . . . a fracas in Taiwan's Legislative Assembly and Molotov cocktails being thrown by angry rioters in the streets of Seoul" (Scott 1989:293–94). Businesspeople portrayed Martin Lee as a political opportunist and his involvement with the democracy movement as a ploy to gain popularity and win a post in an elected government after 1997. One businessperson dubbed him "Martyr Lee" (Roberti 1994:198).

The corporate professionals seized the opportunity for political reform, lobbying for the inclusion of their own professions as functional constituencies. Accountants, for instance, indignant at the omission of their profession from the 1985 White Paper, were determined to be included as a functional constituency in the 1988 White Paper. They submitted petitions to the Office of the Members of the Executive and Legislative Council (Omelco), stressing their large membership (3,211 professional members and 10,414 registered students of accounting), their organization and discipline, their international status, their high standards, and their contributions to public service. They lobbied Legco members and high governmental officials. They held seminars on the Green Paper for journalists, formally requested recognition of their society as a functional constituency, and announced that a survey of their members revealed that 99 percent favored it (*HKSA*, July and Nov. 1986, July and Sept. 1987).

The Service Professionals Respond

Upon the release of the Green Paper, the prodemocracy alliance immediately castigated it as "short-sighted, directionless, and confusing," mainly because it contained too many options on what the Democrats viewed as "trivial matters." They accused the Hong Kong government of backtracking from its 1984 position under pressure from Beijing (*FEER*, June 11, 1987:36).

The Democrats scoffed. The Hong Kong Observers, for instance, argued that it was unlikely that investors would be frightened off by a more representative government (*SCMP*, July 20, 1987). The Joint Declaration never prohibited change before 1997, they argued, "it only called for no change for fifty years in the autonomous Hong Kong SAR after 1997. They also pointed out the unfairness in demanding local developments at the present stage must 'converge' with an unknown, yet to be finalized Basic Law" (M. K. Chan 1991:11). They collected the signatures of 223,886 persons, all of whom supplied their identity card numbers. They held mass rallies, put advertisements in the newspapers, and held a candlelight vigil outside the Legco. Scott (1989:292) notes that support for direct elections came especially from younger, better-educated service professionals. Finally, the political groups commissioned a market research firm to conduct four polls. Each asked a simple question: Are you or are you not in favor of direct elections in 1988? Between 46 and 54 percent of respondents were in favor, between 8 and 12 percent were against, and the remainder were unsure or had no opinion (Miners 1989:30).

Beijing-London Compromises and the 1988 White Paper

The Survey Office Report

The Hong Kong government printed almost two million copies of the forty-eight-page Green Paper, including half a million in English, and distributed them to the public through three hundred outlets around the colony. Advertisements were aired on radio and television, in movie theaters, and in most major newspapers. As Roberti (1994:196) remarks, "this would be the biggest consultation exercise in Hong Kong's history, dwarfing that done on the Joint Declaration."

In addition to the written comments received from business, "leftist" organizations, and the political groups of service professionals, the Survey Office also employed A. G. B. McNair Hong Kong Ltd. to conduct two public opinion surveys. The surveys rigidly followed the confusing list of options set out in the 1987 Green Paper, so the crucial question of direct elections in 1988 was carefully buried (Ching 1994). For example, respondents were asked to choose among the following four options on direct elections:

1. To make no change in the numbers and relative proportions of official, appointed, and elected members.

2. To conclude that direct elections to the Legislative Council are not desirable.

3. To conclude that, in principle, some elements of direct elections are desirable, but that they should not be introduced in 1988.

4. If changes are desired in 1988, to make one or more of the following changes: increase slightly the number of official members; reduce the number of appointed members; increase the number of indirectly elected members; have members directly elected. (Hong Kong Government 1987:55)

The format of the questionnaire, then, all but forced respondents to say that they were against direct elections and made it impossible to say unequivocally that they were in favor of them (Scott 1989:295). Not surprisingly, almost half the respondents were unable to understand the question and so gave no reply (Miners 1989:28).

On November 4, 1987, the Survey Office published a report based on all the submissions received and the views expressed by District Board members and Legco and Exco councilors. The Survey Office received more than 130,000 submissions, compared with 364 for the 1984 Green Paper on representative government and 2,494 on the Joint Declaration. On the crucial question of direct elections to the Legco, the Survey Office reported that 94,270 individuals were opposed and 39,345 in favor. It obtained this result by counting all the 69,557 business and leftist preprinted letters as valid votes and disallowing the democratic political groups' 223,886 signatures (Miners 1989:29; Roberti 1994:205).

The service professionals cried foul. Martin Lee charged that the government had deliberately engineered the result it wanted (Scott 1989:296). Miners (1989:29) concurred: "It is difficult to avoid the conclusion that the Hong Kong government deliberately rigged the survey of public opinion in order to obtain results which would meet with China's approval." The Hong Kong Statistical Society complained that the survey questions were loaded; the questionnaire had made it as difficult as possible for respondents to choose direct elections in 1988 (Roberti 1994:207). Emily Lau charged that the Hong Kong government had "insulted the intelligence of the people. This was a very dangerous political game, like playing with fire would burn you to death" (*Capital,* Mar. 1988:86).

Corporate professionals, too, were targets of the democrats' wrath. From the prodemocracy mass media came complaints about the corporate professionals' lukewarm responses to the Green Paper. The Commercial Radio News described the Hong Kong Institute of Engineers' survey as a disappointing gesture to which three-quarters of the membership did not bother to reply; the *South China Morning Post* described the general response as disappointing and mentioned the Hong Kong Institute of Engineers and the Society of Chartered Accountants in particular (*HK Engineer,* Nov. 1987:4).

Beijing-London Compromises and the White Paper

At the height of the furor in late September, London sought a way out of the impasse. In meetings between Governor Wilson and Vice Foreign Minister Zhou Nan and between the foreign secretaries Geoffrey Howe and Wu Xueqian, London tried to persuade Beijing that direct elections to the Legco were widely accepted in principle in Hong Kong and that London should say so in the coming White Paper. But the Chinese government showed no sign of budging (*FEER,* Oct. 8, 1987:24).

In early December, however, after the Survey Office reported that "the community is sharply divided," Beijing backed away from its opposition to direct elections. Since London was no longer pushing for them, the Chinese officials said they would not object to the introduction of direct elections before 1997 if they were provided for in the Basic Law to be promulgated in 1990. In this respect, Beijing gave the green light to London to introduce a small percentage of direct elections to the Legco in the early 1990s (*FEER,* Dec. 24, 1987).

The White Paper, *The Development of Representative Government: The Way Forward* (Hong Kong Government 1988), published in February 1988, was what Beijing had hoped for. It concluded that although there was wide support for direct elections to the Legco, the community was divided over the timing of the move. Therefore the Hong Kong government decided to postpone direct elections to 1991. "The government's objective is to have prudent and gradual political development and . . . the system in place before 1997 should permit a smooth transition in 1997 and a high degree of continuity thereafter" (*FEER,* Feb. 18, 1988:14). In 1991 only ten seats — many fewer than the democrats wanted — would be directly elected, to replace the ten seats indirectly elected by the District Boards. The only significant changes in the Legco in 1988 were an increase of two seats for functional constituencies (accountants and nurses) and a reduction of two appointed members. Finally, the White Paper confirmed that the governor would continue as president of the Legco for the present.

Senior government officials leaked word that direct elections would not be introduced in 1988, so the public would get used to the idea. To minimize the expected adverse reaction, the government released the White Paper on the eve of the Chinese New Year, the biggest holiday of the year, when almost a million people left to visit relatives in China or to vacation abroad (Roberti 1994:213).

As expected, the White Paper was praised by the business and professional lobby within the Basic Law Consultative Committee. They described it as solid and practical, evidence that the government listened to the wishes of the community (*FEER,* Feb. 25, 1988:21–22).

On the other hand, the White Paper aroused strong feelings among service professionals. To them the introduction of a small number of directly elected Legco members in 1991 was too little, too late. Martin Lee in particular was extremely disheartened, because he had thought the directly elected members would replace appointed members, not councilors indirectly elected by the District Boards. After the electoral college was abolished, the District Boards would cease to be a strategic channel for the Democrats to mobilize the grassroots population to exert influence on policy (Joe Leung 1994:261). The White Paper showed that the Hong Kong government had made sure that it could maintain its appointed majority until 1994 and thus could push unpopular programs through the legislature (Roberti 1994:214).

Service professionals thus felt cheated by the British, who promised them there would be a genuine public opinion poll. The prodemocracy mass media accused the London and Hong Kong governments of buckling under pressure and portrayed the British as a humiliated, lame-duck administration at the mercy of Beijing (*FEER,* Feb. 18, 1988:14).

The Democrats vented their anger and frustration in public protests. Students at the University of Hong Kong burned the White Paper in a public demonstration two days after its publication. Students at Shue Yan College staged a thirty-hour hunger strike. Several hundred people marched through the central business district to protest the lack of substantive political reform in the White Paper. In a petition delivered to Governor Wilson, service professionals charged the government with disregarding public opinion and failing to meet its commitment to develop a representative system of government. They burned copies of the White Paper and a large paper lame duck in front of the Legco building (*FEER,* Feb. 25, 1988:21–23; Mar. 31, 1988:30).

In addition to their attack on the Hong Kong government, service professionals intensified their criticisms on corporate professionals. First, they said it was ironic that accountants held a Legco seat as a new functional constituency. Their reason was that two sitting Legco members who were accountants—Thomas Clydesdale and Kim Cham—were linked to two of Hong Kong's biggest financial scandals of recent years, which had cost taxpayers U.S.$769 million (*FEER,* Feb. 25, 1988:22). Then they pointed to the flawed and unprofessional practices of A. G. B. McNair, the public opinion firm that conducted the two polls on behalf of the Survey Office of the Hong Kong government. The democrats found faults with the design, content, and language of the questionnaire, and likened the way McNair carried out its duties to the "ritual way . . . peasants of Europe of two generations ago faithfully attended Mass and gave their responses in a Latin that they did not understand" (*FEER,* Mar. 10, 1988:32).

Electoral Setbacks

With their failed effort to promote direct elections in 1988, the democrats' enthusiasm for local politics cooled off, and their participation in the District Board and Legco elections in 1988 was significantly diminished (Scott 1989:285). In the District Board elections in March, the turnout rate was only 30 percent, a drop of 7 percent from March 1985. On the other hand, the pro-Beijing forces organized their own neighborhood groups for the District Board elections. The Xinhua News Agency took a friendly role in district affairs. Some prominent District Board members were co-opted into their districts' National Day Celebration committees or invited to visit Beijing. As a result, the pro-Beijing forces gained momentum in their community work and modified service professionals' advantages in local elections. The left-wing Federation of Trade Unions fielded twelve candidates and elected eight. About a third of the nearly 100 pro-Beijing candidates were elected (J. Cheng 1989a:140; Joe Leung 1994:261, 1990:53; S. H. Lo 1997:209; S. Tang 1993:279).

In the Legco election in September 1988, the turnout rate was also about 4 percent lower than the previous Legco election in September 1985. What is more, 13 of the 26 indirectly elected seats in the Legco were filled on an *ipso facto* basis (Cheng 1989b), indicating the consolidation of businesspeople's corporatist democracy system in the Legislature. In the electoral college election of the Legco, the democrats also suffered defeat in the New Territories, Kowloon, Kwun Tong, and Wong Tai Sin by an alliance of conservative businesspeople and pro-Beijing forces. Liberal incumbents like medical doctor Conrad Lam and small businessmen Richard Lai were defeated (*Pai Shing*, Oct. 1, 1988:3–5; Lo 1997:180). As Cheng (1989a:142) reports, the prodemocracy lobby in 1985 won two seats (plus three sympathizers) in the Legco through the electoral college. In 1988, however, it could only secure one solid sympathizer in the Legco through the electoral college system. Thus, the alliance of conservative forces proved to be more aggressive and effective in 1988 than it had before.

Knowing that it was futile to ask the Hong Kong government to democratize the state structure, service professionals shifted their attention to Beijing and the issues of constitutional reform and the Basic Law.

The Basic Law can be broadly divided into three parts. The first deals with the structure of government, the second with economic and fiscal policies, and the third with autonomy issues and the relationship between Hong Kong and Beijing.

Basic Law Politics I: Conflict over the Political Structure

Input in the Drafting Process

Of all the sections of the Basic Law, the most controversial was the one on the political structure of the SAR. Debates on elections to the legislature, the election or appointment of a chief executive, and the relationship between the executive and legislative branches were particularly heated.

Among the Hong Kong representatives on the Basic Law Drafting Committee (BLDC), Martin Lee (a lawyer) and Szeto Wah (an educator and veteran movement leader) were the only ones willing to stand up to Chinese officials. Lee and Szeto found that other Hong Kong drafters would either try quiet persuasion or cooperate with Beijing. As two lone advocates of democratization, Lee and Szeto believed that open confrontation was the only way to make other drafters take their views seriously. Their aggressiveness was born out of a desire to promote populist democracy in Hong Kong (Roberti 1994:166).

When the Political Subcommittee of the BLDC met to discuss the design of Hong Kong's political structure, businesspeople urged preservation of the current probusiness policies under a strong governor (chosen by the business community) as more efficient than a system of checks and balances. Under a populist democratic government, legislation would get bogged down in political battles and policies would change every time the ruling party lost an election. Lee and Szeto, of course, wanted a strong legislature. Otherwise the governor could conspire with the business community and introduce policies aimed at keeping the grassroots population poor and big businesspeople rich (Roberti 1994:172).

The structure of the future government also aroused heated debates in the Basic Law Consultative Committee. In early 1986 several members of business and professional groups on the BLCC met regularly at a social club to draw up a blueprint that would retain the best features of the current system. Vincent Lo, founder of the Shui On Construction Company, was chosen as their spokesman. By August 1986, fifty-seven members (later expanded to eighty-nine) of this "Business and Professional Group of the BLCC" put forward a formal plan for the post-1997 government. The so-called Group of 89 proposal basically called for the continuation of the existing system of corporatist democracy: The chief executive would be indirectly elected by an expanded electoral college made up of 600 people representing eleven sectors: 80 from the Legco; 50 from statutory bodies;

50 from the Urban Council, the Regional Council, and the District Boards; 60 from social, charitable, and sports organizations; 60 professionals; 60 from the labor sector; 80 from the industrial sector; 50 from the commercial sector; 50 from the financial sector; 30 from the religious and education sectors; and 30 civil servants. Only 25 percent of the legislature would be directly elected; 25 percent would be elected through the electoral college and 50 percent through functional constituencies. "The advantages of such a system were obvious," Scott (1989:289) wrote: "it would maintain the disproportionate power of business and economic interests in the political system."

The business Group of 89, equating populist democracy with adversarial politics and free-lunch welfare-state economics, warned that any experimentation with it would frighten away foreign investors. Business especially feared grassroots participation and fulminated endlessly about the dangers of direct elections (Pepper 1997:693). It would be naive, they argued, to think that democracy would enable them to resist Beijing: no political system could stop Beijing if it wanted to interfere in Hong Kong's affairs. Only by maintaining the territory's prosperity and its economic value to China, they insisted, could Hong Kong prevent interference from the mainland (Chu 1996:189).

Later the Group of 89 proposal was released as a pamphlet and incorporated as a possible option in the first draft of the Basic Law. During the campaign to promote this business proposal, Scott (1989:282) pointed out, "all members were asked to contribute $5,000 to the organization and to make themselves available for speaking engagements. The group also hired a public relations firm to make a video which, controversially and somewhat illogically, warned of the dangers of direct elections by showing, among other salutary examples, film clips of South Korean students throwing petrol bombs."

This offensive from the business community helped instigate service professionals in forming a coherent organization to fight back the attacks. It was under such circumstances that a loose alliance called the Joint Committee on the Promotion of Democratic Government (JCPDG) was founded in October 1986. The Joint Committee aimed to campaign for universal franchise and direct elections in the Hong Kong government. The Joint Committee did not have the money or influence that businesspeople had, but many Joint Committee members had extensive contacts within the grassroots population. The Joint Committee was built upon the preexisting network of social movement organizations formed in the 1970s (Sing forthcoming). The Joint Committee consisted of approximately 190 members, including political groups (the Christian Industrial Committee, the Hong Kong Federation of Student Unions, the Hong Kong Association for Democracy and People's Livelihood, the Hong Kong Affairs Society, the Meeting Point, the New Hong Kong Society, the Hong Kong Forum), unions (the Professional Teachers' Union, the Federation of Civil Servants Association, and the Christian Industrial Committee), student bodies (student unions of Hong Kong University, Hong Kong Baptist University, and the Chinese University of Hong Kong), social service organizations (Hong Kong Social Workers General Union, Hong Kong Society of Community Organizations), District Board members, and community organizations (Tsing Yi Concern Group, Shatin Concern Group, Shamshuipo People's Livelihood Concern Group) (Sing forthcoming; Scott 1989:290).

The Joint Committee held a rally at the Ko Shan Theatre in Hunghom in early November 1986. More than 1,300 people attended, including representatives of more than ninety community organizations. Szeto Wah's Professional Teachers' Union became the committee's headquarters. Members of the Joint Committee gradually adopted the label "democracy lobby" and eventually called themselves "democrats" (Jane Lee 1994:273). The Joint Committee held a cartoon exhibition in the New World Center in April 1987, a political forum in July, and in September a rally in Victoria Park at which five thousand people showed up (Sing forthcoming).

The Joint Committee urged the introduction of direct elections to the Legislative Council as well as the formulation of a 190-People Proposal (Roberti 1994:179; Yee and Wong 1987). The 190-People Proposal pushed for a system of *populist democracy:* (1) The chief executive of the post-1997 Hong Kong government was to be elected on the basis of one person, one vote. Popular elections were stressed so as to enhance the legitimacy and authority of the Special Administrative Zone government. (2) The legislature of the post-1997 government would be composed of 50 percent directly elected members, 25 percent from functional constituencies, and 25 percent from geographical constituencies. Direct elections were stressed in making the government more accountable to the grassroots population than proposed under business's Group of 89 proposal. (3) The post-1997 government was to be a legislature-centered government, with the executive branch accountable to the legislature.

Beijing made it clear that it backed the corporate proposal. During the campaign against bourgeois liberalization in April 1987, Deng Xiaoping gave a speech to the BLDC. Deng warned the BLDC that democracy would not be good for the colony, and Hong Kong should not copy the Western system of the separation of powers. "The people who rule Hong Kong must love the motherland and love Hong Kong. Can universal suffrage definitely produce such persons?" Deng was magnanimous but stern: "After 1997, if there are certain people in Hong Kong who curse the CPC and China, we will allow them to do so. However, it is not allowed to turn curses into actions and turn Hong Kong into a base for opposing the mainland under the cloak of 'democracy'. In that case, we will have to intervene" (*Wen Wei Po,* Apr. 17, 1987; Roberti 1994:192). The service professionals got the message: Beijing could intervene in Hong Kong's affairs at any time to protect China's fundamental interests.

Since the gap between the Group of 89 proposal and the 190-People Proposal was so vast, the BLDC finally agreed to include both models in a preliminary draft of the Basic Law and open them to public debate.

Still, so far as the relationship between the governor and the legislature was concerned, the preliminary draft was clearly slanted in favor of business. Chapter 4, on the political system, endorsed an executive-led government. The governor could dissolve the legislature if it insisted on enacting legislation that he refused to sign, or if it failed to approve the budget or to pass "important bills" proposed by the government. On the other hand, the legislature would have no power to investigate the actions of the executive authorities or to call them to testify before its committees. It could impeach the governor by a two-thirds majority, but the decision would have to be approved by the National People's Congress in China (Roberti 1994:216).

The first draft of the Basic Law was released in April 1988. A total of 450,000 copies were printed in Chinese and English. The Consultative Committee spent $385,000 to encourage the people of Hong Kong to submit their views. It prepared a video explaining the background of the Basic Law and sent it to high schools throughout the colony. The two local television stations agreed to air the commercials three thousand times without charge (Roberti 1994:217).

Reactions to the First Draft

The business interests stood firm on their proposal. Vincent Lo claimed that the number of directly elective seats had been increased too rapidly. "We have to move more cautiously because we cannot take chances with our political structure. . . . We believe it [indirect election] is a determining factor in preserving our stability and prosperity" (*Executive,* June 1989:35). The Group of 89 was by now highly organized, and its support stretched into the boardrooms of many of Hong Kong's largest businesses. It sent letters to six hundred influential business and professional organizations asking their views on having an enlarged electoral college elect the governor (Roberti 1994:218).

The Joint Committee for the Promotion of Democratic Government was not idle, either. A "Run for Democracy" on June 13, 1988, was followed by exhibitions, slide and video shows, seminars, dramatic performances, and public opinion surveys at the district level, all aimed at expanding awareness of the draft Basic Law, promoting universal suffrage, and preparing for a letter-writing campaign toward the end of the consultation period. Martin Lee and Szeto Wah even published a booklet proposing alternatives to the draft law. The Consultative Committee received 73,000 submissions on the draft during the five-month consultation period. More than 66,000 responses were organized by prodemocracy groups (Roberti 1994:219–20).

The Drafting Committee's five subcommittees would meet in mid-November to amend the charter before presenting it to the eighth plenum in January 1989. Pressure for compromise was mounting. In September 1988 the business groups went on the offensive again, announcing that the Group of 89 now favored choosing the governor by universal suffrage—as long as there was a 50 percent turnout of eligible voters in the Legco elections to show that people had matured enough politically to choose their own leader. Vincent Lo, showing himself to be a shrewd politician, claimed that the democrats had not made a single concession on the political structure, whereas the Group of 89 had made many (Roberti 1994:223).

Observing the stalemate between Lee and Szeto's democracy lobby and Lo's business camp, a new Group of Educationists led by Cheng Kai-nam (a pro-Beijing leftist) tried to break the deadlock by charting a moderate course. Widely known as the "moderates," Cheng and the Educationists dissociated themselves from the democracy lobby and its open criticisms of Beijing's policies, established good connections with leftist unions and other pro-Beijing groups, and stressed the importance of maintaining a dialogue with Beijing (Jane Lee 1994:276). Cheng and the Educationists met with Martin Lee and the democrats on October 27, but the two groups could not reach a compromise. Vincent Lo's Group of 89 also met Martin Lee's Joint Committee's team on November 9, but the meeting broke up after just ten minutes. Then on November 12, Louis Cha, publisher of the influential *Ming Pao* and co-convener of the BLDC's political committee on constitutional structure, met with the Group of 89, the Educationists, and the democrats' Joint Committee, urging compromise. After more than three hours, the groups had come no closer to a consensus (Roberti 1994:226, 229).

On the eve of the political subcommittee meeting in mid-November, Louis Cha began to promote what he called the Mainstream model. Since Cha claimed that he had incorporated all the major features common to the businesspeople's and the democrats' proposals, and since Cha explicitly said he would like to serve as a mediator, people expected a compromise. To their surprise, the Mainstream model turned out to be very conservative. Cha proposed that the chief executive would be selected not by direct elections but by an expanded electoral college similar to the one proposed by the Group of 89. The first chief executive would be elected by a 400-member committee organized by a preparatory committee appointed by Beijing. The election committee would consist of 100 representatives from each of the following sectors: business and finance; professional bodies; labor, grassroots, and religious organizations; and Legco members and local deputies to the National People's Congress (J. Cheng 1989b:19).

In addition, Cha's model proposed that fifteen of the legislature's fifty-six members (27%) be directly elected in the first term (1997–99). During the fourth term (2007–11) the number of directly elected members would be increased to twenty-three (50%). The rest of the legislature would be indirectly elected via functional constituencies. The issue of "one person, one vote" elections would then be decided by referendum in 2011, fourteen years after the SAR was established. If the measure was passed, the chief executive and all Legco members could be directly elected for the fifth term (2012–15). The people of Hong Kong, then, would have to wait fifteen years after 1997 to have the opportunity to decide whether direct elections would be introduced. And if the referendum was not passed, they would wait ten more years for another opportunity (M. Chan 1991, 1992:21).

Although Cha had acknowledged publicly that his Mainstream model need not be adopted part and parcel by the BLDC, and there was still room for improvement, his model had cast the die to rule out service professionals' last hope for direct elections of the chief executive and Legco members. In fact, the business community seized upon Cha's conciliatory statement by enacting an even more conservative amendment to this model. Hence, Cha Chi-Min, a Hong Kong businessman in the drafting committee, proposed an amendment during the January 1989 meeting that required the referendum to be passed by one-third of all eligible voters and approved by two-thirds of the legislators, the chief executive, and the standing committee of the National People's Congress (Ching 1994:176). In the meeting of the drafters, Martin Lee and Szeto Wah refused to take part in the discussion, because they felt the political subgroup was ignoring the views of the democrats. They sat through the meeting in defiant silence (Roberti 1994:232).

To the service professionals, Cha's Mainstream model was totally unacceptable. It was not one of the alternatives listed in the first draft of the Basic Law, and they had been given no chance to consider its merits during the five-month consultation period. It was even more conservative than the business group's proposal. What angered them most was that Cha used his daily newspaper's editorials to endorse his own model and attack the democrats'. The Hong Kong Journalists' Association called on Cha to resign from the BLDC because he had violated a pledge to keep his political and publishing roles separate. Twenty college students publicly burned copies of Cha's *Ming Pao* outside its offices, and seven students went to Canton to protest the Mainstream model (*FEER*, Dec. 22, 1988:24–25, and Feb. 23, 1989:42).

On December 4, 1988, fifty-four democrats staged a twenty-four-hour hunger strike outside the office of the local branch of the Xinhua News Agency, and the next day Martin Lee led a march from Victoria Park to join the fasters. Some six hundred protesters sang songs and held up banners saying "We want democracy in 1997," "Democracy delayed is democracy denied," and "A whole generation is being deprived of its political rights." When they reached Xinhua, the marchers and hunger strikers tore up copies of the Basic Law and threw them into a trash bin. Szeto Wah himself set them alight (*FEER*, Dec. 22, 1988:24; Roberti 1994:233).

Some democrats carried on a month-long hunger strike in fifty-hour relays in front of the Star Ferry station in downtown Hong Kong. An activist expressed their intense frustration in January 1989: "The Hong Kong people genuinely became fed up with China's overall strategy toward reintegrating Hong Kong. While they were told that their views mattered, in the same breath they were made to realize that China had no interest in what they had to say" (Young 1989:19).

The democrats made their last effort to change the first draft of the Basic Law at the eighth BLDC plenary session in Guangzhou (Canton) in mid-January 1989. Each clause was submitted to a vote. Martin Lee and Szeto Wah offered more than thirty amendments but none received the minimum five votes required for submission to the committee. To show their disgust with the drafting process, Lee and Szeto Wah either voted against all clauses or abstained from voting on all clauses. On the other hand, all the other Hong Kong members of the drafting committee accepted Cha's Mainstream model (*FEER*, Jan. 26, 1989:10).

The Second Draft of the Basic Law

To the disappointment of the democrats, the second draft of the Basic Law endorsed a strong executive and a weak legislature. Strong executive because the chief executive of the SAR could exempt officials from testifying or dissolve the legislature. Weak legislature because the legislature had no role in choosing or dismissing officials. Although the legislature presumably had the power to impeach the chief executive, the final decision rested with Beijing. The SAR budget would be presented to the legislature on a take-it-or-leave-it basis. Revenue and expenditure bills and government policy could not be introduced without the chief executive's approval.

The business community was very pleased with the second draft of the Basic Law. Vincent Lo remarked, "We've come a long way since the first draft, . . . over 100 articles have been amended" (*Executive*, June 1989:34).

Basic Law Politics II: Conflict over Fiscal Policies

Input in the Drafting Process

The chapter on the economy provided another opportunity for the business community to safeguard its interests. The Economy Special Subject Section (ESSS) of the drafting committee, like other subject sections, was strongly business-oriented. All seven of its Hong Kong members were from the corporate sector: Li Ka-shing, Fok Ying-tong, Cha Chi-min, Louis Cha, Wong Po-yan, Sanford Yung, and Lau Wong-fat. In addition, many corporate associations lobbied energetically over the two years of the drafting process to ensure that the articles in the economy section were what they wanted. Consequently, although the articles had been amended and the wording changed several times, the basic assumptions and underlying philosophy of all the versions remained the same—probusiness and anti-welfare.

The policy articles of the chapter on the economy spelled out what the future SAR government must and must not do. It must not permit the growth of public expenditures to exceed the growth of the gross domestic product and it must not implement any exchange control. On the other hand, it must balance the budget, keep taxes low, promote industrial investment, and practice free and open monetary, financial, industrial, commercial, and trading policies. The aim was to control the size of the public sector, to make it impossible for the elected councilors to formulate pro-social welfare policies, to exclude consideration of labor and income redistribution issues, to promote business confidence and stimulate investment, and to protect the interests of big business (Tang 1989).

Reactions to the First Draft

Although the chapter on the economy was highly anti-welfare, it did not receive much criticism from service professionals and employees because their attention was diverted to the chapter on the political structure. And despite its strong business orientation, it received unexpected criticism from the pro-British corporate sector.

Lydia Dunn (the senior member in the Legco), Governor Wilson, and William Purves (chairman of the board of directors of the Hong Kong Bank) considered these provisions too restrictive: future policymakers might need to run up a deficit in the short term to stimulate the economy. They suggested that the policy articles be amended and placed in an appendix to the Basic Law as guiding principles that had no legally binding force (*Executive*, June 1989:35; Tang 1991). However, when the Economic Special Subject Section met in November 1988 to review the suggestions received during the consultation period, it adopted none of the suggestions from the pro-British business sector. Instead, it resolved to retain the policy articles in the main text of the Basic Law. This showed that the pro-British business community failed to articulate its recommendation to Hong Kong Chinese businesspeople with strong ties with Beijing.

In addition, the Economic Subgroup meeting was scheduled right after the Political Subgroup meeting. Since the Hong Kong Chinese business community strongly pushed for the conservative Mainstream model in the political section meeting, they naturally were inclined to endorse the conservative low-tax, antiwelfare policies at the economic section meeting.

The last chance to alter the fiscal policy articles before the finalization of the Second Draft was at the Eighth Plenary Meeting of the entire Basic Law Drafting Committee in January 1989. Before this plenary meeting, corporate professionals made another attempt to amend the chapter on the economy. Peter Wong, a Legco councilor representing the Accounting functional constituency, argued that policy articles on a balanced budget and low taxation would be open to abuse, i.e., those who wanted to avoid or delay tax payments could easily challenge tax assessments in court. Wong warned that Basic Law drafters risked their credibility if they continued to ignore advice from professional experts (*SCMP,* Dec. 21, 1988). Similarly, Liu Yiu-chu, a solicitor who sat on other BLCC sections, argued that the articles in the chapter on the economy had confused long-term and short-term policies. Budget expenditures varied year by year, and this short-term, low-level policy should be determined by the future SAR government and not be included in the Basic Law. Liu also criticized certain influential businessmen for heightening the interest conflicts among various sectors to the constitutional level (Tang 1991). On a similar ground, Martin Lee, a barrister who sat in on other BLCC sections, proposed adding an article allowing the future SAR government to formulate economic policy on its own. Although the proposals from Liu and Lee got substantial support in the BLDC (received 23 and 28 yes votes out of 55), they were both defeated because they needed a two-thirds majority (i.e., 37 votes) to pass an amendment in the BLDC (Tang 1991).

The Second Draft

As a result, the policy articles in the chapter on the economy were downgraded from laws to guidelines, but they were still included in the main body of the document. Unmoved by the suggestions of the pro-British business community and unwilling to follow the service professionals' advice, the Hong Kong Chinese big businesspeople pushed their low-tax, balanced-budget, and anti-welfare points into the second draft of the Basic Law, and later into its final draft (J. Cheng 1989b:31–32).

Basic Law Politics III: Conflict over Autonomy

Input into the Drafting Process

One area of concern was human rights. Lawyers pointed out that the draft provisions failed to fulfill the Joint Declaration's promise that the rights and freedoms of SAR residents would be ensured by law and that the provisions of the two international covenants on human rights would remain in force. The draft had nothing to say about the right to life, to freedom from torture or cruelty, or to freedom from forced or compulsory labor, and the rights that were written into the law were limited. While the draft provided for freedom of speech and of the press, for instance, it made no provision for freedom to seek and receive information and ideas of all kinds (*FEER*, Apr. 7, 1988:58).

Another difficulty was that the National People's Congress was given the power to interpret and amend the Basic Law. If China's legislature could interpret Hong Kong's Basic Law, the charter would offer no protection or guarantees. Whenever Beijing did not like a court ruling, it could simply re-interpret the charter. Martin Lee warned that the effects of such an arrange-ment would seriously undermine the concept of an independent judiciary and Hong Kong's right of final adjudication, because the final appeals court was bound to adopt Beijing's interpretation of the Basic Law. The Hong Kong courts, Lee argued, should have the power to interpret the Basic Law as cases were brought before them. Nevertheless, the Drafting Committee confusingly decided that the Standing Committee of the NPC would have the right to interpret the Basic Law and that the Hong Kong courts would be able to interpret some provisions when they adjudicated cases.

Reactions to the First Draft

In July 1988, three Hong Kong delegations went to London to lobby Par-liament in regard to the draft law. Representatives of the Hong Kong Law Society, the Bar Association, and a group of professionals met with mem-bers of the Foreign Affairs Committee of the House of Commons and urged them to conduct an inquiry on Hong Kong. The issues of concern were the degree of autonomy to be enjoyed by the SAR government, the demo-cratic process, and the SAR government's accountability to the Hong Kong people. Although the Beijing government made no comment on the forth-coming inquiry of the Foreign Affairs Committee, Beijing certainly did not want the British Parliament to interfere in the Basic Law, something that it regarded as China's business (*FEER*, Feb. 16, 1998:17).

In September 1988, nine professional associations (including those of lawyers, doctors, and engineers), together with some members of the de-mocracy lobby and the business Group of 89, issued a joint statement. Since this joint statement was formulated by Hong Kong people of all walks of life, it represented a societal reaction to the First Draft of the Basic Law. Arguing that the Chinese government should delegate more authority to the Hong Kong SAR, this joint statement proposed the following changes in the first draft of the Basic Law:

• The Basic Law should spell out all the national Chinese laws that would apply to Hong Kong.

• Since the first draft undermined the independence of the judiciary by giving the National People's Congress the authority to interpret and amend the Basic Law, the joint statement proposed that powers of the NPC should be more clearly defined, and the SAR courts should be required to ask for clarification from the Standing Committee of the NPC only on issues related to acts of the state and the SAR's relationship with Beijing.

• Before interpreting or amending the Basic Law, the NPC should consult a committee to be made up of Hong Kongers and mainlanders appointed by the NPC's standing committee.

• The clause prohibiting the SAR from passing laws pertaining to "the expression of national unity or territorial integrity" should be dropped (Zhang et al. 1991:213–15).

The Second Draft

To the surprise of the Hong Kong public, the Beijing government was willing to make significant concessions on the relationship between the SAR and Beijing. The second draft basically incorporated all the suggestions in the joint statement, with the result that the SAR had much more autonomy and authority than the first draft accorded it, and the legislature and judiciary had more independence.

The NPC Standing Committee would not, after all, have the power to nullify an SAR law. Beijing could only send proposed laws back to Hong Kong's legislature for amendment. The subcommittee also dropped the clause empowering China's state council to instruct the Hong Kong government to enact laws related to defense and foreign affairs, and laws pertaining to the expression of national unity or territorial integrity. Beijing also listed in Annex III the six Chinese laws that would apply to Hong Kong: laws pertaining to the national capital, anthem, and flag; National Day; national emblems; territorial waters; nationality law; and diplomatic immunity. Though Beijing would not relinquish the Standing Committee's power to interpret the Basic Law, it conceded that Hong Kong's courts could interpret sections of the Basic Law in cases within their own jurisdiction. In cases involving the central government, however, Hong Kong's final appeals court would have to ask the Standing Committee to interpret the relevant sections of the Basic Law, and Hong Kong's courts would be bound by its rulings (*FEER*, Jan. 26, 1989:26). Instead of being prohibited from trying cases involving "defense, foreign affairs, and executive acts," the courts would be allowed to hear all cases except those involving "acts of state" (government policies on national rights). Finally, the subcommittee added a clause stipulating that the Hong Kong government would be responsible for maintaining public order in the SAR (Roberti 1994:23031).

The Ascent of Hong Kong Chinese Big Businesses

What explains the divergent results in the revision process of the Basic Law? Why did certain paragraphs in the sections on the political structure, fiscal policies, and Hong Kong's autonomy get revised while other paragraphs failed to do so?

The critical factor seems to be the orientation of Hong Kong Chinese big businesspeople. First, when these big businesspeople pushed for fiscal conservatism and a balanced budget, they were able to keep this policy in the second draft of the Basic Law, despite strong opposition from the pro-British business sector, the colonial government, and service professionals. Their failure to exert any influence in the Basic Law drafting process reveals the decline of power of pro-British elites and an eclipse of the expatriates' alliance between colonial officials and Hong Kong businesspeople. On the one hand, seizing upon investment opportunities in mainland China, Hong Kong Chinese big businesspeople gained dominance of the economy at the expense of British hongs. On the other hand, since the Hong Kong government would be a lame duck, many Hong Kong Chinese businesspeople defected from pro-British to pro-Beijing. In the late 1980s, the pro-British business community even failed to send any representative to the Basic Law Drafting Committee.

Second, when Hong Kong big businesspeople supported service professionals' proposal on Hong Kong autonomy, the section on the relationship between the SAR and the central government were revised accordingly. Hong Kong big businesspeople, too, wanted a high degree of autonomy and more judicial independence for the post-1997 SAR government so they could have more bargaining chips with the Beijing government.

Third, when Hong Kong big businesspeople opposed service professionals' populist democracy model, this model was deleted from the second draft of the Basic Law. There were hints that Beijing officials preferred that Hong Kong societal forces compromise on the various political proposals, so the resultant Basic Law could have a stronger base of legitimacy. However, big businesspeople were on the offensive, and imposed an even more conservative political model on the drafting committee than the Beijing officials expected (Zhang et al. 1991:148–64). Analysts (Roberti 1994:234) note that there were differences between Xu Jiatun (of Hong Kong's Xinhua News Agency) and Lu Ping (of Beijing's Hong Kong and Macao Affairs Office). Since Xu's base was in Hong Kong, Xu was heavily influenced by Hong Kong's big businesspeople, and he was deeply opposed to too much democracy before and after 1997. On the other hand, Lu from Beijing was more practical and emphasized at the Drafting Committee meetings that the interests of *all* groups had to be looked at.

The pivotal role of Hong Kong big businesspeople in the drafting of the Basic Law shows that they—through the unholy alliance with Beijing—had regained their hegemonic domination over Hong Kong politics, just as they were in control of the colonial government before the emergence of the 1997 issue in the late 1970s.

Conclusion: Constitutional Defeat and Democratic Frustration

Constitutional Defeat

In the early 1980s the service professionals had high hopes for their democracy project. Such terms as *elections* and *accountability* were written into the Joint Declaration. London framed it as a democratic declaration in order to sell it to Hong Kong society and to Parliament. In the mid-1980s, although London proposed only a modest reform to replace the corporatist bureaucracy with a corporatist democracy, the service professionals were still hopeful because the Hong Kong government promised to institute direct elections of the Legco in 1988, and they won landslide victories at the local level in 1985.

Rising expectations in the early and mid-1980s, however, turned to frustration in the late 1980s. Beijing used the "convergence" weapon to slow London's democratic reforms. Then the Hong Kong government renounced its commitment to direct elections in 1988. Despite the 220,000 signatures the service professionals had collected, the Hong Kong government manipulated survey results and declared that Hong Kong society favored postponement of direct elections.

The service professionals did not perform so well in the District Board and Legco elections in 1988. Active intervention by pro-Beijing forces took away some of their grassroots support. Besides, they were too absorbed by constitutional battles to pay sufficient attention to local elections.

When the service professionals' populist democracy model received no support and the drafting committee adopted a conservative model quite similar to the existing system of corporatist democracy, the service professionals thought they had already lost the fight to bring democracy to Hong Kong.

What explains the defeat of the democracy project? First, the antidemocracy forces coalesced in a triple alliance: Beijing-businesspeople-London. Beijing and big businesspeople discovered they had common economic interests and a common opposition. The thriving economic integration between Hong Kong and Guangdong, the increasing investment opportunities in mainland China, the growing threat of the service professionals' welfare program, and the prospect of political instability in Hong Kong brought these strange bedfellows together. Their alliance was institutionalized when big businesspeople were appointed to key posts on the committees charged with drafting Hong Kong's constitution. When London finally agreed to postpone direct elections and crafted a strategic alliance with Beijing and the big businesspeople, the conservative trio was too formidable to tackle.

Second, Basic Law politics absorbed so much of the service professionals' effort that they neglected to consolidate support at the grassroots level (Joe Leung 1994:261). The Basic Law was drafted in mainland China, not in Hong Kong. Despite its vital importance, the draft law was a very complicated, dry, and boring document. It involved technical legal issues (such as how to interpret *autonomy*) of which the grassroots population had little understanding. The drafting process stretched from 1985 to 1989, and service professionals found it difficult to keep the attention of the grassroots population over such a long period when the debates were over such boring matters. Seminars on the Basic Law attracted as few as ten people. Even some journalists referred to it as the "Basic Bore." Press reports were sketchy and confusing because the drafters rarely resolved any important issues. In mid-November 1988, *Ming Pao* published the results of a survey concerning the community's response to the draft Basic Law: 42 percent of the respondents indicated no concern and 10 percent were even unaware that anything was being drafted; 21 percent had read part of the draft but only 1 percent had gone through the whole thing (J. Cheng 1989b; Roberti 1994:181, 218).

Third, the service professionals themselves were lacking in unity. The Joint Committee was a hastily organized response to the businesspeople's offensive, and it failed to grow into a strong political party. Between 1988 and 1989 the three most prominent democratic groups — the Meeting Point, the Hong Kong Affairs Society, and the Hong Kong Association for Democracy and People's Livelihood (ADPL) negotiated to form a political party, but their talks collapsed under the weight of political and ideological differences. The Meeting Point, for example, disagreed with the Hong Kong Affairs Society's tactics in dealing with Beijing, and the ADPL claimed to be more specifically representing the interests of the lower-income people. As a member of the democratic camp has remarked, "the incentive was not strong enough to unite all democrats together and form a political party at that time" (Yu 1997:96). In the end, the Meeting Point decided not to join a united political party, and the ADPL's leader said he had not received an invitation from Martin Lee to do so (E. Lau 1991:163; *FEER,* Dec. 14, 1989:38; J. Lee 1994:278).

Fourth, the service professionals had not developed a farsighted program to challenge the antidemocracy forces (J. Cheng 1989b). The Joint Committee stumbled when it asked that only 50 percent of the legislature's members be directly elected. Had it asked for 100 percent in the first place, it would certainly have had more political space to bargain, negotiate, and compromise. But as Joseph Cheng (1989b:17) said, "no one within the movement's leadership dared mention a revision of its position in late 1986, and the movement was neither prepared to negotiate for the best deal possible nor well prepared for confrontation." As the democracy movement refused to revise its position in any way, its opponents called it inflexible and insincere in seeking a compromise; after all, other political groups had made concessions.

In short, a restricted, corporatist democracy was the product of the strong alliance of Beijing, businesspeople, and London, the populist alliance's neglect of the grassroots population, a divided prodemocracy lobby, and poor tactics.

Democratic Malaise

The democratic forces were so frustrated that signs of an emigration crisis were visible by early 1988. Governor Wilson admitted that the number of emigrants had sharply increased, from an average of 20,000 in the early 1980s to 45,000 in 1988. The typical émigré was under thirty-five, had five to ten years of work experience, had a university degree, earned around U.S.$32,000 to $51,000 a year, and worked in a middle-class profession (*FEER,* Apr. 7, 1988:66). As Joseph Cheng (1989b:7) explained, the emigrants were largely professionals who had the means to leave, "and their political sensitivity and strong feeling for freedom and democracy exacerbate[d] their pessimism regarding the territory's future." He lamented that pessimism led some activists to drop out of the democracy movement. A former chairman of the Meeting Point and the leader of the New Hong Kong Society, for example, quit the movement for fear of offending Beijing. Many activists were absorbed in plans for emigration, and were planning to develop their critics' role overseas.

Hong Kong society was increasingly divided between those who wanted to emigrate and those who planned to stay. Those who had the means to emigrate were doing their best to accumulate wealth, liquid assets, personal skills, and professional qualifications before they left. Those who could not emigrate or who had hopes of advancing their fortunes in Hong Kong kept a low political profile and said nothing in an effort to avoid any post-1997 reprisals. Those who decided to stay had benefited from the emigration crisis. They could get higher salaries, quicker promotions, and more fringe benefits in return for their commitment to stay in Hong Kong (*FEER,* Apr. 7, 1988:71). In this respect, emigration had reinforced the triumph of market forces and dampened the democracy movement.

In sum, in the late 1980s the conservative "triple alliance" of Beijing–big businesspeople–London successfully imposed their version of a restricted, corporatist democracy over Hong Kong society. This was a period of democratic frustration for service professionals, tempting them to seek the exit option through emigration. Nevertheless, just as service professionals were ready to give up hope for their democracy project, the Tiananmen incident occurred in mid-1989, tearing the conservative Beijing–big business–London alliance apart and granting the service professionals' democracy project another chance at revitalization.

Part III From Contested Democracy
to Democratic Compromise

6 The Tiananmen Incident and the Rebirth of the Democracy Project

Deep grief, bitter hatred.

> A stark, four-character editorial in *Wen Wei Po*, a pro-
> Beijing newspaper, on China's democracy movement in 1989

[The Tiananmen incident was] so emotional that it ignited the nationalistic
feeling of many Hong Kong Chinese, so appealing that it rekindled the
democratic aspiration of the local populace, and so tragic that it made most
of the Hong Kong people moan, weep, and thunder.

> Leung Sai-wing (1993:201)

The Rebirth of the Democracy Project

The late 1980s had been a period of democratic frustration for service
professionals. Their populist democracy model was defeated in the first and
second drafts of the Basic Law. Many such professionals planned an exit
through emigration, as the democracy project had gone downhill.

Then came the Tiananmen incident in 1989. It is hard to find another
historical event that exerted such a profound impact on Hong Kong's civil
society. In May and June 1989, millions of Hong Kong Chinese took to the
streets to voice their support of the democracy movement in Tiananmen
Square. By mid-1989, the antidemocracy forces as well were so carried away
by this powerful historical event that even big business and the London
government pushed for faster democratization in Hong Kong. It looked as
though third-wave democracy had finally spread from the Philippines, Taiwan, and South Korea to mainland China and Hong Kong.

This chapter starts with a brief discussion on the origins and nature
of the Tiananmen incident in mainland China. Then it examines how the
Tiananmen incident suddenly led to a rebirth of the democracy project in
Hong Kong in the early 1990s. In particular, this chapter shows how the
Tiananmen incident empowered prodemocracy forces and weakened antidemocracy forces, leading to the party formation of service professionals
and their landslide victory in the Legislative Council elections in 1991.

The Tiananmen Incident in 1989

Political Changes in China

In 1987, reformers in the Chinese Communist Party (CCP) went on the offensive to eliminate the fetters on production the state had inherited from the socialist system. To get rid of outmoded economic institutions, reformers called for a strategy of coastal development, national unification, enterprise reforms, and price reforms. In order to eliminate opposition to the above proposals, they called for special political reforms. Party Secretary Zhao Ziyang advocated "separation of powers both among central government organs and between central and local governments, an end to lifetime tenure in office for political leaders, constitutional definition of the scope of individual autonomy, the vesting of true political supremacy in the National People's Congress, and the abolition of limits on political discussion" (Nathan 1990:9). These measures challenged the authority of Party officials and state bureaucrats, whose privileges depended on collaboration between the planned and market economies.

The reformers' assault on state socialism created all kinds of problems. The decentralization of foreign trade brought an influx of foreign imports and speculation in foreign currency; the enterprise reforms encountered so much resistance that they were quickly discarded; and the price reforms led to rampant inflation and panic buying. The problems that sprang from wholesale economic reform triggered unrest that almost blew the CCP apart in 1989. The radical reforms eroded the CCP's support in the cities. City people in general were dissatisfied over the high inflation rate and the rapidly rising cost of living in 1988 and 1989; state workers complained about the erosion of their entitlements (such as free health care and housing), and new workers had none at all; and the influx of people from the countryside in search of work led to serious unemployment and crime.

The Democracy Movement

After their exposure to the Western lifestyle, members of the new middle class could no longer be satisfied with the nondemocratic policies of the CCP. Wanting the privileges enjoyed by their Western counterparts, they demanded freedom, autonomy, status, high salaries, and job mobility. Thinking themselves better equipped to carry out reform than aging Party members, they pushed for the amnesty of political prisoners, democratic elections, a multiparty system, and protection of human rights.

These structural conflicts in the economy and society, coupled with a succession crisis and conflict between Party Secretary Zhao Ziyang and Premier Li Peng, converged in the Tiananmen incident in 1989. The incident was precipitated by the death in April of Hu Yaobang, the former Party secretary who endorsed wholesale economic reform. Later that month Western-oriented students seized the opportunity of Mikhail Gorbachev's visit to demand freedom, democracy, and human rights. The students' hunger strike quickly turned into a large-scale urban protest to challenge the legitimacy of the CCP.

Premier Li Peng imposed martial law in Beijing on May 20, 1989, but the crowds defiantly barred the army's entry into Tiananmen Square for almost two weeks. When the CCP was unable to resolve the crisis by peaceful dialogue, it resorted to force. In the account of Chan and Lee (1991:117), "the troops and tanks forced their way into Tiananmen Square during the late hours of June 3 and the early hours of June 4, killing a huge but undisclosed number of people."

The Chinese democracy movement had failed because the military was too strong for the urban masses to resist and because the various student organizations were not unified, lacked guidance from establishment professionals, and had not formed an alliance with the working class and peasants. It is reported that workers and students had serious differences on the goals and strategies of the democracy movement (So 1992; So and Hua 1992).

By mass arrests, prosecutions, and a slashing of university enrollments the CCP drove the democracy movement underground and its leaders into exile. There was a deep sense of fatalism and alienation among Chinese students and professionals in the aftermath of Tiananmen.

What was the impact of the Tiananmen incident on Hong Kong's democracy?

Revitalizing Democratization

Thanks to the power of the mass media, the democracy movement in China became an obsession in Hong Kong between April and June 1989. As Chan and Lee (1991:131) point out, "television instantaneously brought scenes of joyous marches, hunger strikes, and tanks into their living rooms, as a powerful reminder that whatever China did in Beijing was inescapably pertinent to Hong Kong's well-being."

During the high tide of the Chinese democracy movement in May, the people of Hong Kong responded with political mobilization and patriotism. They took to the streets to voice their support for the Beijing students. Forty thousand people braved the winds and rain of Typhoon Brenda on May 20; an estimated one million (about one-sixth of the colony's population) showed up on May 21, and there were numerous mass rallies later. Many protesters wore yellow headbands that said "Support the Beijing Students" and T-shirts scrawled with "Long Live the Democracy Movement." On May 27 more than 150 entertainers, among them most of Hong Kong's big pop stars, held a twelve-hour concert to raise money for the students in Beijing. The U.S.$1.5 million they collected brought the total raised in Hong Kong to more than U.S.$3 million. By participating in collective action, the people of Hong Kong demonstrated their understanding that their fate was linked to that of the protesters in mainland China. Patriotic songs were the order of the day as the compatriots joined their hopes for Hong Kong's future to the democratic hopes of China's students (*FEER*, June 1, 1989:17, and July 20, 1989:20; Roberti 1994:251, 254).

On June 4, when the news reached Hong Kong that troops had moved into Tiananmen Square, a crowd estimated to number more than 200,000 gathered at the Happy Valley Race Course to mourn for the students. They sat for five hours and listened to emotional speeches by activists in the democracy movement, community leaders, and movie stars. Martin Lee wore a black headband. Others dressed in the traditional black and white of mourning. On June 5 there was a run on Chinese banks in Hong Kong as depositors closed their accounts. On the evening of June 6, cars and buses covered with prodemocracy stickers converged on the commercial area of Mong Kok. Protesters honked their horns and shouted anti-Beijing slogans. By midnight, traffic was paralyzed. When youths trashed some shops, the police moved in with batons and tear gas. The violence went on for more than four hours (Roberti 1994:256–58; Wilson 1990:222).

In sum, Hong Kong society was drastically transformed by the Tiananmen incident in mid-1989. The event shook the political landscape nearly upside down (Tang 1993:250). As S. W. Leung (1993:201) explains, "it was so dramatic that it drew around the clock coverage by Hong Kong mass media, so emotional that it ignited the nationalistic feeling of many Hong Kong Chinese, so appealing that it rekindled the democratic aspiration of the local populace, and so tragic that it made most of the Hong Kong people moan, weep, and thunder."

The historical event of the Tiananmen incident, then, profoundly impacted Hong Kong's democratization. First, it greatly empowered service professionals; their democracy project was given a chance for rebirth after its near-fatal defeat in the Basic Law struggles. Since these professionals took the lead in organizing mass protests, they emerged as the popular leaders against authoritarianism. They were no longer seen in the mass media as fame-hungry, status-seeking, and self-interested politicians. In fact, Martin Lee, Szeto Wah, Yeung Sum, and Lau Chin-shek emerged as "highly visible, widely accepted, charismatic" leaders promoting the cause of democratization in Hong Kong (Tang 1993:293).

Second, the Tiananmen incident led to an explosion in Hong Kong's civil society. Many nascent civic organizations were formed at the height of the incident. Lau Kin-chee and Wong Yiu-chung formed the Tiananmen Democracy University (TDU) to spread democratic consciousness and practices to every corner of society. Tsang Kin-shing, who led the Democracy Platform, later was elected to the Legco (S. H. Lo 1997:168–71). The students' movement was resurrected. In April 1989 the Hong Kong Federation of Student Unions (HKFSU) sent four delegates to Beijing to observe the action in Tiananmen Square. Students raised funds, led demonstrations, and provided Beijing students with current Hong Kong newspaper reports concerning the democracy movements in Hong Kong and China. In May the HKFS, together with other political groups (such as the Hong Kong Professional Teachers' Union [HKPTU], the Christian Industrial Committee [CIC], and the Hong Kong Social Workers General Union [HKSWGU]) called for the democracy movements in Hong Kong and China to support each other. In mid-May, Hong Kong students organized marches, a hunger strike, and mass rallies in Victoria Park (Wong forthcoming).

In late May the student movement was transformed into a popular movement and grew speedily under the leadership of a new organization called the "Hong Kong Alliance in Support of the Patriotic Democratic Movement in China," under the leadership of Szeto Wah as president and Martin Lee as vice president. In 1989 the Hong Kong Alliance comprised 216 student unions, political groups, labor unions, cultural organizations, and community and grassroots organizations. Most leaders of the Hong Kong Alliance had been leaders of the Joint Committee for Democracy (which engaged in the political battles of the 1988 direct elections and the drafting of the Basic Law in the late 1980s). The Alliance received millions of dollars in donations from people of all walks of life in May and June 1989. It was the first time the democratic forces had had so much money at their disposal. In May they set up a Hong Kong Resources Center in Tiananmen Square to coordinate the distribution of the resources they had collected to support the Beijing democracy movement. Hong Kong Chinese were highly visible in the square. After the crackdown in June, the Hong Kong Alliance used the donations to help mainland democrats flee China. After the Tiananmen incident, the Alliance gave birth to a quasi-political party called United Democrats, whose members publicly declared that they were morally committed to promote democratization because they did not trust the Beijing government (M. Chan 1991:18; Wong forthcoming).

Third, the Tiananmen incident divided the antidemocracy forces. Moved by the large-scale demonstrations they witnessed and worried about the prospect of Beijing's intrusion into Hong Kong's politics, many big businesspeople became prepared to accept a faster pace of democratization. Councilors in the Legco and the Exco achieved a democratic consensus for the direct election of half of the Legco members in 1995 and of the entire legislature in 2003 (*FEER*, June 1, 1989:18). London and the British expatriate officials in Hong Kong, too, seemed to have changed their minds about democratization. On June 30, London's Foreign Affairs Committee called for more rapid speed toward direct election of the Legco than the draft Basic Law provided.

Fourth, the Tiananmen affair cost Beijing its credibility. Mainland Chinese drafters canceled a visit to Hong Kong, and Louis Cha (who formulated the conservative Mainstream model adopted in the draft Basic Law) resigned in protest against Beijing's suppression of the student demonstrators. The leftist presses, unions, and schools in Hong Kong were paralyzed; even the Party press publicly pledged support for the students in Tiananmen Square (Chan and Lau 1990). For example, Hong Kong's Communist presses broke Party ranks to endorse the student movement in China. *Wen Wei Po*, a procommunist newspaper funded by Beijing, published a stark, four-character editorial, "Deep grief, bitter hatred," on May 21, 1989, the day after martial law was declared in Beijing. Many noncommunist presses began to adopt an anticommunist framework. Members of pro-Beijing unions, among them Cheng Yiu-tang (chair of the HKFTU and member of the Basic Law Consultation Committee and the National People's Congress) and vice chair Tam Yiu-chung (member of the Basic Law Drafting Committee and the Legco), along with Cheng Kai-nam (chair of the Hong Kong Citizens Forum), were at the front of the May protest marches. Employees of the Xinhua News Agency published a letter calling for Premier Li Peng to step down. Xu Jiatun himself dealt a blow to the pro-Beijing forces by leaving for the United States (M. Chan 1992:23, 1994; Chan and Lee 1991; Roberti 1994; Wilson 1990:220). As Tang (1993:277) points out, "the pro-

China forces failed to provide either moral or political leadership at this critical historical juncture."

Fifth, the protest marches after the Tiananmen incident expanded support for the service professionals among the grassroots population. Whereas the democracy project's demonstrations had attracted an average turnout of about 500 before the Tiananmen incident, they now attracted up to 1.5 million. Threatened by rapid inflation, growing unemployment, an impending influx of workers from the mainland, and the escalation of real estate prices, the grassroots population was increasingly receptive to the service professionals' program.

Finally, the Tiananmen incident consolidated a new Hong Kong ethnic identity vis-à-vis a Chinese national identity. In Ming-Kwan Lee's (1995: 125) survey in 1990, more than half (56.6%) of respondents regarded themselves as "HongKongers," only 25 percent as "Chinese." In fact, the past forty years since World War II had seen the gradual shedding of a refugee mentality, the acquisition of a sense of commitment to the territory, and the emergence of a "Hong Kong" ethnic identity. But the "HongKonger" identity emerging during the Tiananmen incident possessed an anti-Beijing component, asserted against a taken-for-granted "Chinese" identity. Lee's survey showed that a tiny portion of the Hong Kong respondents (less than 10%) neither trusted the Beijing government nor were prepared to regard "political allegiance to the PRC" as a necessary criterion for "Chineseness." Tam's (1996:9) survey in 1994 also reports that 90 percent of the interviewees felt negatively about the Beijing government, particularly on its supposed lack of rules on law and freedom. In addition, the Hong Kong Chinese were not ready to identify with their counterparts across the border. In this respect, an emerging "HongKonger" identity facilitated the forging of a populist alliance between service professionals and the grassroots population against Beijing.

Businesspeople's Reaction: Democracy and Passports

The Omelco Consensus

The Unofficial Members of the Legco and the Exco, moved by the mass demonstrations and other evidence of strong sentiment for democracy, rethought their position on direct elections. Lydia Dunn called four special meetings of the Office of the Members of the Executive and Legislative Councils (Omelco) to discuss the issue. Many businesspeople in the Omelco were now prepared to accept a much faster pace of democratization than that proposed by the draft Basic Law. Although Martin Lee and Szeto Wah had wanted at least half the legislature directly elected in 1991 and the entire body in 1997, they eventually reached a compromise with their business colleagues: the so-called Omelco Consensus proposed that one-third of the Legco be elected in 1991, 50 percent by 1995, and 100 percent by 2003. The chief executive of the SAR would be directly elected no later than 2003 (*FEER*, June 8, 1989:18; Roberti 1994:253–54).

This strategic alliance between service professionals and businesspeople on the issues of democratization, however, was transient and fragile. As the emotions aroused by the Tiananmen incident subsided, businesspeople gradually backed away from rapid democratization. Although they avoided unnecessary confrontation with the democrats, their participation in events that commemorated the deaths of June 4 was low-key, if they participated at all (Tang 1993:281).

In the aftermath of the Tiananmen incident, many businesspeople and corporate professionals with ties to Britain initiated a "Hong Kong People Saving Hong Kong" campaign. Cheng Hon-kwan, who represented the engineers' constituency in the Legco, charged that "Britain has both a moral obligation and a constitutional responsibility to support its subjects in their hour of need. We believe that the British Government ought to provide all 3.25 million BDTC [British dependent territory citizen] or BNO [British national overseas] passport holders an assurance or insurance policy by granting to them the right of abode or the right of entry" (*HK Engineer*, July 1989:11). If Hong Kong people could leave to live in Britain, they reasoned, they would have no reason to fear the Beijing government and would continue to work and invest in Hong Kong. At a special Omelco meeting on June 14, it was unanimously agreed that Lydia Dunn and Allen Lee, as the senior members of the Exco and the Legco, should go to London to persuade Parliament to restore the right of abode in Britain in order to maintain confidence in Hong Kong (*FEER*, July 6, 1989:30).

The corporate sector decided to take a belated lead in pushing for the "right of abode" issue, because its members saw the Tiananmen crisis as an opportunity to set themselves up as champions of Hong Kong people. During the Chinese democracy movement in May, they saw their status, power, and leadership gradually eroded, as the Hong Kong public enthusiastically demonstrated for the cause of democracy and allied with the democratic lobby. The Tiananmen crisis in June, therefore, not only enabled the corporate forces to regain political domination over the democrats, but also enabled them to regain ideological hegemony by redefining the issue of "the right of abode in Great Britain" as the most prominent issue in Hong Kong.

The ROAD Project

In the aftermath of the Tiananmen incident, a small group of accountants, managers, and corporate directors called a meeting with twenty hours' notice on how to restore the confidence of Hong Kong's people and maintain its prosperity and stability (*Capital*, July 1989). Four items were on the agenda:

1. Request the British government to grant holders of British passports in Hong Kong the same rights as those enjoyed by British citizens.

2. Make certain that the British government will carry out its moral responsibility to enable Hong Kong's citizens to secure a passport in any democratic country, so they need not worry.

3. Institute a democratic government through elections before Beijing resumes sovereignty in 1997.

4. Unite the Hong Kong population to achieve these goals.

They decided to focus first on the second item, as it was concrete and therefore more easily understood by the public than the democratization issue. Having settled that matter, the corporate professionals adopted the name ROAD (Right of Abode Delegation) for their organization (Wong forthcoming).

In contrast to service professional organizations, this corporate ROAD possessed the following characteristics. ROAD's organizers had been educated in Britain; many were licensed to practice there and in the Commonwealth and held British passports. Their movement was not confined to Hong Kong but extended to Britain, the Commonwealth, and elsewhere. They commanded abundant resources; they could easily pay $50,000 to start a mass media campaign. Rather than form an alliance with other community groups, ROAD joined the business alliance.

London's Hong Kong Policy

Since London could not possibly invite 3.25 million Hong Kongers to come to live in the United Kingdom (Britain's minority population would double!), it needed to formulate policies to restore confidence in Hong

Kong to avoid the accusation that it was washing its hands of its erstwhile colony.

The Foreign Affairs Committee (FAC) of the House of Commons immediately called for an acceleration of democratization as the best and surest base for Hong Kong's future. On June 30, 1989, the FAC released its recommendations:

1. Direct election of half the sixty-member Legco in 1991 and the entire body by 1995.

2. Election of the SAR's first chief executive by a democratically constituted electoral college six months before the transfer of sovereignty on July 1, 1997, and of subsequent chief executives by universal suffrage.

3. Introduction of a bill of rights to ensure consistency with international covenants on human rights.

4. No stationing of Chinese troops in Hong Kong.

5. Any proposed amendments to the Basic Law should have the consent of the National People's Congress in China, the Legco, and the Chief Executive in Hong Kong (*FEER*, July 13, 1989:11).

However, the FAC's report was not binding on the London government.

Despite this display of good intentions, anti-British sentiment continued to rise. When Foreign Secretary Geoffrey Howe arrived for a visit apparently intended to show Hong Kong's people that the British government did care about them, several thousand vocal protesters were on hand to greet him at the airport. A bigger crowd rallied at a central park and later marched on Government House. When Howe addressed a group at a lunch hosted by the governor, he was heckled by some elected District Board members. Lee Wing-tat, a District Board chairman, remarked, "Howe would be better off not saying Britain was a staunch friend of Hong Kong. I do not feel Britain is a friend at all. . . . Not shouldering its moral obligation to Hong Kong—this is just hypocrisy" (quoted in S. H. Lo 1997:11). The elected members put up a banner: "Shame on the Thatcher Government—Irresponsible and Hypocritical Government." Then they walked out shouting, "Shame! Shame!" to a round of applause (*FEER*, July 13, 1989:10; Roberti 1994:264–65).

Under pressure from Hong Kong and from Parliament, London finally agreed to a package of measures to restore public confidence in Hong Kong: the speeding up of democratization, the introduction of a human rights bill, the granting of U.K. citizenship to selected Hong Kong people, the launching of massive infrastructure projects (a new airport and container terminals), and the substantial expansion of postsecondary education.

The Nationality Proposal

The House of Lords debated Hong Kong emigration on June 21. The Lords were split on whether British nationals in Hong Kong should be granted the right of abode in the United Kingdom, though most agreed that Britain had a moral responsibility to them. MacLehose, the former governor of Hong Kong, called for an amendment to the Nationality Act within two years' time to grant Hong Kong people the right of abode.

Prime Minister Thatcher tried to rally support for Hong Kong emigration at the British Commonwealth Conference in Kuala Lumpur, at the European summit in Madrid, and at the Group of Seven economic summit in Paris in October and November 1989. At the same time, Governor Wilson visited the United States and tried to persuade its government to grant immigrant status to the people of Hong Kong without requiring them to leave the colony. The British government sought the agreement of friendly Western states and the Commonwealth to provide more passports to Hong Kongers and called for the continuation of international scrutiny of Hong Kong's affairs after 1997 (*FEER*, Oct. 19, 1989:26; Nov. 30, 1989:12–13), but its appeals received little support.

In December 1989, the Thatcher government announced that Britain would grant full citizenship to 50,000 carefully selected Hong Kong families, for a maximum of 225,000 people. It was a unique gesture: it enabled those who qualified to acquire the full rights of British citizenship without taking up residence in Britain. Thus they could choose to live in Hong Kong until 1997, secure in the knowledge that they could then leave at any time (*FEER*, Dec. 28, 1989:10–11; Skeldon 1990–91:512).

Most offers of British nationality would go to corporate professionals (26,486 business managers, accountants, engineers, and computer experts) and state officials (13,300 in sensitive and professional services); only 5,814 would go to doctors, lawyers, and teachers. The British government expected as many as 750,000 people to apply, but only 50,000 passports would be available; members of the immediate families of successful applicants would be listed on their passports. Applicants would be judged according to the following point system: age (200 points), experience (150 points), education/training (150), special circumstances (150), knowledge of English

(50), British links (50), and community service (50). A special category was established for 500 key entrepreneurs, invited by the governor to apply without the need to meet the points requirements (*FEER*, Apr. 19, 1990:18–19). Since it was the business community and corporate professionals that strongly pushed for citizenship, this measure naturally favored them.

Reactions in Hong Kong

The corporate sector warmly welcomed the nationality proposal. A chairman of a group of big companies that had lobbied for the right of abode described it as going a considerable way toward meeting the needs of Hong Kong's people. However, the service sector was more skeptical. Many service professionals perceived the measure as a reluctant handout from the departing colonial power and, as such, an insult to Hong Kong (Skeldon 1991:242). Lo Lung-kwong of the Hong Kong People Saving Hong Kong campaign charged that it was selective and divisive: it would lower morale in the civil service, most of whose 180,000 members were not offered citizenship. Moreover, the category of "500 key entrepreneurs" was criticized as elitist, as the very rich already had the money and connections necessary for emigration without having to rely on special privileges conferred by the Governor of Hong Kong (*FEER*, Dec. 28, 1989:10–11). Ming-kwan Lee (1995:124) remarks that the nationality measure complicated the identity profile of Hong Kong Chinese and sowed seeds of mutual distrust in the community. Questions such as "Have they received any overseas passports?" and "Are they as loyal and committed to Hong Kong as we are?" would certainly be raised in election campaigns in the 1990s.

Beijing's Hong Kong Policy

In sum, a strategic alliance was built during the Tiananmen incident among service professionals, the grassroots population, businesspeople, the London government, and even some leftist supporters for the promotion of democratization in Hong Kong in mid-1989. This democratic alliance surely alarmed Beijing. Beijing not only worried about its inability to control the colony, but now also feared that Hong Kong's democracy had become so strong that it would spread across the border to revitalize the Chinese democracy movement on the mainland. Subsequently, Beijing adopted a much-hardened policy toward Hong Kong's democratic movement than before the Tiananmen incident.

Although there had been calls in Hong Kong and London for Beijing to delay passage of the Basic Law, Beijing resolved that there would be no delay and that Hong Kong would not be given more democracy and greater protection of human rights because of the Tiananmen incident. Therefore, while the consultation period for the second draft of the Basic Law would be extended to the end of October 1989, the Basic Law would be promulgated in early 1990 as planned (Roberti 1994:267).

In addition, Beijing tried to ban the use of Hong Kong as "a subversive base against China" while it continued to co-opt corporate leaders and fortify leftist organizations. Beijing warned the Hong Kong public not to interfere in China's domestic affairs. Jiang Zemin, the newly elected general secretary of the Chinese Communist Party, remarking that "well water should not interfere with river water," implied that under Beijing's "one country, two systems" proposal, the Chinese government would not interfere in Hong Kong's domestic affairs and Hong Kong should not meddle in China's (*FEER*, Aug. 3, 1989:29).

Beijing attempted intimidation of the pro-democracy forces by publicly attacking their leaders. On June 6, 1989, Lee Cheuk-yan, a union leader and a representative of the Alliance who had been sent to Beijing, was arrested at Beijing Capital Airport while boarding a flight bound for Hong Kong. Lee was released on June 8 only after signing a confession. In addition, Beijing accused Martin Lee and Szeto Wah in its official newspaper *The People's Daily* on July 21, 1989. Lee and Szeto were chair and vice chair respectively of the Hong Kong Alliance in Support of the Patriotic Democratic Movement in China. The Alliance called on the People's Liberation Army to overthrow the "Deng XiaoPing–Li Peng –Yang Shangkun regime" and helped Chinese dissidents to escape overseas after the Tiananmen incident. Thus, in *The People's Daily*, Lee and Szeto were accused of trying to subvert the Chinese Government, and warned that they would be arrested and charged if they ever set feet on the mainland. Lee and Szeto were also expelled from participation in the Basic Law Drafting Committee. Zhang Junsheng, the vice director of the New China News Agency, warned that Lee and Szeto might not be allowed to sit on the post-1997 legislature because of their "anti-China" stance and opposition to the Basic Law. The Hong Kong leftist bookstores were also forbidden to sell "counterrevolutionary" books or those written by prodemocracy writers (Chan and Lee 1991:132–33; Lo 1992:15; Lo 1997:211; Wong forthcoming).

Beijing dismissed the democratization and emigration proposals of the Omelco members as part of a British conspiracy that aimed to perpetuate British interests at the expense of Chinese sovereignty. Beijing insisted that the Basic Law Drafting Committee not even consider "the Omelco Consensus." As Chan (1991:22) further notes, "the *Comments on the Basic Law (Draft)* issued by Omelco in October 1989 had to be sent via British diplomatic channels to the Chinese authorities who regarded this a British-'tinted' reflection of local views."

Reactions to the Nationality Measure

In response to Thatcher's discussion of the Hong Kong issue at summit meetings in October and November 1989, Beijing said that Britain's motive was to use international pressure to frustrate China's effort to resume sovereignty over Hong Kong. *The People's Daily* rejected Britain's suggestion that Hong Kong should be monitored internationally and become part of the Commonwealth after 1997 (*FEER*, Nov. 30, 1989:13).

Britain's offer of citizenship to selected Hong Kongers, according to Beijing, was another ploy to perpetuate its rule beyond 1997; the nationality package would either drain away the talent required to keep Hong Kong prosperous or leave behind a group of people whose loyalty was to Britain rather than China (Skeldon 1990–91:513). Beijing was especially disturbed by the prospect that senior officials of the Hong Kong government would hold British passports; administration would grind to a halt if they decided to leave en masse after 1997.

As a counterattack, Beijing warned that even if Hong Kong Chinese acquired the right of abode in Britain, they would still be regarded as Chinese nationals. Under Chinese law, Hong Kong Chinese can acquire foreign nationality only if they settle abroad or renounce their Chinese nationality. To give weight to its displeasure, Beijing stipulated in the Basic Law that Hong Kong residents with the right of abode in another country could not become senior officials of the SAR (*FEER*, Dec. 28, 1989:10).

The Promulgation of the Basic Law

Divisions in the Business Sector

After the Tiananmen incident, the business sector was no longer solidly opposed to direct elections. Many businesspeople, including Vincent Lo of the Group of 89, rethought their opposition to democracy. Since it occurred to them that a democratic government might help to safeguard

Hong Kong from Beijing's intrusion into local politics, they were willing to compromise with the democracy forces. The outcome was the so-called 4-4-2 model, under which directly elected seats in the legislature would be increased to 40 percent, and the remaining seats would be shared by functional constituencies (40%) and an electoral college (20%) from 1995 to 2001 (M. Chan 1994).

On the other hand, some businessmen remained committed to the conservative model. Lo Tak-shing, a former Exco and Legco member and the founder of the New Hong Kong Alliance, visited Beijing after the Tiananmen incident. Lo's Beijing visit aroused the suspicion of other big businesspeople who thought that the former was an opportunist courting favor with Beijing officials (Lo 1997:149). Lo proposed a bicameral legislature, consisting of a "functional house" and an "elected house." The functional house would be composed of representatives of business and professional groups. Half of the elected house would be elected indirectly by members of the District Boards and the two municipal councils and the other half by universal suffrage. Lo figured that the elected house would probably be dominated by the democrats and the functional house by the conservative businesspeople. A bill would have to be passed by each house separately before it could become law, so the businesspeople could block any radical proposal introduced by the democrats (Roberti 1994:272). As Ming Chan (1991:23) observed, Lo's bicameral model not only would split the legislature into two tiers but would enable an indirectly elected upper house to exercise veto power over measures passed by a lower house that had been at least partially elected by the public. Lo's model was sharply criticized by the democracy forces, but the local leftist organizations and the Beijing government liked it (*FEER*, Oct. 12, 1989:26).

When Lo Tak-shing and the democrats were unable to agree, the drafting process lost its momentum. London and Beijing were left to do the final patching up.

The Changing Sino-British Relationship

The Sino-British relationship obviously worsened in the aftermath of the Tiananmen incident. Beijing strongly condemned London for speeding up democratization in Hong Kong, passing the human rights bill, and granting British passports to almost a quarter of a million Hong Kong residents, and it even threatened to refuse to take back the illegal immigrants from the mainland that the Hong Kong government repatriated in October

1989. Beijing further condemned the Hong Kong government's decision to allow Yang Yang, a mainland Chinese swimmer seeking asylum, to leave Hong Kong for the United States (S. H. Lo 1991).

Yet Beijing badly needed London's cooperation during the transition to 1997. Without the support of both the business community and its local leftist organizations, Beijing had little option but to craft a strategic alliance with London at this critical juncture. Otherwise, the Basic Law might not converge with the proposed democratic reforms in Hong Kong. The five-year effort of drafting the Basic Law would have been for nothing.

A strategic Beijing-London alliance was initiated when London took special action to pacify Beijing in late 1989. William Ehrman, political adviser to the Hong Kong government, wrote to the Xinhua News Agency to explain that

the Hong Kong government has no intention of allowing Hong Kong to be used as a base for subversive activities against the People's Republic of China. Xinhua should have noticed the arrest of the April 5th Action Group [an anti-Beijing radical organization] outside their National Day reception. . . . The Hong Kong government has recently rejected a proposal for a permanent site for a replica statue of democracy. No group in Hong Kong has any more tolerance than the law allows. (*SCMP*, Oct. 26, 1989:1)

London arranged several secret visits to Beijing by Governor Wilson, Foreign Secretary Douglas Hurd, and Percy Cradock, now personal adviser to Prime Minister Thatcher, to explain its policy to Chinese officials between November 1989 and January 1990 (Ching 1994:182). At the beginning of the negotiations, London was pressing for more rapid democratization. Wilson explained that the Exco and Legco councilors had reached a consensus on introducing twenty elective seats in 1991 and thirty in 1995. But Beijing insisted that the pace was far too fast and that it could not even consider the Omelco Consensus model. Finally, London and Beijing reached a last-minute compromise on the 1991 and 1995 elections, which was incorporated into the Basic Law. London reassured Beijing on the issues of subversion and internationalization, and Beijing was willing to increase the number of elective seats in Hong Kong (Cradock 1994:230; Hong Kong Government 1994b:8). The final Basic Law was, as Chan (1991:26) put it, "a bilateral Sino-British secret deal. Neither the expressed views of the local populace as 'collected' in the final round of the BLCC consultation nor as 'reflected' by local BLDC members were genuinely taken into consideration by the Beijing government."

Finalization of the Basic Law

On the one hand, the British government agreed to insert into the Basic Law two controversial new clauses related to subversion and internationalization. Article 23 required the SAR legislature to pass laws prohibiting acts of subversion against the central government. Another clause prohibited political activities by foreign or international political organizations and groups in Hong Kong, and prohibited local political groups from establishing links with foreign political organizations or groups (*FEER*, Feb. 1, 1990:16). As Roberti (1994:277) notes, this clause could prevent Chinese dissidents from using Hong Kong as a base of subversion against the central government after the hand-over.

On the other hand, with agreement on the 1997 "convergence" of election arrangements, the British government was able to increase the number of directly elected seats in the 1991 Legco from zero to eighteen and functional constituency seats from fourteen to twenty-one, while reducing the senior civil servants' official seats from ten to three and those of appointed members from twenty to seventeen. In 1995, the last election before the hand-over, there would be no more appointed members or official seats. Then the number of functional constituency seats would increase from twenty-one to thirty and directly elected seats from eighteen to twenty, and the ten remaining seats would be selected by an election committee (Scott 1992:10; see also Table 6). As Scott (1995:202) says, "the Basic Law is a profoundly antidemocratic document." Beijing wanted a restricted, corporatist democracy that would enable it to rule Hong Kong through surrogates and collaborators in big business. The functional constituencies, with their small electorates, allowed for greater manipulation in the selection of business and pro-Beijing candidates than the large electorates that chose the occupants of directly contested seats (Scott 1992:11).

Beijing was willing to increase the proportion of foreigners in the Legco from 15 percent to 20 percent, and Beijing and London reached an understanding on a "through train": the legislature's members elected in 1995 would serve as the first legislators of the Hong Kong Special Administrative Region (SAR) until 1999, if the 1995 legislature was constituted according to the Basic Law (Scott 1995:203). Then, as Chan (1992:25) remarks, "the SAR political system will evolve at a snail's pace over the next decade with half of the legislature directly elected by 2007."

The Basic Law was promulgated in early 1990 by Beijing and London, with very little direct input from Hong Kong. But of course big business

TABLE 6. *Mode of selection of Legislative Council members specified by 1988 White Paper, Omelco Consensus model, and Basic Law*

	Number	Percent
1988 White Paper		
Government officials/appointed	31	56.4%
Functional constituencies	14	25.5
Electoral College	10	18.2
Total	55	100.1%
Omelco Consensus model		
1991		
Government appointed	20	33.3%
Functional constituencies	20	33.3
Direct election	20	33.3
Total	60	100.0%
1995–1997		
Functional constituencies	30	50.0%
Direct election	30	50.0
Total	60	100.0%
1999		
Functional constituencies	30	33.3%
Direct election	60	66.6
Total	90	100.0%
2003		
Direct election	90	100%
Basic Law		
1991		
Government officials/appointed	21	35.0%
Functional constituencies	21	35.0
Electoral College	18	30.0
Total	60	100.0%
1995–1999		
Functional constituencies	30	50.0%
Direct election	20	33.3
Election Committee	10	16.6
Total	60	100.0%
1999–2003		
Functional constituencies	30	50.0%
Direct election	24	40.0

TABLE 6. *Continued*

	Number	Percent
Election Committee	6	10,0
Total	60	100.0%
2003–2007		
Functional constituencies	30	50.0%
Direct election	30	50.0
Total	60	100.0%

Source: Adapted from *Far Eastern Economic Review,* Feb. 1, 1990:19; Mar. 1, 1990:14.

had already imprinted its own policies on it. Although a few members of the business sector had rethought the pace of democratization during the Tiananmen incident, on the whole these people saw no particular need to ask for revision when the emotion of Tiananmen died down and Beijing affirmed its commitment to the business community. The service professionals, however, lost faith in Beijing's promise of a high degree of autonomy after the Tiananmen incident. They perceived the whole Basic Law drafting exercise as merely a political show to deceive the Hong Kong public (S. H. Lo 1992:16). If Beijing could declare martial law and move tanks into Tiananmen Square, how could a piece of paper called the Basic Law protect the rights and freedoms of Hong Kong society? Moreover, the service professionals knew that the grassroots population had neither interest nor faith in the Basic Law. A mass rally held on October 29, 1989, on the draft Basic Law was attended by fewer than five hundred people. That was a far cry from the heady days of May and June, when up to a million people showed up for public demonstrations. The Basic Law Consultative Committee received only 6,522 submissions before the deadline of October 30, 1989. A poll conducted in late October found that seven out of ten people had no confidence that Beijing would stick to the Basic Law (Roberti 1994:275).

In fact, the final promulgation of the Basic Law on April 4, 1990, was an anticlimax. By then the mass media had shifted their attention to the passage of the nationality legislation by the British Parliament on April 5, 1990 (Zhang et al. 1991:241). Already the Basic Law had fallen short of the quasi-sacred status that other constitutions attained. The Basic Law was polluted by Beijing's actions in Tiananmen Square.

Still, the legal and constitutional frameworks for post-1997 Hong Kong were now in place. Within minutes of the announcement that Beijing had officially passed the Basic Law, the Hong Kong government announced that eighteen directly elected seats in the legislature would be filled by direct election in 1991 (Roberti 1994:287–88), setting up a new wave of electoral politics in the aftermath of the Tiananmen incident.

The 1991 Election

Party Formation and Political Labels

Of the sixty members of the Legco, only eighteen were to be directly elected. Still, the prospect of running for those eighteen directly elected seats prompted the formation of political parties. The first one formed was the United Democrats of Hong Kong (UDHK), established on April 23, 1990, by Martin Lee and Szeto Wah, who still led the Hong Kong Alliance in Support of the Patriotic Democratic Movement in China. As such, the United Democrats were labeled "anti-Beijing" because of the group's overlapping leadership role in the Hong Kong Alliance and the latter's support for the democratic movement in China. In 1990, the United Democrats included 220 activists who were also members of the Meeting Point (MP), the Hong Kong Affairs Society (HKAS), and the Association for Democracy and People's Livelihood (ADPL). The United Democrats were mostly service professionals from the ranks of social workers, teachers, university professors, independent union activists, church leaders, and lawyers. Eighty percent of its members possessed a higher education degree. The core leaders of the United Democrats included lawyer Martin Lee, social work professor Yeung Sum, medical doctor Ng Sung-man, teacher Lee Wing-tat, union leader Siu Yin-ying, and educators Ng Ming-yum and Szeto Wah. The United Democrats' platform was to speak up for the interests of Hong Kong, safeguard Hong Kong's rights against Beijing's interference, maintain a high degree of autonomy for Hong Kong, and support a social welfare system (Jane Lee 1994:280, 283; Lo 1997:155–60).

Second, the businesspeople splintered after 1989. Some liberals representing the small business and expatriate sectors who wanted to hasten democratization formed the Hong Kong Democratic Foundation (HKDF) on June 24, 1990, under the leadership of Jimmy McGregor. McGregor represented the Hong Kong General Chamber of Commerce in the Legco, but he was not in tune with the organization's strong business orientation. He wanted to set up an independent, multiracial political organization committed to developing a pluralistic democracy (S. H. Lo 1997:149, 153). Although the HKDF was in the democratic camp, it did not enjoy grass-roots support. Only a few of its members were elected to District Boards in 1991. Since most members were small businesspeople and corporate professionals, they were against what they regarded as the socialist policies of other democratic groups. As Patrick Shiu, the chair of the General Committee, remarked, "Strictly speaking, they [other liberal groups] are advocating socialism" (*Hong Kong Standard,* Oct. 13, 1992). Furthermore, the HKDF managed to establish a good relationship with Beijing (Cheng 1994:294; J. Lee 1994:278; S. H. Lo 1997:154).

Third, many businesspeople still worried about welfare spending and adversarial politics. Some formed the Liberal Democratic Federation (LDF) on November 6, 1990, with the objective of supporting candidates to run in the 1991 elections. Most members of the LDF were well-known business-people and members of the Legco and the Urban Council, including Philip Kwok, Stephen Cheong, Maria Tam, James Tien, and Hu Fa-kwong. Philip Kwok spelled out the platform of the LDF clearly: "We felt that the commercial and industrial sector should play a role in this transition period. We need to catch up [with the prodemocracy forces] and to cope with Legco's direct elections in 1991. . . . We hope that Hong Kong's future will be supported by businessmen. Thus, in our political platform, there are two major points: maintaining commercial and industrial prosperity, and building up Sino–Hong Kong relations on the basis of mutual trust" (quoted in S. H. Lo 1997:163–64). With its call for a harmonious relationship with Beijing, the LDF became a target for co-optation by Beijing (Jane Lee 1994:279).

Finally, a couple of pro-Beijing groups emerged. The New Hong Kong Alliance (NHKA), established by pro-Beijing businesspeople and profes-sionals, formulated a conservative political model to prevent the democrats from dominating the legislature. The Hong Kong Citizens' Forum (CF) was established by Cheng Kai-nam (a pro-Beijing schoolteacher) and Tam Yiu-chung (a leader of the pro-Beijing Federation of Hong Kong Trade Unions). The Citizens' Forum supported Chinese nationalism and aimed to run pro-Beijing candidates in 1991. Its political agenda was to establish regular and frequent dialogue with Beijing and avoid further criticism of the Chinese leadership so that the transition in 1997 would go smoothly (Jane Lee 1994:279–80).

In all of these developments we can see the profound impact of the Tiananmen incident on Hong Kong's democratization. Before 1989, the terms *democracy* and *democrats* had not received widespread acceptance in

Hong Kong society. After a million people marched to support the democracy movement in China, however, the terms *democracy* and *democrats* became hegemonic in Hong Kong's political discourse. It was not only service professionals who declared themselves to be democrats; big business and pro-Beijing forces found it expedient to adopt the democratic label, to speak the democratic discourse, to play democratic games. Conservatives called themselves the Liberal Democratic Federation and the Hong Kong Democratic Foundation in efforts to appeal to the democratic sentiments in Hong Kong society. The mass media, however, were not deceived. They still called these groups "probusiness" and "pro-China" in order to distinguish them from the real democrats. Joseph Chan (1993:57–58) notes that all such labels have connotations that may evoke either sympathy or rejection. Once a label is attached to a group or a person, establishing another label or changing the connotation of the old one takes great effort.

Mobilizing the Grassroots Population

Ming Chan (1992:27) observed that the United Democrats had a large organized labor component among its top leadership. Six of the thirty Central Committee members, including Szeto Wah and Lau Chin-shek, were leaders of major independent unions and veterans of labor actions and community movements. Many core members had long experience in community organizing and election campaigns. Ng Ming-yum of Tuen Mun, Lau Kong-wah and Wong Hong-chung of Shatin, and Man Sai-cheong of Eastern Hong Kong were typical examples. When these activists joined the United Democrats, they brought their local networks and power bases with them (Tang 1993:290). Leung Sai-wing (1993:223), too, points out that the success of the United Democrats' candidates was due in part to their long-term efforts in community construction, district improvement, and social movements.

Interest in the local community and the grassroots population was revitalized with the coming of direct elections in 1991. The securing of support and endorsements from neighborhood organizations (livelihood concern groups or district groups), the setting up of six local party chapters at the community level, and the mobilization of protests against government policies were the principal strategies of democratic candidates. Lui (1993b:341) remarked that the political penetration and institutionalization of the United Democrats at the community level even replaced local livelihood organizations by making them redundant.

The United Democrats articulated a set of pro-welfare and anti-Beijing issues to appeal to the grassroots population. After analyzing campaign materials and platforms, Ming-kwan Lee (1993:240–41) reported that the United Democrats' candidates scored very high on pro-welfare issues: increasing the supply of public housing, subsidizing nursery schools, endorsing a progressive income tax system, demanding a bigger welfare budget, institutionalizing a central provident (retirement) fund, opposing the importation of labor, favoring the strengthening of labor rights through unionization and collective bargaining, tightening the regulations of public utility companies, and "greening" the environment. Based on in-depth interviews with Legco candidates, Jane Lee (1993:300) reports that most candidates chose to focus on attacking government policies directly affecting everyday livelihood and welfare programs. By demonstrating their commitment to improve the general welfare, these candidates used a set of common expressions, such as "to fight for," "to guarantee," "to protect," and "to take care of" the interests of the grassroots; or "to urge," "to monitor," "to supervise," or "to oppose" government on some specific social legislation and policies, such as the importation of labor and price increases. Stephen Tang (1993:149) finds that supporters of the United Democrats came from the grassroots population living in public housing as well as service professionals who enjoyed a relatively higher occupational status and were relatively well educated. In this respect, the United Democrats were now able to forge a populist alliance with the grassroots population through the institutionalization of direct elections in 1991.

Subsequently, the United Democrats decided to mount a full-scale grassroots campaign for the 1991 direct elections. As Chan (1994:172) points out, Szeto Wah, the well-known local union leader, gave up his safe education functional Legco seat to contest the direct election seat in the Kwun Tong–East Kowloon constituency, a manufacturing town and working-class neighborhood. Martin Lee yielded his legal profession functional Legco seat to run in the Hong Kong Island East constituency. Other democratic figures and grassroots activists also ran on the UDHK ticket.

To counteract the democrats' grassroots electoral mobilization, businesspeople formed political organizations to facilitate internal communication and pool resources for election activities. Since they had depended on British patronage in the past, had never run in a direct election before, and held little appeal for the grassroots population, many conservative business candidates attempted to forge an alliance with the leftist pro-Beijing candidates (M. Chan 1992:25).

Like the businesspeople, pro-Beijing forces were rich in resources, as they demonstrated when they enlisted a thousand campaign workers for Cheng Kai-nam. The leftist unions fielded their own candidates (Tam Yiu-chung and Chan Yuen-han) and officially endorsed and contributed to candidates fielded by other leftist organizations and the businesspeople's Liberal Democratic Foundation. The pro-Beijing media launched a campaign to discredit the United Democrats (M. Chan 1992:29; J. Cheng 1994:291).

Many pro-Beijing candidates appropriated the democrats' pro-welfare stand in an effort to appeal to the grassroots population. In fact, pro-Beijing candidates (such as Cheng Kai-nam and Chan Yuen-han) were found to be as pro-welfare as the United Democrats. They were distinguished only by their conciliatory approach to Beijing (M. K. Lee 1993:245).

Election Outcome

In the functional constituencies' indirect election on September 12, 1991, many democratic activists won easily in the contests for the functional seats in the Legco. Cheung Man-kwong, a UDHK member who succeeded his mentor, Szeto Wah, won the educators' seat. The UDHK also gained a seat in the health care constituency without opposition. The two founders of the Hong Kong Democratic Foundation (HKDF) were reelected to the medical seat and the Chamber of Commerce seat, respectively. Still, since twelve of the twenty-one functional seats were uncontested and reserved for business and corporate professionals, the business sector did rather well despite their poor showing in contests for directly elected seats (M. Chan 1994:173–74; Scott 1996:4).

With respect to the first direct election of the Legco on September 15, 1991, the voters' turnout was a record, more than 750,000 (or 39.15%) of 1.91 million registered voters (J. Cheng 1994:291). Moreover, the direct elections brought party politics to life. Of fifty-four candidates who contested the eighteen seats in nine two-seat election districts, thirty-four were fielded by political groups or announced the support of some political organization. Of the eighteen candidates eventually elected, fifteen were affiliated with parties (Louie 1993:157–58).

The democratic activists won a landslide victory, capturing two-thirds of the popular votes and sixteen of the eighteen directly elected seats. The winners were twelve of the fifteen United Democrats' candidates, two of the three Meeting Point candidates, the single candidate from the ADPL, and an independent candidate who was formerly the chair of the Journalists' Association and a strong democrat. The remaining two directly elected seats were won by moderates (M. Chan 1994:174; Scott 1992:4).

In addition, democratic activists were the top vote-getters. The four highest vote getters were: Martin Lee, 74.6 percent; Szeto Wah, 70 percent; Lau Chin-shek, 62.2 percent; Dr. Lam Kui-shing, 51 percent. On the other hand, all leftist and conservative business candidates lost. The Liberal Democratic Federation gained only 5 percent of the vote, the pro-Beijing candidates only 8 percent (M. Chan 1994:174; Hook 1993:846). Having elected none of their candidates, they were in a considerably weakened position.

Since the democrats won sixteen directly elected seats and five of the twenty-one functional constituencies, they formed a fairly solid democratic camp in the Legco together with a few other liberal-minded independents. By the end of 1991, service professionals' United Democrats thus emerged as the most prominent political organization in the Hong Kong polity. Joseph Chan (1993:58) finds that the United Democrats were the only political party that succeeded in attracting those voters who were particularly active in consuming election news and interpersonal exchanges. Chan also argues that the ideal of democracy, however vague it may be, appeared to have taken roots among some electors. These electors generally had a higher sense of political involvement and cared to discuss and even persuade people about election matters.

What explains the remarkable success of the democrats in 1991? Since the pro-Beijing candidates were as outspokenly pro-welfare as the United Democrats, a pro-welfare stand in itself cannot explain it. Many analysts argue that the China factor, clearly on the agenda during the election campaigns, powerfully shaped the results. Lau Chin-shek, for instance, challenged his leftist opponent, Chan Yuen-han, by asking her opinion about helping participants in the 1989 democracy movement to flee China (S. W. Leung 1993). Various surveys indicated that voters had acquired a Hong Konger identity; they could not trust the Beijing government after the Tiananmen incident; they feared Beijing's intervention in Hong Kong's affairs; and they preferred a more responsive and autonomous Hong Kong government. That was why they voted against pro-Beijing candidates and supported those United Democrats who were outspoken in their criticism of Beijing (Lam and Lee 1992:88–105; Tsang 1993:150).

Why did the businesspeople and corporate professionals do so poorly? Businesspeople had little experience in community organizing and grassroots mobilization. They never claimed to seek a mass base and remained a collection of notables with ties to Beijing and the colonial government (Scott 1992:23). Thomas Wong (1993) points to the undercurrent of distrust and ambivalence aroused by the business sector. He found that 45 percent of the respondents to his survey disagreed with the idea that business leaders were honest and dependable. Lee Ming-kwan (1995:129) also reported that the overwhelming majority (75%) of his respondents agreed that "the wealthy people and the big bosses already have their escape hatches arranged; they are here only to make the last killing."

Governor Wilson's Balance of Power

Despite their landslide victory, democratic activists were still a minority in the Legco, because eighteen of the sixty members were appointed by the Governor, twenty-one were indirectly elected by functional constituencies, three were officials (the Chief Secretary, the Financial Secretary, and the Attorney General), and only eighteen were directly elected (J. Lee 1994:271; Scott 1992).

In order to counterbalance the growing influence of the democratic activists in the Legco, Beijing openly declared that the United Democrats were unacceptable to China. In response, Governor Wilson appointed eighteen businesspeople and corporate professionals to the Legco, sixteen of them with clear antidemocratic leanings (M. Chan 1997:578). Beijing warned that the Hong Kong government should appoint no United Democrats to the Executive Council.

By November 1991, twelve appointed Legco members and eight indirectly elected members (four of them previously appointed) formed the Cooperative Resources Center (CRC), which in 1992 became the conservative probusiness Liberal Party. The convener of the CRC was Allen Lee, and its key members included Stephen Cheong, Selina Chow, Ngai Shiu-kit, Lau Wong-fat, Edward Ho, Peggy Lam, and Peter Wong. The CRC courted such groups as the Business and Professionals Federation, the Liberal Democratic Federation, and the rural power brokers in the Heung Yee Kuk (*Hong Kong Standard*, Oct. 21, 1992). The CRC was intended as a joint secretariat to provide support and a gathering place for like-minded conservative businesspeople not directly elected to the Legco. Its aim was to curb the influence of prodemocracy forces in the Legco (M. Chan 1994:175). In early October 1991, Governor Wilson appointed or reappointed four core members of the CRC to the Exco, demonstrating his firm commitment to perpetuate the administration's alliance with businesspeople.

Alarmed by the democrats' election victory, most businesspeople quickly shifted back to urging less haste in establishing democracy and imposing more restrictions on its practice. In June 1992, CRC members joined with pro-Beijing conservatives to defeat, 24 to 22, a motion reaffirming the Omelco Consensus model. Of the eighteen CRC members present to vote down the prodemocracy motion, ten were Legco councilors in 1989 who had supported the Omelco Consensus model then. As Ming Chan (1994:177) remarked, their retreat from their own commitment was a part of the CRC's repositioning as a pragmatic political group friendly to Beijing. It was no coincidence that the CRC received red-carpet treatment on a formal visit to Beijing in June 1992.

To prepare themselves for the election in 1995, fifty-two prominent pro-Beijing figures set up a political party called the Democratic Alliance for the Betterment of Hong Kong (DABHK) on July 10, 1992, with funds provided by local China-owned companies (M. Chan 1994:176).

The Tiananmen Incident and Hong Kong's Democracy

In the late 1980s the prodemocracy forces were in disarray. The service professionals' populist democracy proposal was defeated and the big businesspeople's corporatist democracy was written into the Basic Law. But in 1989 the Tiananmen incident opened up a whole new era for the democrats. First, the conservative triple alliance of Beijing, London, and Hong Kong big business was torn apart. London defected by asking for more rapid democratization; even some big businesspeople and pro-Beijing forces voiced their opposition to the Beijing regime in mid-1989.

Second, there was an empowerment of service professionals. They had formally adopted the label of "democrats." Their political groups were now solidified into the "United Democrats." They deepened their community networks and articulated a pro-welfare platform to appeal to the grassroots population. The populist alliance between service professionals and the grassroots population was further institutionalized at the ballot box in the first direct election of the Legco in 1991. The landslide electoral victory of the democrats showed that they were strongly supported by the grassroots population, giving the democrats a mandate to push forward their populist democracy project.

Third, the symbolic significance of the Tiananmen incident was that it imposed a democratic discourse on the Hong Kong polity. In the post-Tiananmen era, every political group put a democratic label onto itself in order to appeal to the democratic sentiment in Hong Kong society. Not only did service professionals call themselves "United Democrats," but big businesspeople also adopted the label of "Liberal Democratic Foundation" and were forced to participate in electoral competition. Even the pro-Beijing forces were put on the defensive; they, too, had to appropriate service professionals' pro-welfare platform in order to compete for votes. However, the label of "pro-Beijing forces" put them at a disadvantage, and they failed to win any seat in the 1991 Legco election.

Finally, observing the revitalization of the democracy project in Hong Kong and worrying that this project might spill over to the mainland, Beijing quickly hardened its policy toward the democrats in Hong Kong. Martin Lee and Szeto Wah were accused of trying to subvert the Beijing regime; the United Democrats (despite their electoral victory) were seen as a group of rebels threatening the Beijing government. Thus, Beijing pressured London not to appoint any United Democrat member to the Executive Council of the Hong Kong government. Beijing also showed no intention of having a dialogue with this rebel group.

The next chapter will discuss how this hard-line Beijing policy had laid the foundation for a contested democracy in the 1997 transition.

7 | Patten's Electoral Reforms and Contested Democracy

> I think there is quite a lot I can do to broaden and deepen democracy in Hong Kong without necessarily taking on the Chinese on things which they have said they won't accept. They still might not much like the agenda I put forward, but I think we'll be in rather better country when it comes to maneuvering.
>
> Governor Chris Patten (quoted in Dimbleby 1997:95)

> Chris Patten's power will be gradually diminishing. In other words, the people of Hong Kong will not listen to him any more. . . . It's a disastrous situation for Hong Kong, for Britain and for China. And for what? For a few seats in the legislative assembly.
>
> Allen Lee, leader of the Liberal Party (quoted in Dimbleby 1997:174)

Toward a Contested Democracy

The Basic Law—which spells out the legal and constitutional framework of the post-1997 Hong Kong SAR government—was almost five years in the making. The recruitment of Hong Kongers into the Drafting Committee, the drafting process itself, the setting up of another committee to solicit input from the public—all these exercises were aimed at enhancing the legitimacy of the Basic Law. Yet almost overnight its credibility was undermined by the Tiananmen incident in 1989.

The most serious challenge to the legitimacy of the Basic Law, however, came from the British in the early 1990s. In an effort to stamp out anti-British feeling in Hong Kong, Governor Patten promised to advance democratic reforms before the hand-over in 1997. However, since the political structure of Hong Kong had largely been settled by the Basic Law, Patten had to exploit its loopholes and gray areas in order to change the electoral rules for the Legislative Council (Legco).

Patten's last-minute electoral reforms not only intensified the conflict between Beijing and London and realigned political alliances in Hong Kong but also threatened the legitimacy of the Basic Law. Beijing declared that the last Legislative Council elected under Patten's electoral reforms would be dissolved and replaced by a Provisional Legco immediately after the hand-over on July 1, 1997. Prodemocracy forces charged that a Provisional Legco would be illegal because the Basic Law made no provision for it. The Democrats planned to challenge the Provisional Legco in the Hong Kong courts, and the British threatened to take the matter to the World Court. As Sorensen (1993) laments, feuding over election rules had laid the foundation for a contested democracy and democratic breakdown in more than one developing country.

The aim of this chapter is to examine how in the early 1990s key political actors—London, Beijing, big business, and prodemocracy forces—had failed to arrive at a consensus to institutionalize the rules of electoral competition in Hong Kong. This chapter will first study the nature of Patten's electoral reforms. Then it will look into the pattern of the Beijing-London conflict. Finally, it will investigate how such a conflict led to the empowerment of the democrats, the deepening of the unholy alliance between Beijing and Hong Kong's big business, and a contested democracy in Hong Kong.

London's Democratic Reforms

London Changes Its Position

The Sino-British relationship sharply deteriorated during this last phase of colonial rule. From 1984 to 1991, London generally cooperated with Beijing. The British were willing to postpone the introduction of direct elections until 1991 (the year after the promulgation of the Basic Law), as Beijing demanded; they were willing to "consult" Beijing on all major matters straddling 1997 in order to get Beijing's approval for the new airport project. Prime Minister John Major went to Beijing in September 1991 for the signing of the new airport memorandum, marking the first significant break in the West's isolation of China after the Tiananmen incident. Yet after his visit, Major decided to remove David Wilson (an exponent of the cooperative policy), appointed Chris Patten as the last governor of Hong Kong, proposed new democratic reforms, and adopted a confrontational stance toward Beijing.

London introduced its new democratic reform package at a time when the political structure of Hong Kong had largely been settled by the terms of the Basic Law. The scope for constitutional reform in the early 1990s, therefore, was seriously restricted, and it was almost too late for London to make a significant change in Hong Kong's political structure.

Why, then, the sudden shift in London's policy in 1992? It may have resulted from the diminishing influence of the old China hands in the Foreign Office, who always advocated cooperation with China, and the growing influence of politicians over British policy toward Hong Kong (Sum 1995).

Miners (1993) suggests that Patten, a politician who had risen from the ranks by winning elections, believed passionately in democracy, community welfare, and the maximum feasible participation of the people in the government. Patten acknowledged that "my lifelong belief in market economics being socially responsible has had some effect on my attitude to issues like the development of community programmes, the development of welfare, the development of assistance for the disabled and so on" (Tambling 1997:368). His democracy project was publicized at the Conservative Party conference at Blackpool in 1993, and London's about-face may have been an effort to improve the party's image. The party was in turmoil over immigration, yet London knew there would be no flood of Hong Kong Chinese into Britain after 1997 because of the passage of the Nationality Act several years before.

As the report of the House of Commons' Foreign Affairs Committee (1994) acknowledged, world opinion had shifted massively against China since the Tiananmen incident in 1989, so London had less need to concern itself about Beijing's opposition to reforms. And Suzanne Pepper (1997:702) remarks that if the truth could be known, it would doubtless develop that London's new initiative in 1992 was due primarily to its assumption of the speedy downfall of China's Communist government after the collapse of the Soviet Union. If indeed the British made such an assumption, Pepper (1995) suggests, they may have been concerned about how history would judge them if they did not make an extra effort to prepare their last colony for self-rule. As Patten himself stressed, "it's important that Britain departs from Hong Kong in as honourable and dignified a way as possible" (Tambling 1997:363).

Crafting a New Alliance

To enhance his bargaining power with Beijing, Patten needed strong support from Hong Kong society. Upon his arrival, Patten immediately set up a new business council. But since big business had already developed strong ties with Beijing through trade and investment, Patten had little success in securing their support. Many corporate chiefs, in fact, wrote the

Business Council off in private as a "Patten publicity stunt" (*Asiaweek*, Dec. 7, 1994:28).

Patten then tried to craft a new populist alliance with the service professionals, who had emerged as a significant political force since the Tiananmen incident. Patten (1996:281) justified such an alliance by the fact that "Hong Kong had a first-world economy, but very third-world social and community services. Without in any way wrecking our economy or introducing (as though it would be high on my agenda) 'socialism', I sensed that Hong Kong did have to improve the provision for those in need, because otherwise the tensions between the 'haves' and 'have-nots' would create, themselves, problems of political and social balance."

First, Patten announced ambitious programs for improving social welfare, social security, education, health, public housing, and environmental protection—programs that would greatly increase the demand for service professionals. Patten proposed to hire enough teachers to reduce the average class size to twenty; public housing authorities would build an average of a hundred new flats a day; spending on health would rise by almost 5 percent a year. As a result, annual public spending would rise by 21 percent in real terms over the five years to 1997 (Dimbleby 1997:115).

Second, Patten offered tax breaks to more than 90 percent of Hong Kong's salaried employees. Service professionals would certainly welcome a tax break, as they were hard-pressed by double-digit inflation and soaring housing prices in the early 1990s.

Third, when nine Unofficial Members of the Executive Council (Exco), all of whom had been appointed by Governor Wilson, offered their courtesy resignations when Patten took office, seven were surprised to have their offers accepted. Those dropped from the Exco included Allen Lee, Selina Chow, Edward Ho, and Rita Fan, the four founding members of the probusiness Cooperative Resources Center, which was the prototype of the Liberal Party (Miners 1994a). Patten replaced them with service professionals who were more sympathetic to democratization. Miners (1996:254) observes that Patten's Executive Council contained fewer businesspeople than ever before. In 1995, four of nine nongovernmental members were businesspeople, compared to six of nine in 1991 and seven of eight in 1986.

Finally, Patten adopted a more open style of leadership: he took to the streets, shook hands with local residents, gave interviews to journalists, and dispensed with some of the secrecy that had always surrounded the Hong Kong governorship (Ching 1993).

Promoting a Democratization Discourse

Patten replaced Wilson's "convergence" discourse with a new democratization discourse to redefine state-society relations in Hong Kong. Sum (1995) points out that Patten treated citizen participation as an essential condition for Hong Kong's future prosperity. In his policy speech to the Legco in October 1992, Patten (1992:30) emphasized that "the best guarantee of Hong Kong's prosperity for as far ahead as any of us can see or envisage is to protect our way of life. . . . An integral part of this way of life . . . is the participation of individual citizens in the conduct of Hong Kong's affairs." For Patten, subsumed under citizen participation were such concepts as a lower voting age, the replacement of corporate votes by individual votes, a wholly elected legislature, direct representation, accountability, and the rule of law.

Sum (1995) notes that Patten's reconstruction of a democratization discourse not only deepened the moral claim of his project but also introduced a new twist by emphasizing the responsibility of the Hong Kong people. Through Patten's discourse, the London government was reconstructed as a moral protector engaging in a Pax Britannica–style "exit in glory," while the Hong Kong people were reconstructed as needing to be more assertive and the Beijing government reaffirmed as an external constraint on the democratization of Hong Kong.

With regard to policy, Patten's democratic proposals included both a noncontroversial administrative reform and a highly contentious election reform (Patten 1993).

Administrative Reforms

First, Patten ended the overlapping of membership between the Exco and the Legco. Lam (1993) has explained that the existing dual membership could not enhance either a competent executive or an independent legislature. Dual commitments were bound to lead to conflicts of interest, because the Exco and the Legco have separate and distinct responsibilities. The Exco was designed to advise the governor on a wide range of issues. Policies developed by the Exco are presented to the Legco for review. The Exco, therefore, should be purely an advisory body with no link to or influence on the Legco (Lo 1995). The Legco is intended to be independent and expected to be an effective check on the executive branch to prevent abuses of power and poor administration. As Miners (1994a) points out, this separation between the two councils removed an important means for the government to exercise influence over legislators. Exco members now ceased to attend in-house meetings of the Legco and to act as conveners of the Legco's subject panels.

Second, whereas the governor served as the president of the Legco before 1993, the Legco now elected one of its own members to that post in order to enhance its effectiveness as an independent legislature. In addition, the Legco now had full authority to develop its committee system to carry out legislative and supervisory functions (Lam 1993).

Third, the new relationship between the administration and the Legco would be characterized by accountability. Lam (1993) points out that the administration would be required to explain policy and proposals, and respond to criticism and queries raised by the Legco. Patten instituted a "Governor's question time" in the Legco: for one hour each month, Patten came to the Legco to answer, without preparation, any questions on government matters that were put to him (Miners 1993).

In sum, as Miners (1993:5) observes, the Hong Kong system of government in the final years of British rule "more closely resemble[d] that of the United States, where the executive is always liable to be frustrated by a legislature which has the power to refuse to grant it money or the laws which it needs, but is unable to turn it out of office, or compel it to follow the policies which the majority of the legislature prefers."

Electoral Reforms

After his popularity rating soared, Patten was ready to take on Beijing. Without consulting Beijing in advance, Governor Patten sparked the Sino-British conflict in October 1992 with electoral proposals designed to increase the pace of democratization in Hong Kong. His strategy was to adhere to the wording of the Basic Law, with its provision for only twenty seats to be filled by popular election, but he exploited various loopholes and filled in the many gray areas in the document. As Patten acknowledged, there was "quite a lot of space, quite a lot of elbow room between the Joint Declaration and the Basic Law. What I propose to do is to find all those bits of elbow room for bedding down democracy or extending it" (Dimbleby 1997:96). Patten's (1992) proposals can be summarized as follows:

- *Lower voting age.* Patten proposed to lower the voting age from twenty-one to eighteen to increase the number of young voters.

- *Single vote, single seat.* Since the Democrats objected to the 1991 system of two-member districts, Patten proposed to give each elector a single vote for a single directly elected representative in a one-seat election district.

- *Functional constituency revisions.* Before 1992, the twenty-one functional constituencies in the Legislative Council were decided largely on a corporate basis; e.g., each bank had a vote in the financial constituency. Patten proposed to replace corporate votes by the votes of the individuals who owned or controlled the corporations. For example, all directors of companies that were members of the General Chamber of Commerce would be able to vote, instead of the companies themselves. In addition, Patten wanted to redefine the nine new functional constituencies so that each would include the entire population working in that sector. This move would broaden the franchise from a few thousand corporate bodies to around 2.7 million people.

- *Stronger local administration.* Patten suggested abolishing all appointments to the nineteen District Boards and the two Municipal Councils, so that all their members would be directly elected.

- *The Election Committee.* Those elected to the District Boards would then make up a committee to elect the remaining ten members of the Legislative Council. The Basic Law, however, stated that the Election Committee should be elected indirectly by corporate bodies, members of the Legco, and representatives in the National People's Congress and the Political Consultative Conference.

In other words, under Patten's plan, all members of the Legislative Council would be directly or indirectly elected by the people of Hong Kong in 1995. Following the categories of the Basic Law, Patten could claim that his proposals for constitutional reforms were quite compatible with the provisions of the Basic Law (Patten 1992).

Patten's Strategy

Patten lobbied for his proposals in late 1992. Sum (1995:72) observes that Patten attempted to dominate the discursive space by combining the practices of "mediatization," legitimization, and intellectualization. Patten initiated mediatization practices when he appointed the director of government information services as his private press secretary. This move enabled Patten's project to reach the grassroots population quickly in the form of official press releases. He deployed legitimization practices when he explained his package through innovative practices such as his question time in the Legco, town hall meetings with the public, radio phone-in programs, and interviews with the mass media. He used intellectualization when he explained and argued for his proposals in debates and interviews, with his English wit and humor, knowledge and subtlety, eloquence and versatility.

Patten's democratic proposals sparked new activism in civil society. In late 1992, a Joint Association of People's Organizations (JAPOD) was formed, consisting of members of thirty pressure groups such as the Hong Kong Professional Teachers' Union (HKPTU) and the Christian Industrial Committee (CIC). The JAPOD demanded that half of the seats in the legislature be filled by popular election in 1995 and 1997, and it openly pledged its support of Patten's package as its baseline. In mid-1993, Emily Lau, one of the most outspokenly critical members of the Legco, formed Full Democracy (FD) in 1995. FD consisted of more than twenty radical grassroots organizations, including the Hong Kong Federation of Student Unions (HKFSU). Dissatisfied with the relatively conservative stance of the political parties and JAPOD, the FD demanded a fully directly elected legislature in 1995 (Sing forthcoming).

In late 1992, forty human rights and service professional groups organized public support for Patten's proposals through political advertisements, press conferences, public meetings, and demonstrations outside the Xinhua News Agency. Opinion polls conducted in late 1992 showed that a clear majority approved of Patten's proposals and his performance, although a majority also wished to avoid confrontation with China (Craddock 1994; Lam 1993).

Patten flew to London to secure the blessing of the British government. After the meeting, John Major and Douglas Hurd expressed their full backing for Patten's reforms and reiterated that the reform package did not violate the Joint Declaration, the Basic Law, or the seven Sino-British diplomatic letters exchanged during 1990–91. By mid-November 1992, the Canadian, Australian, and U.S. governments also publicly stated their support for greater democracy in Hong Kong (Luk 1992).

Conflict between Beijing and London

Beijing's Violation and Nationalism Discourse

As expected, Beijing's reaction to Patten's proposals was highly negative. Patten was given a cold reception when he visited Beijing in October 1992.

Beijing made it clear that unless Patten withdrew his proposals, it would take drastic action with regard to both the political system and the airport project. Beijing regarded Patten's proposals as a plot to prevent China from regaining sovereignty over Hong Kong, to plant pro-British elements in the political establishment after 1997, and to spread the virus of democracy to the mainland (Cradock 1994; Li 1995).

According to Sum (1995), Beijing countered Patten's democratization discourse with a discourse clustered around "violation," "nationalism," and "negative metaphors." First of all, Beijing accused Patten of "three contraventions": violating the Joint Declaration of 1984, the Basic Law of 1990, and the agreement and understandings reached between the British and Chinese in 1990. The first contravention: without prior consultations with the Chinese, the British suddenly and unilaterally publicized Patten's constitutional package. In doing so they violated clause 5 of the Joint Declaration. The second contravention: the proposed electoral arrangements (the Election Committee and the new functional constituents) of the Legco were major changes to the existing structure, and thus violated clause 3 of the Joint Declaration, which stated that political development in Hong Kong was to be incremental and gradual. The third contravention: the Basic Law stipulates that a District Board is not a political organization, yet Patten proposed to enlarge the power of the District Boards by allowing their members to elect ten Legco councilors as members of the Election Committee. Beijing further accused London of breaching the agreement and understanding reached between the two foreign ministers, as evidenced by their exchange of letters in early 1990 (Lam 1993; K. K. Leung 1995; Ministry of Foreign Affairs 1996).

Beijing also employed a discourse of pragmatic nationalism (Sum 1995). The *Beijing Review* (Feb. 7–20, 1994:33), for instance, invoked the "historical shame" China suffered when "Hong Kong was plundered . . . during the Opium War, which the British launched to invade China"; the Chinese would "never forget this shame," and until it was wiped out, "the Sino-British relationship [could] never become harmonious." This "historical shame," then, justified Hong Kong's reunification with the Chinese motherland and the redefinition of the Hong Kong Chinese as an inseparable part of the people of China. The nationalism Beijing proclaimed was its own; Hong Kong's right to self-determination had no part in it. Beijing's nationalism discourse was constructed around the desire to regain Hong Kong as a prosperous and stable gateway for the modernization of mainland China. The *Beijing Review* (Jan. 3–9, 1994:17) stressed that "after China assumes the exercise of sovereignty over Hong Kong in 1997, the existing social and economic system there will not be changed. The Basic Law also stipulates that the previous capitalist system and the way of life shall remain unchanged for 50 years in Hong Kong."

Beijing relied on negative metaphors to construct an unfavorable image of Patten and his reform package (Sum 1995:74). *Wen Wei Po,* Beijing's semiofficial newspaper in Hong Kong, called Patten a "serpent," a "prostitute," a "two-headed snake," and "sinner of the millennium" as it attacked London's hypocrisy in introducing democracy to Hong Kong after 150 years of colonial rule, its indecency in violating the signed agreement and mutual understanding, and its criminality in creating obstacles to China's reunification with Hong Kong.

Besides using an anticolonial, nationalistic, and negative metaphor discourse, Beijing cultivated its own grassroots political group, the Democratic Alliance for the Betterment of Hong Kong (DABHK). The DABHK, in fact, was inaugurated the day after Patten's arrival in Hong Kong in 1992. Through the DABHK, Beijing hoped to extend its united front work to the grassroots population. Although the unholy alliance with Hong Kong's big capitalists was still the focus of the united front, Beijing wanted to broaden it to encompass the million-odd workers, now that they could vote. The DABHK, therefore, was designed as a grassroots party that could mobilize support to compete with the service professionals' United Democrats at the ballot box. The chair of the DABHK was Tsang Yok-sing, the principal of what used to be known as a "patriotic" high school. The DABHK's core leaders included the pro-Beijing union leaders Tam Yiu-chung and Chan Yuen-han, and the majority of its members were from pro-China organizations. The DABHK had financial backing from local China-funded enterprises and the endorsement of the Hong Kong and Macao Affairs Office. Thus the DABHK was not lacking in resources. Its office in Wanchi was more than 3,000 feet square, and it paid rent of over U.S.$19,000 a month (Mainland Affairs Committee 1995:66). Endorsing Beijing's view, the DABHK criticized Patten for "inventing a cunning new device in the constitutional package that will enable him to go beyond the pace of political reform set by the Basic Law" (*SCMP,* Oct. 11, 1992:2). The DABHK acted as a pro-Beijing patriotic grassroots party in the Hong Kong political arena, recruiting members, offering seminars, holding press conferences, and contributing commentaries to the mass media to promote Hong Kong's reunification with the motherland. Tsang Yok-sing proclaimed, "We are pro-China and pro-Hong Kong. We support China's policy toward Hong Kong" (*Hong Kong Standard*, Oct. 14, 1992).

Beijing also fought back on the economic level. On November 30, 1992, Beijing threatened that "contracts, leases, and agreements" signed by the Hong Kong government would not be honored after 1997 unless they had been approved in advance by China (Luk 1992). The multibillion-dollar airport project was now in financial limbo. As all infrastructure projects and public utilities in Hong Kong are operated by private companies under government license, Beijing's edict sent a chill through all businesses involved in communications, transport, and public utilities (Dimbleby 1997:164). Beijing's move was intended to force the business community to take a firm stand against Patten's electoral reforms.

In the midst of this political conflict, the Hong Kong stock market experienced violent fluctuations, plunging more than a thousand points (almost 20 percent) in three days in December 1992 (Economic and Business Report 1993; *FEER*, Dec. 17, 1992). Patten appealed to Beijing to make a concrete counterproposal so that Hong Kong's citizens could decide what kind of future government they wanted, but Beijing was reluctant to do so. It found Patten's proposed political reforms so wholly unacceptable that the package had to be dropped before Beijing would agree to any talks with London. Beijing further insisted that the Legco must not be involved in the resolution of the agreement, and the Hong Kong officials on the British negotiation team were to serve only as "experts" rather than as full members representing the Hong Kong government (Lam 1994). Instead of working with London to resolve the conflict, Beijing stepped up its united front work in the territory. In March 1993, Beijing appointed a second batch of forty-nine Hong Kong Affairs Advisers—business leaders, retired civil servants, and professionals.

The Sino-British conflict was intensified when Patten's proposals were published in the government gazette in early 1993. Just before the Legco was to debate the proposals, however, Beijing agreed in April 1993 to hold talks after London agreed that the talks should be based not on Patten's 1992 proposals directly, but on the Sino-British Joint Declaration, the Basic Law, and "previous understandings" reached through diplomatic exchanges.

The Talks

The seventeen rounds of talks in Beijing from April to November 1993 nevertheless failed to produce any concrete results because Beijing proved unyielding on all issues. John Burns (1994) points out that the two sides disagreed on three major issues:

1. *The through train.* London pressed Beijing to establish objective criteria before the 1994–95 elections to determine who could ride the through train beyond 1997, but Beijing insisted that this was a matter for the Preparatory Committee for the Special Administrative Region (SAR) to decide in 1996.

2. *The functional constituencies.* Although London compromised by narrowing the scope of functional constituencies to one million voters, Beijing still insisted that voters must be limited to clearly identifiable corporate bodies.

3. *The Election Committee.* London and Beijing disagreed on the composition of a committee to elect ten members to the legislature in 1995. London argued that the committee should be made up of locally elected members; Beijing insisted that it consist of functional constituencies and appointed members.

Beijing and London at first agreed to start with the easier part and then move on to the more difficult part. The negotiations, however, broke off after the seventeenth round in November 1993, when the two sides failed to reach agreement not only on the three major issues but also on three other "simple issues": the lowering of the voting age, the one-seat, one-vote system for the twenty directly elected seats, and the abolition of appointive seats on the lower councils (Lam 1994).

Why did the talks break down? Cradock (1994) suggests that Beijing's unwillingness to yield may have reflected uncertainty about the successor to Deng Xiaoping: no Beijing officials had enough confidence to be flexible. In addition, Patten appeared to suffer from technical constraints. He had long warned that time was running out; if the talks led nowhere, he would have to present his proposals to the legislature as soon as possible in order to make preparations for the District Board elections in September 1994, the elections for the Urban and Regional Councils in March 1995, and the Legco elections in September 1995. Furthermore, Patten was under pressure by the Democrats to present his proposals to the legislature. The Democrats were always worried that Patten would yield to Beijing. Martin Lee complained that the governor had "talked a great deal but delivered nothing," and Lee no longer trusted Patten to fight for democracy (Dimbleby 1997:234).

The Second Kitchen

In an effort to discredit Patten's reform package, Beijing repeated its threat not only to sack any Legco member elected under a system it did not approve but also to dismiss the other two tiers of government (the District Boards and the Municipal Councils). Thus Beijing announced that on July 31, 1997, all persons elected to those three bodies would cease to hold office, and a new three-tiered structure of government would be reestablished in accordance with the relevant stipulations in the Basic Law. The announcement signaled the end of the "through train" agreement spelled out in the Basic Law, by which legislators elected in 1995 could stay in office until 1999, thus invalidating the design for the pre- and post-1997 "convergence" of institutions and personnel (Dimbleby 1997:235).

In addition, Beijing accelerated preparations for a shadow government, called the "second kitchen," to be installed when Hong Kong reverted to Chinese sovereignty. In June 1993, Beijing appointed fifty-seven members to the Preliminary Working Committee (PWC) for the Hong Kong Special Administrative Region Preparatory Committee. The PWC had five subcommittees covering political, economic, legal, cultural and educational, and security issues. The political and legal subcommittees were instructed to have their members immediately embark on plans for an alternative body to the legislature elected in 1995 under the Patten proposals (Economist Intelligence Unit 1994).

Furthermore, Beijing tried to consolidate its unholy alliance with big business. During March and May 1994, Beijing appointed the third batch of Hong Kong Advisers, the first group of 274 District Affairs Advisers, and another thirteen members of the powerful Preliminary Working Committee. These appointees included pro-China DABHK members, District Board chairs, vice chancellors of major universities, former members of the Hong Kong civil service, and big businesspersons (Lo and McMillen 1995). In order to isolate the prodemocracy forces, no member of the United Democrats was appointed to the Preliminary Working Committee. Only two low-profile Democrats were among the 500 District Affairs Advisers. Moreover, only three of the thirty Hong Kong representatives in the Preliminary Working Committee were from the grassroots. Even Tam Yiu-chung, leader of the Hong Kong Federation of Trade Unions and an active PWC member, adopted a low profile in bargaining and speaking for local workers' interests (Wong 1997:110, 128).

The Enactment of Patten's Proposals

Patten held firm against Beijing's offensive and proceeded with his reform proposals without China's blessing. His new tactic was to split his election proposals in half. In December 1993, the Legislative Council was first to be asked to consider three "simple issues." When they were easily passed in February 1994, Patten immediately presented three "major issues" for debate, and he declared July 1994 to be the deadline for passing them.

At the Legco session in late June 1994, only twenty-three legislators could be counted on as firm votes in favor of Patten's three major issues; another twenty-three would definitely vote against them (Economist Intelligence Unit 1994). The Democratic Party was still committed to an increase in the number of directly elected seats from twenty to thirty rather than to Patten's modest reforms. To complicate the situation, the legislators were required to vote for fourteen amendments to Patten's bill, the most dangerous of which had been proposed by business's Liberal Party.

Twenty-four hours before the decisive vote, it looked as though Patten's bill would fail. Not only had the Legco's pro-Beijing bloc confirmed publicly that it would almost certainly support the Liberal Party's amendment, but the independents seemed likely to follow suit. In view of the closeness of the vote, Patten was asked to allow the local members to decide for themselves, without official interference (the three Official Members of the Legco are bound by law and custom to support the Governor). Patten refused. The Liberal Party's amendment was defeated, 29 to 28. Thus after a record seventeen-hour marathon debate from June 29 to June 30, Patten's reform proposals survived by just one vote. Without the three official votes, his bill would have fallen to the business sector's amendment. Patten won technically but perhaps lost morally. Allen Lee, the leader of the Liberal Party, protested: "He didn't win. He bulldozed it through. He won by one vote. He didn't let the Hong Kong people decide. He's been lying to the Hong Kong people. And finally he uses the three official votes to get it through" (Dimbleby 1997:255, 264–65; DeGolyer 1994).

During the session, there were forces pushing the Patten proposal in a more democratic direction. At the urging of the "United Ants" (a small group that proclaimed itself the watchdogs of the Democratic Party), Emily Lau, an independent democrat, proposed that all sixty seats of the Legco should be opened to direct elections; her bill, too, was defeated by just one vote (Miners 1994b:2).

In August 1994, the National People's Congress responded to Patten's victory by passing a resolution to dissolve the last colonial-era Legco on June 30, 1997. In December 1994, the political subcommittee of the Preliminary Working Committee proposed to set up a Provisional Legislature to avoid a legislative vacuum after the transfer of sovereignty in 1997 (Li 1995). For Beijing, a Provisional Legislature was necessary because London had been uncooperative and destroyed the mechanism of the "through train" — the arrangement under which the members elected to office in the 1995 election could stay in the Legco until 1999 (Liang 1995).

In addition, the Preliminary Working Committee wanted to speed up the election of the Chief Executive for the SAR government. The early selection of the Chief Executive was aimed to undermine the authority of the British–Hong Kong administration, render it impotent in introducing major structural or policy changes in the last phase of transition (Lo 1995).

Empowerment of the Democrats

Party Formation

This new round of decolonization politics further revitalized the democracy movement in Hong Kong. Although Patten's reform was a top-down initiative (Sum 1995), and although some members of the prodemocracy forces complained that his proposals were still not democratic enough to bring real reforms to Hong Kong (Ching 1993), the United Democrats and the Meeting Point welcomed the wide representation of the proposed functional constituencies as well as the democratic composition of the proposed election committee (Lam 1993). Backing the Patten proposal, Martin Lee of the United Democrats accused Beijing of designing "an authoritarian system with power concentrated in the hands of a Beijing-appointed chief executive subject to few checks or balances from the legislative or judicial branches" (Lee and Boasberg 1994:48).

Moreover, Patten's proposals had opened up new political space for service professionals to push anew their democracy project. In particular, Patten's proposals prompted the formation of new parties. According to Lo Chi-kin, secretary general of the Meeting Point, the political reforms introduced by Governor Patten polarized the community and left less room for the development of a moderate party such as the Meeting Point (Yu 1997:97). Thus, under intense party competition, the Meeting Point faced obstacles to its development because of the relative weakness of its grassroots support. In order to prepare for the coming District Board elections in September 1994, the Urban and Regional Council elections in March 1995, and the Legco elections in September 1995, the Meeting Point merged with the United Democrats to form the Democratic Party in April 1994. The manifesto of the Democratic Party said it would seek further consolidation of the democratic forces, strive for a high degree of autonomy and an open, democratic government, and promote welfare and equality in Hong Kong. In addition, the party tried to appropriate the discourse of nationalism for its own purposes. Thus its manifesto stated: "We care for China and, as part of the Chinese citizenry, we have the right and obligation to participate in and comment on the affairs of China" (*SCMP,* Apr. 19, 1994:6). It called for condemnation of the Tiananmen incident and for an amendment of the Basic Law to allow full direct elections of the SAR chief executive and the Legco (*Ming Pao,* Oct. 3, 1994).

Nevertheless, the Association for Democracy and People's Livelihood (ADPL), another smaller prodemocratic group, was turned down by the United Democrats and the Meeting Point as a founding member of the Democratic Party. The reason was that the ADPL was too pro-Beijing to be included in the Democratic Party. This step taken by the Democratic Party not only intensified its rift with the ADPL, but also sowed the seeds of non-cooperation (Li 1995).

Legislative Politics

By the early 1990s, the Democratic Party had become a formidable force in the legislature. After the 1991 election, elected members became the majority in the Legco, while appointed members and government officials became the minority. Introducing a new breed of members into the Legco had transformed its mode of operation. There were new rules, allowing more debates on motions and adjournment, a new secretariat, and new standing committees. Consensus was dead and the era of adversarial politics had taken over (Lam 1994; Miners 1994a).

Patten's introduction of his reform package in 1992 had moved the Legco further to the center of the political stage. Several indicators showed the empowerment of the Legco. First, it gained independence from the executive branch. After the end of overlapping memberships between the Exco and the Legco, the executive branch had to be more proactive in communicating with Legco members. Chris Patten led the way, and he spent a lot of time meeting political groups and Legco members (Lo 1995). Whereas before 1991 senior civil servants could be confident that any bill endorsed by the Exco would eventually pass through the Legco, they now had to lobby Legco members to get their policies approved. Lobbying Legco councilors, in fact, was not confined to civil servants. Business organizations' consultants were also quite active in attempting to influence policy and legislation (*Asiaweek*, Dec. 7, 1994:23).

Second, after the meeting of the subject panels of the Legco was conducted in public and under the scrutiny of the media, Legco members frequently interrogated civil servants and forced them to reveal information that they would have preferred to remain secret. For example, Miners (1994a) reports that in April 1994, the Security Panel of the Legco compelled the commissioner of the Independent Commission against Corruption (ICAC) to give evidence in public to justify his dismissal of Alex Tsui, the most senior Chinese investigator on his staff, and conducted its own detailed inquiry into the case. In the same month, legislators decided to set up their own inquiry on a police raid on the Whitehead detention center, in which 250 Vietnamese refugees were injured. These inquiries pointed to the deficiencies of government operations and put pressure on the government to improve its performance (Miners 1994b:3).

Third, the new Bills Committee insisted on amendments that might alter the original content of a draft bill approved by the Exco (Miners 1994a). For example, the New Territories Land Bill in November 1993 was intended to clarify the right of inheritance to land in the New Territories, but legislators objected that the bill perpetuated the discriminatory practice of recognizing only male descendants' right to inherit land. The government finally agreed to introduce amendments to the bill to give equal rights of inheritance to men and women, despite protests from the rural areas of the New Territories.

Fourth, private members' bills proliferated. Although Legco members had always had the power to introduce their own bills, they had rarely exercised it. From 1991 through 1995, however, many Legco members proposed bills that would have direct impact on government policy. During 1994–95, for example, Anna Wu introduced several bills seeking to end various forms of discrimination and to promote equal opportunity. Martin Lee introduced a bill to end political censorship of films. His party colleague Michael Ho introduced a bill to empower the Legco to control the quota of imported labor. Lee Cheuk-yan introduced a bill to improve the terms of maternity leave (Lo 1995). Through amendments and private members' bills, service professionals therefore were able to articulate their interests, such as equal opportunity, anticensorship, and gender equality, to the Legco.

Finally, many government bills were defeated. In the 1991–92 session, the first session after the introduction of direct elections, the government lost only one motion (for a court of final appeal) out of 34 motions and bills. In 1992–93, however, the government lost 6 of 38; in 1993–94, 19 of 86; and in 1994–95, 31 of 151. Clearly the Legco had become more assertive in making its own decisions apart from the executive branch (Leung and Law 1997:22).

Even though the Legco was more powerful than before, there were still considerable limitations on its power (Miners 1994a). The Legco's constitutional powers were largely negative ones. The Legco could reject government legislation, refuse to authorize any government expenditure, and repeal existing legislation, but it could not force the government to introduce new policies or spend money if the government did not want to do so. In addition, the Legco was weakened by the government's power to deny it the information it needed to criticize policies effectively and monitor government operations (Miners 1994b:6). Policy secretaries could refuse to answer questions on the grounds that the matter concerned security, that it was under discussion with China, or that it involved commercially sensitive information.

Deepening the Beijing-Business Alliance

Economic Integration Intensifies

In the early 1990s, Hong Kong manufacturers continued to relocate their businesses across the border to Guangdong Province. It was estimated that as many as five million people in the Pearl River Delta were employed in factories controlled by Hong Kong interests. As a result, the manufacturing sector's contribution to Hong Kong's GDP continued to fall while that of the service sector continued to increase. In 1993 manufacturing's share of Hong Kong's workforce was only 17.7 percent, while services accounted for 60 percent (Hong Kong Government 1994a:2).

What was new in the early 1990s was a wave of infrastructure and real estate investment from Hong Kong's big businesspeople in mainland China. Weakened by the Tiananmen incident, Beijing was desperate to boost its economy with Hong Kong investments. Beijing was willing to open up the land market and sign contracts for numerous large-scale infrastructure projects with Hong Kong companies (So 1995b).

Therefore, many big businesspeople began to shift their investment strategy from globalization to mainland investment. Li Ka-shing's Hutch-inson-Whampao, for example, acquired a 50 percent stake in the Shanghai Port Authority, a 35 percent stake in the Guangzhou–Zhuhai Superhigh-way, and a project to build the container terminal in the Pudong area of Shanghai and Hainan Island. Cheng Yu-tung's New World Development entered into joint ventures with China to build hotels, golf courses, and an expressway in Guangzhou (Sum 1995). Even some old British hongs were tempted to follow their Chinese counterparts and invest in China. Swire reopened its Shanghai office (closed since 1949), said it would invest in a container port in Shekou, and built Coca-Cola bottling plants in China; China Light and Power negotiated an ambitious power-generation deal in Shandong (*FEER*, Oct. 7, 1993:87; Jan. 6, 1994:44–45). As many as 176 com-panies listed on the Hong Kong stock exchange in the early 1990s were involved in more than 800 projects on the mainland. The projects involving the most money were infrastructure schemes and property developments (Burns 1994:61–62).

In addition, mainland China and Hong Kong were each other's biggest investors and trade partners. In the first six months of 1995, half of the colony's exports to China and three-quarters of its imports involved opera-tions of Hong Kong–run firms in China. Mainland companies, meanwhile, were conservatively estimated to account for 15 percent of Hong Kong's economy. By the late 1990s, mainland companies were expected to domi-nate the banking, transport, construction, tourism, and external trade sec-tors of Hong Kong. The Bank of China group, for example, controlled 23 percent of all bank deposits in the colony in 1994, second only to the 33 per-cent controlled by the Hong Kong & Shanghai Banking Corporation and its subsidiary Hang Seng Bank.

Observing a vibrant economic climate in Hong Kong, *Fortune* maga-zine in November 1994 named Hong Kong the world's top city for business, because the territory was at the vortex of an economic boom that would transform not only China but all of Asia, and indeed the world. At an international business conference held in Hong Kong in 1995, 97 percent of 150 corporate leaders surveyed believed the territory would remain a busi-ness powerhouse after the change-over, while 84 percent said they were optimistic about its future. Of 533 members of the American Chamber of Commerce in Hong Kong surveyed in September 1995, 91 percent said they were optimistic about the business environment over the next five years (*Asiaweek*, June 23, 1995:24; *FEER*, Dec. 7, 1995:72).

The Unholy Alliance Strengthens

The victory of the service professionals in 1991, Patten's welfare and electoral reforms, and the growing power of service professionals in the Legco
galvanized the big business sector. Elites of the Cooperative Research Center (CRC) whom Patten had removed from the Exco in 1992 formed a
political party to reposition themselves to represent business's interests.
Following London's lead in appropriating the democratic discourse, these
probusiness CRC members called their organization the Liberal Party. Its
aims were to promote political stability, enhance the investment environment, and ensure a smooth transfer of sovereignty in 1997 by working
with Beijing. The Liberal Party stressed the importance of educating Hong
Kongers about China so that better mutual understanding would be developed. The so-called Liberals wanted to minimize democratic reforms, and
of course social welfare measures were anathema to them (Lo 1997:165–66).
Of all the political parties, the Liberals had the most resources. The party
collected over U.S.$1 million in donations in 1993. Their full-time staff was
twice the size of the United Democrats'. Many members of their staff were
experts in elections, hired in Great Britain. However, the Liberal Party was
not highly organized. Although it had close to 1,500 members, they frequently quit the party when controversies arose. Needless to say, the Liberal Party had little support among the grassroots population because of its
probusiness platform (Mainland Affairs Committee 1995:62, 81–82). The
Liberal Party would not win many directly elected seats in the geographical constituencies, but it was still powerful in the functional constituencies,
which had narrower electoral bases.

Since December 1992 the Liberal Party reversed its earlier support of
the colonial regime and acted like an opposition party, criticizing Patten's
democratic reforms, attacking government policies, and voting against
them in order to build up an image to rival that of the prodemocracy service professionals (Miners 1994a).

The assault by Patten and the Democratic Party on the business community pushed big business to the side of Beijing (*Asiaweek*, Dec. 7, 1994:28).
For many businesspeople, that meant becoming advisers to Beijing on
Hong Kong affairs or members of the influential Preliminary Working
Committee (PWC). Top business figures, such as the industrialist T. K. Ann,
the tycoons Henry Fok and Li Ka-shing, and the banker David Li, were
recruited to the PWC. Thus the committee and the ranks of Hong Kong Affairs Advisers provided critical institutional links for the unholy alliance.

Aside from high-power committee appointments, Beijing also applied the carrot-and-stick approach to enlist the support of Hong Kong Chinese capitalists (deLisle and Lane 1997:57). Businesspeople understood that Beijing would reward its supporters and punish its opponents. The award of government contracts for lucrative infrastructure projects to established friends of Beijing was one of the carrots; Xinhua's virulent attack on Jardine & Matheson for its support of Patten's electoral reforms was one of the sticks.

Many businesspeople sought to legitimize their pro-Beijing stand on the grounds of patriotism. As David Chu, the director of Wah Tak Fung Development, explained: "I label myself as pro-China, but my definition is not that simple. My explanation is that I am a Chinese who wants to help China and Hong Kong, which will be a part of China as well. I do my best to help China to develop into a greater state. I want to make China better" (quoted in Lo and McMillen 1995:111). For David Chu, Hong Kong must have a good working relationship with China regardless of the type of regime in power. Many businesspeople remarked that Beijing was willing to listen to local views, especially on fiscal and monetary matters (*FEER*, Dec. 7, 1995:74). Because of their relations with Beijing, businesspeople were highly confident of Hong Kong's future. "You may say I am extremely optimistic," Chu said. "I fully expect things to be better after 1997. I expect Chinese people will be able to rule Hong Kong even better when the British have left. . . . When Hong Kong is ruled by Hong Kong people, we'll be so proud" (quoted in Dimbleby 1997:294).

Even the General Chamber of Commerce shifted its allegiance to Beijing. In 1994 it ousted the prodemocracy legislator Jimmy McGregor from its board. For the first time it joined other business associations in celebrating Chinese National Day on October 1, 1995. Swire Pacific was willing to sell part of its ownership of the lucrative Cathay Pacific Airlines to two Chinese firms at a huge discount in order to develop a good relationship with Beijing (Huang 1997:105). Brian Hook (1997:565) remarks, "Many of the hongs took a pragmatic line because they were aware that the restoration of sovereignty to China was not confined to matters of government but had economic dimensions too." As 1997 approached, many former pro-British businesspeople explicitly declared their loyalty to Beijing and were rewarded by important positions in the post-1997 government. By the mid-1990s, Hong Kong big business's unholy alliance with Beijing had displaced its traditional expatriate alliance with London (*FEER*, Dec. 7, 1995:73; A. Cheung 1997:730).

The Growing Conflict between Patten and Big Business

Feeling their power now that they had a party as well as an alliance with Beijing, big business began to criticize Patten's democratic reforms in public. Miners (1996:254) remarks that almost all big businesspeople, both European and Chinese, voiced their opposition to Patten's reforms. Vincent Lo, president of the Business and Professionals Federation (BPF) — a think tank and pressure group of 150 invited business members — confided that most of its members were "expressing grave concern about [Patten's] proposals and what they would do to Hong Kong" (quoted in Dimbleby 1997:136). They lamented that Patten's ambitious social program would sap Hong Kong's "spirit of diligence" and turn it into a "welfare society." They feared Patten would increase government spending and raise taxes — dark clouds that could spoil the territory's favorable business climate. Echoing their concerns, Beijing officials criticized the increase in welfare spending as "runaway welfarism"; the Patten regime was "driving recklessly toward a fatal crash" (M. Chan 1997:577).

The pro-Beijing forces saw Patten's electoral proposals as seriously undermining Hong Kong's stability and prosperity. His democracy-widening efforts would ensure that the Legco elected in 1995 would be dominated by populist, pro-grassroots politicians (*Asiaweek*, Dec. 7, 1994: 22–26).

Big business was worried, too, about Patten's confrontational approach to Beijing. The BPF issued a statement in favor of "convergence" with the Basic Law: "Democracy is important, but it is not the only goal. A smooth transition is more important. . . . The BPF strongly believes a smooth transition in 1997 and convergence with the Basic Law is in the best interest of the territory. Our future lies in a sound working relationship with China" (*SCMP,* Nov. 22, 1992:1; Dimbleby 1997:158). One business leader commented that Patten's "constitutional package is a plan which may be beautiful to some people but lacks structure, the structure being the Basic Law, which is to become effective after 1997" (*Hong Kong Standard,* Dec. 2, 1992:3). Thus businesspeople asked Patten to overhaul or even withdraw the democratic reforms to avoid further confrontation with Beijing.

In early 1996, the rivalry between Governor Patten and the business community finally became public. In answer to a query in *Newsweek,* "What motivates the rich people to do Beijing's bidding?" Patten posed his own question: "Why is it that privileged people sign up to arrangements whose sole intention is to choke off the voice of those who by every measure represent the majority of public opinion? Well, I'll say this: they wouldn't be doing it if most of them didn't have foreign passports in their back pockets" (quoted in Dimbleby 1997:356). In response, Nellie Fong, a Hong Kong executive, drafted a letter denouncing Patten for the leaders of the seven chambers of commerce to send to the Prime Minister in London. The letter stopped short of demanding Patten's recall, but expressed profound disappointment at the remarks quoted in *Newsweek*. The business community declared that Patten "has, through his unjustified attacks on the business community, ended up doing Hong Kong a great disservice" (Dimbleby 1997:357). Sonny Lo (1996:169) notes that the businesspeople who had been nurtured, promoted, and protected by the British colonialists up to the mid-1980s turned out to be the most critical opponents of Governor Patten's electoral reforms.

The Electoral Struggles of 1994–1995

Economic Blues in Hong Kong

Despite the growing economic power of the businesspeople and their confidence in the future of the territory, Hong Kong society experienced unemployment, inflation, and soaring housing prices as a result of industrial restructuring and an overheated economy. First, an estimated 600,000 jobs dropped out of the manufacturing sector since the relocation of Hong Kong's industry to the mainland in the 1980s (Ngo and Lau 1996:275). In 1995, Hong Kong's unemployment rate was officially 3.5 percent, its highest in a decade, but survey findings of the Hong Kong Federation of Trade Unions showed that the unemployment rate in the third quarter of 1995 stood at 13 percent, almost four times the official figure (Chiu 1996:437). As manufacturing jobs were relocated across the border to South China and Hong Kong became a service economy, it was not unusual for workers to go to work in the morning and find the premises empty and the management flown (M. Chan 1995:52). It was difficult for displaced industrial workers to get work in the service sector because the requirements were so different. As a result, a growing reserve of industrial workers were trapped in part-time or secondary work, or with none at all. Many workers, after months of searching, were forced to accept considerably lower wages than they had made before (Cheng 1997:xxxix; Ngo and Lau 1996:262–63). The number of people on welfare rose above 110,000 in 1995 from 83,000 in mid-1993. With inflation running more than 9 percent in 1995, the working poor were getting desperate. Demonstrations were held daily outside government offices, and local protests grew more fierce. In November 1995, when some thousand residents protested against their flooded, rodent-infested living quarters, one threw a dead rat toward Governor Patten as he inspected the site (Chai 1993:129; *FEER,* Nov. 9, 1995:36).

Second, despite the increasing economic integration of Hong Kong and mainland China, their financial integration hardly progressed. Using the colony as their base, Hong Kong businesses in China built up not only a large trade surplus but also massive holdings of Hong Kong dollars. In 1992, these overseas holdings totaled some U.S.$807.7 million, or more than the Hong Kong banking system's entire demand deposit base. These Hong Kong dollars were repatriated to Hong Kong through the interbank market, but the local financial institutions were either unable or unwilling to lend them back to China. Instead, lending remained overwhelmingly concentrated on Hong Kong–based assets, notably mortgage lending. As a result, the housing market became so overheated that the prices of small flats rose some 30 percent in both 1992 and 1993. The high cost of private housing turned many service professionals into a "sandwich" middle class: they earned too much to be eligible for public housing but too little to be able to purchase private housing (*FEER Yearbook* 1993; Economist Intelligence Unit 1994; Chai 1993:139).

Third, workers from mainland China, the Philippines, India, and Pakistan poured into Hong Kong. A foreign construction worker could be hired for $19 a day, whereas a Hong Konger commanded $45 (*Asiaweek,* Oct. 20, 1995:44). The Hong Kong government's decision, under pressure from big business, to import laborers (most of them from Guangdong Province) was vocally opposed by the labor unions, which were well aware that imported labor would further depress employment opportunities for local workers, lower wages, and strain the already inadequate housing supply (Chan 1995:52).

At the same time, many highly educated people returned to Hong Kong after securing residency in Australia, Canada, and the United States. In the early 1990s, not only had emigration of service professionals fallen, but 20 percent of those who emigrated in the 1980s now returned (*FEER,* Mar. 31 and May 12, 1994). After securing foreign passports, the returning service professionals were not intimidated by Beijing. They gave new impetus to the democracy movement in Hong Kong (Skeldon 1990–91:513).

The 1994 District Board Elections

Nearly 700,000 voters turned up in the September District Board elections. The turnout rate was 33.1 percent, up six-tenths of a percentage point over the last District Board election, in 1991 (Liang 1994).

Although Beijing repeatedly said that all three tiers of government would be dismantled in 1997, it still encouraged its supporters to participate in the 1994 and 1995 elections. The declared aim was to "accumulate experience" with an eye to the post-1997 future (Pepper 1997:698).

Political parties actively participated in the 1994 District Board elections because they regarded them as a warm-up exercise for the Legco election in 1995. A record 757 candidates entered into competition for 346 District Board seats. The major political groups fielded nearly half of the candidates: the Democratic Party nominated 133, the ADPL 40, the pro-China Democratic Alliance for the Betterment of Hong Kong (DABHK) 83, and the pro-business Liberal Party 88. But no party sought to field enough candidates to capture the majority of seats on all eighteen District Boards (Liang 1994).

The Democratic Party won 75 seats (a success rate of 56%), the ADPL 29 (a success rate of 73%), the DABHK 37 (a success rate of 45%), and the Liberal Party only 18 (a success rate of 20%). Over half of the seats were occupied by nonaligned candidates (Li 1995).

The election results showed that political parties did not take full advantage of the abolition of appointed seats on the District Boards because the constituencies were small and potential candidates few. Clearly the so-called Liberals had little grassroots support in local elections (Li 1995). That may explain why businesspeople strongly opposed democratic reforms and tried to slow the pace of democratization. According to *Asiaweek* (Dec. 7, 1994:28), "for many businesspeople, 1997 cannot come soon enough. After the hand-over, they will only need to deal with China. With their strong ties to Beijing, they find that a relief."

The 1995 Legco Elections

Of the sixty Legislative Council members in the 1991–95 term, three were Officials, eighteen were appointed by the Governor, twenty-one were elected by functional constituencies, and eighteen were elected by geographical constituencies. In 1995, however, the appointment system in the Legco came to an end. Both the Official and the appointed seats were abolished. As a result, of the sixty Legco members, thirty were to be elected by functional constituencies, twenty by geographical constituencies, and ten by an Election Committee composed of directly elected District Board members. This was to be the first ever fully elected legislature in Hong Kong (Kuan 1996:1; Lo Chi-kin 1995).

Despite its objections to Patten's reforms, Beijing saw fit to field candidates. It did not want prodemocracy parties to sweep into power unchallenged, enact laws that could undermine Hong Kong's traditional probusiness policies, and even establish political rights that could be used to agitate against Beijing. Beijing backed the DABHK with money and votes. The Bank of China and other PRC state corporations in Hong Kong provided economic resources, and the pro-Beijing Hong Kong Federation of Trade Unions (HKFTU) mobilized the grassroots constituency.

Two issues stood out in 1995. First was autonomy. The Democratic Party invoked the Hong Konger identity and the anti-Beijing sentiment. It presented itself as a Hong Kong party determined to safeguard Hong Kong's interests against Beijing's intrusion. It argued that more popularly elected members in a stronger Legco were the best guarantees of Hong Kong's autonomy after 1997. However, as memories of Tiananmen had faded by 1995, the Democrats' anti-Beijing line may have been less attractive to the voters than it had been in 1991. On the other hand, the DABHK argued that dialogue rather than confrontation would best promote Hong Kong's interests. The DABHK campaigned as the party best able to defend Hong Kong's interests because of its ability to work with Beijing. The DABHK's slogan was "Love Hong Kong, love China." Beijing's supporters argued that if more of them won, Beijing might even be prepared to leave the legislature alone after 1997 (*FEER*, Sept. 14, 1995:26–27).

Second came the bread-and-butter issues: unemployment, the importation of labor, inadequate social security and welfare, and dilapidated public housing. With the unemployment rate rising and the property market in the doldrums in 1995, the service professionals' welfare agenda was highly appealing to the grassroots population. According to a survey of Legco candidates conducted by the University of Hong Kong, the Democratic candidates received a rating of 7 (10 represented the highest degree of support) on commitment to a welfare society, while the probusiness Liberal candidates registered 1.75 (Lam 1995). Businesspeople criticized the Democratic Party for raising expectations to levels that might harm Hong Kong's free-market spirit. Yet the DABHK sought to appeal to the electorate on the same issues (*FEER*, Apr. 20, 1995:29).

Eighteen candidates were vying for ten seats on the Election Committee; sixty-one candidates competed for twenty-one functional constituency seats (nine seats were uncontested); and fifty candidates were running in twenty single-member election districts in the geographical constituency (Kuan 1996:2). As Scott (1996:16) remarks, the campaign generally was rather bloodless. The positions of the major candidates were well known, and election regulations kept spirited campaigners in check. Despite Beijing's repeated warning that the winners would be out as soon as the British left, 920,567 people (35.8 percent of eligible voters) turned out to vote in the Legco election (*FEER*, Sept. 28, 1995:16).

The prodemocracy forces again swept the directly elected seats. The Democratic Party took nineteen seats out of a total of sixty. Its chairperson, Martin Lee, collected 80 percent of the votes in his constituency, the highest for any candidate. Scott (1996:21) argues that the Democratic Party won because it represented the voters on both the anxiety about Beijing's intentions and welfare and livelihood issues. Similarly, Li (1996) suggests that voters who were pro–Hong Kong and favored a collective mode of consumption voted for the democrats. However, Joseph Cheng (1996) remarks that Hong Kong people voted for the candidates in the prodemocracy camp, not in the expectation that it would capture the government, but rather that it would achieve some degree of checks and balances. With support from like-minded independents, the Democratic Party could probably put together up to thirty votes in the sixty-seat Legco. The victory of the Democratic Party in the Legco election would make Beijing feel more insecure and thus more determined to disband the Legco in 1997 (*Asiaweek*, Sept. 29, 1995:34; *FEER*, Nov. 9, 1995:36).

The pro-Beijing DABHK picked up six seats, mainly in the small functional constituencies representing occupational groups and from the Election Committee. Among its well-known leaders, only Chan Yuen-han was directly elected. Tsang Yok-sing, Tam Yiu-chung, and Cheng Kai-nam ran fairly close to their Democratic opponents but lost in the end (*FEER*, Sept. 28, 1995:16–17; S. H. Lo 1997:210).

Despite its dismaying showing in direct elections, business's Liberal Party still managed to secure ten seats in the Legco through mostly indirect elections in functional constituencies and the Election Committee (Kuan 1996:3). With the support of pro-Beijing forces and other "independents" in the Legco, businesspeople could muster enough votes to block any radical proposal of the service professionals.

Results in the geographical constituency's election revealed the emergence of a populist alliance between prodemocracy forces and the grassroots population. The democratic faction attracted 739,412 votes, or 63.7 percent of the votes. The pro-China faction received only 299,996 votes, or 32.9 percent. The conservative business faction received 15,216 votes, or 1.7 percent. As Lam (1995) remarks, these figures show that the grassroots population supported the democratic faction, which advocated a faster pace of democratization, genuine autonomy, and better social welfare under a capitalist economy.

Obviously, Beijing was not happy with the growing power of the democrats in the Legco. The New China News Agency in Hong Kong declared that the election outcome was unfair and unreasonable. Premier Li Peng announced that Beijing would not recognize any political structure that violated the Joint Declaration and the Basic Law. The Hong Kong and Macao Affairs Office confirmed that Beijing's decision to disband the Legco on June 30, 1997, was firm; it would not be changed by the election results (Dimbleby 1997:304).

Political Realignment in 1995–1996

London Shifts Position Again

Curiously, the passage of Patten's proposals in the Legco in June 1994 signaled a new phase of the Beijing-London relationship. The tense and confrontational relationship gradually faded away, and the two governments were again on speaking terms on transitional matters (Cheng 1995).

In July 1994, just a month after Patten's reform victory, the Sino-British Joint Liaison Group quickly produced agreements on the financial package for the new airport and the disposal of military lands. The group also made progress on some of the two hundred–odd unchanged laws to reflect the shift of status from Britain's colony to China's SAR (DeGolyer 1994).

In mid-May 1995, Michael Heseltine, president of the Board of Trade, put together a team of prominent British industrialists for a high-profile trade mission to China. Foreign Secretary Douglas Hurd commented, "This year saw the largest trade mission to China yet — more than a hundred representatives of more than seventy companies. Our exports [to China] shot up during 1993 by 72 percent. The trend is continuing this year. We are the largest European investors in China, with almost US$2 billion worth of new British investment in China in 1993 alone" (Hurd 1996:58). Hurd further remarked that "Michael [Heseltine] sees this immense market growing at a huge rate. He sees the Germans and the French powering in there with huge delegations, and he wants to do the same" (quoted in Dimbleby 1997:278). The showpiece of the trade mission was a meeting between Heseltine and Li Peng. Both Beijing and London viewed the mission as an important landmark in the process of a gradual restoration of good relations between the two nations. After the mission returned, Heseltine asserted that British trade with China should take precedence over Patten's reform politics. To avoid severely damaging this relationship in the months ahead, Heseltine claimed, Patten had to be prevented from causing yet another showdown with Beijing over the issue of the appeals court (Dimbleby 1997:281).

As a result, in June 1995, Beijing and London finally agreed on terms for setting up a Court of Final Appeal in the territory to replace Britain's Privy Council as the highest judiciary authority for Hong Kong. Despite Governor Patten's repeated statement that the court had to be set up at least a year before the hand-over to build up experience and credibility, now London agreed that the court would not become operational until July 1, 1997, the first day of Chinese rule. London agreed to limit the court's jurisdiction, excluding ill-defined "acts of state" issues, such as national defense matters and foreign affairs. The court was to comprise four local judges and one overseas judge, a formula that London once had rejected on the ground that more overseas judges were needed to ensure an independent judiciary (*Asiaweek*, June 23, 1995:32; *FEER*, June 22, 1995:20). To Martin Lee (1996:240), "the Court of Final Appeal agreement represented a U-turn in British policy, with a reversion to appeasement and the line peddled by Sir Percy Cradock." Lee believed Patten "betrayed the Hong Kong people's trust in him. When he came, it was like a breath of fresh air. He effectively took over from us our banner for democracy . . . [now] I feel terrible" (quoted in Dimbleby 1997:288).

In October 1995, Foreign Minister Qian Qichen paid a visit to his new British counterpart, Malcolm Rifkind, and the two reached some agreement to smooth Hong Kong's transition to Chinese rule. Qian's London visit underlined the fact that any policy for Hong Kong would now be set in London and Beijing (Maxwell 1995). The two agreed on several key issues: London would establish a liaison office in Hong Kong to work with the SAR Preparatory Committee, a body Beijing set up in January 1996 to oversee the formation of the first post-1997 government of Hong Kong; informal meetings were to be held in Hong Kong between senior civil servants and Chinese officials on transition matters; and they would form a joint committee to plan a solemn, grand, and decent hand-over ceremony. Furthermore, when Qian brushed aside London's demand that the new Legco serve out a full four-year term, Rifkind did not press the issue (*Asiaweek*, Oct. 20, 1995:35).

When Beijing and London started to work directly together for the 1997 transition, Patten became marginalized. Percy Cradock remarked, "You now have the spectacle of the incredible shrinking governor." Patten's principal role now was to block the Democrats' efforts to pass laws that would breach Britain's treaty with Beijing and thus would anger China. In a policy address to the Legco in October, Patten threatened to use his veto power if he judged the government's legislative program to be jeopardized by private bills. His public approval rating fell below 50 percent for the first time since he took office in 1992 (*Asiaweek*, Oct. 20, 1995:35; *FEER*, Oct. 26, 1995:20).

What explains Beijing's shift of position? It may have resulted from a geopolitical shift in Beijing's diplomacy in mid-1995. Dismayed by Washington's decision to allow a "private" visit by Taipei's president to the United States and what seemed like escalating U.S. efforts to hem Beijing in, Beijing did not want at the same time to confront the British over a key issue such as Hong Kong. Or it may have been a pragmatic move. The changeover was too near to allow declining confidence to continue to hollow out Hong Kong. Cradock explained that the Chinese "don't want a chaotic transition, for their own interests" (quoted in Adams 1995:9). Furthermore, Hong Kong's businesspeople had been lobbying hard for Beijing's green light for various infrastructural projects straddling 1997, and the "second kitchen" policy was far from popular in Hong Kong (Cheng 1995).

What explains London's adoption of a relatively more cooperative policy toward Beijing? Doubt was growing in Britain as to the wisdom of Patten's pressing home the electoral reforms in the face of China's opposition. Brian Hook (1997:563) points out that doubt was pervasive in sections of the business community that feared their share of the China trade was jeopardized by a program that could not survive beyond 1997. On that point, Martin Lee remarked, the British had again sacrificed Hong Kong's political rights for their own commercial interests (*Asiaweek*, June 30, 1995:38). "To me," Martin Lee (1996:40) said, "there was no doubt this [Court of Final Appeal] agreement was related to the visit by the then British Minister of Trade, Michael Heseltine, to Beijing in the spring of that year. Mr. Heseltine signed numerous trade agreements between Britain and China, and a few days later there was an announcement on an agreement for the setting up of the Court of Final Appeal. To my mind, it was likely that, in return for the trade agreements, Britain had compromised and given China control over the arrangements for setting up the Court of Final Appeal." In addition, as Hong Kong's businesspeople openly complained about Patten's policy, London was under pressure to maintain cooperation with Beijing to safeguard Hong Kong's economic interests.

For Neville Maxwell (1995), the change of British foreign secretaries accentuated the governor's isolation. Douglas Hurd had backed Patten during the crisis over the Court of Final Appeal. Hurd's replacement by Malcolm Rifkind tilted the balance in the Foreign Office, which was always divided over the wisdom of Patten's challenges to Beijing. Cheng (1995) lamented that London felt under pressure when such allies as Australia and Canada were eager to expand trade with China.

Service Professionals Remain Defiant

Despite London's change of position, the service professionals still defied Beijing. In mid-1994, leading members of the Democratic Party vigorously attacked Frederick Fung of the ADPL for accepting an invitation to be Beijing's adviser on Hong Kong affairs. In May 1995, Christine Loh, an independent democrat, demanded in the Legco that Beijing be asked to clarify the Communist Party's future role in the territory. If the Party were to become more active, Loh warned, "it would make Hong Kong hostage to a distant Politburo, which still has only hazy ideas of how modern economies work" (*Asiaweek,* May 19, 1995:27). In June 1995, Martin Lee called the Court of Final Appeal agreement a "sellout" and a "joint Sino-British violation of the Joint Declaration" (*Asiaweek,* June 30, 1995:38). As a protest, the Democratic Party launched an unprecedented vote of no confidence against Governor Patten in the Legco in July 1995. But with the support of probusiness, pro-Beijing members, the Court of Final Appeal bill passed by a margin of nearly 2 to 1 (*FEER,* Aug. 10, 1995:26). In September 1995, after winning his election bid, Martin Lee said, "The elections are a mandate for democratic government in Hong Kong and real constitutional, legal and human-rights reforms to ensure basic freedoms after 1997." He would be using the twenty-one remaining months of British rule, he said, to pass laws buttressing freedom of the press and freedom of speech, and to implement policies to end the importation of labor and to set up a mandatory provident (retirement) fund for all Hong Kong employees (*Asiaweek,* Sept. 29, 1995:39). "This may well be our last-ditch effort to build enough democracy into Hong Kong's still undemocratic colonial legacy to preserve the rule of law, our way of life and Hong Kong's role at the heart of the Pacific Rim" (Lee 1995:6). In October 1995, after London and Beijing reached an accord, Lee complained that "Britain is prepared to betray the Hong Kong people in the interests of trade" (*FEER*, Oct. 19, 1995:17).

There were few signs of a rapprochement between the Democrats and Beijing in 1996. Members of the Democratic Party even joked that Martin Lee was sticking to a simple diet these days in preparation for being thrown in jail in 1997. Szeto Wah prepared to operate outside the system after 1997. Beijing, in its continuing efforts to undermine the Democrats, considered new voting rules to make it more difficult for them to prevail in the Legco. In addition, Beijing shut the Democrats out of all advisory bodies set up to prepare for Hong Kong's transition to Chinese rule (*FEER*, Apr. 20, 1995:28).

The Roots of Contested Democracy

In the late 1980s, as we have seen, London joined the conservative alliance of Beijing and big business. They agreed on a restricted, corporatist democracy that favored business interests and wrote this political model into the draft Basic Law. Then the Tiananmen incident tore the conservative alliance apart. In the early 1990s, London formally defected to the democracy camp.

Trying to craft a strategic alliance with the democracy camp, Governor Patten appointed a few prominent service professionals to the Legco and Exco, adopted pro-welfare policies, implemented administrative reforms, and proposed a controversial reform package to add more populist elements to the corporatist democracy model.

However, since the Basic Law was already promulgated and had received the blessing of Patten's predecessor, Patten's democratic reforms could not possibly go beyond the constitutional framework. So he simply reinterpreted the wording and gray areas of the Basic Law to fit his purposes. Patten redefined "functional constituency" in such a way that it would broaden the franchise from a few thousand corporate bodies to around 2.7 million people, and suggested that the victors in local elections elect the remaining ten members of the Legco.

How should Patten's democratic reforms be evaluated? On the one hand, they advanced the service professionals' democracy project. Patten's reforms helped elevate the United Democrats to a formal Democratic Party. His policy strengthened the Democrats' pro-welfare platform and consolidated their populist alliance with the grassroots population. A surge of public spending brought more teachers per pupil, more nurses and doctors, more hospital beds. There were thirteen new clinics, a new Comprehensive Social Security Assistance Scheme (the first in Hong Kong's history), a Disability Discrimination Ordinance, and more than five thousand "care and attention" beds for the elderly. Even the environment had been improved: pollution in the rivers of the New Territories was down by 70 percent; most cars now used catalytic converters and ran on unleaded petrol (Dimbleby 1997:365). Thanks to Patten's reforms, the Democrats controlled almost half of the Legco seats after 1995.

Many other things indicated that the democracy project had established itself in Hong Kong's civil society. First, Patten made the Hong Kong government more open and accountable. Thanks to the controversy over his proposals, the mass media devoted extensive coverage and commentary to political affairs. Surveys conducted by the Hong Kong Transitions Project in August 1993 and February 1994 showed that nearly 90 percent of Hong Kong people considered themselves informed about government policies that affected them (DeGolyer 1994).

Second, political participation through regular channels greatly expanded. As Michael DeGolyer (1994) remarks, at election time nearly every street in Hong Kong was festooned with signs, posters, banners, and placards. Every mailbox received more than one flyer, and thousands of store owners put up campaign posters, or allowed them to be put up. At least two political opinion surveys appeared every week. Voting had become a socially acceptable behavior.

Third, Patten's reform project further enhanced the prestige of the Democrats; the most popular legislative councilors were Martin Lee, Szeto Wah, Lau Chin-shek, and Emily Lau, and the Democratic Party was the most popular party, according to the polls (Chung 1994). In sum, by the mid-1990s, the traditional image of political apathy of Hong Kong Chinese who were only interested in economic well-being could no longer be an accurate description of the rising tide of heated debate and active participation in the democracy movement. The roots of democracy in Hong Kong thus had grown much deeper since the arrival of Governor Patten in 1992 (M. Chan 1996:20–21; Dimbleby 1997:350).

On the other hand, Patten's reforms promoted a contested democracy in Hong Kong. In response to his reforms, Beijing strengthened its unholy alliance with big business by appointing them as Hong Kong Advisers and to the Preliminary Working Committee. Arguing that the new electoral rules violated the Basic Law, Beijing seized on Patten's reforms as an excellent opportunity to purge democratic activists from the Legco. On June 30, 1997, popularly elected members of the Legco would be forced to step down; there would be no "through train" from 1995 to 1999. In December 1996 a new SAR Provisional Legislature, selected by Beijing appointees, would be in place to discard or amend laws protecting human rights and permitting peaceful demonstrations.

Had Patten's reforms not been proposed and carried out, Hong Kong would still have a restricted democracy. But perhaps it would have been a more stable restricted democracy, because all the political actors, including the service professional Democrats, were forced to accept, to a certain extent, the electoral rules of the Basic Law. In the absence of Patten's reforms, the Democrats would still have won landslide victories at the ballot box because of the populist alliance, though they would have remained a minority in the Legco for at least fifteen years after 1997 because of the structural limitations established by the Basic Law. Nevertheless, the political transition in 1997 might have been less turbulent without Patten's reforms.

However, by manipulating and reinterpreting the Basic Law, Patten had undermined its legitimacy. The Basic Law was not sacred anymore, and its electoral rules were now subject to negotiation. Furthermore, Patten's reforms created a group of Legco members who saw Beijing as usurping their rights, with a popular mandate to serve their terms from 1995 to 1999. As Emily Lau remarked: "We have been elected for four years. I don't see why we should be thrown out by the Chinese government in 1997" (*FEER,* Sept. 28, 1995:17). Naturally, these Legco members condemned the Provisional Legco as illegitimate and unconstitutional. Their body had not even been written into the Basic Law!

What made matters worse was that London suddenly shifted its position again in 1995 and tried to mend its differences with Beijing, backed away from its support for Patten's reforms, and no longer declared the Provisional Legco illegitimate (only unnecessary and unjustified), thus leaving service professionals to fight a lonely battle with Beijing.

In sum, as July 1, 1997 approached, Hong Kong society was divided into two big camps: the unholy alliance of Beijing and the big business and leftist organs in Hong Kong, and a populist alliance of service professionals and the grassroots population. Instead of focusing on winning elections and working within electoral rules, the two camps debated and reinterpreted the Basic Law, laying the foundation for a contested democracy in 1997.

8 | Hand-over Politics and Democratic Compromise in the Transition

> The Democratic Party has always been supportive of the Chinese resumption of Hong Kong's sovereignty and "one country, two systems." Although the Democratic Party has disagreed with some of the contents of the Basic Law, it has clearly stated that it accepts the legitimacy of the Basic Law. Although the Democratic Party has a different view toward the Beijing government, it always insists on using peaceful means to express its opinion and will not threaten social stability.　　　Lo Chi-kin, member of the Central Committee
>　　　　　　　　　　　of the Democratic Party (*Outspoken*, Aug. 1996:6)

> At a protest zone near the Convention Center where the handover ceremony was held in the evening of June 30, 1997, about 20 protesters shouted slogans such as "Down with [Premier] Li Peng, the Butcher of June 4th Slaughter." The protesters' chants were merely drowned out by Beethoven's Fifth Symphony from police loudspeakers on a flyover near the protest zones. No arrest took place.　　　　　　　　　　　　hknews@ahkcus.org, July 2, 1997

A Smooth Transition on July 1, 1997

In the early 1990s, Hong Kong seemed to be heading toward a contested democracy. The Basic Law was plagued by the Tiananmen incident and Patten's electoral reforms. Hong Kong society was divided into two camps: the prodemocracy camp of service professionals (which received the blessing of the colonial government and won the support of the grassroots population at the ballot box) and the antidemocracy camp of big businesspeople (which was strongly endorsed by Beijing and its Hong Kong supporters). Legislators popularly elected in 1995 were asked to step down as soon as Beijing resumed sovereignty on July 1, 1997. Hong Kong Democrats were determined to contest the Provisional Legislature in court. Some Democrats even threatened to chain themselves to pillars in the Legislative Council building on the night of June 30 to avoid being forced to resign. As Leung and Law (1997:18) remark, "Ideological and perhaps social cleavages were taking shape and mobilization either for or against government policies was frequent. Political instability seemed inevitable in the countdown to 1997 and beyond."

As the date of the hand-over drew near, the global mass media expected political confrontation on July 1, 1997. The U.S. media, in particular, tended to present a "Communist repression" scenario to interpret the 1997 transition. The emphasis of American journalists was that Hong Kong was a free, capitalist society that respected human rights and the rule of law. The Beijing government, however, was taken as an authoritarian Communist regime that would not hesitate to use force to repress dissent. The American mass media frequently invoked images of the bloodshed from the 1989 Tiananmen incident when they covered the 1997 event. In such a pessimistic interpretation, Hong Kong society would suffer after 1997. Beijing would impose its authoritarian rule over Hong Kong, as shown by Beijing's threat to purge the popularly elected legislature in Hong Kong right after the hand-over on July 1, 1997, by the effort of the Provisional Legco to restore the old colonial laws in order to suppress human rights in civil society, and by the worry that the Democratic Party might not be allowed to compete in post-1997 elections (Ching 1997b).

However, contrary to the U.S. mass media's expectation, the "Communist repression" scenario failed to materialize after the July 1, 1997, transition. A new election was to take place in mid-1998 to replace the Provisional Legislature; the Democratic Party was still allowed to participate in the post-1997 election; political protests still took place during and after the July 1, 1997 transition, some protesters even shouting, "Down with Li Peng!" (the Premier of the Chinese Communist Party).

To Ian Perkin (1997:227), the chief economist of the Hong Kong General Chamber of Commerce, the transition seemed to be a "time of celebration" for Hong Kong's business community. Hong Kong, with an average per capita income of U.S.$23,200, enjoyed a higher standard of living than Australia, Canada, and the United Kingdom. Even during the political storm between Governor Patten and Beijing in the early 1990s, Hong Kong's gross domestic product (GDP) had grown by almost 25 percent, exports by almost 66 percent, and investments by more than 40 percent. In mid-1997 the Hong Kong stock market soared to 16,000 points in July, compared with about 10,000 a year earlier. Property values skyrocketed; prices of private homes rose 78 percent from 1991 to 1995. The growth rate of the GDP picked up; budget surpluses were projected for 1997 and beyond; inflation was at a ten-year low. The capital flight and brain drain that had dominated the newspapers' front pages in the early 1990s had not materialized; in fact, the return flow of former emigrants expanded as 1997 approached. It was reported that for every hundred people who had left Hong Kong in 1995, sixty returned (Cheng 1997:xxxviii; Dimbleby 1997:366; Nyaw and Li 1996; Chiu and Lui forthcoming).

What explains the smooth transition on July 1, 1997? This chapter argues that a democratic compromise was achieved among Beijing, the Hong Kong SAR government, and service professional democrats. Just before the July 1 critical transition, these forces considerably moderated their stands toward the democracy project. They were willing to compromise and work out a commonly accepted deal toward democratization. In this respect, the crucial research questions are: Why did Beijing shift from a hard line to a moderate stand on Hong Kong's democracy? Why did service professional democrats not fight harder for their democracy project? Why did big business agree to accept the democratic compromise instead of pushing harder for their antidemocracy policies?

This chapter will first examine the battles between pro- and antidemocracy forces over the hand-over politics of setting up a Preparatory Committee, and of the election of the first Chief Executive and the Provisional Legislature of the SAR government. Then this chapter will explain why Beijing, the Democratic Party, and the first SAR government were willing to work out a democratic compromise during the July 1, 1997 transition.

Hand-over Politics

The Preparatory Committee

In January 1996 the 150-member SAR Preparatory Committee was set up to install a 400-member Selection Committee to produce the first SAR chief executive and a 60-member Provisional Legislative Council.

The formation of the Preparatory Committee signaled that the 1997 transition had reached its final, critical phase of hand-over politics from British to Chinese rule. Once the Preparatory Committee was formed, the agenda for the transition would be set principally by Beijing at the expense of London. Since Britain's cooperation had become a minor concern for Beijing, Beijing was free to make major decisions by itself (the *yi-wo-wei-zhu,* or "take myself as the master" strategy). Foreign Secretary Malcolm Rifkind, on a visit in January 1996, in effect warned the people of Hong Kong not to harbor any illusions about the final phase of the transition (Kuan 1997:52; Louie 1996:60).

Of the 94 Hong Kong appointees to the 150-member Preparatory Committee, more than 50 were big businesspeople. Collectively, they controlled twenty-one companies whose stocks were traded on Hong Kong's stock exchange and accounted for 36 percent of its capitalization. The pro-Beijing political groups were also strongly represented on the Preparatory Committee: the One Country, Two Systems Economic Research Institute held eight seats, the Democratic Alliance for the Betterment of Hong Kong (DABHK) four, the Hong Kong Progressive Alliance five, and the Liberal Democratic Federation five. Joseph Cheng (1997:xliii) comments that the Chinese authorities apparently wanted to cultivate a number of pro-Beijing groups and avoid dependence on any one of them. On the other hand, members of the Democratic Party were frozen out. Even the moderate Association for Democracy and People's Livelihood (ADPL) received only two seats (S. H. Lo 1997:212).

On March 24, 1996, a vote was taken on whether to set up a provisional legislature to replace the current Legco in July 1997. Only Frederick Fung, chair of the ADPL, cast a dissenting vote. Director Lu Ping was so angry that he said Fung would not be allowed to sit in the Provisional Legislature, nor would he be allowed to sit on the Selection Committee, whose job was to choose the members of the Provisional Legislature and the Chief Executive. Lu backtracked later, however: he had merely expressed his personal views, he said, not the view of the Beijing government (Ching 1996).

In April 1996, in an effort to gain support, the Preparatory Committee held a widely publicized "consultation," seeking suggestions on how to set up the Selection Committee. The consultation drew more than 1,400 people to a two-day session and an even larger number of written suggestions. Nevertheless, since all members of the Preparatory Committee had been appointed by Beijing, little support was forthcoming. An opinion poll in June 1996 revealed that 56 percent of the respondents had "no confidence" in the Preparatory Committee, 27 percent had "extremely low" confidence, and 12 percent had "low" confidence (*SCMP,* June 24, 1996).

The Selection Committee

In response, the Preparatory Committee launched a campaign to build a good image. Ching (1997a:36) describes its public relations blitz: full-page ads in both Chinese- and English-language newspapers called on the public to express their views, whatever they might be, to the Preparatory Committee offices in Hong Kong and Beijing. Its efforts generated as many as 5,833 candidates, among them elites from all sectors of the community, for the

400 seats on the Selection Committee. Many retired politicians and former senior government officials applied, apparently in an attempt to show their support for the Beijing government (J. Cheng 1997:xli; Kuan 1997:53).

As Cheng (1997:xli) laments, the Preparatory Committee maintained control throughout the election of members of the Selection Committee. They rejected the proposal that various interest groups nominate a number of candidates: people who wanted to join the Selection Committee had to compete as individuals; there was no need for anyone to be accountable to an organization. The Director's Panel had ample discretionary power in drawing up the final list of candidates to be voted on by the full committee. Five of the ten members of the Director's Panel were from the mainland and five from Hong Kong. The criteria for inclusion in the list of candidates were unclear and the selection process was conducted in secret. The Hong Kong directors themselves were eligible for nomination. Finally, the fifty-six mainland members of the Preparatory Committee could vote as a bloc, thus ensuring that their votes would be decisive (Johannes Chan 1996:38).

When the 400-member Selection Committee was set up by the Preparatory Committee on November 2, 1996, big business was again overwhelmingly represented. Despite a formal scheme to allocate seats to four constituencies—business, professional, grassroots, and political—businesspeople occupied more than half the total seats, and grassroots constituencies were heavily underrepresented. Selection Committee members included the real estate tycoons Li Ka-shing, Lee Shau-kee, and Walter Kwok, the gambling magnate Stanley Ho, the movie mogul Run Shaw, and the infrastructure developer Gordon Wu.

Kuan (1997:54) notes that loyalty to Beijing was again rewarded. The Hong Kong Progressive Alliance, a pro-Beijing business and professional group that had done poorly in the 1995 elections, got the largest number of seats (forty-seven) on the Selection Committee. The DABHK received forty-two seats, the Liberal Democratic Federation eight, and the Hong Kong Federation of Trade Unions sixteen (J. Cheng 1997:xliii).

Johannes Chan (1996:38) notes that many members of the Preparatory Committee who had nominated themselves were elected. Candidates for chief executive had declared their candidacies before the election of the Selection Committee. Those who drew up the lists of candidates for the Selection Committee may have borne in mind the people most likely to vote for the candidate they preferred for chief executive; thus the choice of chief executive may have already been determined before the election process.

The Chief Executive

As Foreign Minister Qian Qichen said at the first plenary session of the Selection Committee, the election of Hong Kong's chief executive by its people was unprecedented. During more than 150 years of British colonial rule no government had consulted the Hong Kong people on the appointment of any governor (C. Y. Cheung 1997:1).

As closed-door lobbying in the Selection Committee was supplemented by public campaigns, the election of the chief executive became a media event. Several candidates put forward their names for nomination. Each candidate needed to secure the support of fifty members of the Selection Committee. The contest turned out to be more competitive than many people expected.

When the business tycoon Peter Woo started the race in September 1996 with an American-style campaign, the other three contenders (the shipping magnate Tung Chee-hwa, outgoing Chief Justice Sir Yang Ti-liang, and retired Appeals Court Judge Simon Li) were forced to follow suit. All candidates visited social, political, and economic organizations, toured housing projects, markets, and even temporary housing areas, and of course gave interviews to the media and attended the Selection Committee's question-and-answer sessions, broadcast live, to explain their platforms. It would not be fair to say that the selection of the chief executive election lacked transparency (C. Y. Cheung 1997:4; Kuan 1997:54).

Whatever they may have thought about the candidates, however, the people of Hong Kong had no voting power. It was the 400-member Selection Committee that had the right to vote. The composition of the Selection Committee strongly favored candidates of a pro-Beijing business background. It was only natural that the committee picked Tung Chee-hwa as chief executive. On November 15 Tung secured 206 of the committee's 400 votes, former Chief Justice Yang Ti-liang 82, Peter Woo 52, and Judge Simon Li only 43. Since the rules called for each candidate to secure nominations from 50 members of the Selection Committee to stay in the race, Judge Li was disqualified. Judging by the nomination votes, the election of the first chief executive was already a foregone conclusion on November 15. Election day, December 11, 1996, was an anticlimax: 320 members of the Selection Committee voted for Tung, 42 votes went to Yang, and 36 to Woo (C. Y. Cheung 1997:4).

In Kuan's (1997:54) account, Tung was born in Shanghai in 1937. After six years in England, he spent a decade in the United States, where he worked mostly for his father's shipping company. Tung finally inherited the shipping empire in 1982, when shipping was in a global slump. His debt-ridden business was bailed out in 1986 with Chinese money. Beijing appointed Tung a Hong Kong Adviser in 1992 and Patten made him a member of the Executive Council the same year. In January 1996, Tung was named vice chairman of the Preparatory Committee and singled out for a handshake by President Jiang Zemin at a reception. Despite his public offices and Beijing's endorsement, Tung remained little known to the public until the campaigns in late 1996. Tung seemed to promote the Singapore model: he extolled Confucian virtues, promised special attention to such issues as housing, advocated a greater role for government in economic development, and expressed conservative views on contentious issues such as restoring the old colonial laws on civil protests (hknews@ahkcus.org, July 2, 1997).

The Provisional Legislature

The Selection Committee also chose a pro-Beijing, business-oriented Provisional Legco to replace the current elected Legco. The selection was highly controversial: fully 70 percent of the 130 candidates and 85 percent of those eventually selected were themselves members of the Selection Committee. This suggests that the Selection Committee selected its own members to serve on the Provisional Legco. Ten of the committee members who claimed Legco seats had lost on pro-Beijing tickets in the popular elections of 1995.

The election of the Provisional Legco in 1997 therefore lacked legitimacy. Although thirty-three of the thirty-four Legco members who had nominated themselves were selected, C. Y. Cheung (1997:2) notes that the old Legco members had received more than 1.38 million popular votes in 1995, when a record 920,000 people voted in the twenty directly elected geographical constituencies. However, the members of the Provisional Legislature were elected by the 400 appointed members of the Selection Committee. In addition, twenty-six prodemocracy Legco members elected in 1995 refused to participate in or recognize the legitimacy of the Provisional Legco. Thus the Provisional Legco can be seen as a major retrogression in the democratic development of Hong Kong.

In sum, the 1996 elections epitomized "democratic elections with Chinese characteristics." Commentators noted that they bore a close resemblance to elections across the border. Instead of a step toward open elections with mass participation, the 1996 elections were characterized by controlled candidacy, limited voting rights, a fixed candidate-seat ratio, and procedures hidden from public view (J. Chan 1996: 39; Louie 1996:64).

The Executive Council

Tung appointed eleven ex officio members to serve on the Executive Council of the first SAR government in late January 1997. Sir Chung Sze-yuen, a veteran former senior adviser to colonial governors, was appointed convener of the Executive Council. Two members of Patten's Executive Council — Rosanna Wong (chief of the Housing Authority) and Raymond Chien (representing business) — would straddle the July 1 transition.

Also included in the Executive Council were former Chief Justice Yang Ti-liang; the head of the Better Hong Kong Foundation, Nellie Fong; and the vice chair of Beijing's Federation of Trade Unions, Tam Yiu-chung. In fact, most members of the Exco were prominent businesspeople who sat on Beijing-appointed panels and committees responsible for the hand-over.

No one in the democratic camp was included in Tung's Exco (hknews@ahkcus.org, Jan. 27, 1997). The Democrats commented that Tung's Exco consisted solely of conservative businesspeople and "old colonial batteries" (people who used to serve in the former colonial administration). The Exco was just a continuation of old colonial rule. The public thus could hardly expect this team to strive for human rights and freedom (hknews@ahkcus.org, Jan. 27, 1997). By an odd twist, the appointment of many former colonial elites to Tung's Exco infuriated some traditional pro-Beijing elites. Dorothy Liu Yiu-chu, for instance, criticized Beijing for "wrongly co-opting 'opportunistic patriots,' thus undermining united front work" (Wong 1997:124).

The Democrats' Offensive

The Democrats were not pleased by the political developments before the hand-over. They waged public protests, engaged in foreign lobbying, challenged the Provisional Legco in court, and tried to push through pro-welfare and prolabor measures in the Legco.

Public Protests

On December 11, 1996, prodemocracy activists scuffled with riot police outside the Hong Kong Convention Centre, where the Selection Committee had voted for a chief executive to rule Hong Kong after 1997. The prodemocracy activists—Emily Lau, Andrew Cheng, and Lee Cheuk-yan, all Legco members—erected a "tomb of democracy" outside the building and shouted, "Oppose the phony election!" When police arrived, they lay down in the road and were dragged away. The police detained them for more than four hours (hknews@ahkcus.org, Dec. 11 and 14, 1996).

On December 16, 1996, the Democratic Party said it would burn all 114,589 signatures it had gathered in support of Szeto Wah's campaign as unofficial candidate for chief executive. The party boasted that while the chief executive of the first post-1997 government was selected by only 400 members of a committee appointed by Beijing, Szeto Wah had been chosen by 114,589 people in Hong Kong. The signatures had to be burned to ease the public's fear of retaliation after the hand-over (hknews@ahkcus.org, Dec. 16, 1996).

On December 20, members of the Democratic Party chanted, "Oppose the Provisional Legislature, oppose the rubber stamp!" outside the local branch of the Xinhua News Agency. The Provisional Legislature, they claimed, was illegal and unconstitutional—it was not even mentioned in the Basic Law (hknews@ahkcus.org, Dec. 20 and 22, 1996).

On January 20, 1997, a legal panel of the SAR Preparatory Committee decided to repeal or amend twenty-five laws protecting human rights and permitting peaceful demonstrations. Prodemocracy groups described the Preparatory Committee's move as a blow to democracy that would dent international confidence in post-1997 Hong Kong (hknews@ahkcus.org, Jan. 20, 1997).

Despite their protests, the democratic forces were increasingly sidelined. Their protests did not receive the public support they expected because the Preparatory Committee's elections of the chief executive and the Provisional Legislature stole the media's attention (Kuan 1997:52).

On April 20, a Sunday, more than a thousand Hong Kongers took to the streets to protest the curbs on civil liberties that the SAR planned to enforce after the hand-over. If Tung's plans went ahead, after July 1 local political groups would be barred from accepting foreign donations, and they would have to secure permission from the police before they could hold a demonstration. Until then, they had only to notify the police of their intentions. Tung, who launched the plans in early April, invited the public to submit comments by the end of the month, but protesters called the "consultation" a sham. Brandishing red and green banners, protesters chanted, "No to fake consultation" as they marched from Victoria Park to the Central business district. The march was organized by the Hong Kong People's Alliance for Human Rights, comprising thirty local nongovernmental organizations (hknews@ahkcus.org, Apr. 21, 1997).

On June 1 the Hong Kong Alliance in Support of the Patriotic Democratic Movement organized a demonstration to commemorate the deaths of the students in the Tiananmen incident of June 4, 1989. The Alliance estimated that seven thousand people joined in the demonstration. The protesters carried placards in the funeral colors of black and white, and shouted demands that the Chinese government reassess its verdict on the June 4 incident. Others held up signs calling for the release of the Chinese dissidents Wang Dan and Wei Jingsheng. A mock coffin bore a painted message: "The dictatorship of butchers will leave a stink that will last ten thousand years." The Alliance vowed to continue to hold annual candlelight vigils at Victoria Park after the hand-over (forum@ahkcus.org, June 3, 1997; H-ASIA@h-net.msu.edu, June 2, 1997).

Foreign Lobbies

Due to the globalization of Hong Kong's economy and emigrant population, there was also a globalization of Hong Kong politics during the 1997 transition. Martin Lee went to Europe in February 1997 to express concern that China was set to roll back Hong Kong's freedom after the hand-over. Lee urged the European Union to oppose Beijing's plan to dilute Hong Kong's human rights laws and dismantle its elected legislature (hknews@ahkcus.org, Feb. 13, 1997).

In April Martin Lee and other Democrats conducted a fund-raising campaign in the United States and collected over U.S.$500,000 from Hong Kong's emigrant communities. In Washington, Lee received a human rights award and spoke with President Bill Clinton and Vice President Al Gore. The Clinton administration expressed concern over the deterioration of human rights in Hong Kong, and Secretary of State Madeleine Albright assured Lee of "strong U.S. support for continued full political and civil rights and the way of life of the people of Hong Kong" (hknews@ahkcus.org, Apr. 21, 1997).

In response, Beijing predictably accused Lee of trying to incite international meddling in Hong Kong's affairs. Shen Guofang, speaking for the Foreign Ministry, said that Martin Lee "depends on foreigners to interfere in Hong Kong issues and indulges in spreading rumors and lies to try to blacken Hong Kong" (hknews@ahkcus.org, Apr. 15, 1997).

Chief Executive Tung Chee-hwa, too, accused Lee of badmouthing Hong Kong. "Is there any need to go abroad to blacken Hong Kong's name? Is there any need for foreigners to come to Hong Kong to tell us, the Hong Kong people, what to do in the future? Why can't we be the master of our own destiny and fate?" (hknews@ahkcus.org, Feb. 13, 1997). Tung proposed a law that would ban overseas contributions to political parties, and he invoked the Basic Law's clause prohibiting political activities by foreign or international political organizations and barring local political groups from establishing links with such groups.

Since Martin Lee's patriotism was already under hostile scrutiny, it seemed doubtful that he would be allowed to play any public role in Hong Kong after the hand-over. There was the fear that Tung might even use his executive authority to exclude the Democrats from any electoral process that China might put in place in Hong Kong (Dimbleby 1997:404).

Court Challenges to the Provisional Legislature

The decision to establish a provisional legislature met with strong opposition from the democratic forces. Beijing's rationale was that because Governor Patten's democratic reforms in 1992 violated agreements between China and Britain, the Legco "through train" had been derailed. If a legal vacuum in the SAR government was to be avoided, a provisional legislature was required before the first SAR Legco was set up after the hand-over. Beijing further argued that the National People's Congress's decision in April 1990 that the Preparatory Committee "shall be responsible for preparing the establishment of the Region" provided the legal basis for the formation of the Provisional Legco, for it implied that if necessary the Preparatory Committee could set up a provisional legislature to assist in the establishment of the HKSAR (C. Y. Cheung 1997:2).

The Bar Association, however, argued that no matter what the Provisional Legislature was called, it was in essence still the first legislature of the SAR, and should be constituted according to the relevant articles in the Basic Law and the 1990 NPC decision. Both of these documents specified that the first Legco would be composed of sixty members, twenty chosen by geographical constituencies in direct elections, ten by an election committee, and thirty by functional constituencies. The absence of a through train could not justify the composition and formation of the first Legislative Council in a manner different from that prescribed in the 1990 NPC decision. The legality of the Provisional Legislature must be grounded in the relevant statutory documents, not on the basis of political expediency. In addition, doubts about the legality of the Provisional Legislature and the validity of any actions it took would diminish confidence in the legal system of Hong Kong as a whole. In these circumstances, any laws that the Provisional Legislature adopted would be open to challenge in the courts, and its very existence posed a threat to stability (M. Chan 1996:6; C. Y. Cheung 1997:3; C. K. Lo 1996; Conner 1997).

Echoing the concerns of the Bar Association, the Democrats argued that because the Provisional Legislature had no constitutional rationale, it was an unlawful body. Nowhere in the Basic Law could a constitutional basis for a provisional legislature be found. So in June the Democratic Party launched a challenge to the Provisional Legislature in court. The suit was dismissed, however. The courts, ruled Judge Raymond Sears, could not be used to settle political battles. The Provisional Legco and its chair, Rita Fan, had done nothing unlawful. If the interim body was considered unlawful, the judge went on, Attorney General Jeremy Mathews should have brought the case on behalf of the government. Any legal challenges to laws passed by the interim body would have to come after July 1, 1997 (hknews@ahkcus.org, June 12, 1997). In July a Hong Kong appeals court presided over by Chief Judge Patrick Chan Siu-oi ruled that it was not for the court to judge the legality of a body set up with the authorization of the National People's Congress, the supreme power on the mainland. The Democrats, of course, condemned the court's decision as "bowing to power" (hknews@ahkcus.org, July 30 and Aug. 1, 1997).

Legislative Politics

The directly elected councilors in the democratic camp, seeing time running out for a transition to representative government before the handover, inundated the Legco with private member bills in 1996 and the first half of 1997. In March 1996, the independent labor union leader Leung Yiu-chung made a motion to condemn the Preparatory Committee as a puppet of the Chinese government. The motion was carried by a vote of 23 to 22. The vote showed that a substantial number of sitting legislators in the democratic camp were adamantly opposed to Beijing's plan to replace the popularly elected legislature with an appointed provisional legislature on July 1, 1997 (Ching 1997a:33).

Most of the private members' bills aimed to make up for lost time in securing labor and welfare rights. Total employment in manufacturing stood at 460,000 by the end of 1996, down from 808,900 in 1989. The income gap had increased. While middle managers' real income had increased an average of 4.8 percent a year from 1989 to 1995, rank-and-file craftsmen's and workers' real income had dropped 0.22 percent per year (Chiu and Lui forthcoming). In the winter of 1996, as many as seventy poor elderly persons had died of the cold. To the surprise of many people and perhaps of government officials, most of the victims were not homeless street people but elderly persons who lived alone (Chiu 1996:442). This tragedy sent a strong signal that something had gone wrong in prosperous Hong Kong. Despite a per capita GDP that ranked among the highest in the world, Hong Kong's income disparities were among the widest among developed countries. The number of people receiving comprehensive social security assistance (CSSA) increased 23 percent, from 104,807 in December 1994 to 129,245 in December 1995. Statistics point to growing poverty and new areas of concern, such as an increase in the number of single-parent families and the working poor, as a result of the restructuring of Hong Kong's industries (Chiu 1996:442; Kuan 1997:58; Ngan 1997:417).

The year 1996 witnessed an increasing number of debates on the role of government in social welfare, accompanied by class actions for legislation to extend the rights of labor. Both proponents and opponents were very vocal. Business's Liberal Party called upon the Hong Kong government to review its welfare spending, claiming that its growth had created a serious financial burden. Labor's representatives and democratic forces countered that labor's welfare had always lagged behind economic growth and that real wages had actually declined (Kuan 1997:57–59).

The DABHK, despite its support of Beijing, aligned itself with the democratic forces on labor and welfare issues. With the DABHK's support, the prodemocracy forces gathered enough votes to override the Liberal votes on labor and welfare issues. The legislature was able to pass private members' bills outlawing unfair trade practices and sex discrimination, forcing employers to give priority to local workers in hiring, scrapping schemes to import labor, and reining in an increase in transportation fares. Labor, too, saw improvements in the provisions for severance pay and bonuses for long service, and pay during maternity leave was increased from two-thirds to four-fifths of an employee's normal wages (Louie 1996:63; Ngo and Lau 1996: 261, 273). As the DABHK might have expected, its cooperation with the Democrats on labor and welfare issues cost it support from the pro-Beijing camp. Since Beijing placed business's interests over those of the grassroots, it appointed fewer DABHK members to the Selection Committee than members of other pro-Beijing business organizations (Wong 1997:122–23).

In addition, in Patten's annual address in October 1996, he took specific issue with the "Hong Kong is going broke because of the welfare burden" thesis. He decided to cut back the labor importation scheme that had allegedly contributed to the growth of unemployment. Patten's budget gave welfare spending a bigger boost than economic services (Kuan 1997:59).

Finally, in a last stand against a possible crackdown after the hand-over, in late June 1997 the lame-duck legislature passed laws minimizing punishment for political dissent after British rule ended. The prodemocracy legislators scraped together sufficient votes to strike down proposed provisions against subversion and secession. By 23 votes to 20, the Legislative Council—which would die with British rule at midnight on June 30, 1997—amended laws to state clearly that only violence, not vocal dissent, would be a punishable offense (hknews@ahkcus.org, June 24, 1997).

The prolabor legislators also seized the opportunity to present seven private members' bills. They sought protection for union activities; employees' rights to consultation, representation, and collective bargaining; and control of the composition and activities of trade unions. In addition, they called for extra statutory holidays; they supported measures against age discrimination; and they proposed amendments to unfair dismissal laws and the Occupational Deafness Compensation Scheme (hknews@ahkcus.org, June 20, 1997).

The Provisional Legislature Fights Back

Fighting back against the Democrats' social welfare and labor offensives, the business community worked with pro-Beijing forces in the Provisional Legislature to gain a stronger say over public policies and human rights issues.

Reinstating the Old Colonial Laws and Freezing Last-Minute Bills

About two weeks before the hand-over, the Provisional Legco approved new restrictions on civil liberties, voting to limit demonstrations and political fund-raising after Hong Kong came under Chinese rule. By voice votes, the legislators passed laws allowing the police to ban any demonstration deemed a threat to national security—calling for independence for Tibet or Taiwan, for instance. They also prohibited political parties from receiving foreign donations and banned defacement of the Chinese flag (hknews@ahkcus.org, June 14, 1997).

Although the Provisional Legco was supposed to be only a stopgap body to produce urgent legislation until the elections in 1998, it pushed through a significant body of important legislation with great haste and minimal debate. Right after the hand-over, the Provisional Legco proved to be a quick-acting rubber stamp for everything the executive deemed administratively or politically convenient. For example, the Provisional Legco unilaterally modified the Hong Kong residency rules. The Basic Law stipulates that children of Hong Kong residents born in China have the right to live in the Hong Kong SAR; the Provisional Legco passed a law that permits them to stay in Hong Kong only if their status has been endorsed by the government (elau@hknet.com, Aug. 3, 1997).

With no consultation and scant debate, the Provisional Legislature also froze labor legislation passed by the previous legislature just before the hand-over. This legislation related to workers' right to collective bargaining, the use of funds by trade unions for political purposes, the prevention of discrimination against union members, and extension of the Bill of Rights Ordinance to the private sector. Obviously, the labor legislation did not suit the business groups that dominated the Provisional Legco. Business's main objection was that it would weaken Hong Kong's economic competitiveness. The freezing of the labor laws prompted a protest by five hundred people led by prodemocracy activists and union leaders. They called the Provisional Legco a "tycoon dictatorship" and viewed the suspension as a big setback "in the rule of law, workers' interests, and democracy" (*International Herald Tribune*, Aug. 27, 1997:7; *China News Digest*, July 16, 1997).

Changing the Voting Methods

The Provisional Legislature made three major changes in the system for election to the Legislative Council. Their main intent was to circumscribe the influence of prodemocracy forces, to make sure they would win no more landslide victories (Louie 1996:64–65; National Democratic Institute 1997).

First, the single-seat and the first-past-the-post systems in the geographical constituency elections of 1985 were abandoned in favor of a system of proportional representation, though not as that term is usually understood. To fill the twenty directly elected seats, Hong Kong was to be divided into five geographical constituencies, each to elect three to five legislators. Candidates endorsed by either a party or a coalition would run in each district. The number of seats allocated would depend on the percentage of votes they secured.

Second, the Provisional Legislature changed the voting method for functional constituencies; the pre-Patten method of corporate voting was restored. Representatives of eligible corporate entities were authorized to vote on behalf of their organizations. The nine new constituencies that Patten created in 1995 were completely reorganized and their franchise was substantially restricted. Instead of having more than 2 million people eligible to vote in 1995, the 1998 Legco functional constituencies would have no more than 200,000 corporate votes.

Third, the composition of the electoral college responsible for electing ten members to the legislature was completely changed. Its members, instead of being persons elected to the District Boards, would be chosen from an 800-member committee, 200 members to be drawn from each of four sectors: (1) the industrial and financial sector; (2) the professions; (3) labor, social services, and religious services; and (4) the Chinese representative organs, such as the National People's Congress and the People's Political Consultative Conference (hknews@ahkcus.org, Sept. 28, 1997).

The voting system was changed to ensure that the post-1997 government would have a strong executive and a relatively weak legislature. The functional constituencies ensured that business interests were well represented and the ten "selected" seats filled by the electoral college would ensure that Beijing's interests were also represented. On the other hand, the proportional representation system in the geographical electoral seats could increase competition among prodemocracy forces. As Emily Lau points out, "given that the elections would be by proportional representation and the voters can only cast one vote, it is inevitable that candidates from the Democratic Party and The Frontier [another prodemocracy organization] will compete in the same constituency" (elau@hknet.com, Sept. 26, 1997). In addition, since the geographical constituencies were now larger than before, more funds would be needed for publicity and other campaign expenses. Thus the change would benefit candidates and parties that were resourceful and supported by the business community or Beijing (forum@ahkcus.org, June 2, 1997). Furthermore, the candidates of parties less popular than the Democrats could still win some seats, thus depriving the Democrats of the landslide victories they could otherwise expect.

With these new electoral rules, prodemocracy candidates, however popular, could no longer form a majority bloc in the Legco. At best, prodemocracy legislators could be a moral force, using the Legco as a platform to air their views. When the chips were down, prodemocracy legislators would always be outvoted, as they were in the second half of the 1980s.

Although big business used the Provisional Legco to fight back the Democrats' offensive, Beijing and the first SAR government were willing to work out a compromise with the Democratic Party in order to achieve a smooth transition on July 1, 1997.

Beijing's Moderate Posture before the Hand-over

Beijing adopted a moderate policy toward Hong Kong in hand-over politics. As Kuan (1997:52) points out, Beijing was interested in a "smooth" transition, which could mean anything from preventing the least disruption of its efforts to fill the future SAR government with patriots and their bedfellows to galvanizing maximum support for those efforts.

Working with the British

In April 1996, Foreign Minister Qian Qichen met with his British counterpart, Malcolm Rifkind, to discuss hand-over matters. Both men publicly reaffirmed that the Provisional Legislature was a closed matter. Beijing further announced that it would respect British authority in Hong Kong before the hand-over. Beijing would delay launching the Provisional Legislature, have it meet in China rather than in Hong Kong, and confine its work to "preliminary preparations," not "formal decisions and actions," before going into formal session on July 1, 1997. Beijing gave public assurances that the Provisional Legislature would not become a second center of power in Hong Kong before the hand-over (Kuan 1997:53).

During a trade mission to China, Michael Heseltine said that "our interest and the Chinese interest in Hong Kong are identical, and . . . we have to bring about the transfer of Hong Kong in the condition of prosperity and stability." As Dimbleby (1997:359) remarks, Heseltine was the only Western politician of note who had managed to complete a visit to China in recent years without making one mention of human rights, even in private conversations with the Beijing leadership.

Lobbying the Democrats

As soon as the Preparatory Committee was set up, its deputy secretary general, Shiu Sin-por, asserted that China was prepared to deal with the Democratic Party: "It is a reality that the Democratic Party represents a certain portion of Hong Kong people. The Chinese government knows it very well" (Ching 1997a:31).

In April 1996, during the consultation exercise conducted by the Preparatory Committee, Beijing tried to mend fences with the Democratic

Party in order to achieve a smooth transition. An invitation to participate in the consultation meeting was sent to the Professional Teachers' Union (PTU), headed by Cheung Man-kwong and Szeto Wah. A formal dialogue between Beijing and PTU leaders therefore could be interpreted as a breakthrough. But after Cheung and Szeto publicly made uncompromising statements against the Provisional Legislature, their invitations were withdrawn (Cheng 1997:xlvii; Ching 1996:45).

Although Beijing made it clear that it found the electoral system used in 1995 unacceptable, it did not terminate that system together. Instead, Beijing promised that the Provisional Legislature would operate until the formation of the first legislature of the SAR, but no later than June 30, 1998. Elections for a properly constituted Legco would take place in May 1998 (Ching 1997b:59; Conner 1997:89).

In an interview with ABC News, Lu Ping said that the Democratic Party could continue to exist and participate in elections after 1997. "I think they can continue to exist if they abide by the law," Lu said. "I don't think there will be any difficulty for them" (Ching 1997a:37). Lu's statement could be taken as another overture by Beijing to the Democrats.

In August 1996, when the Preparatory Committee sought nominations for the 400-member Selection Committee, Vice Premier Qian Qichen made another conciliatory gesture to the Democrats: even members of the Democratic Party, once deemed subversive because of their links to the Tiananmen movement, were welcome to apply to serve on the Selection Committee. Qian further stressed that people who held different opinions on the path and speed of Hong Kong's democracy could discuss Hong Kong affairs with the aim of working out a compromise, so long as they supported Beijing's resumption of sovereignty and hoped for Hong Kong's stability and prosperity. Qian's slogan, "Work for consensus, tolerate small differences," was publicized in *Outspoken,* the official magazine of the Democratic Party, in August 1996. Still, the Democrats refused to join the Selection Committee because they remained opposed to Beijing's decision "to scrap Hong Kong's elected legislature and replace it with a hand-picked version." As a result, there was no breakthrough to establish a dialogue between Beijing and the Democratic Party (Cheng 1997:xlvii).

The Through Train for Top Civil Servants

In February 1997, Chief Executive Elect Tung submitted a list of principal officials of the Hong Kong government to Beijing for approval. Tung's list consisted of all eighteen current policy secretaries (except Attorney

General Jeremy Mathews, who could not meet the requirement of Chinese nationality) and five department heads. A few policy secretaries had offended Beijing in the mid-1990s by their strong backing of Patten's democratic reforms, and there were speculations that they would not be acceptable to Beijing.

To everyone's surprise, Beijing swiftly accepted every official on Tung's list, even those who had pushed for Patten's reforms. The passengers on the through train to the SAR government turned out to be the top civil servants. Analysts interpreted this gesture as Beijing's way of keeping its promise not to interfere in post-1997 affairs. Prices on the Hong Kong stock exchange rose after this news got out (hknews@ahkcus.org, Feb. 24, 1997). Hook (1997:566) predicted that continuity in the civil service without interference from Beijing would contribute much to the stability, prosperity, and progress of the Hong Kong SAR into the twenty-first century.

Furthermore, in March 1997 Beijing made it clear that after 1997, it would be up to the Hong Kong government to draft its own budget; Beijing would not be involved (Ching 1997b:66). This statement confirmed that Beijing would honor its commitment to Hong Kong's autonomy.

Tolerating Protests against Beijing

Addressing Hong Kong's elite, President Jiang Zemin repeatedly told Hong Kongers that they were to govern themselves, that their fate was in their own hands, that Hong Kong—a place so utterly different from the rest of China—would chart its own course. "Hong Kong will continue to practice the capitalist system . . . with its previous socioeconomic system and way of life remaining unchanged and its laws remaining basically unchanged while the main part of the nation persists in the socialist system" (hknews@ahkcus.org, July 2, 1997). Up to the end of 1997, it seemed that Beijing was keeping its promise not to intervene in Hong Kong's political affairs.

During the transition there were many public demonstrations challenging the Beijing government. On the evening of the hand-over ceremony, June 30, 1997, the radical April 5 Action Group carried a large paper model of a Chinese tank to remind people of the June 4 incident and marched from Wan Chai subway station to a protest zone near the Convention and Exhibition Centre, where the hand-over ceremony was held. When the twenty or so protesters shouted slogans such as "Down with Li Peng, the butcher of June fourth!" and "Remember the June fourth slaughter!" their chants were drowned out by Beethoven's Fifth Symphony from loudspeakers on a police aircraft flying over the protest zone. President Jiang Zemin and Premier Li Peng were attending the ceremony inside the Convention and Exhibition Centre. Li may have heard the chants when he entered the building, but Beijing took no action beyond Beethoven. A Hong Kong police spokesman was defensive about the incident: "There are many people celebrating the hand-over around the area. We just want to play some nice music for the public. We have no intention of covering the voices of the protesters" (hknews@ahkcus.org, July 2, 1997).

On July 1 about three thousand protesters participated in a demonstration organized by the Hong Kong Alliance in Support of the Patriotic Democratic Movement in China. Beijing branded the Alliance subversive because it had championed the cause of democracy during the Tiananmen incident. The protesters wore T-shirts and carried signs saying: "Don't forget June 4" and "Build a democratic China." They chanted, "Put an end to one-party dictatorship!" and called for the immediate release of jailed dissidents, a reversal of the verdict on the democratic movement in Beijing, and punishment for those responsible for the crackdown. The protesters delivered a manifesto to the new chief executive's office, calling on Beijing to release its political prisoners. However, the demonstration was peaceful. Hong Kong police cleared two lanes of traffic to permit the protesters to deliver their manifesto and made no attempt to stop them (hknews@ahkcus.org, July 4, 1997).

What Explains Beijing's Moderation?

When we look back to the early 1990s, we see that Beijing was forced to take a tough stand toward Hong Kong because of the turmoil of the Tiananmen incident, because of the challenges posed by Patten's electoral reforms, and because of the uncertainty about the leadership of the Chinese Communist Party. In 1997, however, when the emotion of the Tiananmen incident had died down, when the British colonial government had become a lame duck, and when the core leadership of the Chinese Communist Party stabilized after the death of Deng Xiaoping in February 1997, Beijing could afford to ease its stand on Hong Kong.

Economically, Lo (1997:324) explains that as Hong Kong becomes an international city, where foreign countries and mainland Chinese corporations are keen to protect their economic interests and maintain the territory's political stability, Beijing officials will probably refrain from taking strong actions against Hong Kong democrats. In addition, while Beijing was using the slogan "one country, two systems" in an attempt to lure Taiwan back to the fold, any political repression in Hong Kong would jeopardize its mission (Ching 1997b:65). Beijing wanted to show Taipei how well it treated Hong Kong and how much autonomy it allowed. Beijing had made the mistake of starting a nine-day missile test off the coast of Taiwan in early 1996, not only causing the United States to send naval forces into the area but inducing the Hang Seng index to plunge 820 points (7.3%), one of the largest reverses recorded in the Asia-Pacific region (Dimbleby 1997:351). Since reunification by force was not working, Beijing needed to treat Hong Kong well in order to achieve peaceful reunification with Taiwan.

Furthermore, in mid-1997 the whole world was watching the hand-over in Hong Kong. As John Major stated well, "Every member of the international community, all Hong Kong's friends and partners around the world, in both hemispheres and five continents, will be watching to see that the letter and spirit of the Joint Declaration are honoured, now, next year and for fifty years beyond. And we will be making sure that they do" (Dimbleby 1997:340). Intensive media coverage of the hand-over event surely pressured Beijing to moderate its stand on Hong Kong.

For all of these reasons, Beijing will try to keep its commitment to allow Hong Kong a high degree of autonomy. As Ching (1997b:64) comments, "China did not spend two years negotiating the Joint Declaration, five years drafting the Basic Law, and many more years negotiating other agreements with the idea that it would tear them all up on July 1."

The Moderate Stand of the First SAR Government

Working with the Democrats

During his election campaign in October 1996, Tung distanced himself from Patten's reforms and criticized the governor obliquely for initiating them without Beijing's approval, but still he promised that the June 4 commemorative activities would be permitted after 1997, as long as they were peaceful and lawful. He called on the Democrats to be more constructive by supporting the Provisional Legislature rather than mounting a legal challenge to it (Dimbleby 1997:375–76).

Despite their political differences, Tung managed to open a communication channel to the Democratic Party, justifying it as "compensation" for the probable exclusion of the Democrats from his Executive Council. He agreed to meet with the Democrats every two months, more often if necessary. As Tung explained, "It is necessary to continue our dialogue regularly to enhance our mutual understanding" (hknews@ahkcus.org, Jan. 10, 1997).

In addition, Tung tried to work with the Democrats on human rights issues. The Provisional Legislature proposed a variety of measures to outlaw any organization that had not registered with the police. Political groups would not be able to accept funding from abroad, and, for the sake of public order, no demonstration of more than thirty people would be permitted in the absence of a formal notice at least seven days in advance, and a statement from the police that they had no objection. These proposals provoked anger among Hong Kong society during a three-week consultation period in May 1997. In order to work with the Democrats, Tung's office released a statement modifying the proposals: political organizations would, after all, be able to accept donations from abroad, but only from individuals, not from foreign organizations; and although the police would retain the power to ban public gatherings, it would not be necessary for protesters to secure a statement of no objection beforehand (Dimbleby 1997:427–28).

Tung was also committed to tolerate political protests in Hong Kong after 1997. Yip Hua-kwok, whom Tung appointed as his special consultant, said, "Don't expect that there will be no protests and demonstrations after July 1. If there are demonstrations and protests, let them go on. For they will prove to the world that Hong Kong is a free and open city, full of vigor, freedom, democracy. Of course, the basic premise is to obey the Basic Law" (1997:4). Yip may have served as a broker between Tung and the Democrats, as he had long been a supporter of the Meeting Point before its merger with the Democratic Party in 1994.

Keeping the Basic Law's Democratic Promises

During the transition, Tung assured Secretary of State Madeleine Albright that the right to hold street protests would be preserved under Chinese rule, and he stressed that preparing for the elections in 1998 was the most important task of the Provisional Legislative Council (hknews@ahkcus.org, July 2, 1997).

In September 1997, Tung went to Southeast Asia and the United States to lobby for support of the new government. His trip, described as an official goodwill mission, was clearly intended to reassure American and other investors that Hong Kong would continue to be a good place for investment and that democracy—if not quite there yet—was coming. The Provisional Council, he explained, already had some elected members, and their numbers would grow. The Hong Kong SAR would move toward democracy step by step, in accordance with the Basic Law.

Tung faced tough questions from reporters, but the business community and other conservative figures welcomed him warmly. Caspar Weinberger (1997:37), former secretary of defense in the Reagan administration, commented that "Mr. Tung handled this trip well. He is reasonable, articulate, and a very smart and successful businessman. He is good at being reassuring."

A Welfare Package for the Grassroots Population

As soon as he was sworn in as chief executive, Tung promised a wide range of social policies aimed to defuse the grievances of the grassroots population. Tung promised to solve Hong Kong's housing problem—his aim was to achieve a home ownership rate of 70 percent in ten years. He wanted to reinvigorate the school system by upgrading teachers' qualifications and ensuring full-day school sessions at the primary level. He proposed a mandatory retirement fund and established a government commission for the elderly (hknews@ahkcus.org, July 2, 1997).

In Tung's policy speech to the legislature in October 1997, he also dealt extensively with social welfare issues for the grassroots population when he put forward a development package for business. To meet his target of 85,000 flats a year, Tung presented a "rolling" five-year program to allocate 380 hectares for private housing and 285 hectares for public housing. Some 250,000 flats now leased in public housing would be sold to tenants over the next ten years, and 6,000 families would benefit each year from a new "home starter" scheme that would provide mortgages of about H.K.$600,000.

To increase the quality of education, kindergarten teachers would be at least 60 percent qualified teachers by the year 2000; 60 percent of primary schools would become whole-day schools by 2002; and 700 more native English-speaking language teachers would be provided for secondary schools.

To help the elderly, Tung increased their welfare allowance by H.K.$380 a month. Twelve health-care centers for the elderly would be set up in 1998–99 and twenty-three more social centers for them would be established between 1998 and 2002. An "elderly volunteer program" would be established to encourage senior citizens to participate in community life. A Mandatory Provident Fund Scheme was to be in operation by 1998 to provide a nest egg for today's workers before they became tomorrow's retirees (hknews@ahkcus.org, Oct. 8, 1997).

The Democrats complained that Tung had said nothing about freedom and human rights, nothing about democratization except that Legco elections would be held May 24, 1998. They were also frustrated because Tung had taken the social welfare issues from their own agenda. Housing, education, and the elderly were the key issues on which the Democrats had won the support of the grassroots population in 1995. When Tung took the initiative in addressing those issues, the Democrats were put on the defensive. Now they had to worry about losing support in 1998 (hknews@ahkcus.org, Oct. 8, 1997).

A Developmental Package for the Business Community

When Tung promoted welfare measures for service professionals and the grassroots population, he also delivered a developmental package for the business section. In his maiden policy speech to the legislature in October 1997, he unveiled an ambitious plan to launch Hong Kong into the information age while promising that it would be a caring city. In an epic two-hour speech titled "Building Hong Kong for a New Era," Tung explained how Hong Kong could improve its competitive position and develop cutting-edge technology. He would construct the Science Park, the Second International Technology Center, and the Fourth Industrial Estate. He would establish a high-level framework to coordinate major infrastructure improvements, business investments, and cooperation between Hong Kong and Guangdong Province. To create a highly educated workforce, Tung would launch a five-year development program to bring the young into the computer age and put H.K.$5 billion in a special education fund to improve teaching quality in the schools. Furthermore, he promised that he would in no circumstances consider raising taxes in 1998 to finance those massive undertakings (hknews@ahkcus.org, Oct. 8, 1997).

Tung's policy address received unanimous acclaim from the Provisional Legislative Council, the pro-Beijing political parties, and the business community. Allen Lee (Li Peng-fei), chairman of the Liberal Party, lauded Tung's economic policies as appropriate for Hong Kong, especially the proposal to set up a bureau for information technology. Ambrose Lau Honchuen, chair of the Hong Kong Progressive Alliance (HKPA), said that the Alliance recommended the development of higher value-added economic activities and that Tung's speech had given clear guidelines toward this goal. The Federation of Hong Kong Industries chair, Henry Tsang, described Tung's policies as "proactive" and said they would be beneficial to Hong Kong's long-term development as an international center for finance, trade, industry, and the service sector (hknews@ahkcus.org, Oct. 8, 1997).

Knowing that after 1997 the Hong Kong government would be supported ideologically by an executive-led ethos and facilitated institutionally by constraint of political parties and electoral politics (A. Cheung 1997:737), Tung could afford to take a moderate stand toward the democracy forces to enhance the legitimacy of his SAR government.

The Moderation of the Democratic Party

Mild Protests on Hand-over Day

In the early 1990s, influenced by the 1989 Tiananmen incident, the Democratic Party adopted a strong pro-welfare program and a critical stand toward Beijing. In response, Beijing denounced some Democratic Party leaders as subversive, and Beijing officials refused to communicate with the Democratic Party. Pro-Beijing forces labeled the Democratic Party "pro-British, anti-Beijing, and trouble-makers in Hong Kong" (*Outspoken,* Jan. 15, 1996:7). There was a fear that the Democratic Party would not be allowed to participate in post-1997 elections in Hong Kong.

Subsequently, in early 1997, Martin Lee of the Democratic Party revealed that some party members threatened to chain themselves to pillars or to chairs in the Legislative Council building on the night of June 30, 1997. Many Democrats were elected in 1995 to serve four-year terms, and they felt they had a right to stay in the Legco after the hand-over to prevent the Provisional Legco from taking over (hknews@ahkcus.org, July 4, 1997). However, in the end the party backed away from such a militant confrontation and settled for a hand-over rally on the balcony at midnight. They counted down the last ten seconds to midnight with shouts of "Long live democracy! Fight for democracy!" Martin Lee and other key party members condemned the Provisional Legco and called for its swift dismissal. The balcony protest attracted the media and was broadcast all over the world, but the Democratic Party had missed a golden opportunity to stage a militant protest that would have captured even more of the world's attention (hknews@ahkcus.org, July 2, 1997).

Why did the Democrats abandon their plans for a more militant protest? They may have been swayed by Tung's personal appeal not to make any "confrontational moves." In addition, the Chief Executive Office arranged for a car to take the Democratic Party leaders — Martin Lee, Yeung Sum, and Cheung Bing-leung — to the rally at the Legco building right after they attended the hand-over ceremony in the Convention Centre up to about midnight (forum@ahkcus.org, July 15, 1997; hknews@ahkcus.org, June 5, 1997).

The Democrats' moderation was also a product of their striving for a consensual ideological platform, the radicals' departure from the party, their lack of power to mobilize public opinion to support confrontation, and resigned acceptance of their minority position.

Striving for a Consensual Ideological Platform

The Democratic Party's ideological platform changed drastically after 1995. Martin Lee said that he was working for a "new consensual politics" based on three kinds of cooperation in the Legco: cooperation among political parties, between the Legco and the executive branch, and between Hong Kong and Beijing. Cheung Man-kwong and other party leaders even spoke of building a new alliance beyond class and party lines. In this framework, enlightened pro-Beijing forces and farsighted capitalists would work together with the Democrats (*Outspoken,* Jan. 15, 1996:3,6).

Martin Lee justified this new consensual politics on the grounds that the Democrats' nineteen votes in the sixty-member Legco were hardly enough to get their program passed unless they formed a strategic coalition with other parties. If the Democrats could cut down unnecessary disputes in the Legco and turn to compromise and lobbying — without betraying the party's basic principles, of course — they would find it easier to carry out their program. They needed to work with the government, too, Lee said. It would not do for the Democrats to be always in opposition to the government, for then the government would be paralyzed and Hong Kong would suffer. The Democrats should be brave enough to support any good government program and to work for the support of the majority of the Legco members to get a good program passed (*Outspoken,* Jan. 13, 1996:4).

From then on, although the Democrats still criticized Beijing for replacing the democratically elected legislature with the appointed Provisional Legislature, they began to highlight what they had in common with Beijing in an effort to achieve tactical cooperation on the hand-over. Yeung Sum, the party's vice chair, said that the Democratic Party had no disagreement with Beijing's two premises: certainly they supported Beijing's resumption of sovereignty and hoped for Hong Kong's stability and prosperity. As early as 1984, he pointed out, when most people were still hesitating to take a stand, many members of the democratic camp had declared publicly that they supported "Chinese resumption of Hong Kong's sovereignty and democratic reunification" (*Outspoken*, Aug. 1996:4).

Lo Chi-kin, a member of the Central Committee of the Democratic Party, also emphasized that "the Democratic Party has always been supportive of the Chinese resumption of Hong Kong's sovereignty and 'one country, two systems.' Although the Democratic Party has disagreed with some of the content of the Basic Law, it has clearly stated that it accepts the legitimacy of the Basic Law. Although the Democratic Party takes a different view of the Beijing government, it always insists on using peaceful means to express its opinion and will not destroy social stability. Thus, the elements of a consensus have long existed" (*Outspoken*, Aug. 1996:6). The many Democrats who once had belonged to the Meeting Point could easily cultivate moderation, because the Meeting Point had developed a harmonious relationship with Beijing until the Tiananmen incident (*Hong Kong Standard*, Oct. 15, 1992).

This new consensual stand may have been a response to Beijing's declaration that a new election would take place in 1998 to replace the Provisional Legislature and that the Democratic Party would be allowed to participate in elections. In preparation for the post-1997 elections, then, the democratic forces adopted a less confrontational and more accommodating political style to obtain political space for themselves in the Hong Kong SAR.

Radicals Quit the Democratic Party

During this critical phase of hand-over politics, the democratic forces were far from united (Cheng 1997:xlix). In August 1996, a radical group called the Frontier was founded by Emily Lau, Lau Chin-shek, and Lee Cheuk-yan. Emily Lau was a former journalist with the *Far Eastern Economic Review;* Lau Chin-shek and Lee Cheuk-yan were leaders of Hong Kong's independent labor movement. With a diverse membership of about a hundred (mostly service professionals, students, and labor unionists), the Frontier was loosely organized. It had no chairperson, only a spokesperson.

The Frontier positioned itself as a political moral force. It was staunchly anticommunist and hoped to mobilize the grassroots population to engage in street protests and other confrontations. As Emily Lau said, the Frontier was composed of people "who are determined to prove that in spite of the turbulent political changes and the threat of dire consequences for those who dare to speak their minds, there are people who adhere to their principles and ideals" (elau@hknet.com, June 22, 1997). It seemed to the Frontier's leaders that many in the democracy camp had already compromised their principles in exchange for better relations with the future sovereign. Their views on Beijing and grassroots mobilization were a hidden source of friction with the democracy forces. That was why Lau Chin-shek and Lee Cheuk-yan decided to join the Frontier. The role of the Frontier was to put pressure on the Democrats not to compromise on the principles of democracy, human rights, and the rule of law — to stop being so moderate.

On July 1, 1997, the Frontier declined to join the Democrats' balcony protest; they preferred to be with the people, they said, rather than with the international media. They joined a second rally in Statue Square organized by the Hong Kong People's Coalition for an Alternative Hand-over, which included grassroots, human rights, and antidiscrimination groups, and they organized a rally of their own around the Legislative Council building. They wrapped the building with yellow banners as a token of their wish to return to it one day (hknews@ahkcus.org, July 2, 1997).

Other radical democratic groups, too, tried to organize street protests, but none of them were able to mobilize a large group of followers. The usual turnout was only a few dozen committed cadres. Still, in the post-1997 elections the radical leaders of the Frontier expected to capture votes that otherwise would go to the Democrats (C. Leung 1997:52, 56–57; hknews@ahkcus.org, July 3, 1997).

Only Voting Power, Little Mobilization Power

Observing the split in the prodemocracy forces, Beijing no longer considered the Democrats a serious threat. Beijing still anticipated opposition and protests from them, but it did not believe they could mobilize much support among the grassroots population. In fact, Beijing thought the Democratic Party probably attracted more attention in the West than at home.

The diminishing power of the Democratic Party to mobilize protests ironically was the result of its success in formal politics. Its victories in 1991 and 1995 enabled the party to play a key role in the legislature. As Cheng (1997:xlix) points out, in many ways their electoral success positioned the Democrats as a party of the political establishment, and their strongest influence was felt through constitutional channels. Similarly, S. W. Leung (1996:234) remarks that more detrimental to the party's strength was "the reluctance at building up linkages between the party and socioeconomic organizations, such as labour unions and other pressure/interest groups." After getting used to engaging in consensus politics to articulate their platform through the establishment, the Democrats were reluctant to go back to the street strategies that many of its founders had adopted in the 1970s and 1980s.

The switch to consensus politics alienated some junior members of the Democratic Party. Members based in the District Boards warned that cooperation with the establishment contradicted the the party's platform of support for the grassroots population. The divergence of views on such issues as labor rights and collective protests between the labor union leader Lau Chin-shek and other core leaders in the Democratic Party reflected fundamental differences in outlook (C. Leung 1997:54).

Since most of the Democratic Party leaders had started their political careers by organizing protests in the 1970s, their close connections with social movement organizations created expectations among the grassroots population that the party would continue to lead them in opposing government policies. Thus the party's consensus politics in the mid-1990s disappointed many grassroots organizations and led them to steer clear of institutional politics (Lui and Chiu forthcoming). Even some student unions (especially the Chinese University Student Union) became critical of the Democratic Party. They complained that the party had betrayed its commitment to the grassroots population, and in doing so had left them no room to maneuver and crippled their movement. After the mid-1990s, many student unions withdrew support from the Democratic Party (*Outspoken,* June 1996:9–10).

The Democrats' consensus politics had indeed weakened the grassroots organizations. The Democratic Party had drawn leaders, resources, and media coverage from them. The Joint Association of People's Organizations (JAPOD) and Full Democracy (FD) could draw at most a few hundred people to their protest activities. The JAPOD was reduced to staging small-scale street dramas and drawing caricatures mocking the conservatives (Sing forthcoming).

One of the Democratic Party's biggest problems was lack of money. Yu (1997:109) points out that the party had three major sources of funds: its members' annual dues, donations, and government subsidies for the three-tier councilors. Since the party had fewer than a thousand members and annual dues were less than U.S.$30, the most it could collect was less than U.S.$30,000, which could not even sustain the operations of a local branch for a year. Since the Democrats had failed to develop good relations with the business sector, few businesspeople donated money to the party. As a result, government subsidies to the three-tier councilors became the major source of revenue for the party's daily operations. The purging of Democrats from the Legislative Council, the Urban and Regional Councils, and the District Boards in mid-1997 thus caused the party enormous financial hardship. Its leaders must have breathed a sigh of relief when Tung modified the Provisional Legislature's bill to allow them to receive donations from individuals overseas.

Public Support for a Confrontational Strategy Dwindles

The Democratic Party's moderation may also have stemmed from lack of support for a confrontational strategy during the hand-over. The leaders believed that participation in the Selection Committee would give them no influence over the process of setting up the first Hong Kong SAR government, so they declined Beijing's invitation to join the committee. Beijing and the business community then attacked their refusal as hostile and confrontational. Many Hong Kong people, in fact, would have liked to see the Democratic Party work with Beijing for a smooth transition in 1997. In two separate surveys (*Ming Pao*, Aug. 12, 1996; *Hong Kong Economic Daily*, Aug. 15, 1996), more than 60 percent of the respondents believed the Democratic Party should join the Selection Committee.

Even some members of the democratic camp wanted to develop a more cordial relationship with Beijing. The moderate Hong Kong Association for Democracy and People's Livelihood, with about 120 members and one seat in the Legco after the 1991 election, won four seats in 1995. As its name implies, the ADPL stressed such social issues as housing and welfare, but it strove to maintain a dialogue with Beijing and to operate within the establishment. That was why Beijing chose two ADPL leaders to serve on the powerful Preparatory Committee. Although Fung Kin-kee, the leader of the ADPL, cast a lone vote against the formation of the Provisional Legislature in March 1996, he later changed his mind and encouraged ADPL members to run for seats in it (C. Leung 1997:58–59; hknews@ahkcus.org, Aug. 13, 1997).

Hong Kong society, too, may have developed a more positive view of Beijing, because the year before the transition was marked by growing Chinese nationalism. In September 1996 Hong Kong was the scene of massive demonstrations against the Japanese occupation of the Diaoyutai Islands. Some 50,000 people showed up in Victoria Park to eulogize Chan Yuk-cheung, who had died when he jumped into the water off the main island of the archipelago, where a lighthouse had been erected by a right-wing

Japanese group. Touched by Chan's patriotic act, the Democratic legislators Albert Ho and Tsang Kin-shing worked with the pro-unification New Party in Taiwan to send another expedition to the Diaoyutai Islands. They were able to plant China's five-star red national flag alongside a Republic of China flag (the one used in Taiwan). As Nyaw and Li (1996:xxxv) observe, in the midst of the hand-over, Hong Kong society was experiencing an identity crisis. While Hong Konger feelings ("we are not mainlanders") were still prevalent, many Hong Kong people were also deeply nationalistic and were outraged by Japan's occupation of the Diaoyutai Islands.

Resigned to Being a Minority Party

After being purged from the Legislative Council in 1997, the Democrats had no choice but to prepare to survive as an opposition party in the political wilderness. They had to face the hard reality of being a permanent minority party riven by dissention over its policy toward Beijing, which might intensify after 1997. More members might, like Chan Choi-hi, defy the party to seek a seat in the Provisional Legislature, especially since he won (C. Leung 1997:55).

Still, the Democratic Party will not fade away. Its core leaders are firmly committed to the democratization of Hong Kong. Martin Lee is still very popular. He and his colleagues still have enough voter appeal to win directly elected seats in the legislature. The Democratic Party still draws enormous support from overseas Hong Kong emigrants as well as from the United States. So the SAR government needs to build a cordial relationship with the Democrats to keep them from being cornered into protesting in the streets and becoming a destabilizing force (C. Leung 1997:56; hknews@ahkcus.org, July 4, 1997).

So there is hope for the Democratic Party. Under the Basic Law, the pace of democratization will be governed by a fixed timetable. Half of the legislature's sixty seats will be elected by geographically based constituencies in 2003. As the years go by, the Legco will have more and more directly elected members and the Democratic Party will have more influence.

Taking the long view, a hopeful Martin Lee declared: "I think that there is in Hong Kong enough momentum behind the development of representative government and civil society to make those things in the long term unstoppable. You can wind up the Legislative Council, but you can't actually wind up the sixty to seventy per cent of the population which still supports the Democratic Party" (quoted in Dimbleby 1997:350).

Toward a Democratic Compromise

Up to the mid-1990s, Hong Kong was headed toward a contested democracy. The constitutional framework of the post-1997 government had been contested. Hong Kong society was divided into two big camps. Beijing was determined to dismantle the existing legislature and replace it with a provisional one. No member of the Democratic Party was appointed to the committee that would select the first governor and the members of the Provisional Legislature. The big businesspeople were on the offensive, restoring old colonial laws in order to curb human rights and workers' welfare.

In response, the Democratic Party protested against Beijing's policies on the anniversary of the Tiananmen incident. The party collected signatures to show that the grassroots population did not favor a provisional legislature, and it challenged the Provisional Legislature in court on the grounds that it was unconstitutional. It seemed, therefore, that the pro- and anti-democracy forces were headed for a showdown in mid-1997.

The Western media envisioned an authoritarian scenario in Hong Kong after the transition. The Democratic Party would be outlawed. The press would be censored, "subversive" organizations would be banned, dissidents would be imprisoned. Beijing would rely on its unholy alliance with big business to rule Hong Kong with no input from the Democrats. In this scenario, 1997 would be an authoritarian transition from a British colony ruled by expatriates and big business to a Communist Chinese colony ruled by Beijing and big business.

The Western media's scenario has thus far failed to materialize. No violent political confrontation, no outright political repression, and little political censorship took place in mid-1997. Instead, a democratic compromise was achieved among Beijing, the Hong Kong SAR government, and the democracy camp during this critical transition from British to Chinese rule. What explains this democratic compromise?

First, Beijing drastically toned down its opposition to the Democratic Party after 1996. Although Beijing denounced some Democratic leaders as subversive and refused to communicate with them, and although in the aftermath of the Tiananmen incident it even intimated that the Democratic Party would be outlawed after 1997, Beijing suddenly invited Democratic leaders to participate in the consultation exercises of the Preparatory Committee, welcomed them to the Selection Committee, and assured them that they would be allowed to compete in elections after 1997. Furthermore,

Beijing tolerated political protests in Hong Kong, even when the protesters shouted offensive slogans against Beijing leaders.

Beijing's moderate stand toward the Democrats in the mid-1990s was a result of the waning of the emotions aroused by the Tiananmen incident, the hope of luring Taiwan to the negotiation table, and the intense media attention to the transition. Too, the consolidation of China's core leadership after the death of Deng Xiaoping enabled Beijing to compromise. If Deng had still been alive and the Beijing leadership in disarray, it is unlikely that Beijing would have reversed its opposition to the Hong Kong Democrats. As it was, Beijing had all the cards it needed to win the game in Hong Kong, so it could relax its control during the critical transition period in the interest of smoothing its resumption of sovereignty.

The first SAR government of Tung Chee-hwa also moderated its stand toward the democratic camp in mid-1997. Although the Democratic Party was not represented in either the Provisional Legislature or the Executive Council, Tung still maintained a channel of communication with Democratic Party leaders, meeting with them every two months. Just before the transition, Tung even appealed to them personally not to disrupt the transition ceremony. He kept his promise to tolerate political protests after July 1, 1997, and he proposed to increase government spending on housing, education, and the elderly to mollify the grassroots population. Knowing that the post-1997 government would have a strong executive and a weak legislature, Tung could afford to work with the Democrats in order to enhance his legitimacy in Hong Kongers' eyes.

Third, the Democratic Party adopted a moderate stand toward Beijing and the Tung government. The Democrats' protest at the moment of the transition was peaceful, and they were willing to participate in the 1998 elections, even though the Provisional Legislature had so drastically changed the electoral rules that they saw little possibility of gaining a majority. Further, the Democratic Party emphasized that it would always support Beijing's resumption of sovereignty and always hope for Hong Kong's stability and prosperity. This was enough to assure Beijing and the Tung government that they could work with the Democrats. The defection of several radical leaders in the mid-1990s made it easier for the party to moderate its opposition to the government.

Having been the dominant party in the mid-1990s, it had neglected to maintain its links with grassroots organizations. Although many Democratic Party leaders could still attract voter support, they realized that their ability to mobilize the grassroots population was limited now. Since the Hong Kong public generally wanted a smooth rather than a confrontational transition, the Democrats concentrated their energy on the 1998 elections rather than on street protests. The many Democrats who had once belonged to the Meeting Point, which embraced Chinese nationalism and developed a good relationship with Beijing, were able to adopt a nationalist agenda without being condemned as opportunists or betrayers. What the Democratic Party hoped for was election victories down the road. As the Basic Law stipulates an increasing number of directly elected seats in the Legco, the Democrats had reason to believe their influence in the government would grow.

Fourth, big business was willing to go along with the compromise with the Democrats. The Basic Law and the new electoral rules imposed by the Provisional Legislature ensured business's dominance of the post-1997 legislature. Since the Democratic Party could not become a majority in the legislature, the business community was confident that it could defeat any bills that threatened its interests. Hong Kong's robust economy in mid-1997 also facilitated a compromise between the Democrats and the business community. With ample budget reserves and facing a strong economy, Tung's government was able to develop a package that could satisfy both the grassroots population and the business community.

Finally, Patten's electoral reforms had been one of the decisive factors that led to the contested democracy in Hong Kong of the early 1990s. By 1997, however, the colonial government had become a lame duck. London was again cooperating with Beijing. As a result, Beijing and Tung's SAR government were able to work out a compromise with the Democrats without interference from London and the colonial government.

In mid-1997, therefore, a new antagonistic alliance emerged in Hong Kong. Although the political actors were still ideologically divided, although they publicly opposed one another on policy questions, and although they developed no explicit pact, they achieved a tacit understanding on some procedural and ground rules for the democratic transition in Hong Kong.

First, with regard to political participants, there was an agreement to include all politically significant actors in the post-1997 elections. Not only the moderate Democratic Party but also the radical Frontier organization was allowed to run for election in 1998. Even though the democrats had been purged from the Provisional Legislature in 1997, they were allowed to reenter Hong Kong's political elections. Beijing may have calculated that political inclusion was a better strategy than pushing the democrats to street protests.

Second, the political actors shared an underlying tactical consensus about the rules of the electoral game and the worth of existing political institutions. The Democratic Party conceded that it no longer challenged the Basic Law and the new electoral arrangements made by the "illegal" Provisional Legislature. In addition, the Democratic Party agreed to compete under the new rules of governance. On the other hand, Beijing and the SAR government agreed to tolerate protests, dissent, freedom of the press, and free electoral competition after 1997.

Third, the political actors shared a consensus on basic ideological values. The Democratic Party worked toward a class compromise when it endorsed business's values of economic prosperity and political stability, and it worked toward a national compromise when it endorsed Beijing's resumption of sovereignty from the British. On the other hand, Beijing and the SAR government embraced the democrats' demand that Hong Kong's legislature and government would soon be completely elected in the near future, in accordance with the stipulations in the Basic Law.

Fourth, the political actors competed on the basis of restrained partisanship, and they cooperated tactically to contain especially explosive issues and conflicts. It seems that the political actors extended tactical guarantees not to threaten each other's vital interests and to forgo their capacity to harm each other. Thus the Democratic Party staged only a peaceful protest during the July 1 transition ceremony, when Hong Kong was under the scrutiny of the global mass media. After July 1, 1997, there were indications that the Democratic Party restrained itself from shouting insulting slogans to Beijing leaders during their protests. On the other hand, Beijing and the SAR government tolerated the Democrats' conducting a Tiananmen memorial on June 4 and their fund-raising activities overseas.

Fifth, the political actors perceived decisional outcomes in positive-sum or politics-as-bargaining terms. The Democratic Party was still hopeful that it could win many seats in the legislature, while Beijing and the SAR government used the elections to increase their legitimate rule in Hong Kong and to lure Taipei into national reunification talks.

Finally, democratic compromise was achieved through restricting the scope of representation in order to reassure the traditionally dominant class that its vital interests would be respected. Although no longer hegemonic as it was before the 1980s, the business community could still maintain dominance in the Hong Kong government and legislature through functional constituencies, seats returned through the electoral committee, and the new rule of proportional representation in direct elections. Subsequently, big businesspeople tactically agreed to work with the democrats in future elections because business is the beneficiary of the post-1997 political system.

In sum, an "antagonistic alliance" emerged in Hong Kong when warring factions of disunified political actors deliberately reorganized their relations by negotiating compromises on their most basic disagreements. Beijing, service professional democrats, and big businesspeople tactically agreed on the rules of governance, on the basis of mutual guarantees for the vital interests of those involved. Still, this alliance was antagonistic in the sense that Beijing, service professional democrats, and big businesspeople were deeply divided on ideological and policy issues. They publicly criticized one another, and aimed to outcompete one another in the electoral arena.

What are the implications of this political settlement and democratic compromise on the future of democratization in Hong Kong? We will discuss this topic in the next chapter.

9 | Conclusion

This book examines the origins and development of the democracy project in Hong Kong. In particular, it attempts to explain the metamorphosis of the Hong Kong state from a nondemocracy before the 1980s to a restricted democracy in the late 1980s and a contested democracy in the early 1990s. It also laments the democratic compromise during the critical transition in 1997.

The Genesis of the Democracy Project

As Hong Kong became a newly industrializing economy, it gave rise to a new generation of college students. In the early 1970s, the college students initiated a nationalist movement, calling for identification with the Chinese motherland and campaigning to make Chinese the official language in Hong Kong. When many student activists entered the service professions after graduation, they radicalized those professions and started a community movement criticizing the policies of the colonial government. They formed pressure groups to address the grievances of the grassroots population.

This book argues that earlier nationalist and community movements served as a prelude to the democracy movement of a decade later due to a continuity of values and beliefs, leadership and organizational forms, and strategies of protest among the three movements. Nevertheless, the nationalist and community movements failed to articulate a discourse of democracy because the Hong Kong government was still a nondemocracy ruled jointly through an expatriate alliance between British colonial officials and pro-British big businesspeople.

In the early 1980s, when London negotiated with Beijing over the future of Hong Kong, big businesspeople and the mass media hoped that some-how colonial rule might continue. To counteract this pro-British offensive, Beijing proposed a package it called "Hong Kong People Ruling Hong Kong" in an effort to craft a strategic alliance with the service professionals. The service professionals responded by becoming politicized, forming political groups, developing a pro-welfare platform, and pushing for a democratic reunification with mainland China. After an economic crisis prompted London to accede to Beijing's demands, London pushed for the insertion of such terms as *election* and *accountability* in the Joint Declara-tion in an effort to sell the package to the Hong Kong service professionals and the British Parliament. Thus began the democracy project in Hong Kong. However, it was more a case of muddling through than a grand in-auguration, because the democratic terms were slipped into the Joint Dec-laration at the last moment and were not defined or clarified in any way. Moreover, London covered up its disagreement with Beijing on this critical issue, thus presenting the misleading impression that Beijing, too, endorsed a Western-style democratic system in Hong Kong after 1997.

The Formation of a Restricted Democracy

Once London let the democracy genie out of the bottle, it proposed a modest democratic reform in 1984. Alarmed by the prospect of losing their political hegemony in the Hong Kong government, big businesspeople in the Legislative Council (Legco) and the Executive Council (Exco) managed to slow the democratization process and restrict it to a system of corpo-ratist democracy, thus guaranteeing their monopolistic representation in the Legco through functional constituencies and indirect elections. Still, the limited democratic openings did give the service professionals a mea-sure of power. They enthusiastically participated in elections, mobilized community support, publicized their pro-welfare platform to appeal to the grassroots population, and won landslide victories against traditional busi-nesspeople in District Board elections. Some even got selected for the Legco through indirect elections. The entry of a small number of service profes-sionals transformed the legislative process. Consensus politics was replaced by oppositional politics as service professionals in the Legco increasingly challenged government and business policies.

For the democratic forces, however, rising expectations in the mid-1980s turned into frustration in the late 1980s. Their growing power triggered an unholy alliance between big businesspeople and Beijing. Beijing and the big businesspeople then used the process of drafting the Basic Law to imprint a restricted, corporatist democratic system into Hong Kong's miniconstitution. The service professionals did put up a fight for their populist democratic system—they wanted the Hong Kong government to fulfill its promise to hold direct elections in 1988, and they protested the businesspeople's restricted democracy model both in the Basic Law Drafting Committee and in the streets. But the conservative alliance of Beijing, big businesspeople, and London was too strong to be overcome. The service professionals lacked unity and strategic planning, and they made the fatal error of failing to mobilize the grassroots population around issues concerning the Basic Law. Their populist package was defeated. As the restricted democracy system was written into the constitution, many service professionals became so discouraged that they thought of emigrating and setting up a democratic front overseas.

From Contested Democracy to Democratic Compromise

The conservative alliance was torn apart by the Tiananmen incident in 1989. At the height of the incident, some big businesspeople and pro-Beijing forces turned against the Beijing regime, and even London defected by asking for democratization to be speeded up. Service professionals emerged as popular leaders during the Tiananmen protests; having taken to calling themselves "democrats," they went on to join forces as the United Democrats. They deepened their community network and articulated a pro-welfare platform to appeal to the grassroots population. Through this populist alliance, they won a landslide victory in the first direct elections to the Legco in 1991. The symbolic significance of the Tiananmen incident was that it imposed a democratic discourse on Hong Kong politics. Every political group, even the big businesspeople's conservative organizations, took on a democratic label in an effort to appeal to the widespread democratic sentiments in the early 1990s.

In the mid-1990s, London did an abrupt about-face. It stopped cooperating with Beijing and adopted an antagonistic stance. In 1992, Governor Patten crafted a strategic alliance with service professionals by appointing them to the Legco and promoting a pro-welfare policy. Then Patten reinterpreted the gray areas of the Basic Law to fit the populist democracy system espoused by the service professionals. The support of London and the Hong Kong government further empowered the service professionals. They formed the Democratic Party and won another victory in the 1995 election. Alarmed by the alliance of service professionals and London, big businesspeople were pushed back to Beijing. In response, Beijing consolidated the unholy alliance by appointing them as Hong Kong Advisers in the Preliminary Working Committee and the Preparatory Committee, which handled transition affairs. Furthermore, Beijing announced that it would dismantle the popularly elected legislature and replace it with a provisional one in 1997, because Patten's reforms had violated the Basic Law. Big businesspeople on the Preparatory Committee were pushing for the restoration of old colonial rules that inhibited political protests and rolled back labor rights.

Hong Kong society then was polarized into two camps: those who supported the alliance of Beijing and big businesspeople versus those who supported the populist alliance of service professionals and the grassroots population. Instead of focusing on winning elections and working through electoral rules, the two camps debated and reinterpreted the Basic Law, laying the foundation for a contested democracy in 1997.

However, contested democracy did not materialize during the critical transition period. On the one hand, Beijing announced that new elections to the Legislative Council would take place as early as mid-1998. Beijing also assured the Democratic Party that its members would be allowed to run for election in the post-1997 SAR government. Furthermore, the chief executive elect, Tung Chee-hwa, successfully maintained a channel of communication with the Democrats and personally appealed to them for a smooth transition on July 1. On the other hand, the Democratic Party was weakened by the departure of radical members to form a new Frontier organization and by the pro-welfare stand of Tung's SAR government. Knowing that its strength was in the ballot box rather than in street demonstrations, the Democrats accepted a class compromise with Beijing, the SAR government, and big businesspeople, even though they knew they would be a minority party in the post-1997 legislature.

During the critical July 1 transition in 1997, a consensus among political actors emerged in Hong Kong. Although still ideologically divided and publicly opposed to one another on policy questions, they achieved a tactical understanding on the procedural and ground rules for Hong Kong's democratization.

Toward a Societal Explanation

Bringing the Societal Forces Back In

The power dependency explanation of Hong Kong's democracy (Kuan 1991; S. K. Lau 1995) characterized Hong Kong as a dependent polity controlled by London and Beijing: London and Beijing set the rules of democratization, denying the people of Hong Kong any role in shaping their own future. Advocates of this explanation have tended to see the local elites as power-seeking and preoccupied with "pure" political issues, subject to manipulation by Beijing and London, and Hong Kong's masses as alienated from politics. Consequently, focusing on the structural outcome of democratization, they take a pessimistic view of democracy's prospects in Hong Kong.

More recent research, however, points to the crucial role of societal forces and their shifting alliances in Hong Kong's democratization. Hong Kong's societal forces, rather than dancing to the tunes of Beijing and London or playing the role of spectator, are seen as agents making strategic decisions that affected the course of democratization. Instead of seeing the elites as power-seeking and preoccupied with pure political issues, we can now trace the economic interests and value commitments of the elites and see why some actors were more prone than others to raise socioeconomic and livelihood issues in their quest for democratization. And when we look beyond the final structural outcomes, we can see how societal forces and their shifting alliances complicated the genesis and transformation of the democracy project in Hong Kong.

The big businesspeople played a critical role in blocking democratization. Their interests alone were represented in the colonial government before the 1980s. No wonder Hong Kong was known as a capitalist paradise! In the mid-1980s big businesspeople, through their control of both the Exco and the Legco, restricted the scope of democratization so that functional constituencies and indirect elections still guaranteed that their interests would prevail. In the late 1980s, big businesspeople managed to write their restricted, corporatist democracy model into the constitution through an unholy alliance with Beijing. In the early 1990s, they openly criticized Patten's electoral reforms, laying the groundwork for a contested democracy in 1997. In the mid-1990s, they started another offensive to restore old colonial laws limiting human rights through the Preparatory Committee and the Provisional Legislature. Except for a brief moment at the height of the Tiananmen incident in 1989, big businesspeople consistently acted as a strong force blocking the democracy project.

Opposing them were the service professionals, who emerged in the late 1970s as a new political force to challenge the welfare policies of the colonial government. In the early 1980s they proposed a "democratic national reunification" and pushed London and Beijing hard to write some democratic terms into the Joint Declaration. By the mid-1980s they had grown into an opposition force inside the government when they won seats in the Legco. In the late 1980s, they pushed for direct elections in 1988 and for inclusion of their populist democracy model in the constitution. They failed, but their project was revitalized by the Tiananmen incident and Patten's electoral reforms. Seizing upon the opening of direct elections, service professionals emerged as popular leaders speaking for the interests of Hong Kong; they cultivated a populist alliance, and they won landslide victories in the geographical constituencies in 1991 and 1995. Ironically, however, their entry into legislative politics weakened their links to grassroots organizations and social movements. In order to secure enough votes to have their policies passed in the legislature, the Democrats moderated their political platform, worked with pro-Beijing people, and ultimately focused on institutional channels rather than on street protests.

Even the grassroots population was not so passive as many observers supposed. Though for historical reasons they failed to emerge as a class, they were politically active in presenting their grievances through the community movement in the late 1970s. They were attracted to the pro-welfare issues of service professionals in the 1985 elections, and they chose service professionals to represent them in the legislature. Although the technical issues of the Basic Law debates failed to engage their attention in the late 1980s, they again lent strong support to the pro-welfare, anti-Beijing platform of service professionals in the early 1990s, giving them a popular mandate to push for democratization. In 1997, the growing demands of the grassroots population even led Tung to adopt a pro-welfare package in an effort to pacify them.

State-Societal Alliances

Beijing and London, to be sure, were two powerful actors in Hong Kong's democratic politics. Yet they did not dictate the evolution of democratic politics as they pleased. They needed the support of Hong Kong's societal forces and frequently entered into alliances with them in efforts to carry out their policies. The alliances were of two kinds: institutional and strategic.

An institutional alliance is one formalized through political institutions. London, for instance, ruled Hong Kong through an expatriate alliance with pro-British businesspeople. London and the British hongs had a common interest in maintaining Hong Kong's political stability and Britain's dominance of its economy. This expatriate alliance was institutionalized through the appointment of British and pro-British businesspeople to the Legco and the Exco, thus guaranteeing business's monopolistic representation in the government. This institutional alliance was highly stable for over a century. However, it began to crack during the negotiation process in the early 1980s, as London decided to hand over the sovereignty of Hong Kong to Beijing in 1997.

In the late 1980s, a new unholy alliance between Beijing and Hong Kong Chinese businesspeople gradually replaced the traditional expatriate alliance of London and pro-British businesspeople. Beijing and big businesspeople had a common interest in mainland investments as well as in maintaining Hong Kong's prosperity and stability. This alliance was institutionalized through the appointment of big businesspeople to the Basic Law committees in the late 1980s and to the Preliminary Working Committees, the Preparatory Committee, and the Provisional Legislative Council in the 1990s, thus again guaranteeing business's continued dominance in the government of the SAR. This unholy alliance, like the earlier expatriate alliance, was highly stable. Even though it was shaken by the Tiananmen incident, the rising power of service professionals and Patten's political reforms in the 1990s quickly restored and consolidated it.

A populist alliance, too, was emerging in the early 1990s. Service professionals and the grassroots population had common interests and value commitments in promoting welfare policies, especially when the lives of the urban masses were threatened by Hong Kong's restructuring from a labor-intensive manufacturing economy to a service economy and by the prospect of the importation of mainland Chinese and foreign workers. This populist alliance was forged through the establishment of direct elections to the Legco, which guaranteed that the voice of the people would be heard. The alliance took shape when the Democrats won landslide victories in the 1991 and 1995 elections. At the same time, however, victory at the ballot box served to weaken the populist alliance, for as the Democrats focused on the legislature, their attention to community affairs dwindled. The populist alliance, then, was institutionalized only at the ballot box, not at the level of community mobilization. To weaken the populist alliance, big businesspeople adopted the strategy of restricting the franchise.

During the critical transition in 1997, an antagonistic alliance among Beijing, the SAR government, and service professionals developed in efforts to craft a democratic compromise. There was no explicit pact, but this antagonistic alliance was institutionalized through the new electoral rules to take effect in mid-1997. Beijing and the SAR government allowed service professionals to reenter the race for seats in the Legislative Council, and service professionals promised to uphold the Basic Law and work for prosperity and political stability. Big businesspeople were willing to go along with this compromise because their dominance in the post-1997 government was assured. However, the alliance was antagonistic in the sense that these political actors remained ideologically divided, they publicly opposed one another's policies, and they strove to outcompete one another in elections after 1997. So long as the political actors respect the basic electoral rules and compete on the basis of restrained partisanship, their alliance will endure; if they disregard the vital interests of any of the parties involved, it will fall apart.

Unlike an institutional alliance, a strategic alliance is based merely on political convenience at a particular historical conjuncture. During the negotiation process in the early 1980s, Beijing tried to craft a strategic alliance with service professionals in an effort to win the battle of public opinion. Both Beijing and service professionals wanted national reunification and an end to colonial rule. This strategic alliance quickly fell apart as service professionals discovered that Beijing did not share their orientation toward their democracy project.

In the mid-1980s, London also wanted to craft a strategic alliance with Beijing to prepare for a graceful retreat. This strategic alliance, however, was highly unstable; it was on and off several times as it was battered by the Tiananmen incident and Patten's reforms. Beijing was suspicious of a conspiracy to continue colonial rule, but was willing to mend its differences with London temporarily in the face of the pressing need for a smooth transition in 1997.

At the height of the Tiananmen incident in 1989, some big businesspeople, and even some pro-Beijing forces, wanted to craft a strategic alliance with service professionals to quicken the pace of democratization. But this strategic alliance dissipated as the trauma of the Tiananmen incident faded and business's interests became threatened by the service professionals' pro-welfare program.

Structural Constraints and Historical Opportunities

In sum, contrary to the observers who identify London and Beijing as the main structural constraints on the democracy project, we have seen the crucial role played by alliances between state and societal forces in blocking the democratization of Hong Kong.

Up to the 1980s, the democracy project was suppressed by the expatriate alliance between British officials and British hongs. In these circumstances, service professionals could at best start a community movement to address the grievances of the urban poor, but they failed to inject a democratic discourse into Hong Kong politics. Had there been no expatriate alliance, the liberal governor Murray MacLehose, who promoted many welfare and community-oriented policies, might have instituted more democratic reforms at the local level in the 1970s.

In the late 1980s, the unholy alliance succeeded in restricting the democracy project to a quasi-corporatist democracy that favored business. Had there been no economic integration between Hong Kong and mainland China in the 1980s, Beijing would not have befriended Hong Kong's big businesspeople. It is therefore doubtful that these businesspeople actually preferred a restricted democracy, because such a political system could have facilitated Communist control from Beijing.

However, four historical events galvanized societal forces in Hong Kong to challenge these structural constraints. First, the negotiations over the future of Hong Kong in the 1980s helped bring on an economic crisis, crack the expatriate alliance, start the decolonization process, and imprint some democratic terms in the Joint Declaration. The genesis of the democracy project, therefore, owed much to the negotiations over the 1997 hand-over issue. Had the negotiations not happened, it is doubtful that the democracy project would have gotten started as early as the mid-1980s.

Second, when the Tiananmen incident exploded in 1989, a conservative constitution had been written and the prodemocracy camp was already in disarray. But Tiananmen revitalized prodemocracy forces and weakened their opponents, enabling service professionals effectively to challenge the restricted democracy in the Basic Law. Had there been no violence in Tiananmen Square, the conservative coalition would have remained intact to exercise hegemony over prodemocracy forces.

Third, when London suddenly did an about-face in the early 1990s, Governor Patten manipulated the rules of the Basic Law, extended the franchise, and engaged in a war of words with Beijing. Beijing, in response, decided to purge the popularly elected legislature and condemn the Democrats as pro-British. Had Patten not instituted electoral reforms, Hong Kong's transition would have been much more peaceful.

Finally, in 1996 both Beijing and the service professionals suddenly moderated their hostility, negotiated their basic disagreements, and tactically agreed on the governance of the SAR. It seems that Beijing, the service professionals, and the big businesspeople so valued a smooth transition that they would rather work with one another than risk turbulence. Had a smooth transition on July 1, 1997, not been so urgent, it is doubtful that the basic disagreements among Beijing, service professionals, and big business could have been resolved so peacefully.

We have seen, then, that both pro- and antidemocracy forces have deep-rooted institutional bases. Historical events, however, were on the side of the prodemocracy forces. Yet the politics of the negotiation process, the Tiananmen event, Patten's electoral reforms, and the critical July 1, 1997 transition were not enough to consolidate democracy in Hong Kong.

Why not? Why were the democratic forces in Hong Kong frustrated when their neighbors in Taiwan and South Korea managed to achieve breakthroughs?

Hong Kong's Democratization from the NIE Perspective

Hong Kong, like the other East Asian newly industrializing economies, had most of the prerequisites for democratization. Its robust economy makes possible high levels of urbanization, education, literacy, and media exposure. It has considerable wealth and a large middle class, and it lacks extreme income inequalities. The movement for democratization came at roughly the same time in Hong Kong, Taiwan, and South Korea. Yet there are also profound differences among them with regard to autonomy, the state-business relationship, labor activism, class alliances, national reunification, and the role of historical events in the development of the democracy project. Those differences explain the diverse paths that democratic development took in the three NIEs.

Taiwan: Democracy from Above

Among the three East Asian states, Taiwan was the strongest and had the most autonomy. It is often described as a party-state, because a powerful Leninist party permeated its structure, economy, and society. It was also an alien state because the Guomindang (GMD, the Nationalist Party) imposed its rule on the native Taiwanese when it was defeated by the Chinese Communists on the mainland in 1949. The mainlanders in the GMD, fearing the ambitions of the Taiwanese for self-sufficiency and independence, maintained a large state sector (about 16% of Taiwan's GDP in the early 1970s) to keep the reins of economic power in their own hands. The GMD also had deeply penetrated civil society, so it could curb the development of any organized opposition. Under martial law, civil liberties were severely limited (there was no freedom of assembly, for instance) and the media were strictly censored. Moreover, government surveillance and the strong threat of repression were central mechanisms of the GMD's labor control (Gold 1986; So and Chiu 1995; So and Hua 1992; Tien 1992).

Although the Taiwanese state was developmentally oriented, it was not state enterprises but small- and medium-sized firms (S&M firms) that made up Taiwan's export sector. Of the 260,000 business enterprises in Taiwan, 98 percent were considered S&M firms, employing 70 percent of all employees and accounting for 65 percent of exports. But the small business sector was not linked to the Taiwanese state: the GMD neither paid serious attention to the trade associations organized by the S&M firms nor sought their advice in formulating economic policies. Getting no support from the state, the S&M firms had to rely on self-financing or informal money markets for credit. They also complained that the state failed to supply them with information on trends in international trade (Hsiao 1993; Shieh 1992).

Although capital accumulated at a rapid rate, Taiwan's "economic miracle" was achieved at the expense of social expenditures, so that such problems as income inequalities, environmental pollution, industrial safety, traffic congestion, consumer fraud, and human rights violations became endemic. By the early 1970s, opposition to the GMD regime began to emerge. Instead of waging a class struggle, however, the opposition took the form of an ethnic struggle against mainlanders' domination of native Taiwanese (Bello and Rosenfeld 1992; Wachman 1994).

A new generation of indigenous Taiwanese intellectuals began to demand their rights to political participation and representation in the state, freedom of speech, and the lifting of martial law. They complained of violations of human rights; they used such new magazines as *China Tide* to resurrect the struggle against despotism that had begun during the Japanese occupation of Taiwan; they started a native literature focusing on the lives of indigenous Taiwanese people; and they organized a Dangwai (non-GMD) political group to challenge the GMD in elections. United by their Taiwanese language and culture, this new generation of intellectuals forged an ethnic alliance among Taiwanese S&M businesspeople, the new middle class, and labor against the mainlanders' GMD in the late 1970s and 1980s. The Dangwai expressed their claims in the streets, on the floor of the legislature, and in their writings. In response, the GMD shut down their magazines, suppressed their street demonstrations, and imprisoned their leaders (G. Chen 1982; Chiou 1986).

In the mid-1980s, however, the state experienced a crisis of legitimacy when the Western states severed diplomatic ties with Taiwan to recognize China and a series of economic and political scandals broke. At this historical juncture the aging strongman Chiang Ching-kuo persuaded the GMD conservatives to promote democratic reforms from above. The GMD lifted martial law, released political prisoners, legalized a multiparty system, informally recognized the Democratic Progressive Party (DPP), and liberalized the mass media (Chou and Nathan 1987; T. J. Cheng 1989; Myers 1987; Copper 1987). Democratic reforms would polish the GMD's image, and its legitimacy would be increased if the oppositional forces were included in the electoral game. Besides, with its monopoly of the mass media, its enormous resources, and the credit for economic development, the GMD could guarantee its own victory in elections and stay in power (So and May 1993; Haggard and Kaufman 1995).

The lifting of martial law stimulated the emergence of organized interest groups. When the easing of restrictions on strikes and street demonstrations allowed interest groups to demonstrate, a "contentious" civil society emerged and social movements proliferated—a consumer movement, an environmental movement, a farmers' movement, a women's movement, a labor movement, a student movement, a shelter movement (Hsiao 1996).

Since the GMD took the initiative in paving the way for democracy when it was still strong, it managed to dominate the transition, easing up where and when it deemed fit, and kept the pace and direction of the reforms relatively well controlled. After the GMD regained its legitimacy through democratization, it began to formulate a new policy toward the mainland. It allowed home visits and tourism, and even tolerated indirect trade with the mainland and investment there. The dynamics of democratization and integration with the mainland then became fused. A new Taiwanese identity emerged to contest the dominant Chinese national identity, and opposition forces openly articulated the Taiwan independence platform to challenge the mainland when it called for national reunification. Big business became more active in politics, and found itself in conflict with the GMD on the issue of direct trade with mainland China. To break the unholy alliance between big business and Communist China and persuade big business to stay in Taiwan, the GMD relaxed pollution regulations and sweetened tax incentives—moves that made social activists increasingly critical of the GMD and big business. Finally, mainland reunification issues divided GMD leaders and created new political alignments among pro- and anti-unification forces, forcing the Taiwanese state to be more responsive to demands from civil society.

In the early 1990s, the GMD further promoted the Taiwanization of the party apparatus, increased government spending on some welfare measures, incorporated big business in the state's decision-making process, and held strategic negotiations with opposition parties in an effort to dilute the antagonism between mainlanders and Taiwanese and gain support from the new middle class, businesspeople, and moderate elements in the opposition parties (Hsiao and So 1993, 1996).

As a result, a democratic consolidation occurred in Taiwan in the mid-1990s. The GMD was able to achieve a constitutional reform and open up the parliamentary body, two major cities' mayors, the Taiwan provincial governor, and the presidency for election. Most important, the GMD won the highly competitive presidential election in 1996 at the ballot box. Once the GMD competed effectively for votes in an open electoral system and did not hesitate to hold strategic negotiations with opposition parties, it seems that democratic reforms were firmly institutionalized in Taiwanese society. In fact, researchers have already begun to shift their attention from the study of democratic breakthroughs and consolidation to the examination of the economic consequences of democratization (T. J. Cheng 1996; Haggard and Kaufman 1995).

South Korea: Democracy from Below

Like the Taiwanese state, the state in South Korea was developmentally oriented. Economic growth, productivity, and competitiveness were at the top of the state's agenda (Amsden 1989). Nevertheless, the Korean state did not have a strong political party that could secure grassroots support, nor did it have a strong leader who could unify the state and party for democratization. Thus the Korean state relied on a strong dose of authoritarianism to maintain its control over civil society. During the regime of Park Chung Hee, for example, strikes were banned, existing unions outlawed, dissenting newspapers and magazines closed down, protesters arrested, and political activists jailed (Choi 1989).

The state-business relationship in South Korea also differed from that in Taiwan. Whereas Taiwan had a large state sector and S&M business-people had no part in the state's decision making, in South Korea the state cultivated a small number of conglomerate business groups (*chaebols*) as its clientele. The state supported the *chaebols'* economic monopolies and granted them credits and export licenses in exchange for a steady supply of political funds. As Eckert (1993) remarks, despite their wealth, Korean big businesspeople remained a decidedly unhegemonic class, estranged from the very state and society in which they continued to grow. On the one hand, the *chaebols* were frequently disciplined by state officials through withdrawal of loans and licenses if they did not meet the specified stringent performance requirements for export. On the other hand, the *chaebols* were the focus of intense popular resentment because of the aggressive and selfish way their owners had accumulated wealth (Koo 1993a). Kim Woo Choong, chairman of the Daewoo Group, complained: "Our country's businessmen have not been able to acquire public esteem. On the contrary, [they] have been denounced or kept at a safe distance with feigned respect" (quoted in Eckert 1993:95). This *chaebol*-bashing phenomenon emerged, as Koo (1993b) explains, because the *chaebols* exploited labor to the maximum extent possible under the protection of an authoritarian capitalist state. In these circumstances, for which they were neither culturally nor ideologically prepared, Korean workers developed impressive class consciousness and organization.

Despite the admiration of outsiders for the "Korean miracle," then, South Korea's economic achievements never brought it popular support. The regimes of Park Chung Hee (1961–79) and Chun Doo Hwan (1980–87) were continuously plagued by student demonstrations, dissident movements, and labor protests. Cheng and Kim (1994) point out that throughout the 1960s and 1970s, university campuses were shut down for at least a month every year by student demonstrations against the authoritarian Park regime. In the 1980s, the student demonstrations became better organized and more violent (Han 1989). The incidence and frequency of violence increased as the suppression of the Chun regime intensified, producing "a vicious cycle of opposition and suppression."

Whereas the opposition movements in Taiwan focused on the ethnic conflict between mainlanders and Taiwanese, the Korean opposition took place along the class divide between the state and the *chaebols* on the one hand and the middle and working classes on the other. Despite the repression of workers, their high concentration in the *chaebols*' large-scale heavy industries provided favorable conditions for a militant labor movement. The labor movement became explosive when it developed close ties to political movements outside industry and was supported organizationally and ideologically by the *minjung* (the people's or the masses') movement of the new middle class. *Minjung* became a powerful opposition discourse and a political symbol, and provided a new identity for all who participated in political, social, and cultural movements in opposition to the authoritarian state (Koo 1993b, 1993c).

In the mid-1980s, the merger of the labor and *minjung* movements led to democratic breakthroughs in South Korea. The torture-killing of a Seoul National University student, revealed in January 1987, intensified the struggle against the regime. There were 3,749 strikes in 1987. Chun's announcement that a presidential election would be postponed until his term expired brought massive demonstrations. According to news reports, more than 300,000 people demonstrated, and the street demonstrations kept escalating until they had grown too big and widespread to be controlled by the police alone. Finally, by June 1987, Roh Tae Woo, chair of the ruling party, admitted defeat, accepted practically all the demands of the opposition movement, and agreed to hold a direct presidential election at the end of 1997. In contrast to the Taiwanese experience of initiating democratic reforms from above by a strong party leader, the Korean experience typifies the promotion of democracy from below—the transition from authoritarian rule occurred because of unstoppable strikes and street demonstrations by civil society (Cheng and Kim 1994; Hsiao and Koo 1997).

Oppositional elites negotiated to merge their parties into one dominant party (the Democratic Liberal Party, or DLP) in 1990, and a civilian government under Kim Young Sam was elected in 1993. In 1996, after a radical shakeup of the military establishment, two former military presidents— Chun and Roh—were even put in jail.

Democratic transition, however, was accompanied by the deradicalization of middle-class politics. Hsiao and Koo (1997) observe that many members of the middle class felt threatened by labor's militancy after the democratic transition. As the *minjung* movement waned, the middle class began to promote its own interests (Koo 1991). Thus a new Citizen Coalition for Economic Justice was formed to correct economic injustice, to protect the environment, to ensure a clean election, to fight against gender inequality, and to raise civil consciousness. The new social movements and the regional loyalty of the middle class became prominent issues in Korean electoral politics. In the mid-1990s, as the military fell under civilian control and electoral rules became institutionalized, there was little doubt that South Korea had not only negotiated the transition to democracy but consolidated it.

Hong Kong: Embattled Democracy

Whereas in South Korea and Taiwan the state intervened extensively in the marketplace to direct industrialization according to its own priorities, in Hong Kong the colonial state left investment decisions to the private sector. Certainly, the state assisted private capital accumulation in a variety of ways, most notably in provisions for the infrastructure (such as the maintenance of a low-tax business environment, the expansion of the public education system, and the massive public housing program), but Hong Kong was still a far cry from the developmental states portrayed in the statist literature. Haddon-Cave (1984) thus describes Hong Kong's economic policy as "positive non-interventionism."

Furthermore, the pattern of the state's relationship with business was not the same in Hong Kong as in Taiwan and South Korea. Whereas Taiwanese big businesspeople were excluded from the state altogether and Korean *chaebols* were merely the clientele of the authoritarian state, Hong Kong's big businesspeople maintained an alliance with the colonial state for over a century. This state-business alliance was never seriously challenged until the emergence of a new generation of service professionals in the 1970s. Even then, Hong Kong's community movement was much weaker than the oppositional movements in Taiwan and South Korea. The numbers of the participants, the strength of their organizations, and the violence of their confrontations were on a much smaller in scale in Hong Kong than in Taiwan and South Korea. An ethnic bond united the native Taiwanese and a *minjung* discourse united the Korean middle and working classes against their authoritarian states; no equivalent bond or radical discourse united the Hong Kong service professionals with the grassroots population. Although Hong Kong workers received low wages, they were still better off than their Korean counterparts in large *chaebol* enterprises under strict, repressive labor laws. In addition, the multitude of small firms, high labor turnover, and ideological divisions between pro-Beijing and pro-Taipei factions weakened the labor unions in Hong Kong. Moreover, Hong Kong protesters had fewer grievances than their counterparts in Taiwan and South Korea. Although the Hong Kong state was a nondemocracy, it was not authoritarian. In comparison with Taiwan and South Korea in the 1970s, Hong Kong experienced little repression or bloodshed and had no political prisoners. Although Hong Kong was not a welfare state, the MacLehose administration in the 1970s did provide some welfare measures, such as public housing, to mitigate urban grievances. These factors may explain why the Taiwanese and South Korean oppositional movements were able to articulate a democratic discourse much earlier than the community movement in Hong Kong.

In sum, the structural conditions for democratization were much less favorable in Hong Kong than in its neighboring states, because the colonial state's conservative alliance with big businesspeople was stronger and the service professionals' populist alliance with the grassroots population was weaker.

Furthermore, whereas democratization occurred before national reunification in Taiwan, democratization and national reunification occurred together in Hong Kong. In Taiwan, therefore, the GMD had a much freer hand to promote democracy from above, without interference from Beijing. In Hong Kong, where democracy was a product of national reunification and decolonization, Beijing and London had a chance to shape the course of democratization. Their negotiations over the future of Hong Kong in the early 1980s served as a catalyst to inject democracy into Hong Kong society. The talks simultaneously politicized service professionals and created a crack in the expatriate alliance. Nevertheless, the democratic structure that emerged in Hong Kong was neither directed from above, as in Taiwan, nor pushed from below, as in South Korea; it simply muddled through. London used the democracy project as a tactical means to sell the Joint Declaration to Hong Kong service professionals and the British Parliament. London and the Hong Kong government had no intention of carrying the democracy project through. After the Joint Declaration was signed, the Hong Kong government was a lame duck, and it felt no need to manipulate the course of democratization to stay in power, as the GMD state in Taiwan did.

Had there been no economic integration between Hong Kong and mainland China, Hong Kong big businesspeople might have formed an ethnic alliance across class lines (like that in Taiwan) to safeguard Hong Kong's interests. But the very rapid economic integration between Hong Kong and mainland China prevented the formation of such ethnic alliances. Instead, mainland economic integration cultivated an "unholy alliance" between Hong Kong Chinese big businesspeople and Beijing, greatly strengthening Hong Kong Chinese businesspeople's economic power and social status at the expense of those of the British hongs. Once this unholy alliance was formed, bourgeois dominance was restored in Hong Kong. When London forsook its democracy promise and joined the conservative camp in the late 1980s, the Beijing–big businesspeople–London conservative alliance left little room for the democratization of Hong Kong. After their unsuccessful attempt to install direct election of the legislators in the Hong Kong government, Hong Kong's service professionals were in no position to challenge the almighty conservative alliance. The product of this imbalance between pro- and antidemocracy forces was a restricted, corporatist democratic system written into the constitution.

In the early 1990s, Taiwan and South Korea were on their way to democratic consolidation, as their opposing parties agreed to abide by electoral rules, and there was direct election of their presidents and legislative councilors. However, Hong Kong was on its way to a contested democracy, because the Tiananmen incident had, overnight, revitalized the democracy project through demoralizing the Beijing regime and injecting a democratic discourse into Hong Kong politics. Furthermore, London defected to the democracy camp, proposing electoral reforms, uniting service professionals into a democratic party, and enabling the democrats to forge a populist alliance with the grassroots population on an anti-Beijing, pro-welfare platform at the voting box. In the early 1990s, the democrats were considerably strengthened, able to contest the rules of restricted democracy imposed by the conservative alliance of Beijing and big businesspeople.

However, this new impetus toward the democracy project in the early 1990s failed to lead to a democratic consolidation like that of Taiwan and South Korea. Although the Hong Kong democrats had strength at the voting box, they were weak in mobilization power. Used to having institutional channels to promote its policy, the Democratic Party neglected linkages with community organizations and social movements. After the departure of the radicals inside the party, the Democratic Party agreed to have a democratic compromise with Beijing and big businesspeople, even though it knew that it would only be a minority party in the legislature.

Theoretical Implications

The above discussion on Hong Kong's democracy provides the following implications for the literature on democratization. First, the Hong Kong case shows that democratization is not purely a political phenomenon, because it is embedded in the economy and the national reunification process. In Hong Kong, democratization occurred side by side with economic relocation and national reunification with China. Hong Kong's economic integration with mainland China triggered both the formation of an unholy alliance between Beijing and Hong Kong big capitalists, as well as the intensification of the grassroots population's distress over unemployment and inflation. While the unholy alliance was strong enough to narrow the scope of democracy and slow its progress, the grassroots population's distress continued to generate support for service professionals' pro-welfare, prolabor agenda at the ballot box. Thus integration with the mainland generated both conservative forces to obstruct democratization and popular forces to promote it. The path of democracy would have been radically different otherwise.

Second, the Hong Kong case shows that the sequence of democratization and national reunification matters. In Taiwan, democratization occurred before the issue of national reunification became prominent. The GMD, therefore, had a freer hand to promote the mode of democracy it liked. In Hong Kong, where the democracy project was conceived during the negotiation process, most electoral reforms were proposed after the colony's future had been settled. Beijing then felt it had a right to intervene in Hong Kong's political affairs because it would resume sovereignty in 1997.

Third, the Hong Kong case shows also that the positive role of the British in promoting democracy in Third World countries has been greatly exaggerated. Britain's rule of law and its system of representation are said to have laid the foundation for democratic government in the postcolonial era. In Hong Kong, it is obvious that democratization was never high on Britain's agenda as it negotiated with Beijing. British electoral reforms in the late 1980s were halfhearted. Governor Patten's electoral package in the early 1990s was too little, too late. In fact, it was the waning of the British factor that helped consolidate the democratic compromise in the mid-1990s.

Fourth, the Hong Kong case shows, too, that business's role in Third World democracy also has been exaggerated. In the third-wave literature, business's role in democratization has seldom been analyzed because business is often lumped with the middle class. Since middle-class service professionals were promoters of democratization, it is often assumed that big businesspeople also played a positive role in the process. Yet Hong Kong's big businesspeople were the key opponents of the democracy project. The expatriate alliance opposed it; the unholy alliance opposed it. Only when business's dominance of the Hong Kong government was assured did big businesspeople go along with the democratic compromise with the service professionals.

Finally, the Hong Kong case shows that although service professionals were key promoters of the democracy project, they could not accomplish the task by themselves. Their strength lies in the development of an alliance with the grassroots population at both the ballot box and the community level. Hong Kong's Democratic Party was moving toward a community mobilization mode in the early 1990s. However, the Democrats' success at the ballot box and their absorption in legislative politics so distracted them from community work that their radical members decamped in disillusionment and their power to mobilize grassroots support evaporated. Eventually the Democrats accepted a compromise with Beijing, the SAR government, and the business community, even though they knew they would be a minority party for a long time to come.

In short, the Hong Kong case shows that democratization is more than a purely political phenomenon, that the sequence of democratization and national reunification matters, that the positive roles of the British and business are greatly exaggerated, and that the service professionals must gain the support of the grassroots population at both the ballot box and the community level if they are to overcome the tendency to compromise the democracy project. That being the case, what lies in store for Hong Kong now that it has become Beijing's SAR?

Whither Hong Kong's Democracy?

Democratic compromise during the July 1, 1997 transition reproduced the mode of restricted corporatist democracy that Hong Kong practiced in the late 1980s. Business and pro-Beijing forces played dominant roles in the SAR government, and the Democratic Party was only a minority party in the Legislative Council.

Will Hong Kong move toward an authoritarian scenario? When service professionals protest against the SAR government and Beijing, will the police try to suppress them? If they do, there may be violent clashes, massive arrests, and unstoppable riots, followed by a bear market, a sharp drop in real estate prices, a massive out-migration of service professionals, capital flight, inflation, and panic buying at supermarkets. In that event, Beijing may send troops to restore order, suspend the Basic Law, outlaw the Democratic Party, institute press censorship, ban "subversive" organizations, and take political prisoners. After peace is restored, Beijing may rely on an unholy alliance with big business to rule Hong Kong without any input from service professionals.

Since this authoritarian scenario hinges on an outbreak of violent confrontations, massive riots, and a serious economic crisis, it is highly unlikely to take place in the near future. Besides, Beijing would hesitate to militarize Hong Kong for fear of undermining the prospects for peaceful reunification with Taiwan and doing untold damage to its efforts to achieve economic modernization at home (Yahuda 1993:251).

Then will Hong Kong move instead toward a democracy-from-below scenario, like that in South Korea? For example, if the Democratic Party gets fed up with perpetual defeat in legislative politics, it may decide to go outside the institutional arena once again to stage public demonstrations in the streets. The Democrats could mobilize community organizations, social movements, and the grassroots population for one violent protest after another. After months of such unrest, the business-dominated SAR government would be forced to step down. The Basic Law could be amended to establish direct elections of the chief executive and the Legislative Council to meet the Democrats' demands. Knowing that it is futile to resist demands from the civil society, Beijing and the big businesspeople could reluctantly accept a populist mode of democracy in Hong Kong. This scenario hinges on the empowerment of the populist alliance through street protests and massive demonstrations. It seems highly unlikely, though, because street protests in Hong Kong in the post-1997 era draw only a few hundred protesters, at most a few thousand.

So it seems that a restricted, corporatist democracy will prevail in Hong Kong for at least a few more decades. Yet as long as the Democratic Party is permitted to function, it will play a crucial role in promoting democratization, because of its strong grassroots support at the ballot box. Since the Basic Law stipulates that elections will play a significant role in allocating political power, elections will not be abolished altogether. Thus, while a restricted, corporatist democracy project will survive, it will be under constant challenge from service professionals and the grassroots population.

Service professionals will push for prolabor, pro-welfare policies, defend human rights, and challenge business's and Beijing's dominance in the government. Although democracy may not develop so quickly as it did in Taiwan and South Korea, in time Hong Kong may be neither a capitalist paradise nor a timid Special Administrative Region of the People's Republic.

References

Books and Articles

Adams, J. S. 1995. "Interview with Sir Percy Cradock." *Asian Affairs: Journal of the Royal Society for Asian Affairs* 26:7–9.

Almond, Gabriel A., and Sidney Verba. 1963. *The Civic Culture: Political Attitudes and Democracy in Five Nations.* Princeton: Princeton University Press.

Amsden, Alice. 1989. *Asia's Next Giant: South Korea and Late Industrialization.* New York: Oxford University Press.

Baker, Hugh D. R. 1983. "Life in the Cities: The Emergence of Hong Kong Man." *China Quarterly* 95:469–79.

Bello, Walden, and Stephanie Rosenfeld. 1992. *Dragons in Distress: Asia's Miracle Economies in Crisis.* San Francisco: Institute for Food and Development Policy.

The Birth of the Basic Law. 1990. Hong Kong: Wen Wei Po.

Bonavia, David. 1985. *Hong Kong 1997: The Final Settlement.* Hong Kong: South China Morning Post.

Burns, John P. 1994. "Hong Kong in 1993: The Struggle for Authority Intensifies." *Asian Survey* 34:55–63.

Burton, Michael, and John Higley. 1987. "Elite Settlements." *American Sociological Review* 52:295–307.

Campbell, Duncan. 1980. "A Secret Plan for Dictatorship." *New Statesman,* Dec. 12, p. 8.

Castells, Manuel, L. Goh, and R. Yin-Wang Kwok. 1990. *The Shek Kip Mei Syndrome: Economic Development and Public Housing in Hong Kong and Singapore.* London: Pion.

Chai, B. Karin. 1993. "The Politicization of Unions in Hong Kong." Pp. 121–58 in *One Culture, Many Systems: Politics in the Reunification of China,* edited by Donald H. McMillen and Michael E. DeGolyer. Hong Kong: Chinese University Press.

Chan, Johannes. 1996. "Representation in Dispute—Who Will Rule Hong Kong?" *China Forum,* Winter, pp. 4–7, 38–39.

Chan, Joseph Man. 1993. "Communication, Political Knowledge and Attitudes: A Survey Study of the Hong Kong Electorate." Pp. 41–62 in *Hong Kong Tried Democracy: The 1991 Elections in Hong Kong,* edited by Siu-Kai Lau and Kin-

Shuen Louie. Hong Kong: Hong Kong Institute of Asia-Pacific Studies, Chinese University of Hong Kong.

Chan, Joseph Man, and Chin-Chuan Lee. 1991. *Mass Media and Political Transition: The Hong Kong Press in China's Orbit.* New York: Guilford.

Chan, Ming K. 1991. "Democracy Derailed." Pp. 3–33 in *The Hong Kong Basic Law,* edited by Ming K. Chan and David J. Clark. Armonk, N.Y.: M. E. Sharpe.

———. 1992. "Under China's Shadow: Realpolitik of Hong Kong Labour Unionism Toward 1997." Pp. 15–36 in *Politics and Society in Hong Kong Towards 1997,* edited by Charles Burton. Toronto: Joint Centre for Asia Pacific Studies.

———. 1994. "Decolonization Without Democracy: The Birth of Pluralistic Politics in Hong Kong." Pp. 161–81 in *The Politics of Democratization: Generalizing East Asian Experience,* edited by Edward Friedman. Boulder: Westview.

———. 1995. "All in the Family: The Hong Kong–Guangdong Link in Historical Perspective." Pp. 31–63 in *The Hong Kong–Guangdong Link: Partnership in Flux,* edited by Reginald Yin-Wang Kwok and Alvin Y. So. Armonk, N.Y.: M. E. Sharpe.

———. 1996. "The Politics of Hong Kong's Imperfect Transition: Dimensions of the China Factor." Paper presented at the Annual Meeting of the Association for Asian Studies, Honolulu, April.

———. 1997. "The Legacy of the British Administration of Hong Kong: A View from Hong Kong." *China Quarterly* 151:567–82.

Chan, Ming K., and Tuen-yu Lau. 1990. "Dilemma of the Communist Press in a Pluralistic Society: Hong Kong in the Transition to Chinese Sovereignty, 1988–1989." *Asian Survey* 30:731–47.

Chan Yu-xiang. 1989. *Zuori Jinri Chen Yu-xiang* [Yesterday's and today's Chen Yu-xiang]. Hong Kong: Guang Jue Jing.

———. 1990. *Xiang Gang Sin Sheng Dai* [The new generation of Hong Kong]. Hong Kong: South China Press.

Chao, Linda, and Ramon H. Myers. 1998. *The First Chinese Democracy: Political Life in the Republic of China on Taiwan.* Baltimore: Johns Hopkins University Press.

Cheek-Milby, Kathleen. 1989. "The Civil Servant as Politician: The Role of the Official Member of the Legislative Council." Pp. 256–91 in *Hong Kong: Challenge of Transformation,* edited by Kathleen Cheek-Milby and Miron Mushkat. Hong Kong: Centre of Asian Studies, University of Hong Kong.

Chen, Edward K. Y. 1980. "The Economic Setting." Pp. 1–50 in *The Business Environment in Hong Kong,* edited by David G. Lethbridge. Hong Kong: Oxford University Press.

Chen, Guying. 1982. "The Reform Movement among Intellectuals in Taiwan since 1970." *Bulletin of Concerned Asian Scholars* 14 (3):32–47.

Chen, Jing-xiang. 1985. "XiangGang Di XueSheng YunDong" [Hong Kong's student movement]. Pp. 177–203 in *Hong Kong in the Mid-Eighties,* edited by Joseph Y. S. Cheng. Hong Kong: University Publisher.

Cheng, Joseph Y. S. 1984a. *Hong Kong in Search of a Future.* Hong Kong: Oxford University Press.

———. 1984b. "The Future of Hong Kong: Surveys of the Hong Kong People's Attitudes." *Australian Journal of Chinese Affairs* 12:113–42.

———. 1986. "The 1985 District Board Elections in Hong Kong." Pp. 67–87 in *Hong Kong in Transition*, edited by Joseph Y. S. Cheng. Hong Kong: Oxford University Press.

———. 1989a. "The 1989 District Board Elections — A Study of Political Participation in the Transition Period." Pp. 117–49 in *Hong Kong: Challenge of Transformation*, edited by Kathleen Cheek-Milby and Miron Mushkat. Hong Kong: Centre of Asian Studies, University of Hong Kong.

———. 1989b. "The Democracy Movement in Hong Kong: Difficulties and Prospects." Paper presented at the conference "Hong Kong towards 1997 and Beyond," Honolulu, Jan. 26–27.

———. 1994. "Hong Kong's Legislative Council Elections: Review of 1991 and Planning for 1995." Pp. 291–316 in *25 Years of Social and Economic Development in Hong Kong*, edited by Benjamin K. P. Leung and Teresa Y. C. Wong. Hong Kong: Centre of Asian Studies, University of Hong Kong.

———. 1995. "Sino-British Negotiations and Problems of the British Administration." Paper presented at the conference "Hong Kong and Its Pearl River Delta Hinterland: Links to China, Links to the World," University of British Columbia, Vancouver, May.

———. 1996. "Political Participation in Hong Kong in the Mid-1990s." Pp. 13–44 in *The 1995 Legislative Council Elections in Hong Kong*, edited by Hsin-Chi Kuan et al. Hong Kong: Hong Kong Institute of Asia-Pacific Studies, Chinese University of Hong Kong.

———. 1997. "Introduction." Pp. xxxvii–lv in *The Other Hong Kong Report 1997*, edited by Joseph Y. S. Cheng. Hong Kong: Chinese University Press.

Cheng, Tun-Jen. 1989. "Democratizing the Quasi-Leninist KMT Regime in Taiwan." *World Politics* 41:471–99.

———. 1996. "Economic Consequences of Democratization in Taiwan and South Korea." Working Papers in Taiwan Studies, American Political Science Association.

Cheng, Tun-Jen, and Eun Mee Kim. 1994. "Making Democracy: Generalizing the South Korean Case." Pp. 125–47 in *The Politics of Democratization: Generalizing East Asian Experience*, edited by Edward Friedman. Boulder: Westview.

Cheung, Anthony B. L. 1987. "Xin Zhong Chan Jie Ji De Mao Qu Yu Zheng Zhi Ying Xiang" [The rise of the new middle class and its political impact]. *Ming Bao Yue Kan* 253 (Jan. 10): 10–15.

———. 1994. "Hong Kong Pro-Democracy Parties' Role and Function." *Meeting Point Forum*, July, pp. 1–3. (In Chinese.)

———. 1997. "Rebureaucratization of Politics in Hong Kong: Prospects after 1997." *Asian Survey* 37:720–37.

Cheung, Chor-Yung. 1997. "Constitution and Administration." Pp. 1–14 in *The Other Hong Kong Report 1997*, edited by Joseph Y. S. Cheng. Hong Kong: Chinese University Press.

Ching, Frank. 1985. *Hong Kong and China: For Better or For Worse*. New York: China Council of the Asia Society and the Foreign Policy Association.

———. 1993. "Politics, Politicians and Political Parties." Pp. 23–37 in *The Other*

Hong Kong Report 1993, edited by Po-King Choi and Lok-Sang Ho. Hong Kong: Chinese University Press.

———. 1994. "Toward Colonial Sunset: The Wilson Regime, 1987–92." Pp. 173–97 in *Precarious Balance: Hong Kong Between China and Britain, 1842–1992,* edited by Ming K. Chan. Armonk N.Y.: M. E. Sharpe.

———. 1996. "From the Joint Declaration to the Basic Law." Pp. 33–50 in *The Other Hong Kong Report 1996,* edited by Mee-Kau Nyaw and Si-Ming Li. Hong Kong: Chinese University Press.

——— 1997a. "China–Hong Kong Relations." Pp. 29–48 in *The Other Hong Kong Report 1997,* edited by Joseph Y. S. Cheng. Hong Kong: Chinese University Press.

———. 1997b. "Misreading Hong Kong." *Foreign Affairs* 76 (3): 53–66.

Chiou, C. L. 1986. "Politics of Alienation and Polarization: Taiwan's Tangwai in the 1980s." *Bulletin of Concerned Asian Scholars* 18:16–28.

Chiu, Hungdah. 1987. "Introduction." Pp. 1–22 in *The Future of Hong Kong: Toward 1997 and Beyond,* edited by Hungdah Chiu, Y. C. Jao, and Yuan-li Wu. New York: Quorum Books.

Chiu, Hungdah, Y. C. Jao, and Yuan-li Wu. 1987. *The Future of Hong Kong: Toward 1997 and Beyond.* New York: Quorum Books.

Chiu, Sammy W. S. 1996. "Social Welfare." Pp. 431–48 in *The Other Hong Kong Report 1996,* edited by Mee-Kau Myaw and Si-Ming Li. Hong Kong: Chinese University Press.

Chiu, Stephen. 1995. *The Politics of Laissez-faire: Hong Kong's Strategy of Industrialization in Historical Perspective.* Hong Kong: Hong Kong Institute of Asia-Pacific Studies, Chinese University of Hong Kong.

Chiu, Stephen, and Tai-Lok Lui. Forthcoming. "Conclusion." In *Social Movements in Hong Kong,* edited by Stephen Chiu and Tai-Lok Lui. Hong Kong: University of Hong Kong Press.

Chiu, Stephen, and David Levin. Forthcoming. "Contestatory Unionism: Trade Unions in the Private Sector." In *Social Movements in Hong Kong,* edited by Stephen Chiu and Tai-Lok Lui. Hong Kong: University of Hong Kong Press.

Choi, Jang Jip. 1989. *Labor and the Authoritarian State: Labor Unions in South Korean Manufacturing Industries, 1961–1980.* Seoul: Korea University Press.

Chou, Yangsun, and Andrew Nathan. 1987. "Democratizing Transition in Taiwan." *Asian Survey* 27:277–99.

Chu, Cindy. 1996. "The 'New Era's Patriotic United Front,' the Hong Kong Question, and Implications for China's Reform." Dissertation, University of Hawaii at Manoa.

Chui, Ernest Wing-Tak. 1989. "Policy versus Politics: Implications of the Politicization of Social Workers in Hong Kong." *Asian Journal of Public Administration* 11:216–30.

Chung, Robert T. Y. 1994. "Public Opinion." Pp. 103–23 in *The Other Hong Kong Report 1993,* edited by Donald H. McMillen and Si-Wai Man. Hong Kong: Chinese University Press.

Conner, Alison W. 1997. "Legal Institutions in Transitional Hong Kong." Pp. 85–112 in *The Challenge of Hong Kong's Reintegration with China,* edited by Ming K. Chan. Hong Kong: University of Hong Kong Press.

Copper, John. 1987. "Politics in Taiwan, 1985-86: Political Developments and Elections." In *Survey of Recent Developments in China (Mainland and Taiwan), 1985-1986,* edited by Hungdah Chiu. Occasional Paper/Reprint Series in Contemporary Asian Studies, School of Law, University of Maryland.

Cottrell, Robert. 1993. *The End of Hong Kong.* London: John Murray.

Cradock, Percy. 1994. *Experiences of China.* London: John Murray.

———. 1996. "Sino-British Relations over Hong Kong." *Chinese Law and Government* 29 (1): 51-56.

Davies, Stephen N. G. 1977. "One Brand of Politics Rekindled." *Hong Kong Law Journal* 7:44-80.

———. 1989. "The Changing Nature of Representation in Hong Kong Politics." Pp. 36-76 in *Hong Kong: The Challenge of Transformation,* edited by Kathleen Cheek-Milby and Miron Mushkat. Hong Kong: Centre of Asian Studies, University of Hong Kong.

DeGolyer, Michael E. 1994. "Politics, Politicians, and Political Parties." Pp. 75-101 in *The Other Hong Kong Report 1993,* edited by Donald H. McMillen and Si-Wai Man. Hong Kong: Chinese University Press.

deLisle, Jacques, and Kevin P. Lane. 1997. "Cooking the Rice without Cooking the Goose: The Rule of Law, the Battle over Business, and the Quest for Prosperity in Hong Kong after 1997." Pp. 31-70 in *Hong Kong under Chinese Rule,* edited by Warren Cohen and Li Zhao. New York: Cambridge University Press.

Diamond, Larry. 1989. "Introduction: Persistence, Erosion, Breakdown, and Renewal." Pp. 1-52 in *Democracy in Developing Countries: Asia,* edited by Larry Diamond, Juan Linz, and Seymour Martin Lipset. Boulder: Lynne Rienner.

Dimbleby, Jonathan. 1997. *The Last Governor: Chris Patten and the Handover of Hong Kong.* London: Little, Brown.

Di Palma, Giuseppe. 1990. *To Craft Democracies.* Berkeley: University of California Press.

Draft Agreement between the Government of the United Kingdom of Great Britain and Northern Ireland and the Government of the People's Republic of China on the Future of Hong Kong. 1984. Hong Kong: Government Printer.

Dunn, Lydia. 1989. "The Role of Members of the Executive and Legislative Councils." Pp. 77-90 in *Hong Kong: The Challenge of Transformation,* edited by Kathleen Cheek-Milby and Miron Mushkat. Hong Kong: Centre of Asian Studies, University of Hong Kong.

Eckert, Carter J. 1993. "The South Korean Bourgeoisie: A Class in Search of Hegemony." Pp. 95-130 in *State and Society in Contemporary Korea,* edited by Hagen Koo. Ithaca: Cornell University Press.

Economic and Business Report. 1993. *Asia Pacific Review 1993/94.* London: Kogan Page.

Economist Intelligence Unit. 1994. *Country Report: Hong Kong, Macau.* London: Economist Intelligence Unit.

Eitel, E. J. 1895. *Europe in China: The History of Hong Kong from the Beginning to the Year of 1882.* Hong Kong: Kelly & Walsh.

England, Joe, and John Rear. 1981. *Industrial Relations and Law in Hong Kong.* New York: Oxford University Press.

Etzioni-Halevy, Eva. 1997. "Introduction." Pp. xxiii–xxxv in *Classes and Elites in Democracy and Democratization*, edited by Eva Etzioni-Halevy. New York: Garland.

Faure, David. 1997. "Reflections on Being Chinese in Hong Kong." Pp. 103–20 in *Hong Kong's Transitions, 1842–1997*, edited by Judith Brown and Rosemary Foot. New York: St. Martin's Press.

Field, G. Lowell, John Higley, and Michael G. Burton. 1990. "A New Elite Framework for Political Sociology." *Revue Européene des Sciences Sociales* 28:149–82.

Fung, Ho Lup. 1982. "Introduction" and "Society for Community Organization: The Past Ten Years." Pp. 7–14 in *People's Power in This Decade*, edited by Society for Community Organization. Hong Kong: Society for Community Organization.

Ghai, Yash. 1991 "The Past and the Future of Hong Kong's Constitution." *China Quarterly* 128:794–814.

Gold, Thomas B. 1986. *State and Society in the Taiwan Miracle*. Armonk, N.Y.: M. E. Sharpe.

Haddon-Cave, Philip. 1984. "Introduction." Pp. xv–xx in *The Business Environment in Hong Kong*, edited by David G. Lethbridge. New York: Oxford University Press.

Haggard, Stephan, and Robert R. Kaufman. 1995. *The Political Economy of Democratic Transitions*. Princeton: Princeton University Press.

Halliday, Jon. 1974. "Hong Kong: Britain's Chinese Colony." *New Left Review* 87:91–113.

Han, Sung-Joo. 1989. "South Korea: Politics in Transition." Pp. 267–303 in *Democracy in Developing Countries: Asia*, edited by Larry Diamond, Juan Linz, and Seymour Martin Lipset. Boulder: Lynne Rienner.

HK Federation. 1982. [Hong Kong Federation of Student Unions (Xianggang Zhuanshang Xuesheng Lianhui)]. *Xianggang Jiaoyu Taoushi* [Seeing through Hong Kong's education system]. Hong Kong: Guang Jue Jing.

HKU 66 Editorial Committee [Hong Kong University 66 Editorial Committee]. 1977. *Hong Kong University 66: Review and Preview*. Hong Kong: Hong Kong University Student Union.

HKU Student Union [Hong Kong University Student Union (Xianggang Daxue Xueshenghui)]. 1987. *Xianggang Jiaoyu Zhidu Quanmian Jiantao* [Hong Kong education system comprehensive review). Hong Kong: Jinling.

Home Affairs Branch. 1980. *Information Paper for Chief Secretary's Committee, Monitoring of Pressure Group Activities*. Hong Kong: Government Printer.

Hong Kong Government. 1984a. *Green Paper: The Future Development of Representative Government in Hong Kong*. Hong Kong: Government Printer.

———. 1984b. *White Paper: The Future Development of Representative Government in Hong Kong*. Hong Kong: Government Printer.

———. 1987. *Green Paper: The 1987 Review of Developments in Representative Government*. Hong Kong: Government Printer.

———. 1988. *White Paper: The Development of Representative Government: The Way Forward*. Hong Kong: Government Printer.

———. 1994a. *Hong Kong in Figures*. Hong Kong: Government Printer.

———. 1994b. *Representative Government in Hong Kong.* Hong Kong: Government Printer.

———. n.d. *The Legislative Council: Behind the Scenes.* Hong Kong: Government Printer.

Hook, Brian. 1993. "Political Change in Hong Kong." *China Quarterly* 136:840–963.

———. 1997. "British View of the Legacy of the Colonial Administration of Hong Kong: A Preliminary Assessment." *China Quarterly* 151:553–66.

House of Commons, Foreign Affairs Committee. 1994. *Relations between the United Kingdom and China in the Period up to and beyond 1997.* London: Her Majesty's Stationery Office, Mar. 23.

Howe, Christopher. 1983. "Growth, Public Policy and Hong Kong's Economic Relationship with China." *China Quarterly* 95:512–33.

Hsiao, Hsin-Huang Michael. 1993. "Formation and Transformation of Taiwan's State-Business Relations: A Critical Analysis." *Bulletin of the Institute of Ethnology* 74:1–32.

———. 1996. "Social Movements and Civil Society in Taiwan." *Copenhagen Journal of Asian Studies* 11:7–26.

Hsiao, Hsing-Huang Michael, and Hagen Koo. 1997. "The Middle Class and Democratization in East Asia: Taiwan and South Korea Compared." Pp. 312–34 in *Consolidating the Third Wave Democracies: Themes and Perspectives,* edited by Larry Diamond, Marc F. Plattner, Yun-han Chu, and Hung-mao Tien. Baltimore: Johns Hopkins University Press.

Hsiao, Hsing-Huang Michael, and Alvin So. 1993. "Ascent through National Integration: Chinese Triangle of Mainland–Taiwan–Hong Kong." Pp. 133–50 in *Pacific Asia and the Future of the World Economy,* edited by Ravi Palat. Westport, Conn.: Greenwood.

———. 1996. "The Taiwan-Mainland Economic Nexus: Sociopolitical Origins, State-Society Impacts, and Future Prospects." *Bulletin of Concerned Asian Scholars* 28 (1): 3–12.

Huang, Yasheng. 1997. "The Economic and Political Integration of Hong Kong: Implications for Government-Business Relations." Pp. 96–114 in *Hong Kong under Chinese Rule,* edited by Warren Cohen and Li Zhao. New York: Cambridge University Press.

Huber, Evelyne, Dietrich Rueschemeyer, and John D. Stephens. 1993. "The Impact of Economic Development on Democracy." *Journal of Economic Perspectives* 7:71–85.

Huntington, Samuel. 1984. "Will More Countries Become Democratic?" *Political Science Quarterly* 99:193–218.

———. 1991a. "A New Era in Democracy: Democracy's Third Wave." *Current* 335:27–39.

———. 1991b. *The Third Wave: Democratization in the Late Twentieth Century.* Norman: University of Oklahoma Press.

Hurd, Douglas. 1996. "Speech by the Right Honourable Douglas Hurd CBE MP to the Great Britain–China Center: Britain and China—1997 and Beyond." *Chinese Law and Government* 29 (1): 57–64.

Jao, Y. C. 1985. "The Monetary System and the Future of Hong Kong." Pp. 361–95 in *Hong Kong and 1997: Strategies for the Future,* edited by Y. C. Jao. Hong Kong: Centre of Asian Studies, University of Hong Kong.

Jao, Y. C., et al. 1985. *Hong Kong and 1997: Strategies for the Future.* Hong Kong: Centre of Asian Studies, University of Hong Kong.

Karl, Terry Lynn, and Philippe C. Schmitter. 1991. "Modes of Transition in Latin America, Southern and Eastern Europe." *International Social Science Journal* 128:269–84.

King, Ambrose Y. C. 1981. "Administrative Absorption of Politics in Hong Kong: Emphasis on the Grass Roots Level." Pp. 127–46 in *Social Life and Development in Hong Kong,* edited by Ambrose Y. C. King and Rance P. L. Lee. Hong Kong: Chinese University Press.

———. 1991. *The Hong Kong Talks and Hong Kong Politics.* Hong Kong: Hong Kong Institute of Asia-Pacific Studies, Chinese University of Hong Kong. Reprint Series no. 4, from *Issues and Studies* 22 (6): 52–75.

Kitschelt, Herbert. 1993. "Comparative Historical Research and Rational Choice Theory: The Case of Transitions to Democracy." *Theory and Society* 22:412–27.

Koo, Hagen. 1991. "Middle Classes, Democratization, and Class Formation: The Case of South Korea." *Theory and Society* 20:485–509.

———. 1993a. "Introduction: Beyond State-Market Relations." Pp. 1–21 in *State and Society in Contemporary Korea,* edited by Hagen Koo. Ithaca: Cornell University Press.

———. 1993b. "The State, *Minjung,* and the Working Class in South Korea." Pp. 131–62 in *State and Society in Contemporary Korea,* edited by Hagen Koo. Ithaca: Cornell University Press.

———. 1993c. "Strong State and Contentious Society." Pp. 231–50 in *State and Society in Contemporary Korea,* edited by Hagen Koo. Ithaca: Cornell University Press.

Kuan, Hsin-Chi. 1991. "Power Dependence and Democratic Transition: The Case of Hong Kong." *China Quarterly* 128:774–93.

———. 1996. "Introduction." Pp. 1–9 in *The 1995 Legislative Council Elections in Hong Kong,* edited by Hsin-Chi Kuan et al. Hong Kong: Hong Kong Institute of Asia-Pacific Studies, Chinese University of Hong Kong.

———. 1997. "Hong Kong in 1996: Structuring the Future." *Asian Survey* 37 (1): 52–59.

Kwan, Bun-fong [1971] 1982. "Weihu Diaoyutai Lingtu Zhuquan Zai Xianggang" [Defend the sovereignty of Diaoyutai Territory in Hong Kong]. Pp. 22–28 in *XueYun Chunqui: Xianggang Xuesheng Yundong* [Students' movement history: Hong Kong's students' movement], edited by Yuandong Shiwu Pinglun She [Far East Affairs Commentary Institute]. Hong Kong: Yuandong.

Kwok, Reginald Yin-Wang, and Alvin Y. So, eds. 1995. *The Hong Kong–Guangdong Link: Partnership in Flux.* Armonk, N.Y.: M. E. Sharpe.

Kwong, Paul. 1984. "The 1997 Question and Emigrant Problems in Hong Kong." Paper presented at the conference "Aisan-Pacific Immigration to the United States," Honolulu, September.

Lam, Jermain T. M. 1993. "Chris Patten's Constitutional Reform Package: Implications for Hong Kong's Political Transition." *Issues and Studies* 29 (7): 55–72.

———. 1994. "Failure of Sino-British Talks over Hong Kong: Consequences and Implications." *Issues and Studies* 30:95–115.

———. 1995. "The Last Legislative Council Election in Hong Kong." *Issues and Studies* 31 (12): 68–82.

Lam, Jermain T. M., and Ahmed Shafiqul Huque. 1995. "Economic Development and Democratization: Hong Kong's Experience." *Asian Journal of Political Science* 3:49–64.

Lam, Jermain T. M., and Jane C. Y. Lee. 1992. *The Political Culture of the Voters in Hong Kong*, pt. 2, *A Study of the Geographical Constituencies of the Legislative Council.* Hong Kong: City Polytechnic of Hong Kong.

Lau, Emily. 1988. "The Early History of the Drafting Process." Pp. 90–106 in *The Basic Law and Hong Kong's Future,* edited by Peter Wesley-Smith and Albert Chen. Hong Kong: Butterworths.

———. 1991. *Emily Lau Faces Hong Kong.* Hong Kong: Open Magazine. (In Chinese.)

Lau, Siu-Kai. 1982. *Society and Politics in Hong Kong.* Hong Kong: Chinese University Press.

———. 1992a. "Social Irrelevance of Politics: Hong Kong Chinese Attitudes toward Political Leadership." *Pacific Affairs* 65:225–46.

———. 1992b. "Political Attitudes." Pp. 129–57 in *Indicators of Social Development: Hong Kong 1990,* edited by Siu-Kai Lau et al. Hong Kong: Hong Kong Institute of Asia-Pacific Studies, Chinese University of Hong Kong.

———. 1995. "Hong Kong's Path of Democratization." *Asiatische Studien/Etudes Asiatiques* 49:71–90.

———. 1998. "The Eclipse of Politics in the Hong Kong Special Administrative Region." *Asian Affairs* 25:38–46.

Lau, Siu-Kai, and Hsin-Chi Kuan. 1984. "District Board Elections in Hong Kong." *Journal of Commonwealth and Comparative Politics* 22:303–17.

———. 1985. *The 1985 District Board Election in Hong Kong: The Limits of Political Mobilization in a Dependent Polity.* Hong Kong: Institute of Social Studies, Chinese University of Hong Kong.

———. 1988. *The Ethos of the Hong Kong Chinese.* Hong Kong: Chinese University of Hong Kong Press.

Lau, Siu-Kai, and Po-San Wan. 1987. "Research Report on the Trend of Social Change." *Ming Pao Monthly,* no. 9 (Sept.), pp. 3–10.

Lau, Siu-Kai, Hsin-Chi Kuan, and Po-San Wan. 1991. "Political Attitudes." Pp. 129–57 in *Indicators of Social Development: Hong Kong 1988,* edited by Siu-Kai Lau et al. Hong Kong: Hong Kong Institute of Asia-Pacific Studies, Chinese University of Hong Kong.

Law, Ping. 1988. "White Collar Unionism: The Case of Teachers." Pp. 163–66 in *Labour Movement in a Changing Society: The Experience of Hong Kong,* edited by Y. C. Jao et al. Hong Kong: Center of Asian Studies, University of Hong Kong.

Lee, Jane C. Y. 1993. "Campaigning Themes of the Candidates in the 1991 Legislative Council Election." Pp. 297–316 in *Hong Kong Tried Democracy: The 1991 Elections in Hong Kong,* edited by Siu-Kai Lau and Kin-Shuen Louie. Hong Kong: Hong Kong Institute of Asia-Pacific Studies, Chinese University of Hong Kong.

————. 1994. "The Emergence of Party Politics in Hong Kong, 1982–92." Pp. 270–90 in *25 Years of Social and Economic Development in Hong Kong*, edited by Benjamin K. P. Leung and Teresa Y. C. Wong. Hong Kong: Centre of Asian Studies, University of Hong Kong.

Lee, Martin. 1995. "Hong Kong's 1000 Days." *Asian Affairs: Journal of the Royal Society for Asian Affairs* 26:3–6.

————. 1996. "The Fight for Democracy." Pp. 227–32 in *Hong Kong Remembers*, edited by Sally Blyth and Ian Wotherspoon. Hong Kong: Oxford University Press.

Lee, Martin, and Tom Boasberg. 1994. "Broken Promises: Hong Kong Faces 1997." *Journal of Democracy* 5 (2): 42–56.

Lee, Ming-Kwan. 1987. "Hong Kong: The Final Days of a Colonial Polity." *China News Analysis* 1335 (May 15): 1–8.

————. 1990. "Politicians." Pp. 113–30 in *Hong Kong Report 1990*, edited by Richard Wong and Joseph Cheng. Hong Kong: Chinese University Press.

————. 1993. "Issue-Positions in the 1991 Legislative Council Election." Pp. 237–48 in *Hong Kong Tried Democracy: The 1991 Elections in Hong Kong*, edited by Siu-Kai Lau and Kin-Shuen Louie. Hong Kong: Hong Kong Institute of Asia-Pacific Studies, Chinese University of Hong Kong.

————. 1995. "Community and Identity in Transition in Hong Kong." Pp. 119–32 in *The Hong Kong–Guangdong Link: Partnership in Flux*, edited by Reginald Yin-Wang Kwok and Alvin Y. So. Armonk, N.Y.: M. E. Sharpe.

Lee, Ming-Kwan, and Frances Lai. 1988. "Selection Process and Political Behavior in a Colonial Legislature." Paper presented at the Annual Meeting of the International Political Science Association, Washington, D.C., August.

Lee, Wing-tat. 1996. "Social Movements and Party Politics." *Outspoken*, June, pp. 4–5.

Leung, Benjamin K. P. 1990. "Collective Violence: A Social-Structural Analysis." Pp. 143–62 in *Social Issues in Hong Kong*, edited by Benjamin K. P. Leung. Hong Kong: Oxford University Press.

————. 1994. "Class and Politics." Pp. 203–16 in *25 Years of Social and Economic Development in Hong Kong*, edited by Benjamin K. P. Leung and Teresa Y. C. Wong. Hong Kong: Centre of Asian Studies, University of Hong Kong.

————. Forthcoming. "The Student Movement in Hong Kong: Transition to a Democratizing Society." In *Social Movements in Hong Kong*, edited by Stephen W. K. Chiu and Tai-Lok Lui. Hong Kong: University of Hong Kong Press.

Leung, Chris K. H. 1997. "Political Parties." Pp. 49–70 in *The Other Hong Kong Report 1997*, edited by Joseph Y. S. Cheng. Hong Kong: Chinese University Press.

Leung, Hon-chu. 1986. "Political Action in Compressing Space: A Study of Political Activist Groups in Hong Kong." M.A. thesis, Department of Sociology, Chinese University of Hong Kong.

Leung, Joan Y. H. 1990. "Functional Representation in Hong Kong: Institutionalization and Legitimization of the Business and Professional Elites." *Asian Journal of Public Administration* 12:143–75.

Leung, Joe C. B. 1977. "The Community Development Drama: 1968–77." *Hong Kong Journal of Social Work* 11:17–22.

————. 1982. "Social Movement: A Community Worker's Perspective." Pp. 44–46 in *People's Power in This Decade,* edited by Society for Community Organization. Hong Kong: Society for Community Organization.

————. 1986a. "Community Participation: The Decline of Residents' Organizations." Pp. 354–71 in *Hong Kong in Transition,* edited by Joseph Y. S. Cheng. Hong Kong: Oxford University Press.

————. 1986b. "Community Development in Hong Kong: Contributions towards Democratization." *Community Development Journal* 21:3–10.

————. 1990. "Problems and Changes in Community Politics." Pp. 43–66 in *Social Issues in Hong Kong,* edited by Benjamin K. P. Leung. Hong Kong: Oxford University Press.

————. 1994. "Community Participation: Past, Present, and Future." Pp. 252–69 in *25 Years of Social and Economic Development in Hong Kong,* edited by Benjamin K. P. Leung and Teresa Y. C. Wong. Hong Kong: Centre of Asian Studies, University of Hong Kong.

Leung, K. K. 1995. "The Basic Law and the Problem of Political Transition." Pp. 33–49 in *The Other Hong Kong Report 1995,* edited by Stephen Y. L. Cheung and Stephen M. H. Sze. Hong Kong: Chinese University Press.

Leung, Kwan-Kwok. 1993. "Student Politics in Hong Kong: Democracy and Transition." Pp. 159–72 in *One Culture, Many Systems: Politics in the Reunification of China,* edited by Donald H. McMillen and Michael E. DeGolyer. Hong Kong: Chinese University Press.

Leung, Kwan-Kwok, and Kam-yee Law. 1997. "Fractionalization of the 'Party' System in the Hong Kong Transition." *Asian Thoughts and Society* 22 (64): 18–25.

Leung, Sai-Wing. 1993. "The 'China Factor' in the 1991 Legislative Council Election." Pp. 187–236 in *Hong Kong Tried Democracy: The 1991 Elections in Hong Kong,* edited by Siu-Kai Lau and Kin-Shuen Louie. Hong Kong: Hong Kong Institute of Asia-Pacific Studies, Chinese University of Hong Kong.

————. 1996. "The 'China Factor' and Voters' Choice in the 1995 Legislative Council Election." Pp. 201–44 in *The 1995 Legislative Council Elections in Hong Kong,* edited by Hsin-Chi Kuan et al. Hong Kong: Hong Kong Institute of Asia-Pacific Studies, Chinese University of Hong Kong.

Li, Pang-Kwong. 1995. "Elections, Politicians, and Electoral Politics." Pp. 51–65 in *The Other Hong Kong Report 1995,* edited by Stephen Y. L. Cheung and Stephen M. H. Sze. Hong Kong: Chinese University Press.

————. 1996. "1995 Legislative Council Direct Election: A Political Cleavage Approach." Pp. 245–76 in *The 1995 Legislative Council Elections in Hong Kong,* edited by Hsin-Chi Kuan et al. Hong Kong: Hong Kong Institute of Asia-Pacific Studies, Chinese University of Hong Kong.

Liang, Yu-Ying. 1994. "Hong Kong's Recent District Board Development." *Issues and Studies* 30 (10): 137–38.

————. 1995. "Beijing Set on Establishing a Provisional Legislature in Hong Kong." *Issues and Studies* 31 (1): 101–2.

Lipset, Seymour Martin. 1959. "Some Social Requisites of Democracy: Economic Development and Political Legitimacy." *American Political Science Review* 53: 69–105.

————. 1994. "The Social Requisites of Democracy Revisited." *American Sociological Review* 59:1–22.

Lo, Chi-Kin. 1995. "Constitution and Administration." Pp. 1–12 in *The Other Hong Kong Report 1995*, edited by Stephen Y. L. Cheung and Stephen M. H. Sze. Hong Kong: Chinese University Press.

————. 1996. "Constitution and Administration." Pp. 1–12 in *The Other Hong Kong Report 1996*, edited by Mee-kau Nyaw and Si-ming Li. Hong Kong: Chinese University Press.

Lo, Shiu-Hing. 1988. "Decolonization and Political Development in Hong Kong." *Asian Survey* 28:613–29

————. 1989. "Colonial Policy-Makers, Capitalist Class and China: Determinants of Electoral Reform in Hong Kong's and Macau's Legislatures." *Pacific Affairs* 62:204–18.

————. 1990. "Democratization in Hong Kong: Reasons, Phases, and Limits." *Issues and Studies* 26 (5): 100–117.

————. 1991. "The Problem of Perception and Sino-British Relations over Hong Kong." *Contemporary Southeast Asia* 13:200–219.

————. 1992. "The Politics of Cooptation in Hong Kong: A Study of the Basic Law Drafting Process." *Asian Journal of Public Administration* 14:3–24.

————. 1996. "Hong Kong: Post-colonialism and Political Conflict." Pp. 163–81 in *The New Rich in Asia*, edited by David S. G. Goodman. London: Routledge.

————. 1997. *The Politics of Democratization in Hong Kong*. New York: St. Martin's Press.

Lo, Sonny Shiu-Hing, and Donald Hugh McMillen. 1995. "A Profile of the 'Pro-China Hong Kong Elites': Images and Perceptions." *Issues and Studies* 31 (6): 98–127.

Lo, Tak Shing. 1996. "Political Realism." Pp. 268–75 in *Hong Kong Remembers*, edited by Sally Blyth and Ian Wotherspoon. Hong Kong: Oxford University Press.

Louie, Kin-Shuen. 1993. "The 'Party-Identification' Factor in the 1991 Legislative Council Election." Pp. 157–86 in *Hong Kong Tried Democracy: The 1991 Elections in Hong Kong*, edited by Siu-Kai Lau and Kin-Shuen Louie. Hong Kong: Hong Kong Institute of Asia-Pacific Studies, Chinese University of Hong Kong.

————. 1996. "Election and Politics." Pp. 51–66 in *The Other Hong Kong Report 1996*, edited by Mee-kau Nyaw and Si-ming Li. Hong Kong: Chinese University Press.

Lu Fan-zhi. 1985. *Ping ZhongYing ShuangFang Yu JiBenFa WenTi* [Comment on both China and Britain and the issues on the Basic Law]. Hong Kong: Ji Xian.

Lui, Tai-Lok. 1984. "Urban Protests in Hong Kong." M. Phil. thesis. University of Hong Kong.

————. 1993a. "Hong Kong's New Middle Class: Its Formation and Politics." Pp. 247–72 in *Discovery of the Middle Classes in East Asia*, edited by Hsin-Huang Michael Hsiao. Taipei: Institute of Ethnology, Academia Sinica.

————. 1993b. "Two Logics of Community Politics: Residents' Organizations and the 1991 Election." Pp. 331–44 in *Hong Kong Tried Democracy: The 1991 Elections in Hong Kong*, edited by Siu-Kai Lau and Kin-Shuen Louie. Hong Kong: Hong Kong Institute of Asia-Pacific Studies, Chinese University of Hong Kong.

————. 1994. "Searching for a New Path of Social Movement: Reflection on the Path the Meeting Point Took over the Past Eleven Years." *Meeting Point Discussion*, September, pp. 4–5. (In Chinese.)

Lui, Tai-Lok, and Stephen W. K. Chiu. 1997. "The Structure of Social Movements in Contemporary Hong Kong." *China Information* 12:97–113.

————. Forthcoming. "Introduction: Changing Political Opportunity and the Shaping of Collective Action: Social Movements in Hong Kong." In *Social Movements in Hong Kong*, edited by Stephen W. K. Chiu and Tai-Lok Lui. Hong Kong: Hong Kong University Press.

Lui Tai-Lok and Gong Qi-sheng (James Kung). 1985. *Cheng Shi Zong Heng* [Urban movements]. Hong Kong: Guang Jiao Jing.

Luk, Bernard. 1992. "Reactions to Patten's Constitutional Proposals." *Canada and Hong Kong Update* 8:1–4.

Ma Sai. 1982. "Zenyang Kandai Youguan 'Renzhong Guanshe' de Yici Wenti" [How to treat a few questions relating to 'identify with China and pay attention to society']. Pp. 257–79 in *XueYun Chunqui: Xianggang Xuesheng Yundong* [Students' movement history: Hong Kong's students' movement], edited by Yuandong Shiwu Pinglun She [Far East Affairs Commentary Institute]. Hong Kong: Yuandong.

Mainland Affairs Committee. 1995. *A Comparative Study of Hong Kong's Political Parties*. Taipei: Mainland Affairs Committee, Executive Council. (In Chinese.)

Mak, Hoi-Wah. 1988. "White-Collar Unionism: The Case of Social Workers." Pp. 167–74 in *Labour Movement in a Changing Society: The Experience of Hong Kong*, edited by Y. C. Jao et al. Hong Kong: Centre of Asian Studies, University of Hong Kong.

Mathews, Gordon. 1997. "Heunggongyahn: On the Past, Present, and Future of Hong Kong Identity." *Bulletin of Concerned Asian Scholars* 29 (3): 3–13.

Maxwell, Neville. 1995. "Britain Backs Off." *Far Eastern Economic Review*, Nov. 9, p. 39.

Meeting Point (HuiDian). 1984. *MinZhu GaiGe Yu GangRen ZhiGang* [Democratic reform and Hong Kong people ruling Hong Kong]. Hong Kong: ZhuQuang.

Miners, Norman. 1981. *The Government and Politics of Hong Kong*. Hong Kong: Oxford University Press.

————. 1989. "Moves towards Representative Government, 1984–1988." Pp. 19–35 in *Hong Kong: Challenge of Transformation*, edited by Kathleen Cheek-Milby and Miron Mushkat. Hong Kong: Centre of Asian Studies, University of Hong Kong.

————. 1993. "Constitution and Administration." Pp. 1–37 in *The Other Hong Kong Report 1993*, edited by Po-King Choi and Lok-Sang Ho. Hong Kong: Chinese University Press.

————. 1994a. "The Transformation of the Hong Kong Legislative Council, 1970–1994: From Consensus to Confrontation." *Asian Journal of Public Administration* 16:224–48.

————. 1994b. "Constitution and Administration." Pp. 1–8 in *The Other Hong*

Kong Report 1993, edited by Donald H. McMillen and Si-Wai Man. Hong Kong: Chinese University Press.

————. 1996. "Consultation with Business Interests: The Case of Hong Kong." *Asian Journal of Public Administration* 18:245–57.

Ministry of Foreign Affairs, People's Republic of China. 1996. "Facts about a Few Important Aspects of Sino-British Talks on 1994–95 Electoral Arrangements in Hong Kong." *Chinese Law and Government* 29 (1): 21–50.

Myers, Ramon. 1987. "Political Theory and Recent Political Development in the Republic of China." *Asian Survey* 27:1003–22.

Nathan, Andrew. 1990. *China's Crisis*. New York: Columbia University Press.

National Democratic Institute (NDI). 1997. "The Promise of Democratization in Hong Kong: The New Election Framework." NDI Hong Kong Report no. 2, Oct. 23. Http://www.ndi.org/hkrpt.htm.

Ngan, Mary Chan Kam. 1966. "The Two Universities in Hong Kong: An Analysis of Their Aims and Contributions to Our Bi-cultural Community." *Journal of Education* 23:1–10.

Ngan, Raymond M. H. 1997. "Social Welfare." Pp. 411–30 in *The Other Hong Kong Report 1997*, edited by Joseph Cheng. Hong Kong: Chinese University Press.

Ngo, Hang Yue, and Chung Ming Lau. 1996. "Labor and Employment." Pp. 259–76 in *The Other Hong Kong Report 1996*, edited by Mee-kau Nyaw and Si-ming Li. Hong Kong: Chinese University Press.

Nyaw, Mee-Kau and Si-Ming Li. 1996. "Introduction." Pp. xxxi–xliv in *The Other Hong Kong Report 1996*, edited by Mee-Kau Nyaw and Si-Ming Li. Hong Kong: Chinese University Press.

O'Donnell, Guillermo, and Philippe C. Schmitter. 1986. *Transition from Authoritarian Rule: Tentative Conclusions about Uncertain Democracies*. Baltimore: Johns Hopkins University Press.

Overholt, William H. 1985. "Hong Kong after Chinese-British Agreement." *Asian Perspective* 9:257–73.

Patten, Christopher. 1992. "Governor Patten's Policy Speech to Legco." *Canada and Hong Kong Update* 8:1–4.

————. 1993. *Our Next Five Years: The Agenda for Hong Kong*. Hong Kong: Government Printer.

————. 1996. "The Last Governor." Pp. 276–85 in *Hong Kong Remembers*, edited by Sally Blyth and Ian Wotherspoon. Hong Kong: Oxford University Press.

Pepper, Suzanne. 1995. "Hong Kong in 1994." *Asian Survey* 35:48–60.

————. 1997. "Hong Kong, 1997: East vs. West and the Struggle for Democratic Reform within the Chinese State." *Asian Survey* 37:683–704.

Perkin, Ian. 1997. "The Economy." Pp. 227–52 in *The Other Hong Kong Report 1997*, edited by Joseph Cheng. Hong Kong: Chinese University Press.

Przeworski, Adam. 1986. "Some Problems in the Study of the Transition Democracy." Pp. 47–63 in *Transitions from Authoritarian Rule: Comparative Perspectives*, edited by Guillermo O'Donnell, Philippe C. Schmitter, and Laurence Whitehead. Baltimore: Johns Hopkins University Press.

————. 1991. *Democracy and the Market: Political and Economic Reforms in Eastern Europe and Latin America*. New York: Cambridge University Press.

Rafferty, Kevin. 1990. *City on the Rocks: Hong Kong's Uncertain Future.* New York: Viking.

Roberti, Mark. 1994. *The Fall of Hong Kong.* New York: Wiley.

Roy, Denny. 1990. "The Triumph of Nationalism in Peking's Hong Kong Policy." *Issues and Studies* 26 (4): 105–20.

Rueschemeyer, Dietrich, Evelyne Huber Stephens, and John Stephens. 1992. *Capitalist Development and Democracy.* Chicago: University of Chicago Press.

Schumpeter, Joseph A. 1950. *Capitalism, Socialism, and Democracy.* New York: Harper Torchbooks.

Scott, Ian. 1989. *Political Change and the Crisis of Legitimacy in Hong Kong.* Honolulu: University of Hawaii Press.

———. 1992. "An Overview of the Hong Kong Legislative Council Elections of 1991." Pp. 1–28 in *Votes without Power: The Hong Kong Legislative Council Elections,* edited by Rowena Kwok, Joan Leung, and Ian Scott. Hong Kong: Hong Kong University Press.

———. 1995. "Political Transformation in Hong Kong: From Colony to Colony." Pp. 189–223 in *The Hong Kong–Guangdong Link: Partnership in Flux,* edited by Reginald Yin-Wang Kwok and Alvin Y. So. Armonk, N.Y.: M. E. Sharpe.

———. 1996. "Party Politics and Elections in Transitional Hong Kong." Paper presented at the Annual Meeting of the Association for Asian Studies, Honolulu, Apr. 11–14.

Shieh, G. S. 1992. *"Boss" Island: The Subcontracting Network and Micro-entrepreneurship in Taiwan's Development.* New York: Peter Lang.

Shin, Doh Chull. 1994. "On the Third Wave of Democratization: A Synthesis and Evaluation of Recent Theory and Research." *World Politics* 47:135–70.

Sing, Ming. 1996. "Economic Development, Civil Society, and Democratization in Hong Kong." *Journal of Contemporary Asia* 26:482–504.

———. Forthcoming. "Mobilization for Political Change: The Pro-Democracy Movement in Hong Kong (1980–1994)." In *Social Movements in Hong Kong,* edited by Stephen W. K. Chiu and Tai-Lok Lui. Hong Kong: University of Hong Kong Press.

Skeldon, Ronald. 1991. "Emigration, Immigration and Fertility Decline: Demographic Integration or Disintegration?" Pp. 233–58 in *The Other Hong Kong Report 1991,* edited by Yun-Wing Sung and Ming-Kwan Lee. Hong Kong: Chinese University Press.

———. 1990-91. "Emigration and the Future of Hong Kong." *Pacific Affairs* 63:500–523.

———. 1997. "Hong Kong Communities Overseas." Pp. 121–48 in *Hong Kong's Transitions, 1842–1997,* edited by Judith M. Brown and Rosemary Foot. New York: St. Martin's Press.

Smart, Josephine, and Alan Smart. 1991. "Personal Relations and Divergent Economies: A Case Study of Hong Kong Investment in South China." *International Journal of Urban and Regional Research* 15:216–33.

So, Alvin Y. 1986a. "The Economic Success of Hong Kong: Insights from a World-System Perspective." *Sociological Perspectives* 29:241–58.

————. 1986b. *The South China Silk District: Local Historical Transformation and World-System Theory.* Albany: State University of New York Press.

————. 1988. "Shenzhen Special Economic Zone: China's Struggle for Independent Development." *Canadian Journal of Development Studies* 9:313–24.

————. 1990. *Social Change and Development: Modernization, Dependency, and World-System Theories.* Newbury Park, Calif.: Sage.

————. 1991. "Class Struggle Analysis: A Critique of Class Structure Analysis." *Sociological Perspectives* 34:39–59.

————. 1992. "The Dilemma of Socialist Development in China." *Humboldt Journal of Social Relations* 18:163–94.

————. 1993a. "Western Sociological Theories and Hong Kong New Middle Class." Pp. 219–45 in *Discovery of the Middle Classes in East Asia,* edited by Hsin-Huang Michael Hsiao. Taipei: Institute of Ethnology, Academia Sinica.

————. 1993b. "Hong Kong People Ruling Hong Kong! The Rise of the New Middle Class and Negotiation Politics, 1982–1984." *Asian Affairs: An American Review* 20:67–87.

————. 1995a. "New Middle Class Politics in Hong Kong: 1997 and Democratization." *Asiatische Studien/Etudes Asiatiques* 49:91–111.

————. 1995b. "Political Determinants of Direct Investment in Mainland China." Pp. 95–112 in *Emerging Patterns of East Asian Investment in China: From Korea, Taiwan, and Hong Kong,* edited by Sumner La Croix, Michael G. Plummer, and Keun Lee. Armonk, N.Y.: M. E. Sharpe.

————. 1995c. "Recent Developments in Marxist Class Analysis: A Critical Appraisal." *Sociological Inquiry* 65 (3–4): 313–28.

————. 1996. "Class Analysis and Radical Social Theories: Discovering the Missing Link." *Research in Political Economy* 15:1–26.

So, Alvin Y., and Stephen W. K. Chiu. 1995. *East Asia and the World Economy.* Thousand Oaks, Calif.: Sage.

So, Alvin Y., and Muhammad Hikam. 1990. "Class Theory or Class Analysis? A Reexamination of the Unfinished Chapter of Marx on Class." *Critical Sociology* 17:35–56.

So, Alvin Y., and Shiping Hua. 1992. "Democracy as an Antisystemic Movement in Taiwan, Hong Kong, and China." *Sociological Perspective* 35:385–404.

So, Alvin Y., and Ludmilla Kwitko. 1990. "New Middle Class and the Democratic Movements in Hong Kong." *Journal of Contemporary Asia* 20:384–98.

————. 1992. "The Transformation of Urban Movements in Hong Kong." *Bulletin of Concerned Asian Scholars* 24 (4): 31–42.

So, Alvin Y., and Reginald Yin-Wang Kwok. 1995. "Socio-economic Core, Political Periphery: Hong Kong's Uncertain Future toward the Twenty-first Century." Pp. 251–58 in *The Hong Kong–Guangdong Link: Partnership in Flux,* edited by Reginald Yin-Wang Kwok and Alvin Y. So. Armonk, N.Y.: M. E. Sharpe.

So, Alvin Y., and Sai-Hsin May. 1993. "Democratization in East Asia in the Late 1980s: Taiwan Breakthrough, Hong Kong Frustration." *Studies in Comparative International Development* 28 (2): 60–79.

So, Alvin Y., and Suwarsono. 1989. " 'Class' in the Writings of Wallerstein and

Thompson: Toward a Class Struggle Analysis." *Sociological Perspectives* 32:453–67.

Sorensen, George. 1993. *Democracy and Democratization.* Boulder: Westview.

Sum, Ngai-Ling. 1995. "More than a 'War of Words': Identity, Politics, and the Struggle for Dominance during the Recent 'Political Reform' Period in Hong Kong." *Economy and Society* 24:67–100.

Student Unions. n.d. [Zhongda Xue ShengHui, GangDa XueSheng Hui (The student unions of the University of Hong Kong and Chinese University of Hong Kong).] *XiangGang QianTu FengYun* [Uncertainty surrounding the future of Hong Kong]. Hong Kong: Student Unions of the University of Hong Kong and the Chinese University of Hong Kong.

Tam, Larry K. L. 1983. "Problems and Prospects for Hong Kong Major Sector." *Hong Kong Managers* 19:22–26.

Tam, Siumi Maria. 1996. "Youth in Hong Kong: Re-rooting of an Identity." Paper presenting at the Annual Meeting of the Association for Asian Studies, Honolulu, April.

Tambling, Jeremy. 1997. "The History Man: The Last Governor of Hong Kong." *Public Culture* 9:355–76.

Tang, James T. H., and Frank Ching. 1994. "The MacLehose-Youde Years: Balancing the 'Three-Legged Stool,' 1971–86." Pp. 149–71 in *Precarious Balance: Hong Kong between China and Britain, 1842–1992,* edited by Ming K. Chan. Armonk, N.Y.: M. E. Sharpe.

Tang, Shu-Hung. 1989. "The Hong Kong Basic Law (Draft): The Political Economy of the Articles on Economy." Paper presented at the conference "Hong Kong towards 1997 and Beyond," Honolulu, Jan. 26–27.

———. 1991. "Fiscal Constitution, Income Distribution, and the Basic Law of Hong Kong." *Economy and Society* 20:283–305.

Tang, Stephen Lung-Wai. 1993. "Political Markets, Competition, and the Return to Monopoly: Evolution amidst a Historical Tragedy." Pp. 249–96 in *Hong Kong Tried Democracy: The 1991 Elections in Hong Kong,* edited by Siu-Kai Lau and Kin-Shuen Louie. Hong Kong: Hong Kong Institute of Asia-Pacific Studies, Chinese University of Hong Kong.

Thatcher, Margaret. 1993. *The Downing Street Years.* New York: HarperCollins.

Tien Hung-mao. 1989. *The Great Transition: Political and Social Change in the Republic of China.* Stanford: Hoover Institution Press. (In Chinese.)

———. 1992. "Taiwan's Evolution toward Democracy: A Historical Perspective." Pp. 3–23 in *Taiwan: Beyond the Economic Miracle,* edited by Denis F. Simon and Michael Y. M. Kau. Armonk, N.Y.: M. E. Sharpe.

TOYPA [The Outstanding Young Persons' Association]. 1984. *Candid Opinion.* Hong Kong: TOYPA.

Tsai Jung-fang. 1993. *Hong Kong in Chinese History.* New York: Columbia University Press.

Tsang Wing-kwong. 1993. "Who Voted for the Democrats?" Pp. 115–56 in *Hong Kong Tried Democracy: The 1991 Elections in Hong Kong,* edited by Siu-Kai Lau and Kin-Shuen Louie. Hong Kong: Hong Kong Institute of Asia-Pacific Studies, Chinese University of Hong Kong.

Tsim Tak-lung. 1990. "The Implementation of the Sino-British Joint Declaration." Pp. 131–46 in *The Other Hong Kong Report, 1990,* edited by Richard Wong and Joseph Cheng. Hong Kong: Chinese University Press.

Turner, H. A., with Patricia Fosh et al. 1980. *The Last Colony, but Whose? A Study of the Labour Movement, Labour Market, and Labour Relations in Hong Kong.* New York: Cambridge University Press.

Wachman, Alan M. 1994. *Taiwan: National Identity and Democratization.* Armonk, N.Y.: M. E. Sharpe.

Weinberger, Caspar. 1997. "Hong Kong Is Not Taiwan." *Forbes,* Oct. 13, p. 37.

Weiner, Myron. 1987. "Empirical Democratic Theory." Pp. 3–34 in *Competitive Elections in Developing Countries,* edited by Myron Weiner and Ergun Ozbudun. Durham, N.C.: Duke University Press.

Wesley-Smith, Peter. 1987. *Constitutional and Administrative Law in Hong Kong.* Vol. 1. Hong Kong: China and Hong Kong Law Studies.

Wight, Martin. 1946. *The Development of the Legislative Council.* London: Faber & Faber.

Wilson, Dick. 1990. *Hong Kong! Hong Kong!* London: Unwin Hyman.

Wilson, Lord David. 1996. "Learning to Live with China." Pp. 175–84 in *Hong Kong Remembers,* edited by Sally Blyth and Ian Wotherspoon. Hong Kong: Oxford University Press.

Wong, Gilbert. 1991. "Business Groups in a Dynamic Environment: Hong Kong, 1976–1986." Pp. 126–54 in *Business Networks and Economic Development in East and Southeast Asia,* edited by Gary Hamilton. Hong Kong: Centre of Asian Studies, University of Hong Kong.

Wong, Pik-Wan. Forthcoming. "The Pro-Chinese Democracy Movement in Hong Kong, 1976–95." In *Social Movements in Hong Kong,* edited by Stephen Chiu and Tai-Lok Lui. Hong Kong: University of Hong Kong Press.

Wong, Siu-Lun. 1988. *Emigrant Entrepreneurs.* Hong Kong: Oxford University Press.

———. 1994. "Business and Politics in Hong Kong during the Transition." Pp. 217–35 in *25 Years of Social and Economic Development in Hong Kong,* edited by Benjamin K. P. Leung and Teresa Y. C. Wong. Hong Kong: Centre of Asian Studies, University of Hong Kong.

Wong, Thomas W. P. 1993. "The New Middle Class in Hong Kong: Class in Formation." Pp. 273–306 in *Discovery of the Middle Classes in East Asia,* edited by Hsin-Huang Michael Hsiao. Taipei: Institute of Ethnology, Academia Sinica.

Wong, Thomas W. P., and Tai-Lok Lui. 1992. *From One Brand of Politics to One Brand of Political Culture.* Hong Kong: Hong Kong Institute of Asia-Pacific Studies, Chinese University of Hong Kong.

Wong, Wai-Kwok. 1997. "Can Co-optation Win Over the Hong Kong People? China's United Front Work in Hong Kong since 1984." *Issues and Studies* 33 (5): 102–37.

Wong Yiu-chung. 1984. "Five Characteristics of Ruling Elites of Hong Kong." *Hong Kong Economic Journal Monthly* 8 (9): 13–15. (In Chinese.)

Wu, Anna. 1996. "Government by Whom?" Pp. 158–66 in *Hong Kong Remembers,* edited by Sally Blyth and Ian Wotherspoon. Hong Kong: Oxford University Press.

Xianggang de Mingri Zhixing [Hong Kong's future star]. 1985. Hong Kong: Guang Jue Jing.

Xie Jia-ju. 1982. "Fenxi Xianggang de Jiaoyu Zhengce" [Analyze Hong Kong's education policy]. Pp. 37–58 in *Xianggang Jiaoyu Toushi* [Seeing through Hong Kong's education system], edited by Xianggang Zhuanshang Xuesheng Lianhui [Hong Kong Federation of Student Unions]. Hong Kong: Guang Jue Jing.

Xu Jiatun. 1994. *Xu Jiatun Xianggang Huiyilu* [Xu Jiatun's Hong Kong memoirs]. Taipei: Lianjing Chubanshiye.

Yahuda, Michael. 1993. "Hong Kong's Future: Sino-British Negotiations, Perceptions, Organization, and Political Culture." *International Affairs* 69:245–66.

Ye JianYuan. 1985. *QianTu Huo XiWang: Xu JiaTun Deng Lun XiangGang* [Future and Prospect: Writings of Xu Jiatun and Others on Hong Kong). Hong Kong: JinLing.

Yee, Herbert S., and Wong Yiu-chung. 1987. "Hong Kong: The Politics of Daya Bay Nuclear Plant Debate." *International Affairs* 63:617–30.

Yip Hua-kwok. 1997. "Political Merchant — Yip Hua-kwok." *Hong Kong Youth and Tertiary Student Association* 9 (May): 2–5. (In Chinese.)

Young, John D. 1989. "Red Colony: Hong Kong 1997." Paper presented at the conference "Hong Kong towards 1997 and Beyond," Honolulu, Jan. 26–27.

Yu Wing-yat. 1997. "Organizational Adaptation of the Hong Kong Democratic Party." *Issues and Studies* 33 (1): 87–115.

Yuandong Shimu Pinglun She [Far East Affairs Commentary Institute]. 1982. *Xue-Yun Chunqui: Xianggang Xuesheng Yundong* [Students' movement history: Hong Kong's students' movement). Hong Kong: Yuandong.

Zhang Jiefeng et al. 1991. *Bubian, Wushi Nian? Zhongyinggang Jiaoli Jibenfa* [No change for fifty years? China, Britain, and Hong Kong wrestle with the Basic Law]. Hong Kong: Langchao Chubanse.

Periodicals

Asian Business
Asiaweek
Beijing Review
Capital
China News Digest
China Tide
Chinese University Students
Executive
The Express
FEER (Far Eastern Economic Review)
FEER Yearbook (Far Eastern Economic Review Yearbook)
Fortune
Guang Jue Jing [Wide angle]

HK Engineer (*Hong Kong Engineer,* an English-language magazine published in Hong Kong)

HKSA (*Hong Kong Society of Accountants,* an English-language magazine published in Hong Kong)

Hong Kong Economic Daily

Hong Kong Economic Journal Monthly

Hong Kong Standard (an English-language newspaper published in Hong Kong)

International Herald Tribune

Ming Pao

Newsweek

Outspoken (official magazine of the Democratic Party)

Pai Shing [*Baixing*] (a Chinese magazine published in Hong Kong)

The People's Daily

SCMP (*South China Morning Post,* an English-language newspaper published in Hong Kong)

Seventies Monthly

Ta Kung Po [*Dagong Bao*] (a Chinese magazine published in Hong Kong)

Wen Wei Po [*Wenhui Bao*] (a Chinese newspaper published in Hong Kong)

Websites

elau@hknet.com

forum@ahkcus.org

H-ASIA@h-net.msu.edu

hknews@ahkcus.org

Index

Library of Congress Cataloging-in-Publication Data
So, Alvin Y., 1953–
  Hong Kong's embattld democracy : a societal analysis / Alvin Y.
So.
      p.   cm.
  Includes bibliographical references and index.
  ISBN 0-8018-6145-4 (alk. paper)
      1. Democracy — China — Hong Kong.   2. Hong Kong (China) — Social
conditions.   3. Hong Kong (China) — Politics and government — 1997–
I. Title.
JQ1539.5.A91S63   1999
320.95125′09′049 — dc21   99-25083
                                                                              CIP